Russia from the American Embassy

AMERICANS IN REVOLUTIONARY RUSSIA

Vol. 1
Albert Rhys Williams, *Through the Russian Revolution*, edited by
William Benton Whisenhunt (2016)

Vol. 2
Princess Julia Cantacuzène, Countess Spéransky, née Grant, *Russian People: Revolutionary Recollections*, edited by Norman E. Saul (2016)

Vol. 3
Ernest Poole, *The Village: Russian Impressions*, edited by Norman E. Saul (2017)

Vol. 4
John Reed, *Ten Days That Shook the World*, edited by
William Benton Whisenhunt (2017)

Vol. 5
Louise Bryant, *Six Red Months in Russia*, edited by Lee A. Farrow (2017)

Vol. 6
Edward Alsworth Ross, *Russia in Upheaval*, edited by Rex A. Wade (2017)

Vol. 7
Donald Thompson, *Donald Thompson in Russia*, edited by David H. Mould (2018)

Vol. 8
Arthur Bullard, *The Russian Pendulum: Autocracy—Democracy—Bolshevism*, edited by
David W. McFadden (2019)

Vol. 9
Pauline S. Crosley, *Intimate Letters from Petrograd*, edited by Lee A. Farrow (2019)

Vol. 10
Madeleine Z. Doty, *"The Bolshevik Revolution Had Descended on Me": Madeleine Z. Doty's Russian Revolution*, edited by Julia L. Mickenberg (2019)

Vol. 11
David R. Francis, *Russia from the American Embassy*, edited by Vladimir V. Noskov (2019)

Series General Editors:
Norman E. Saul and William Benton Whisenhunt

Russia from the American Embassy

David R. Francis

Edited and Introduction by
Vladimir V. Noskov

ANTHEM PRESS

Anthem Press
An imprint of Wimbledon Publishing Company
www.anthempress.com

First published by Slavica Publishers, Indiana University, USA, 2019

This edition first published in UK and USA 2026
by ANTHEM PRESS
75–76 Blackfriars Road, London SE1 8HA, UK
or PO Box 9779, London SW19 7ZG, UK
and
244 Madison Ave #116, New York, NY 10016, USA

Copyright © 2026 Vladimir V. Noskov editorial matter and selection;
individual chapters © individual contributors

The moral right of the authors has been asserted.

All rights reserved. Without limiting the rights under copyright reserved above,
no part of this publication may be reproduced, stored or introduced into
a retrieval system, or transmitted, in any form or by any means
(electronic, mechanical, photocopying, recording or otherwise),
without the prior written permission of both the copyright
owner and the above publisher of this book.

British Library Cataloguing-in-Publication Data
A catalogue record for this book is available from the British Library.

Library of Congress Cataloging-in-Publication Data
A catalog record for this book has been requested.

ISBN-13: 978-1-83999-712-9 (Hbk)
ISBN-10: 1-83999-712-5 (Hbk)

ISBN-13: 978-1-83999-713-6 (Pbk)
ISBN-10: 1-83999-713-3 (Pbk)

Cover design: Tracey Theriault

This title is also available as an eBook.

CONTENTS

Editor's Introduction   ix
   Vladimir V. Noskov

RUSSIA FROM THE AMERICAN EMBASSY

Introduction   3

I. First Impressions   7

II. German Influence in Russian Affairs   22

III. Treason in High Places   31

IV. Rumblings of Revolutions   47

V. The March Revolutions   53

VI. American Recognition of the Provisional Government   72

VII. The Council of Workmen and Soldiers' Deputies   83

VIII. Significant Changes in the Ministry   98

IX. The Diplomatic and Railway Commission   108

X. The July Revolution   113

XI. The Provisional Government and the Forces of Destruction	120
XII. The Break Between Kerensky and Korniloff	129
XIII. The Bolsheviks Overthrow the Government	144
XIV. The Constituent Assembly Dispersed by Armed Bolsheviks	164
XV. The Diamandi Incident	187
XVI. The Brest-Litovsk Peace	193
XVII. Vologda—The Diplomatic Capital	202
XVIII. Archangel and the Northern Government	224
XIX. Allied Policies in Russia	253
XX. Bolshevism and the Peace Conference	260
XXI. Bolshevism in Principle and in Practice	277
XXII. Russia—The Chief Victim of the World War	285
XXIII. Retrospect	288
Index	293

ILLUSTRATIONS

Furshtatskaya Street	Figure 1
Zinger House	Figure 2
US Embassy at Vologda	Figure 3
US Consulate General at Arkhangel´sk	Figure 4
The American Embassy, Petrograd, 1909–17	Figure 5
Terestchenko	Figure 6
Paul Miliukoff	Figure 6
Michael Rodzianko	Figure 6
The American Railway Commission to Russia and Ambassador Francis at the American Embassy, Petrograd	Figure 7
Alexander Kerensky	Figure 8
N. Prebensen	Figure 9
Sir George W. Buchanan	Figure 9
Count Diamandi	Figure 9
T. Noulens	Figure 9

Ambassador Francis and his staff before the
American Embassy, Vologda, Russia — Figure 10

Last conference of the Allied chiefs in the
American Embassy, Vologda, July 23, 1918 — Figure 11

EDITOR'S INTRODUCTION
Vladimir V. Noskov

David Rowland Francis presented himself as the "United States Ambassador to Russia under the Czar, the Provisional Government and the Bolshevists." Actually, he represented his country before four Russian governments: the Imperial, Provisional, Soviet, and Northern ones. During his stay in Russia, Francis changed his residence three times, moving from Petrograd first, to Vologda, and finally to Arkhangel'sk. He was an eyewitness of the greatest events in the history of Russia: the World War, February Revolution, downfall of the empire, October Revolution, and Civil War. During the two and half years of his residence in Russia, Francis met a lot of prominent people of the time, including Nicholas II, the last emperor of Russia, and Vladimir I. Lenin, the first Soviet leader. Francis's diplomatic experience was unique and had no parallel in the history of Russian-American relations. That is why his memoirs are of special interest for historians and the general public alike.

The most striking feature of his Russian experience is the fact that Francis was not a diplomat at all. Practically nothing in his previous life might have helped him in his ambassadorial work. He was born in Richmond, Kentucky, in 1850, and moved to St. Louis, Missouri, in 1866 to attend Washington University. After graduation he became a clerk, and soon afterward a partner in a commercial house, thus beginning his successful business career. Francis was also an officer or trustee in many banking and philanthropic institutions while rising to prominence in politics, serving as mayor of St. Louis (1885–89) and the youngest governor of Missouri (1889–93). For a short time, he served as secretary of the interior in Grover Cleveland's cabinet. He was a devoted Democrat but opposed William J. Bryan's candidacy in 1896, and he was out of politics for ten years afterwards. Francis married Jane Perry, who belonged to a prominent Missouri family, and they raised six sons.

One of the Francis's most brilliant achievements was his campaign to organize the 1904 World Exposition in St. Louis. On the one hand, it was a typical story illustrating his unusual business and administrative abilities. On the other, the episode was of special importance in Francis's biography because it provided him with his only international experience prior to his appointment to a diplomatic post. This wonderful saga began in the summer of 1889—when Francis began pushing for a world's fair to be held in St. Louis—and lasted for fifteen years. In 1903, Francis made a tour around principal European capitals to encourage foreign participation. He met King Edward VII of Great Britain, French President Emile Loubet, Kaiser Wilhelm II of Germany, and King Leopold II of Belgium. Francis hastened back to St. Louis from Europe, where, at the Dedication Day ceremony, he welcomed members of the diplomatic corps, including British, French, Italian, and Russian ambassadors. The St. Louis Fair lasted for seven months, during which Francis was said to be "the most photographed man in America."[1] The fair was the largest international exposition the world had ever seen at that time, and it was a great financial success.[2] In mid-1906, Francis made another trip to Europe with his companions, where he "was tireless in tracking down monarchs and prime ministers" wherever they might be found.[3]

At the same time, Francis returned to active political life and came around to supporting Woodrow Wilson in 1912. Francis also strengthened his friendship with Charles R. Crane, a wealthy Chicago businessman and prominent Democratic campaign contributor who was a friend of the new president. Crane had the reputation of being one of the most active and influential promoters of rapprochement with Russia. The so-called Crane circle included, among others, such diverse people as journalists Arthur Ruhl and Stanley Washburn, businessmen Frederick M. Corse and Raymond Robins, and the YMCA leader John R. Mott—to list only those persons whom, as well as Crane himself, Francis would later meet in Petrograd. The most outstanding figure among Crane's followers was expert in Russian language and institutions Samuel N. Harper.

On the eve of the World War, the post of US ambassador at St. Petersburg was vacant, and relations between the two powers were rather cool. In July 1914, the ambassadorship in Russia was offered to George T. Marye, an international lawyer and active Democratic supporter, but in early 1916, he was forced to resign as a result of his inability to meet Wilson's expectations. With Crane's assistance, a new ambassador by the name of Governor Francis was appointed, and Harper was named an unofficial advisor to accompany him to Russia.[4] As Francis's biographer wrote, in his mature years, Francis represented "the perfect image of a successful American businessman and civic leader" and was "proud of his contributions to the community, pleased with his accomplishments and with himself." He was "a brash, opinionated, stubborn, smart, sometimes foolish, straight-talking, quick-acted, inde-

---

[1] Harper Barnes, *Standing on a Volcano: The Life and Times of David Rowland Francis* (St. Louis: Missouri Historical Society Press, 2001), 72–75, 123–125, 131, 144.

[2] Robert W. Rydell, *All the World's a Fair: Visions of Empire at American International Expositions, 1876–1916* (Chicago: University of Chicago Press, 1984), 155–183.

[3] Barnes, *Standing on a Volcano*, 168.

[4] Paul A. Goble, "Samuel N. Harper and the Study of Russia," *Cahiers du monde russe et soviétique* 14, no. 4 (1973): 613.

pendent-minded, proud, self-made man...was rich and getting richer, busy with his directorships and his civic duties, regularly traveling the country to speak to large audiences and meet with other powerful men, who were his friends."[5]

Meanwhile, as the editor of his letters noted, "Francis was shrewd and capable in the world he knew, but international diplomacy was not in that world."[6] The Russian ambassador in Washington characterized him as a thriving provincial businessman with a good fortune and great self-assurance.[7] The new American ambassador had little international experience, no theoretical preparation, no practical knowledge, and no diplomatic abilities required for the post. In George F. Kennan's opinion, "Francis was not what you would call a cosmopolitan person. He was a product of the old West, a 'provincial' in the best sense of the term, in whose character there was reflected something of the 'showboat' Mississippi: the vigor, the earthiness, the slightly flamboyant elegance, and the uninhibited enjoyment of the good things of life. His values and opinions were, at his age of 67, firmly established, and were not to be essentially shaken even by the experience of residence in a foreign capital in dramatic times."[8] He was made a diplomat by chance as a consequence of a "Democratic débauche" in the Foreign Service and the demoralization of the State Department, which followed Woodrow Wilson's rise to presidency.

Francis sailed for Russia on April 8, 1916, leaving his family at home. He was accompanied by his African American valet, Philip Jordan. Arthur Ruhl, who crossed the Atlantic on the same steamboat, remembered "his man Friday, Phil, a body-servant of the old-fashioned Southern kind, already mourning, after but a week of foreign ways, for the hot biscuits of St. Louis."[9] Harper, another one of Francis's companions, wrote after several days at sea: "I heard enough of them to realize that our new ambassador was a very blunt, outspoken American, who believed in speaking his mind regardless of the rules of diplomacy."[10]

Francis arrived in Petrograd on the morning on April 15 (28)[11] and was met at the station by the people of the embassy. The staff of the US embassy in the Russian capital consisted of nine men at the time. The senior diplomat was veteran Herbert

---

[5] Barnes, *Standing on a Volcano*, vii, xi, 178.

[6] Jamie H. Cockfield, ed., *Dollars and Diplomacy: Ambassador David Rowland Francis and the Fall of Tsarism, 1916–1917* (Durham, NC: Duke University Press, 1981), 4.

[7] See V. S. Vasyukov, *Vneshniaia politika Rossii nakanune Fevral'skoi revoliutsii* (Moscow: Mysl', 1989), 182.

[8] George F. Kennan, *Russia and the West under Lenin and Stalin* (Boston: Little, Brown, 1960), 50.

[9] Arthur Ruhl, *White Nights and Other Russian Impressions* (New York: Charles Scribner's Sons, 1917), 4.

[10] Barnes, *Standing on a Volcano*, 188.

[11] See n. 95, p. xxvi.

H. D. Peirce, a special agent of the State Department with the rank of minister plenipotentiary who was appointed in 1915 to assist the ambassador in Russia. He served in Russia for seven years, long before his appointment, and his prolonged experience taught him that the "entire social fabric of Russia, the point of view of the Russian mind and its manner of thought, differ widely from our own, and are not susceptible of estimation upon the same basis of comparison."[12] Francis did not have enough time to learn this lesson because his collaboration with the experienced adviser was very short. The next in rank was First Secretary of the embassy Fred M. Dearing, Francis's fellow countryman but his antipode in the realm of diplomacy. Frederick A. Sterling—another Missourian—and John C. White held the posts of second secretary, and John L. Ryan was third secretary.

The staff of attachés to the embassy included a brilliant naval officer, Newton A. McCully, who had been appointed the first permanent US naval attaché with residence in Petrograd and had played a prominent part in Russian-American relations during the World War, 1917 revolutions, and Civil War. By April 1916, McCully had served in Petrograd for a year and a half, was well-acquainted with Russian affairs, and had earned a reputation for being the most experienced and informed member of the embassy staff. A former newspaperman, Henry D. Baker, turned out to be the first US commercial attaché in Russia. He served there from the end of 1914 and was active in promoting closer Russian-American relations in trade and commerce. Military attaché Second Lieutenant E. Francis Riggs had reached the post just recently and was officially presented to the emperor on February 10 (23), 1916. The last addition to the embassy staff was Captain James C. Breckinridge of the Marine Corps. He was assigned to duty as assistant naval attaché at Petrograd on February 16 and arrived there shortly before Francis. All diplomats mentioned above accompanied the ambassador to the official imperial reception, which took place in the Alexandrovsky Palace at Tsarskoe Selo on April 22 (May 5), 1916.[13]

A few months after the reception, almost the whole embassy staff was replaced. In May and June 1916, Attaché Baker and all secretaries were reappointed to other posts. Harper also left Petrograd in August. Dearing—who was very critical of the embassy's work and elaborated plans "to revamp U.S. Embassy"—entered into conflict with Francis, and in the fall of that year, he left Russia without a new appointment in the Foreign Service. In the course of 1916, Secretaries Norman Armour, Sheldon Whitehouse, and Livingston Phelps joined the staff, followed by First Secretary James G. Bailey in early 1917. Of great help to Francis were the appointments of J. Butler Wright as counselor and William C. Huntington as commercial attaché later in 1916.

---

[12] Herbert H. D. Peirce, "Russia," *The Atlantic Monthly*, October 1901, 465.

[13] D. R. Francis to Frank L. Polk, May 9, 1916, in *Dollars and Diplomacy*, 20–22. For the official Russian account of the reception, see B. D. Gal′perina and B. D. Milovidov, comps., *Kamerfuryerskiye zhurnaly 1916–1917* (St. Petersburg: D. A. R. K., 2014), 138–39.

The last imperial Russian foreign minister stated that Francis produced "an impression of not a diplomat, but a businessman, as well as all his embassy staff; even their residence was more like a commercial office than an embassy." In his opinion, only Wright and Huntington looked like real diplomats. "Especially Huntington was able to serve as an example for foreign diplomats."[14]

Counselor Wright arrived at his post on November 4 (17), 1916, and found a staff beset with disorganization and inefficiency. Francis seemed "a rather daft, grandfatherly country gentlemen" with "great sense of nature, good keenness and common sense." But as ambassador, he had "very little conception of the social amenities as regards the Diplomatic Service." As the weeks passed, Wright and many of the embassy staff worried that the ambassador's inexperience might cause him to do something foolhardy and embarrassing. As a result, Wright and his colleagues hovered nervously around him, creating a tense work environment.[15] "Wright performed his duties with great conscientiousness, but found it difficult to strike the right tone in his relation to Francis," Kennan wrote. "In Wright's eyes, Francis personified all the characteristic weakness of the political appointee in a diplomatic position. In Francis' eyes, Wright manifested the worst traits of the career officer."[16]

After the World War erupted, the US embassy in Petrograd was assigned to represent the German and Austro-Hungarian interests in Russia. The main part of this job was to supervise a great number of prisoners of war. To coordinate the POW work, the so-called Second Division of the embassy was created, and a prominent social worker, Edward T. Devine, arrived in March 1916 to head it. The division was assisted by the members of the American Young Men's Christian Associations, headed by Dr. Archibald C. Harte. Devine's frictions with Francis over their respective jurisdiction and his reputation of being pro-German led to his recall, and in October, the former secretary of the St. Petersburg embassy, Basil Miles, replaced him as head of the division. "Mr. Basil Miles, the new head of the Second Division of the Relief Branch of the embassy, has taken charge and gives promise of being very satisfactory," Francis wrote to his wife.[17] Miles was appointed special assistant to the ambassador with the rank of minister plenipotentiary. Soon the Foreign Service "emergency man," William F. Sands arrived in Petrograd as another special assistant to the ambassador to help Miles in his division. On the whole, in early 1917, at least fifty people made up the US embassy in Petrograd: twenty-eight of the regular staff

---

[14] N. N. Pokrovsky, *Poslednii v Mariinskom dvortse: Vospominaniia ministra inostrannykh del* (Moscow: Novoe literaturnoe obozrenie, 2015), 192.

[15] William Allison, *American Diplomats in Russia: Case Studies in Orphan Diplomacy, 1916–1919* (Westport, CT: Praeger, 1997), 51–53.

[16] George F. Kennan, *Russia Leaves the War* (Princeton, NJ: Princeton University Press, 1989), 43.

[17] D. R. Francis to Jane Francis, October 18 (31), 1916, in *Dollars and Diplomacy*, 55.

and twenty-two in the Second Division, making it the largest diplomatic mission in Russia.[18] The staff of the US consulate general in Petrograd consisted of five people, headed by North Winship, an experienced diplomat.[19]

The ambassador is always front and center in his egocentric memoirs; most of the people listed above Francis does not mention in his writings, or mentions only in passing. For example, he writes almost nothing about the Second Division, which completed the majority of the embassy's everyday work. Meanwhile, most of the secretaries and attachés were more informed and experienced in their duties than the ambassador in his. Unfortunately, something of Francis's "awkwardness made itself felt in the ambassador's relations with his career associates," Kennan noted. "He could not help but be aware of their greater familiarity both with diplomatic life in general and with the Petrograd scene in particular. On the other hand, it was difficult for him to seek and accept their opinions without betraying his own ignorance and forfeiting the dignity of his position."[20] Another historian stated: "Apart from his ignoring the appearance of things in a capital rife with rumors about spying and espionage, Francis made additional mistakes due to the unfamiliarity of both setting and role. His outlook was shaped by the shibboleths around which he had fashioned careers in business and the Democratic party."[21]

Arriving in Petrograd, Francis found that the state of the embassy building was a problem. The US embassy rented the mansion of Count Michael N. Grabbe on Furshtatskaya street. The ambassador had his office on the second floor, near two small private rooms that Philip Jordan had furnished as his bedroom and sitting room. But this poorly furnished "palace" was considered a "laughing stock among Russians and diplomats alike," Chargé Charles S. Wilson reported.[22] Francis was appalled at the rundown condition and inadequate furnishing of the embassy, which was described by an eyewitness as looking more like a warehouse than a residence. "It is a large house and susceptible of being made very attractive, but it is out of repair and has little furniture and no furnishing whatever," the ambassador wrote to his son.[23] To the secretary of state, he reported: "The Embassy building is in very poor condition. I am sleeping in the Embassy and taking breakfast here, which is furnished

---

[18] Norman E. Saul, *War and Revolution: The United States and Russia, 1914–1921* (Lawrence: University Press of Kansas, 2001), 69–70.

[19] See *Ves' Petrograd na 1917: Adresnaia i spravochnaia kniga g. Petrograda. Dvadtsat' chetvertyi god izdaniia* (Petrograd: T-vo A. S. Suvorina "Novoe vremia," 1916), 97.

[20] Kennan, *Russia Leaves the War*, 38.

[21] David Mayers, *The Ambassadors and America's Soviet Policy* (New York: Oxford University Press, 1995), 72.

[22] See Saul, *War and Revolution*, 9.

[23] Barnes, *Standing on a Volcano*, 194–95.

by the wife of one of the messengers; my luncheon and dinner I get elsewhere."[24] On May 17 (30), Francis cabled Lansing: "Just completed visits to my colleagues whose elegantly founded, well located embassies put me to shame. Am[erican] Embassy inconvenient ill adapted almost absolutely unequipped."[25] Francis was obliged to advance his own cash to pay for a dining room suite, kitchen utensils and supplies, curtains, and shades.[26] Furthermore, the Francis residence was located "in a fashionable part of the city lying between its center and the Tairide district to the east. Since this latter district included the later Soviet head-quarters at the Smolny Institute, as well as the Parliament building, the American Embassy found itself in the midst of some of the most dramatic and violent happenings of the revolutionary period."[27]

Francis's personal connections in the Russian capital were rather limited. As Kennan noted:

> Francis' taste and habits were the robust and simple ones of the American Middle West at the turn of the century. As such, they bore little affinity to the refined predilections of continental diplomatic society.... [His] preference for an evening's entertainment ran to good cigars, good whisky, and a few cronies around the card table, rather than to large and elegant mixed gatherings. For this reason, as well as by reason of a certain parsimoniousness, he lived for the most part quietly in his Embassy apartment, confining his social life largely to the American colony, taking relatively little part in the social doings of high Petrograd society.[28]

In April 1916, there were 202 American citizens in the Russian capital.[29] Significantly, Francis's first visitor after his arrival was H. Fessenden Meserve, who represented the National City Bank of New York in Russia.[30] Samuel McRoberts, a Missourian and vice president of the bank, also arrived in Petrograd on May 2 (15), 1916, for the purpose of consummating a loan of $50,000,000 to the Russian government.[31] Francis actively supported McRoberts during his visit to Petrograd

---

[24] D. R. Francis to R. Lansing, May 2, 1916, in *Lansing Papers, 1914–1920*, 2: 312.

[25] See Saul, *War and Revolution*, 67.

[26] Barnes, *Standing on a Volcano*, 201.

[27] Kennan, *Russia Leaves the War*, 36.

[28] Ibid., 36–38.

[29] *Izvestiia Obshchestva sblizheniia mezhdu Rossiei i Amerikoi*, 2 (April 1916): 45.

[30] Barnes, *Standing on a Volcano*, 193.

[31] D. R. Francis to R. Lansing, May 20, 1916, in *Lansing Papers*, 1: 149; D. R. Francis to R. Lansing, July 25, 1916, in *Dollars and Diplomacy*, 37.

and helped negotiate a loan, and at the very end of the year, a branch of the National City Bank was opened in Petrograd. Another respected American businessman in the Russian capital was Marion McAllister Smith of Guaranty Trust Company of New York. But the main figure in the local American business community was the representative of the New York Life Insurance Company, Frederick M. Corse. "The tall, fifty-one-year-old Vermonter was fluent in Russian and considered to be the dean of the American colony in Petrograd. He was Francis's closest male friend."[32] It was Corse who initiated the establishment of the American hospital in Petrograd. In December 1916, Francis was personally introduced to each of the wounded soldiers at the hospital.[33] Another group of American residents led by the Meserves and the Smiths had united to sponsor the American Refuge for Refugee Women and Children from the War Zone. Both factions received additional support from the US embassy.

Another circle of the Francis's acquaintances consisted of American wives of Russian noblemen with high social standing: Baroness Frances Ramsay (who was a sister of Sheldon Whitehouse), Countess Lilie Nostitz, Princess Susan Beloselskaya-Belozerskaya, and Princess Julia Cantacuzéne-Speransky, granddaughter of President Grant. Assistant Foreign Minister Vladimir A. Artzimovich, a former consul in San Francisco, was also married to an American. He was America's confidential friend in the ministry but was dismissed in October 1916. There was also the educational and philanthropic *Mayak* (Lighthouse) Society in Petrograd, sponsored by the YMCA and headed by General Secretary Franklin A. Gaylord. Pastor George A. Simons ran the affairs of the American Methodist Episcopal Chapel in Petrograd. In 1915, a branch of the Russian-American Chamber of Commerce and the Society for Promoting Mutual Friendly Relations between Russia and America were established in Petrograd. The society was headed by the former Russian Ambassador to Washington Roman R. Rosen. In June 1916, the society council gave a dinner in honor of the new US ambassador.[34] Nevertheless, Francis was slow to make friends among the Russians. "I gave a Fourth of July reception yesterday," he wrote to his wife. "The guests were mainly, if not altogether, Americans, as Russians do not understand the Fourth of July, and furthermore I have made comparatively few social acquaintances among the Russians."[35]

---

[32] Barnes, *Standing on a Volcano*, 207.

[33] Lyubov Ginzburg, "Rediscovering the 'Living Human Documents' of a Goodwill Initiative: Letters from Russian Soldiers Cared for at the City Hospital of the American Colony in Petrograd, 1914–1918," in *New Perspectives on Russian-American Relations*, ed. William Benton Whisenhunt and Norman E. Saul (New York: Routledge, 2016), 129–31, 135.

[34] *Izvestiia Obshchestva sblizheniia mezhdu Rossiei i Amerikoi*, 3 (September 1916): 34.

[35] D. R. Francis to Jane Francis, July 5, 1916, in *Dollars and Diplomacy*, 31.

Francis's circle of knowledgeable acquaintances, his place in Russian high society, and his influence in governmental lobby were far smaller than that of the British or French ambassadors. Francis "had found himself overshadowed, in his relation to Russian court circles, by his French and British colleagues, who were more experienced, better connected, more at home in the world of dynamic diplomacy and aristocratic social forms."[36] The most influential foreign representative in Petrograd was obviously the British Ambassador Sir George W. Buchanan. The stuffy and proper Englishman sharply contrasted with casual Francis.[37] Next in influence was the French Ambassador Maurice Paléologue, whose meeting with the US ambassador went very poorly because Francis's efforts to avoid giving the slightest hint of partiality in the war irked the French ambassador.[38] "Francis seems to have found no easy approach to his diplomatic colleagues," Kennan noted. "They, for their part, tended either to ignore him or to view him with amusement and condescension. His rare diplomatic dinners…failed to accord with the standards of diplomatic elegance then prevailing in the Russian capital."[39] Francis "was alternately ignored and patronized by his British and French colleagues. He seldom entertained and led an unsociable life in the dilapidated embassy."[40] Both Buchanan and Paléologue rarely mentioned Francis in their memoirs, and so Russian officials did.

The whole term of Francis's stay in Russia may be divided into five periods: the last months of the imperial Russia (April 1916–February 1917), revolutionary turmoil under the Provisional Government (February–October 1917), dawn of the Bolshevik era in Petrograd (October 1917–February 1918), stop-off in Soviet Vologda (March–July 1918), and the final sojourn in Arkhangel'sk occupied by the Allied forces (August–November 1918). Actually, Francis saw five different Russias from his windows: he was made to act in five different historical situations and presents five different images of Russia in his book. That is why his *Russia from the American Embassy* appears to a reader so multifaceted, varied, and even contradictory.

"The mission upon which I have started is a very difficult one," Francis wrote after his appointment.[41] But he was not able to realize then how difficult it would prove! His main assignment in Russia was to negotiate a new commercial treaty instead of the old 1832 treaty abrogated by the US government in 1911. Surprisingly for the instigators of the abrogation, this sanction did not affect Russian policy at

---

[36] Kennan, *Russia Leaves the War*, 16.

[37] Saul, *War and Revolution*, 71.

[38] Benson Lee Grayson, *Russian-American Relations in World War I* (New York: Frederick Ungar, 1979), 79.

[39] Kennan, *Russia Leaves the War*, 38.

[40] Mayers, *The Ambassadors and America's Soviet Policy*, 74.

[41] D. R. Francis to C. S. Hamlin, April 20, 1916, in *Dollars and Diplomacy*, 14.

all. The abrogation had accomplished nothing. Meanwhile, Russian-American relations were "frigid" and the abrogation only added to existing difficulties.[42] Woodrow Wilson himself actively supported the abrogation in his search for votes on the eve of the 1912 election, but in becoming president, he was forced to try to restore normal commercial relations with Russia. Ambassador Marye could not accomplish the task. "[We] need diplomatic and commercial representation in Russia of a standard of excellence which can eradicate a growing suspicion of our sordidness.... [We] need the proper official representation also because at the end of the war we must strive to make a commercial treaty with Russia," the military correspondent Richard W. Child wrote in 1916.[43]

Interested primarily in negotiating a new commercial treaty, Francis accepted the post under the mistaken belief that he could accomplish this end without difficulty. But from the very beginning, he was shockingly disappointed by Russian refusal even to discuss the matter. Instead, Russian Foreign Minister Sergei D. Sazonov several times reminded Francis that "the treaty had been denounced by America and not by Russia."[44] With the treaty his primary interest, Francis was to find his stay in Russia marked by frustration, bitterness, and failure.[45] Actually, the main job of the US embassy in Russia during the World War was the care of German and Austro-Hungarian prisoners of war. Ambassador Marye complained that "operation of the embassy was swamped by the influx of unexpectedly high numbers of POWs; 80 percent of its work was devoted to this issue."[46] The POW work was greater than all other business of the embassy combined, Francis reported in July 1916.[47] "At the end of 1916, the American embassy and consulates in Russia were undertaken to care for more than two million military and civilian prisoners in concentration camps scattered throughout European Russia and Siberia," Countess Nostitz wrote.[48] The need to fulfill these enormous obligations become an unpleasant surprise for Francis, who had little interest in the job. "He would have preferred to ignore the military-prisoner

---

[42] Clifford L. Egan, "Pressure Groups, the Department of State, and the Abrogation of the Russian-American Treaty of 1832," *Proceedings of the American Philosophical Society* 115, no. 4 (1971): 334.

[43] Richard Washburn Child, *Potential Russia* (New York: E. P. Dutton, 1916), 199–201.

[44] D. R. Francis to R. Lansing, May 7 and June 16, 1916, in *Dollars and Diplomacy*, 18, 28–29.

[45] Grayson, *Russian-American Relations in World War I*, 74.

[46] Mayers, *The Ambassadors and America's Soviet Policy*, 69.

[47] See Saul, *War and Revolution*, 45.

[48] Countess Nostitz, *The Countess from Iowa* (New York: G. P. Putnam's Sons, 1936), 172.

issue and was dismayed by the scope of problems in what he called the 'uncongenial task' of representing German and Austrian interests."[49]

Francis had a one-sided view of the internal situation in late imperial Russia, which was influenced by his acquaintances in liberal Russian circles. As Harper noted, the ambassador quickly had "interested himself in the work and views of the people's organizations, whose leaders were soon to head the revolution of March, 1917."[50] The prospect of revolution was first mentioned by him as early as August 1916, when Francis reported to the secretary of state: "I do not think there will be a revolution immediately after the close of the war, [but] if the Court Party does not adopt a more liberal policy by extending more privileges to the people and their representatives in the Duma, a revolution will take place before the lapse of even a few years."[51] In December 1916, Francis wrote: "It is more than interesting to be in the position which I occupy at this time. This is the most critical period of the world's history in my opinion, and Petrograd is occupying a very prominent place in the theater of affairs—in fact it is second to none."[52] Francis anticipated some events of importance in Russian history but was sure that "there is no danger of a revolution before the end of the war."[53] His own position began to strengthen due to the breaking off of diplomatic relations between the US and Germany on February 3, 1917. "The Russians are very much pleased with the stand we have taken and are already beginning to treat us as Allies," Francis reported.[54] A bit later the ambassador repeated to Wilson that he did "not anticipate any revolution…in the immediate future."[55]

On February 23 (March 8) 1917, the revolution in Petrograd did erupt. According to Countess Nostitz, when its outcome had become clear, Francis said to her: "It doesn't surprise me. But all the same I consider my colleagues of some of the other Embassies have made a great mistake in backing up the opposition movement against the Imperial Family. I told them so at our last conference. I said—'Gentlemen, in the Middle States, from where I come, we don't swap horses while crossing a stream.'"[56] After the emperor's abdication, he recognized that "this is undoubtedly a revolution,

---

[49] Mayers, *The Ambassadors and America's Soviet Policy*, 73.

[50] See Barnes, *Standing on a Volcano*, 204.

[51] D. R. Francis to R. Lansing, August 14, 1916, in *Lansing Papers*, 2: 319.

[52] D. R. Francis to P. B. Fourke, December 10 (23), 1916, in *Dollars and Diplomacy*, 71–72.

[53] D. R. Francis to C. Thompson, January 4 (17), 1917, in *Dollars and Diplomacy*, 78.

[54] D. R. Francis to R. Lansing, January 29 (February 11), 1917, in *Lansing Papers*, 2: 321–322.

[55] See David S. Foglesong, "A Missouri Democrat in Revolutionary Russia: Ambassador David R. Francis and the American Confrontation with Russian Radicalism, 1917," *Gateway Heritage* 12, no. 3 (1992): 26.

[56] Countess Nostitz, *The Countess from Iowa*, 195.

but it is the best managed revolution that has ever taken place for its magnitude."[57] A downfall of a thousand-year empire meant the dawn of the new era in Russia and in the history of Russian-American relations, as well as in Francis's diplomatic career.

The US ambassador turned out to be the first foreign diplomat to pose the question of recognition of the Russian Provisional Government. Three days after the emperor's abdication, Francis telegraphed to Washington his reasons for speedy recognition, trying to convince Lansing that it was "the most amazing revolution," which was "the practical realization of that principle of government which we have championed and advocated, I mean government by consent of the governed."[58] In his mind, the Russian Revolution was the equivalent of the American one almost a century and a half before.[59] His decision was influenced also by the new Russian foreign minister, Pavel N. Milyukov, who found in Francis "a credulous interlocutor."[60] Milyukov himself recalled: "The Ambassador from the United States, the dear Francis (who was in no way a diplomat), clearly wanted America to be the first to recognize the Russian revolution, and I willingly entered a little conspiracy with him."[61] As George Buchanan noted ironically, "The United States Ambassador was the first to recognize the Provisional Government officially on March 22, an achievement of which he was always proud."[62]

But Francis was not able to follow the rapid and chaotic sweep of events that led Russia from one crisis to another. His view of the unfolding events was limited and based in illusion. Francis confessed that such "assumptions concerning the Russian situation" which "were least likely to be fulfilled," namely, "that Russian political life would advance at once toward a stable parliamentary system and that Russia would continue to wage war."[63] As Foglesong wrote: "In the euphoria that followed the tsar's abdication, Francis and other U.S. officials neglected the deeper social and economic origins of the revolution, underestimated the strength of the Soviet, and exaggerated the power of the Provisional Government. An inflated notion of the influence and authority of the Duma leaders distorted Francis' perspective and alleviated his con-

---

[57] D. R. Francis to R. Lansing, March 2 (15), 1917, in *Dollars and Diplomacy*, 91.

[58] Francis telegram to Lansing, March 18, 1917, in *Foreign Relations of the United States, 1917*, 1207. (Hereafter referred to as *FRUS*.)

[59] Barnes, *Standing on a Volcano*, 227, 239.

[60] G. N. Mikhailovskii, *Zapiski: Iz istorii rossiiskogo vneshnepoliticheskogo vedomstva, 1914–1920* (Moscow: Mezhdunarodnye otnosheniia, 1993), 1, 280.

[61] Paul Miliukov, *Political Memoirs, 1905–1907* (Ann Arbor: University of Michigan Press, 1967), 439.

[62] George Buchanan, *My Mission to Russia and Other Diplomatic Memoirs* (London: Cassel, 1923), 2: 91.

[63] Kennan, *Russia Leaves the War*, 16.

cern about the unpredictability of the workers and soldiers.... [He] never grasped the degree to which political authority had become fragmented or understood the army's demoralization."[64] Besides, "Francis labored under the haziest knowledge of the ideological divisions within the Marxist and non-Marxist socialist parties."[65] Francis "was sufficiently aware of the plight of the Russian people to welcome jubilantly the overthrow of the Tsar and the coming to power of the Provisional Government," the former Consul DeWitt C. Poole said. With "the members of the Provisional Government Francis had a bridge of understanding, and with them in power over a period of years Francis might have gone down as a pretty successful ambassador." Those pro-Allied liberals, Poole continued, "were well inside the understanding and liking of Francis or any other rather narrowly American American."[66]

On March 25 (April 7), 1917, news of the US entering the war against Germany reached Petrograd. This created a new situation in Russian-American relations and made the US ambassador a popular figure in the Russian capital. "That revolution and our entering the war, so nearly contemporaneous as they were, mark a new era in the history of society," Francis reported. "Our form of government is their model; our taking part in the contest has infused into them a confident spirit and imbued them with a firm determination."[67] As Francis stated a bit later, "In my judgment the American Embassy is respected to a greater extent and has more influence with the Provisional Government and with the people generally than any other mission in Russia."[68] Owing to his position as envoy of Russia's new powerful ally, Francis indeed enjoyed a rather elusive prestige in Petrograd. But his ambassadorial position was compromised and diminished by the flux of special US missions with no clearly defined responsibilities, which were arriving one after another on the Petrograd scene during the summer of 1917.

The first of them were the Railway (Stevens) Commission and the so-called Root Mission. Francis readily supported the former and even tried to direct its activities, but was reluctant as to the advisability of the latter, which was sent by the Wilson administration regardless of the ambassador's opinion. From the very beginning, the issue of confusion of authorities arose. As Root remarked, "It is plain that we can't have three bodies dealing with the Russian Government at the same time—the regular Embassy, the President's Mission & the R. R. Commission."[69] But Wilson

---

[64] Foglesong, "A Missouri Democrat in Revolutionary Russia," 28.

[65] Mayers, *The Ambassadors and America's Soviet Policy*, 77–78.

[66] See Kennan, *Russia Leaves the War*, 17; Foglesong, "A Missouri Democrat in Revolutionary Russia," 28.

[67] Francis telegram, April 21, 1917, in *FRUS, 1917, Supplement 2, The World War*, vol. 1, 36.

[68] D. R. Francis to R. Lansing, April 25 (May 8), 1917, in *Lansing Papers*, 2: 332–334.

[69] E. Root to R. Lansing, May 6, 1917, in *Lansing Papers*, 2: 329.

refused to define the authorities clearly. As a result, Stevens sometimes interfered in diplomatic matters, Root discussed railroad questions, and Francis tried to do everything, maneuvering between two chiefs of missions and different branches of the Russian government. The Root Mission departed Petrograd on June 26 (July 9), leaving behind the US Military Mission, which turned out to be one more quasi-political body representing special army interests. It was headed by Brigadier General William V. Judson.

Probably the most exotic was the American Red Cross Mission—which, to the ambassador's embarrassment, soon arrived in Petrograd. The mission was promoted by Montana copper magnate William B. Thompson, who tried to use it as an instrument of America's support for Russia's continued participation in the war. Neither the ambassador nor the other official representatives on the scene felt that there was a need for such a mission.[70] The result was a deplorable misunderstanding between the ARCM and the US embassy.[71]

One more US agency was created by the Committee on Public Information under the title the American Press Bureau at Petrograd. The CPI was represented by journalist Arthur Bullard, and the committee's associate chairman, Edgar Sisson, who considered himself to be "Special Representative of President Wilson in Russia"—"thus the making of trouble and confusion were implanted firmly in the situation by official Washington before Sisson even arrived in Russia."[72]

After the arrival of the CPI emissaries, the situation with US official representation in Petrograd was confused to the highest degree. Petrograd was "host to high-level U.S. commissions, delegations, and missions that collectively eclipsed the embassy's significance."[73] Francis and "a number of other high-ranking State Department officials already at their posts in Russia did not look favorably on the prospective preemption of their responsibilities by the special commissions. The ambassador and his staff viewed the personnel of the various commissions as Johnnies-come-lately and as too inexperienced to understand either the political complications of the Revolution or the Russian military's failures on the Eastern Front."[74] Bullard described the situation in the following words: "No one of the ambassadors was of strong enough character to dominate and control his own flock. Grouped, about each embassy, there were military missions, secret services, publicity agents, commercial attachés, all busily

---

[70] Neil V. Salzman, *Reform and Revolution: The Life and Times of Raymond Robins* (Kent, OH: Kent State University Press, 1991), 177.

[71] Kennan, *Russia Leaves the War*, 61.

[72] Ibid., 50–51.

[73] Mayers, *The Ambassadors and America's Soviet Policy*, 86.

[74] Neil V. Salzman, ed., *Russia in War and Revolution: General William V. Judson's Accounts from Petrograd, 1917–1918* (Kent, OH: Kent State University Press, 1998), 30.

engaged in trying to serve their country, but with no one to co-ordinate their actions. They were continually getting in each other's way." And, he added, "Our own representatives—embassy, military mission, Red Cross, and consulates—were just as bitterly divided."[75]

At the same time, the ambassador's "neglect of discerning reports" by his more competent and informed subordinates "meant that Francis denied himself real familiarity with the Russian situation."[76] In mid-September, J. Butler Wright noted in his diary that amid rumors "that the 'Bolshevik' sentiment is growing in strength throughout the country everyone, with only the exception of D. R. F., believes that a clash—and a serious one—is bound to occur soon." The counselor was amused by the "glowing reports" of D. R. F., which were not distinguished by brilliant insights or farsighted prescriptions.[77] On the morning of October 26 (November 8), 1917, Francis once more woke up in a completely new country. "Situation here undetermined but this Bolshevik government can not survive and I think will collapse within few days," Francis telegraphed to Washington on the fourth day of the October Revolution.[78] "[The] 'governor,' as Harper and other advisers called Francis—and in character he remained the ex-governor of Missouri, the Show-Me state—was confident that the Bolsheviks would not take power, and then, that they would fall," Albert Rhys Williams explains.[79] With such a view, the ambassador "seemed to have no policy at all except to insist that the Bolsheviks could not last."[80]

Lieutenant Colonel Raymond Robins, who replaced Thompson as the head of the ARCM, and General Judson were in favor of some limited contacts with the Bolshevik government from the very beginning, considering them a matter of necessity. But Francis officially informed Judson on November 7 (20) that "it was my policy to do nothing or permit no act to be performed by anyone connected with the Embassy or under my control that could be construed as a direct or indirect recognition of what is generally known as the 'Bolshevik' government."[81] The start of the Soviet-German peace negotiations at Brest-Litovsk created a new situation. Judson insisted on contact with the Soviet leadership in order to influence conditions of the

---

[75] Arthur Bullard, *The Russian Pendulum* (New York: Macmillan, 1919), 111–13. This title is also available as a reprint. See *The Russian Pendulum: Autocracy—Democracy—Bolshevism*, ed. David W. McFadden (Bloomington, IN: Slavica, 2019).

[76] Mayers, *The Ambassadors and America's Soviet Policy*, 86.

[77] Foglesong, "A Missouri Democrat in Revolutionary Russia," 37–40.

[78] Francis telegram, November 11, 1917, in *FRUS, 1918, Russia*, vol. 3, 207.

[79] Albert Rhys Williams, *Journey into Revolution: Petrograd, 1917–1918* (Chicago: Quadrangle Books, 1969), 82.

[80] Ibid., 196–97.

[81] Salzman, *Russia in War and Revolution*, 136.

armistice, and Francis grew inclined to his opinion, but on November 23 (December 6), Lansing forbade "all direct communication with the Bolsheviks." Under pressure from opposite sides, disoriented Francis either acted in contradiction or preferred not to act at all.

All the significant American representatives in Petrograd jointly agreed to recommend opening informal channels of communication with the Bolshevik government in order to coordinate actions against Germany. The American community was united on one other issue as well: the necessity of replacing the ambassador with someone more reliable and with better judgment.[82] After Francis's conviction was proven wrong by the Bolshevik seizure of power, the sense that the elderly ambassador was tired, confused, and out of touch with Russian reality contributed to a movement by other US envoys in Russia to have him recalled.[83] Sisson, the prime instigator of the recall movement, reported on November 21 (December 4): "Found Ambassador without policy except anger at Bolsheviks, unamenable to arguments or entreaties of his official advisers, military and civil." In his opinion, "no fruitful work can be done here by any division of our Government so long as Francis remains in charge of Embassy." The ambassador "impress[es] every one as a sick man absolutely unfitted to the strain physical and mental of his great post," Sisson added.[84] The next day, Judson wrote in his diary that Francis "seems to me completely exhausted and overwrought by the strain he has recently been under."[85] Two days later, Huntington reported to Harper that Francis was increasingly tired, despondent, and in ill health.[86] Bullard shared the common opinion in his letter to Edward House: "Francis is a sick man entirely overwhelmed by the situation, [and] he has created hopelessly hostile relations with people where it is his obvious duty to seek cooperation."[87] The recommendations for Francis's removal were supported by Basil Miles and William F. Sands, who had already returned to Washington and tried to push the decision through the State Department.[88]

Sir George Buchanan left Petrograd on December 25, 1917 (January 7, 1918), and Francis, being the next in seniority, replaced him as the doyen of the diplomatic corps. His debut in this capacity took place a week later when Francis led the entire corps in its unanimous protest against the arrest of the Romanian minister,

---

[82] David W. McFadden, *Alternative Paths: Soviets and Americans, 1917–1920* (New York: Oxford University Press, 1993), 91–92.

[83] Foglesong, "A Missouri Democrat in Revolutionary Russia," 38.

[84] Kennan, *Russia Leaves the War*, 125–26.

[85] Salzman, *Russia in War and Revolution*, 165.

[86] See Saul, *War and Revolution*, 201.

[87] See McFadden, *Alternative Paths*, 92.

[88] Kennan, *Russia Leaves the War*, 385–86.

Count Diamandy, and all his staff by the Bolsheviks.[89] Lenin responded by pointing to the extremely dangerous situation in which Russian troops found themselves on the Romanian Front. Nevertheless, the Romanians were released the following day and then deported from Russia. Significantly, the unpublished version of Francis's memoirs differs in this particular case from the published one.[90] In the course of further events, Francis was becoming increasingly isolated—from Washington, the Soviet government, and his own staff.[91] On February 7, 1918, Harper concluded that a new ambassador was needed because "men of wide vision and men of action are required at this most critical post."[92] At the same time, Robins was bound to appear in Petrograd as "the real American Ambassador" and, thus, to diminish Francis's prestige and his potential usefulness in the formal ambassadorial position.[93]

By the end of January, the wife of the naval attaché at Petrograd has come to the conclusion that there was "no place for Americans! There is nothing that they can accomplish."[94] That same day, the Soviet delegation at Brest-Litovsk interrupted peace negotiations to give a pretext for the German offensive, which began on February 18, 1918, and created danger for Petrograd.[95] Two days later, at a conference of Allied representatives, the decision was made to abandon the Russian capital. While the Soviet government was preparing to escape to Moscow, the Americans chose Vologda, a railroad junction 300 miles east of Petrograd. There, Francis might decide to continue his way further east to Vladivostok or to go to Arkhangel′sk in northern Russia. On February 24 and 27, the American colony (consisting of more

---

[89] See *FRUS, 1918, Russia*, vol. 1, 477–78; Kennan, *Russia Leaves the War*, 330–42. For other accounts of these events, see Louis de Robien, *The Diary of a Diplomat in Russia, 1917–1918* (New York: Praeger, 1970), 190–94 (French); Flavius Solomon and Andrei Cușco, "How Much Ideology can Diplomacy Endure? The Early Phase of Soviet-Romanian Relations, November 1917–February 1918," *Jahrbücher für Geschichte Osteuropas* 63, no. 3 (2015): 400–407 (Romanian); I.A. Zalkind, "NKID v semnadtsatom godu," *Utro Strany Sovetov* (Leningrad: Lenizdat, 1988), 204 (Soviet).

[90] See Kennan, *Russia Leaves the War*, 338.

[91] Saul, *War and Revolution*, 222–24.

[92] Ibid., 229.

[93] Kennan, *Russia Leaves the War*, 395–96.

[94] Pauline S. Crosley, *Intimate Letters from Petrograd* (New York: E. P. Dutton, 1920), 273. This title is also available as a reprint. See *Intimate Letters from Petrograd*, ed. Lee A. Farrow (Bloomington, IN: Slavica, 2019).

[95] The change of calendars occurred in between. Until February 1918, Russia clung to the Julian (or Old Style) calendar, which was thirteen days behind the Gregorian (New Style) calendar used in Western Europe and the United States. So February 1, OS, turned into February 14, NS.

than sixty people) had left Petrograd.[96] It included the embassy staff, officers of the military mission, people of the Red Cross and YMCA, personnel of the New York City Bank, and some other Americans. Most of the other diplomatic missions followed the Americans or joined them later. Thus, Vologda turned to be the "diplomatic capital of Russia," as Francis termed the city. The theater critic Oliver M. Sayler wrote:

> I went out from Petrograd to Vologda to see Mr. Francis early in March 1918, ten days after all the embassies had fled from the panic-stricken capital. The day I arrived in Vologda, the Ambassador gave out to the Russian press the following statement, which was copied throughout Russia: ... "America still counts itself an ally of the Russian people and we shall be ready to help, no matter what Government organizes a vigorous resistance to the German invasion." ... Here again, with all its genuine sympathy, was the same misunderstanding of the social revolution as a mere political quarrel. Here again was the delusion in which most people outside Russia resisted—the delusion that Russia could fight once more if she wished to.[97]

News of the Brest-Litovsk treaty, concluded on March 3, 1918, quickly reached Vologda. Francis began to "inveigh against Brest-Litovsk," hoping to destroy it, especially after the Murmansk experiment where the Allies cooperated with the local Soviets in joint efforts to organize an anti-German Front. On April 5, Francis telegraphed to Lansing: "Transportation conditions deplorable and require improvement, which we can best render having demonstrated our ability thereof by bettering Soviet government service." The ambassador even suggested "to place American Railway Commission in charge of Soviet government.... Furthermore, in event of Allied intervention from east or west or both, railroad efficiency is essential," he continued. Francis recommended to ignore "mistakes of Soviet government and outrages practiced" in order to "induce Soviet government to ask Allied assistance, so that when Allies enter Russia, will not with Soviet government's refusal, but Soviet government's welcome."[98] By May 2, Francis had decided that the "time for Allied intervention has arrived" because the Russian people were ready to welcome it.[99] On June 4, after the Czecho-Slovak revolt, he made a trip to Petrograd to try to establish contact with anti-Bolshevik forces in the former capital on the assumption that soon,

---

[96] Saul, *War and Revolution*, 234–35.

[97] Oliver M. Sayler, "Russia Looks to America," *North American Review* 209, no. 759 (1919): 191–93.

[98] Francis telegram, April 5, 1918, in *FRUS, 1918, Russia*, vol. 3, 228.

[99] Francis telegram, May 2, 1918, in *FRUS, 1918, Russia*, vol. 1, 519–21.

the Bolshevik power would collapse.[100] In his opinion, the Czecho-Slovak case might justify the intervention of the Allied powers in Russia.[101] "Russian people [are] confidently expecting Allied intervention and will welcome it," Francis stated. "Russian people are expecting America to lead in intervention," he continued. "At the same time these people require leadership and look to us therefore."[102]

During his stay in Vologda and later in Arkhangel´sk, Francis associated with many people who were prominent not only in local affairs, but in all-Russian politics as well. On July 4, 1918, he reported: "I gave a Fourth of July reception to-day. ... [The] feeling in Vologda is very friendly towards the Embassy as it is realized that we have added much to the reputation of the city."[103] But this idyll disappeared two days later when Left Socialist Revolutionaries assassinated Count Mirbach, Germany's envoy to Russia, and an anti-Bolshevik uprising erupted in Moscow, followed by a mutiny in Yaroslavl´. In response, the Extraordinary Revolutionary Staff was created in Vologda. It assumed all powers in the city and stationed a military guard at the door of the embassy. The Soviet government tried to force diplomats to move to Moscow. Instead they decided to escape to Arkhangel´sk, where the Allied intervention was anticipated.

On July 24, 1918, Francis, at the head of the entire diplomatic corps, left Vologda and reached Arkhangel´sk after the Allied forces occupied the city. Arkhangel´sk turned out to be the second diplomatic capital of Russia alongside Moscow. From Arkhangel´sk, Francis "called for large, aggressive military campaigns to reorganize Russian resistance to Germany and eradicate the menace of Bolshevism."[104] Mayers wrote: "There Francis became enmeshed in the affairs of Nicholas Chaikovsky and the anti-Bolsheviks of the area, whose career involved coup, countercoup, and kidnappings."[105] He practiced direct and sometimes crucial personal intervention in local politics, acting more like a governor of Missouri than an ambassador. Francis even pressed (or "advised very categorically," in his own words) the appointments of officials in the Northern Government. But by the fall of that year, he had depleted his own resources of energy and health. The timely arrival of Rear Admiral McCully, who was appointed commander of the American Naval forces in north Russia, saved him. Placed aboard the USS *Olympia* on a stretcher, Francis left Arkhangel´sk for England on November 7, 1918. It was the first anniversary of the October Revolution

---

[100] McFadden, *Alternative Paths*, 136.

[101] Francis telegram, June 11, 1918, in *FRUS, 1918, Russia*, vol. 1, 561.

[102] Francis telegram, June 22, 1918, in *FRUS, 1918, Russia*, vol. 2, 220–23.

[103] Francis telegram, July 4, 1918, in *FRUS, 1918, Russia*, vol. 1, 568.

[104] David S. Foglesong, *America's Secret War against Bolshevism: U.S. Intervention in the Russian Civil War, 1917–1920* (Chapel Hill: University of North Carolina Press, 1995), 295.

[105] Mayers, *The Ambassadors and America's Soviet Policy*, 83.

and four days before the Armistice, signed on November 11, 1918, which ended the World War.

Francis spent the remaining eight years of his life trying to convince the American public that he was right, as he did in his testimony before the Overman Committee and in his memoirs.[106] He published his *Russia from the American Embassy* soon after his official resignation in 1920. But the ambassador's book "proved to be more a defense of his actions in Russia than a historical memoir."[107] Kennan noted, "His political role was not a great one, but his simple, outspoken, American pragmatism provided a revealing contrast to the intensely theoretical controversies that raged around him, and one comes away from the reading of his memoirs with the feeling that America could have been in some ways much worse served, if in other ways better."[108] Russian historian Iurii Got´e stated in his review of Francis's memoirs that documents cited by the author constitute the most valuable part of the book. But "Russia, Russian people, and Russian interrelations were not very comprehensible mystery for him." Francis, in his opinion, was "a foreigner with, perhaps, the most alien psychology to us." The American ambassador was "not able to comprehend neither Russia itself, nor what is going on here." Therefore his memoirs are "not an impartial account of events which took place in Russia in 1916–18, but their reflection in the mind of businessman who to his own surprise become their eyewitness," concluded the reviewer.[109]

David R. Francis died in 1927. Historians differ in their opinions of his legacy. Francis was the "most fascinating, controversial, and, perhaps, misunderstood American in Russia during the revolutionary years," William Allison noted.[110] Consequently, Allison continues, to evaluate "Ambassador Francis is not an easy task. Historians have called him incompetent, misplaced, and more recently, astute and dedicated. His character has generally been praised. His skill as a diplomat, however, has often been criticized."[111] Kennan wrote: "If, as was the case, he was poorly prepared in many ways for this unusual task, one cannot deny him a certain admiration for the spirit in which he accepted and performed it."[112] But even Kennan's carefully balanced study has "not erased the negative portrait of David R. Francis as a nice old fellow who had no experience in diplomacy and was over his head representing

---

[106] Allison, *American Diplomats in Russia*, 44–46.

[107] Ibid., 47.

[108] Kennan, *Russia and the West under Lenin and Stalin*, 50–51.

[109] Iurii Got´e, "Vospominaniia posla Frensisa o Rossii," *Annaly* 3 (1923): 292–93.

[110] Allison, *American Diplomats in Russia*, 13.

[111] Ibid., 47.

[112] Kennan, *Russia and the West under Lenin and Stalin*, 50.

the United States in revolutionary Russia."[113] According to Jamie H. Cockfield, the "problem with his work came in his inability to comprehend and interpret events."[114] David Mayers stated categorically: "Mediocre U.S. diplomacy in St. Petersburg, broken by the accidental appearance of able envoys, culminated in the careers of Marye and Francis."[115] Only David S. Foglesong strays from these opinions with his conclusion that "a careful review of the available evidence suggests the need to revise the common image of Ambassador Francis as a doddering, diplomatic dilettante."[116]

As Kennan wrote many years ago, "It was easy for the members of the American community and the diplomatic corps to ridicule Francis and to deprecate his ability. An injustice had been done to him, an undeserved one, in sending him to such a post at such a time. Only the greatest unfamiliarity with the requirements of normal diplomatic life could have explained a belief that Francis at his age and with his experience and temperament, would have been well equipped to meet those requirements."[117]

This conclusion paved the way for considering the Francis problem as a part of the much broader Wilson problem. It was President Wilson who "thought that all people, whether they be Mexican peons or Russian peasants, whites or orientals, were capable of being trained in the habits of democracy."[118] Lloyd C. Gardner noted, "In both Mexico and Russia, finally, Wilson had started out fighting counter-revolution, and ended struggling to contain and control the very forces he had unknowingly encouraged by condemning reactionary special interests and imperialism."[119] Christopher Lasch explained, "In wartime Russia, Wilsonians sought initially to buttress the pro-Allied liberal-nationalist regime of the March Revolution, in order to save the moral and material strength of a liberalized Russia for the anti-German coalition. Then too, even after failing to prevent the triumph of Russian Bolshevism, the Wilson Administration continued its limited efforts, by means of intervention and diplomacy, to end the single-party rule of the Bolsheviks and hopefully to bring Russia back to the lost liberalism of the March Revolution."[120] As David McFadden concluded, "Wilson's policy was so torn between anti-Bolshevism and anti-interven-

---

[113] Barnes, *Standing on a Volcano*, xii.

[114] *Dollars and Diplomacy*, 4.

[115] Mayers, *The Ambassadors and America's Soviet Policy*, 85.

[116] Foglesong, "A Missouri Democrat in Revolutionary Russia," 39.

[117] Kennan, *Russia Leaves the War*, 40.

[118] Arthur S. Link, *Wilson the Diplomatist: A Look at His Major Foreign Policies* (Baltimore: Johns Hopkins University Press, 1957), 14.

[119] Lloyd C. Gardner, *Wilson and Revolutions, 1913–1921* (Philadelphia: J. B. Lippincott, 1976), 18.

[120] Christopher Lasch, *The American Liberals and the Russian Revolution* (New York: Columbia University Press, 1962), 7.

tion that it was not a Wilson policy at all, but instead a nonpolicy, often determined by subordinates, allies, or events in Russia."[121]

Francis's diplomatic career is a particular case of Wilsonianism, with its liberal illusions and democratic prejudices. That is why his failure as a diplomat may be considered a display of the Woodrow Wilson's greater fiasco, which culminated in the Senate's refusal to ratify the Treaty of Versailles. Francis was an ordinary American politician with a rather narrow provincial outlook. As an American who found himself in Petrograd, he wished to see in Russia another America. But Russia is a world in itself, and a foreign embassy is not the best point for observation. History itself, with the magnitude of events, was against Francis. Nevertheless, he was not the worst of the US ambassadors in Russia. Francis was not, of course, the right man in the right place, but obviously he deserves sympathy, and his memoirs—the closest attention.

Suggested Further Reading

Beatty, Bessie. *The Red Heart of Russia*. New York: Century, 1918.

Beury, Charles E. *Russia After the Revolution*. Philadelphia: George W. Jacobs, 1918.

Bolshevik Propaganda: Hearings Before a Subcomm. of the Comm. on the Judiciary, United States S. 65th Cong. (1919).

Brown, Arthur Judson. *Russia in Transformation*. New York: Fleming H. Revell, 1917.

Brown, William Adams. *The Groping Giant: Revolutionary Russia as Seen by an American Democrat*. New Haven, CT: Yale University Press, 1920.

Bryant, Louise. *Six Red Months in Russia: An Observer's Account of Russia Before and During the Proletarian Dictatorship*. New York: George H. Doran, 1918.

Buchanan, Meriel. *Petrograd: The City of Trouble, 1914–1918*. London: W. Collins Sons, 1919.

Cantacuzène, Princess. *Revolutionary Days: Recollections of Romanoffs and Bolsheviki, 1914–1917*. Boston: Small, Maynard, 1919.

Cumming, C. K., Walter W. Pettit, comps. *Russian-American Relations, March, 1917–March, 1920, Documents and Papers*. New York: Harcourt, Brace & Howe, 1920.

Davis, Malcolm W. *Open Gates to Russia*. New York: Harper & Brothers, 1920.

Dorr, Rheta Childe. *Inside the Russian Revolution*. New York: Macmillan, 1917.

Dubie, Alain. *Frank A. Golder: An Adventure of a Historian in Quest of Russian History*. Boulder, CO: East European Monographs, 1989.

---

[121] David W. McFadden, "Did Wilson Have a Russian Policy?," *Reviews in American History* 24, no. 4 (1996): 628.

Fedotoff White, D. *Survival Through War and Revolution in Russia*. Philadelphia: University of Pennsylvania Press, 1939.

Graham, Stephen. *Russia in 1916*. New York: Macmillan, 1917.

Hard, William. *Raymond Robins' Own Story*. New York: Harper & Brothers, 1920.

Harper, Florence MacLeod. *Runaway Russia*. New York: Century, 1918.

Hasegawa, Tsuyoshi. *The February Revolution, Petrograd, 1917: The End of the Tsarist Regime and the Birth of Dual Power*. Seattle: University of Washington Press, 1981.

Houghteling, James L. *A Diary of the Russian Revolution*. New York: Dodd, Mead, 1918.

Kalpaschnikoff, Andrew. *A Prisoner of Trotsky's*. Garden City, NY: Doubleday, Page, 1920.

Kliefoth, Alfred W. *Bolshevism: By an Eye-witness from Wisconsin*. Milwaukee: American Constitutional League of Wisconsin, 1920.

Marcosson, Isaac F. *The Rebirth of Russia*. New York: John Lane, 1917.

McRoberts, Samuel. *Russia*. Boston: American Institute of Banking, 1917.

[Mott, John R.]. *Recent Experiences and Impressions in Russia: Extracts from Correspondence and Addresses of John R. Mott, Member of the Special Diplomatic Mission of the United States to Russia, May–August, 1917*. New York: YMCA Press, 1917.

Mott, T. Bentley. *Twenty Years as Military Attaché*. New York: Oxford University Press, 1937.

Petrunkevitch, Alexander, Samuel Northrup Harper, and Frank Alfred Golder. *The Russian Revolution*. Cambridge, MA: Harvard University Press, 1918.

Root, Elihu. *The United States and the War, The Mission to Russia, Political Addresses*. Cambridge, MA: Harvard University Press, 1918.

Ross, Edward Alsworth. *Russia in Upheaval*. New York: Century, 1918.

Russell, Charles Edward. *Unchained Russia*. New York: D. Appleton, 1918.

Sayler, Oliver M. *Russia, White or Red*. Boston: Little, Brown, 1919.

Sisson, Edgar. *One Hundred Red Days: A Personal Chronicle of the Bolshevik Revolution*. New Haven, CT: Yale University Press, 1931.

Thompson, Donald C. *Donald Thompson in Russia*. New York: Century, 1918.

———. *From Czar to Kaiser: The Betrayal of Russia*. Garden City, NY: Doubleday, Page, 1918.

United States Special Diplomatic Mission to Russia. *America's Message to the Russian People: Addresses by the Members of the Special Diplomatic Mission of the United States to Russia in the Year 1917*. Boston: Marshall Jones, 1918.

Washburn, Stanley. *The Russian Advance: Being the Third Volume of Field Notes from the Russian Front, Embracing the Period from June 5th to September 1st, 1916.* Garden City, NY: Doubleday, Page, 1917.

Weeks, Charles J. *An American Naval Diplomat in Revolutionary Russia: The Life and Times of Vice Admiral Newton A. McCully.* Annapolis, MD: Naval Institute Press, 1993.

Figure 1. Furshtatskaya Street, 34 (US Embassy at Petrograd, 1909–18).

Figure 2. Zinger House (US Consulate General at Petrograd, 1909–18).

Figure 3. US Embassy at Vologda (1918).

Figure 4. US Consulate General at Arkhangel'sk (1918–19).

RUSSIA FROM THE AMERICAN EMBASSY
APRIL, 1916—NOVEMBER, 1918

BY

DAVID R. FRANCIS

United States Ambassador to Russia under the Czar,
the Provisional Government and the Bolsheviks

ILLUSTRATED

NEW YORK
CHARLES SCRIBNER'S SONS
1921

Copyright, 1921, by
CHARLES SCRIBNER'S SONS
Published August, 1921
Reprinted October, 1921

PRINTED AT THE SCRIBNER PRESS
NEW YORK, U.S.A.

INTRODUCTION

My commission as Ambassador to Russia was dated March 9th, 1916. As I was so long in regaining my health and strength after leaving Russia, I offered to resign the Ambassadorship three or more times, but each time the Secretary of State or the Acting Secretary dissuaded me from presenting my resignation. I have drawn no salary as Ambassador since the 26th of April, 1919, but since then I have held myself subject to being sent back to Russia as American Ambassador in the event a stable government was established there. At no time was there any likelihood of our recognizing the Bolshevik Soviet Government. My resignation as Ambassador to Russia was presented on the 3rd of March, 1921, but I have not had advice of its acceptance up to the present writing. It will be seen, therefore, that my services have covered five years.

During this period I was credited to the Monarchy of Russia thirteen months. I represented the United States with the Provisional Government of Russia for eight months.[1] I remained in Russia from the inception of Bolshevik usurpation and until within five days of the Armistice, when a surgical operation necessitated removal to a hospital in London. Upon leaving the hospital I went by direction of the Secretary of State to Paris, to be present at the meeting of the Peace Conference in February, 1919. My urgent recommendation that I be sent back to Petrograd was under consideration. I was continued as Ambassador to Russia on the inactive list and without pay, holding myself in readiness to return if there should be at any time a favorable decision upon my recommendation.

Bolshevism began to show itself eighteen months before my departure from Russia. I saw its spasmodic manifestations through the summer of 1917, its usurpation

---

[1] The Provisional Government was the supreme governing body of Russia between the February and October Revolutions, created on March 2, 1917, under the chairmanship of Prince Georgy E. Lvov. His first cabinet was dominated by Kadets and their allies and included the only socialist in the person of Alexander F. Kerensky. After the so-called April Crisis, the first coalition cabinet was formed on May 5 with enlarged socialist representation. After the July Crisis, the new coalition cabinet under chairmanship of Kerensky was composed on July 24. It was the second coalition cabinet which proclaimed the Russian Republic on September 1. The last coalition cabinet was created on September 25, 1917, a month before the October Revolution.

of power in the autumn of that year. I was in the midst of Lenin's[2] experiment in government for more than a year. I have seen this monstrosity run its course, to become the world wide danger which my observation at close hand had convinced me it would become. I have kept in close touch with developments in Russia up to the present time, reading most of the articles written by newspaper men and magazine authors who have journeyed to Russia, having obtained the consent of the Soviet Government previous to entering that country.

On the 25th of February, 1917, I sent this cablegram from Petrograd:

Secretary of State,
Washington.

Strictly confidential for President. Understand Customary to tender resignation on beginning of new term. Mine is herewith presented. Thoroughly reconciled to return or entirely willing to remain or to serve in any position where you think can be most effective. Personal interest and inclination subordinated to country's welfare in this critical juncture.

Francis.

I received no reply to the tender of my resignation, but I thought nothing strange of this, as the diplomatic regulations state an ambassador or a minister does not have to resign; he should take the sending of his successor's name to the Senate for confirmation as a removal or recall.

While at Vologda, I received from the Secretary of State, under date of May 24th, 1918, this cable:

The following is for your information: Governor Gardner of Missouri[3] has stated that on account of the recent death of Senator Stone,[4] he desired to appoint you to vacancy in the Senate. In reply the Department has stated that your services are regarded as essential to the Governments relations with Russia, and that you could not be dispensed with at this time.

---

[2] Vladimir I. Lenin (Ulyanov, 1870–1924), Bolshevik leader, founder of the Soviet state, first chairman of the Council of People's Commissars from October 26, 1917.

[3] Frederick Dozier Gardner (1869–1933), governor of Missouri, 1917–21.

[4] William J. Stone (1848–1918), Democratic politician, governor of Missouri, 1893–97; senator from Missouri, 1903–18; chairman of the United States Senate Committee on Foreign Relations, 1913–18. One of six US senators who voted against the war with Germany. Died on April 14, 1918.

The above statement was made by the Department in full confidence of your desire to serve where you are most needed.

Lansing.[5]

This was exceedingly gratifying to me, not only because of the compliment Governor Gardner paid me, but I considered it an answer to my tendered resignation.

Before leaving Petrograd for Vologda, I received two cablegrams from the Department of State. The first one authorized me to leave Petrograd when I considered it unsafe. The second authorized my departure "whenever your judgment so dictates."

On my return to Washington a year later, I asked the Department of State where they expected me to go when they authorized me to leave Petrograd. The reply was, I was expected to go to London and await orders, or to return to Washington. My colleagues all endeavored to return to their own countries, but I cabled my Government that I did not think it wise to leave Russia, and would not do so unless ordered, and I went to Vologda.

After being in Vologda four or five days, the Department cabled me I should remain there until I considered it unsafe, when I could select my own location in Russia, if I thought any place was safe.

While in Archangel, after the Department had been advised of my condition, Secretary of State, cabled me under date of October 11th, 1918:

> The Department regards your devotion to duty as an example of the highest traditions of the Service. In order to be able to continue your valued service, I believe you should proceed at once to London for consultation as to whether surgical assistance can be rendered there. Please take all precautions in your journey. I am asking the Secretary of War for special assistance from the medical officers with Colonel Stewart.[6] Advise me of your departure and your arrival in London. You will leave Poole in charge.[7] Please accept my cordial good wishes for your speedy restoration to active work.
>
> Lansing.

---

[5] Robert Lansing (1868–1928), secretary of state, 1915–20.

[6] George Evans Stewart (1872–1946), colonel, commander of the American Expeditionary Forces in northern Russia, 1918–19.

[7] DeWitt Clinton Poole, Jr. (1885–1952), graduate of University of Wisconsin (1906, BA) and George Washington University (1910, MDip); was engaged in newspaper work, 1906–10. He entered the Consular Service in 1910 and served in Berlin and Paris. Detailed for duty in the consulate general at Moscow on July 17, 1917; detailed to Arkhangel'sk as special assistant to the ambassador with rank of counselor of the embassy on October 5, 1918. Detailed to the Department of State as chief of the Division of Russian Affairs on October 1, 1919–March 1920; acting chief of the division, April 27–November 23, 1921; chief of the division, December 20, 1921–October 1, 1923.

On the 18th of November, 1918, Secretary of State Lansing cabled me through the American Embassy at London:

> As you were advised October 12th, Department plans for you to return to Archangel unless situation changes, but no definite decision will be reached until your health is restored.

From the time of my arrival in Russia, I followed the practice of committing fully to paper the incidents, the interviews, the impressions, in short whatever interested me about Russia, whether official or unofficial. I endeavored to present to the Department of State not always in formal but rather in intimate and confidential detail the quickly shifting changes that were taking place in Russia. These reports are drawn upon extensively in the chapters which follow.

In my personal letters to my family, to friends, to business associates, I wrote of Russia and of Russians, as I might have done in the freedom of a diary. Liberal extracts from these letters have been introduced. From time to time my opinions of Russian leadership and of general conditions were revised, my hopes of governmental reform and stability shattered, my predictions were not realized. The readers of this narrative will discover that. I thought it best to carry them through these different times and perilous changes in the hope that they would reach the same conclusions that I did, and which conclusions have not been changed up to the present time. Those conclusions are that Bolshevism, if it dominates the world, will lead us back to barbarism.

All the enciphered cables are set forth in paraphrases thereof.

I cheerfully acknowledge my obligation, for their valued and helpful assistance, to Mr. Lyman Beecher Stowe[8] and Mr. Walter B. Stevens.[9]

---

[8] Lyman Beecher Stowe (1880–1963), author and editor from New York City, grandson of Harriet Beecher Stowe.

[9] Walter Barlow Stevens (1848–1939), journalist and author, former reporter of *The St. Louis Times*, historian of Missouri and St. Louis. Francis's lifelong friend who induced and helped him to write his memoirs.

Chapter I
FIRST IMPRESSIONS

At two o'clock in the morning on the 28th of April, 1916, with the grinding of brakes and the pushing of people toward the doors, the Stockholm Express came to a stop in the Finland Station[1] of Petrograd,[2] and I realized that my duties as Ambassador from the greatest Republic of the New World to the Court of the mightiest Autocracy of the Old had virtually begun. It was dark and cold. I was alone except for my loyal colored valet, Philip Jordan.[3] I had never been in Russia before. I had never been an Ambassador before. My knowledge of Russia up to the time of my appointment had been that of the average intelligent American citizen—unhappily slight and vague. In order to meet without quailing the heavy responsibilities and the unknown problems which lay before me I needed all the self-confidence born of my experience as Mayor of my City, Governor of my State, Member of the President's Cabinet, and as head for many years of my own business.

Any momentary misgivings I may have felt, however, were soon dispelled by my cordial American greeting from the members of the Embassy staff who had loyally stood by to welcome me since 11 p.m., the hour at which the train had been due.

As I began to familiarize myself with my duties I was appalled at the enormous amount of work and responsibility entailed by my uncongenial task as the representative of German and Austrian interests in Russia. There were at the time one and a quarter million Austrian prisoners and a quarter of a million German prisoners in Russian prison camps. In addition there were about 200,000 interned German civilians and 50,000 Austrians. I had to supervise the care and attention received by these hundreds of thousands of persons and act as the official intermediary between them

---

[1] One of five Petrograd railway stations and the only one in the northern part of the city providing direct communication with Europe through Finland.

[2] St. Petersburg was renamed Petrograd on August 18, 1914, after the outbreak of the war with Germany. On January 26, 1924, after Lenin's death, the city was renamed Leningrad.

[3] Philip (Phil) Jordan (1868–1941), Francis's African American valet, who entered the employ of the Francis family in 1889 and served until his death.

and their governments. This work was conducted from the Austrian Embassy[4] which we had taken over at the time we assumed charge of Austrian interests. It required not only the exclusive services of a large corps of able assistants, known as the Relief Corps,[5] but demanded my personal attention for several hours daily.

Among the first places that I visited was the German Embassy which was also, and for the same reason, under my charge.[6] This capacious and imposing structure had been sacked by the Petrograd populace in 1914 in retaliation for indignities which had been shown the Russian Empress Dowager[7] when she passed through Berlin on her return from Switzerland to Russia after Germany's declaration of war against Russia.[8] The angry crowd had done its work thoroughly. On inspecting this large building I found the luxurious furnishings mutilated and useless, the great mirrors broken, the electric light fixtures twisted out of shape, and even the oil paintings of the German Emperors, Chancellors and Ministers of Foreign Affairs, disfigured beyond repair.

This huge, costly and partially demolished Embassy seemed to me to well symbolize the relations between Germany and Russia. This Embassy had been a part of Germany's long and persistent campaign to gain a dominating influence in Russia. At a pre-arranged meeting in Baltic waters on July 24th, 1905, Kaiser Wilhelm[9] had induced his weak and easily influenced cousin, Nicholas,[10] to sign the secret Treaty

---

[4] The Austro-Hungarian embassy had its residence at the Buturlina Mansion on Sergievskaya Street, 10, not far from the US embassy. After the beginning of the World War, it was placed under American care and made the headquarters of the embassy's "Second Division."

[5] Actually personnel of the US embassy's Second Division, which was created in 1916 for supervision over Austro-Hungarian and German prisoners of war and interned subjects in Russia. It consisted mainly of people of the YMCA and Red Cross and was headed from March 1916 by prominent social worker Edward T. Devine (1867–1948). At the end of October, he was replaced with Basil Miles, who held the rank of special assistant to the ambassador. In early 1917, professional diplomat William F. Sands (1874–1946) arrived in Petrograd to assist Miles. The Second Division ceased its operations after the US entry into the World War; its duties were delegated to the Norway and Denmark legations.

[6] The German embassy at Petrograd was located on St. Isaac's Square, 11. After the beginning of the German-Russian War in July 1914, it was placed under American supervision but was completely ransacked by a mob and deemed unfit for further use.

[7] Maria Fyodorovna (1847–1928), wife of Alexander III, mother of Nicholas II, daughter of King Christian IX of Denmark.

[8] Germany declared war on Russia on July 19 (August 1), 1914.

[9] Wilhelm II (1859–1941), German kaiser, 1888–1918.

[10] Nicholas II (1868–1918), the last emperor of Russia, 1894–1917. He abdicated after the February Revolution on March 2, 1917, was exiled to Siberia, removed to Ekaterinburg, and executed there along with his family and servants on July 16–17, 1918, when the mutinous Czecho-Slovak troops approached the city.

of Bjorke.[11] This Treaty, whose provisions became known several years later, bound the two nations mutually to assist each other against any third party and prohibited the conclusion of a separate peace with a common adversary. This agreement, signed during the Russo-Japanese War, was to become effective at the restoration of peace between Russia and Japan. It also provided that France was not to be informed of the Treaty until after it came into effect, when she should be invited to become a party to it. Obviously this Treaty would have been a breach of faith on Russia's part with her ally, France, and could only have resulted in severing the close relations between those countries and thus strengthening Germany at the expense of both which was, of course, the Kaiser's object. Thanks to Count Witte[12] this mischievous Treaty never went into effect. He was at the time Minister of Finance and the dominating personality in the Government. He succeeded in over-ruling the Czar himself, and checkmating this intrigue of the German Emperor. By so doing, however, he incurred the displeasure of the Czar and the active hostility of the Czarina.[13]

I had heard before leaving America that the Russian Court circles were honeycombed with German spies and German sympathizers. As a result I was on the lookout for the activities of such persons. I also knew that important Russian industries, mines and financial institutions were controlled by German capital. Immediately before the outbreak of the war 49 percent of Russia's foreign commerce was with Germany. In the same year Germany had taken advantage of Russia's weakened condition because of her disastrous war with Japan to force upon her a commercial treaty in which all the advantages were on the side of Germany, and which was effective for ten years, or until the year 1915.[14] The bitterness against Germany was greatly increased by the effects of this treaty. In fact, by the year 1914 the Russian industries that were not under German control were comparatively few. Germany well knew that public sentiment in Russia would never tolerate the renewal of this unfair treaty and that knowledge was one of the immediate causes which induced Germany to force Russia into war in 1914.

The bitterest enmity had grown up since the outbreak of the war, twenty-two months before, between the Russian nobility who were purely Russian and those who were accused of German sympathies. The latter became known as the Court Party

---

[11] Treaty of Björkö, a secret alliance signed on July 11 (24), 1905, by Wilhelm II and Nicholas II. The treaty was not ratified by Russia due to the opposition of leading Russian ministers.

[12] Sergei Y. Witte (1849–1915), minister of finance, 1892–1903; chief Russian plenipotentiary at the Portsmouth peace negotiations, which ended the Russo-Japanese War of 1904–05. Chairman of the Council of Ministers, October 1905–April 1906.

[13] Empress Alexandra Fyodorovna (1872–1918), wife of Nicholas II, daughter of Grand Duke Ludwig IV of Hesse. Original name Alix-Victoria-Helena-Louisa-Beatrice.

[14] Actually the additional convention to the Treaty of Commerce and Navigation between Russia and Germany of January 29 (February 10), 1894, signed on July 15 (28), 1904.

and were headed by the Empress, who before her marriage had been a German Princess from Hesse-Darmstadt, and a cousin of the German Emperor. The Empress was said to have gained such a strong influence over the Emperor that even his mother, the Empress Dowager, to whom he had always been so devoted, could not counteract it. In fact, it was believed that at the behest of his wife the Emperor had required his mother to leave Petrograd. In any case, she had left and was living in Kieff. In addition there were many charges of the direct use of German and Austrian money in high places. The former Minister of War, Sukhomlinoff,[15] had been charged by Grand Duke Nicholas[16] with intentionally aiding the enemy by deliberately failing to provide the troops with arms and ammunition. He had been arrested and imprisoned in the St. Peter and Paul Fortress. His wife, a beautiful and attractive woman,[17] had accepted attentions from a Russian General, who had been charged with taking a bribe of 400,000 roubles from the enemy in return for information concerning Russian troop movements and the Russian lack of ammunition. This General had been tried, convicted and shot. There was at this time a Russian Commission in America for the purchase of arms and munitions.[18] It was commonly believed that a member of this Commission had been bribed to give wrong specifications for ammunition, and that when tried in actual battle it was found this ammunition could not be used. These exposures had naturally made the Russian people extremely anxious and suspicious. The Secret Service of the Empire also had corrupted several of the revolutionary leaders, among whom were Azef[19] and Father Gapon,[20] the leader of the Black Friday

---

[15] Vladimir A. Sukhomlinov (1848–1926), general of cavalry, minister of war, 1909–15. He was dismissed from the post on June 13, 1915, and arrested on April 29, 1916, on the charge of treasonable negligence for inadequately preparing the Russian army for the war. On September 20, 1917, he was sentenced to life imprisonment. On May 1, 1918, he was granted amnesty and allowed to emigrate.

[16] Grand Duke Nikolai Nikolaevich (1856–1929), grandson of Nicholas I, cousin of Nicholas II, general of cavalry, commander in chief of the Russian army, July 20, 1914–August 23, 1915.

[17] Ekaterina V. Sukhomlinova (Goshkevich; in her first marriage Butovich).

[18] The Russian Purchasing Committee in America with residence at New York City was established in October 1915 under the chairmanship of Major General Aleksei V. Sapozhnikov. From May 1916, it was headed by Lieutenant General of Artillery Anatoly P. Zalyubovsky (1859–1936).

[19] Evno F. Azef (1869–1918), a prominent leader of the Party of Socialists-Revolutionaries (SRs), head of its combat organization, and an agent-provocateur of the Russian secret police at the same time.

[20] Georgy A. Gapon (1870–1906), Russian Orthodox priest, popular workers' leader, and secret police provocateur at the same time. He was executed by Socialist Revolutionaries.

demonstration of 1905.[21] Some of these leaders had been induced to make attempts upon the lives of members of the royal family and in some instances had actually committed murders with the knowledge of the Secret Service. The Secret Service was willing to offer up these royal personages as sacrifices in order to obtain justification for suppressing the revolutionary spirit with an iron hand. I shall tell my story from here on largely by means of extracts from confidential letters and dispatches which I sent and received between April 28th, 1916, and November 6th, 1918—the dates marking my active services as Ambassador. Since leaving Russia, while still holding the office, I have been on the inactive list. Although these dispatches and letters, so far from being written with a view to publication, were prepared in most cases for the confidential information of those to whom they were addressed, I shall use them for two reasons: first, because I wish my readers to know that there are no inaccuracies owing to lapses of memory on my part, and second, because it seems to me that many of these accounts have an added interest by reason of the fact that they were written immediately after the stirring events described.

In a letter to my son, Perry Francis,[22] written May 1st, 1916, three days after my arrival in Petrograd, I said:

> On the day of my arrival a note was sent to the Foreign Office asking when I would be received, and on the following day, Saturday, had an audience with Sazonoff, Minister of Foreign Affairs,[23] and also with Sturmer, President of the Council of Ministers, and also Minister of the Interior.[24] My interview with Sazonoff was prolonged through an hour and twenty minutes and was by no means satisfactory. He was exceedingly cordial, but I was disappointed in that he said that Russia was not prepared at this time to negotiate any commercial treaty with our country[25] or any other country until all of the

---

[21] Actually the "Bloody Sunday" of January 9, 1905, when a peaceful workmen's procession led by Father Gapon was shot down by imperial troops while they were marching toward the Winter Palace to present a petition to Nicholas II. The event marked the beginning of the Russian Revolution of 1905.

[22] John Dietz Perry Francis, the ambassador's eldest son (1876–1950).

[23] Sergei D. Sazonov (1860–1927), minister of foreign affairs of the Russian Empire, September 14, 1910–July 7, 1916; minister of foreign affairs of the Denikin and Kolchak governments, 1918–19.

[24] Boris V. Stürmer (1848–1917), graduate of St. Petersburg University, lawyer, director of the Ceremonial Department of the Ministry of Imperial Court, 1879–92. Chairman of the Council of Ministers of the Russian Empire, January 20–November 10, 1916; also minister of interior, March 3–July 7, and afterwards minister of foreign affairs. He was arrested after the February Revolution, died in the prison hospital on August 20, 1917.

[25] Proposed commercial treaty instead of Russian-American Treaty of Commerce and Navigation, signed on December 6 (18), 1832, but abrogated by the US on December 17, 1911.

Allies[26] arrived at some understanding on economic questions. I told him my last advices were to the effect that he was willing and desirous of negotiating a new commercial treaty, to which he replied that he had so stated six months ago, but that not since June or July of 1915 had the subject been broached to him, and now it was too late as the Allies have agreed upon a program which provides for an understanding between themselves not only as to the prosecution of the war, but as to the commercial relations between themselves and friendly, neutral and belligerent countries after the close of the war. Of course, this is strictly confidential and should not be given to the public prints, nor told to anyone except those upon whom you can thoroughly rely. Immediately upon returning to the Embassy,[27] I prepared a cablegram to the State Department of 500 words, informing the Secretary of the situation and expressing my great disappointment. I told Sazonoff, who speaks very good English, that I was greatly disappointed, and in fact decidedly so, because to negotiate such a treaty had been the main object I had had in view when accepting the appointment as Ambassador. The Allies have called an economic council to meet in Paris about June 1st,[28] at which this country will be represented by the Comptroller of the Empire and four other potential officials. It seems, therefore, that the negotiation of a commercial treaty must be postponed until after the council is held; it will continue in session about thirty days. There is no hope, therefore, of negotiating a treaty between our country and Russia before July.

When First Secretary Dearing[29] made the appointment for my initial interview with Minister of Foreign Affairs Sazonoff there was no thought of my also calling upon Baron Sturmer, who was at the time both President of the Council of Ministers and Minister of the Interior, but a message was received at the Embassy the morning of the day I was to meet the Foreign Minister requesting that I call upon Minister Sturmer before going to the Foreign Office. I soon learned that there was friction

---

[26] The powers comprising the Entente—the United Kingdom, France, Russia, Japan, Italy, etc.

[27] From 1909, the US embassy rented the Count Grabbe Mansion on Furshtatskaya Street, 34.

[28] Economic Conference of the Allies was held in Paris on June 14–17, 1916.

[29] Fred Morris Dearing (1879–1963), born in Columbia, MO; a graduate of the University of Missouri, took postgraduate course in jurisprudence and diplomacy at Columbia University. He entered the Foreign Service in 1906; served in Cuba, China, Great Britain, and Mexico; held the post of assistant chief of the Division of Latin American Affairs of the State Department, 1911–13; and then served in Belgium and Spain. On February 2, 1916, he was assigned first secretary of the Petrograd embassy; made counselor of the embassy on July 17, 1916; unassigned from November 7, 1916.

between the two Ministers which undoubtedly accounted for this unusual request. I naturally called upon Sturmer as requested. Although he was exceedingly cordial and expressed himself as very anxious to establish closer relations with my Government, I was by no means favorably impressed by him. His appearance was as German as his name. His mind worked slowly and his temperament was phlegmatic. In short, he impressed me as a dull man. Shortly after my presentation to the Emperor, he called on me at the Embassy. He was again extremely cordial and emphatic in his protestations of a desire for close relations with the United States Government, but I liked him no better. As Minister of the Interior he had charge of the prison camps which it was the duty of the Relief Corps of the American Embassy to inspect. The entire Corps cordially disliked him and when in July, 1916, he was transferred—through the influence of the Empress and Rasputin[30] as I later learned—and made Minister of Foreign Affairs, great was the rejoicing among the members of the American Relief Corps. Shortly after his appointment as Minister of Foreign Affairs he moved into a palatial summer residence on the island in the River Neva opposite the Winter Palace. Here I called one afternoon and met the Baroness Sturmer.[31] During my conversation with her I could not help noticing how the Baron paced up and down the room and every now and again stopped in front of a long mirror in which he surveyed himself with evident satisfaction, while he turned up the ends of his mustaches which were in the style of the German Kaiser.

After my original brief conversation with Baron Sturmer I went to the Foreign Office for my appointment with Minister Sazonoff. He greeted me cordially although he was not as excessively cordial as had been Sturmer. He looked about 55 years old, is slightly under medium height and of a spare build. His nose is rather prominent, his mouth firm set and his chin neither square nor pointed. His face and manner bore evidence of overwork and mental strain. His mind was evidently as alert as Sturmer's lethargic. His replies to my questions were prompt to the point of abruptness. When I told him I had no experience in diplomacy but had accepted the appointment in the hope and expectation of negotiating a commercial treaty between Russia and the United States he arose abruptly from his chair and made the statement given in the letter above. I could well imagine him entering the great Hall of Tsarskoe Selo

---

[30] Grigory E. Rasputin (1869–1916), an illiterate Siberian peasant possessing powerful mystic and hypnotic abilities who won a great confidence of the imperial couple due to his care of their fatally sick son, Aleksei. Became a figure of great influence in high society and governmental circles, turned into a symbol of the "dark forces" governing the late Russian Empire. He was killed on December 17, 1916, by a group of monarchists comprised of Prince Felix F. Yusupov, Vladimir M. Purishkevich, and Grand Duke Dmitry Pavlovich.

[31] Elizaveta V. Strukova.

Palace[32] on the fateful night of July 31st, 1914, with his quick firm step to tell the Emperor that Germany had declared war. The royal family and some prominent members of the nobility were attending an entertainment at the Palace when the Foreign Minister entered, and went direct to his Majesty, took him to one side, told him the ominous news and then left the hall with him while the entertainment continued and the guests were left to speculate on what had happened.

Within ten days of my arrival in Petrograd I determined to make the acquaintance of the American colony,[33] so I invited the Americans to tea at the Embassy on a Sunday afternoon. The invitations were generally accepted and the guests remarked that they had not realized there were so many Americans in Petrograd. They seemed greatly pleased and were, in fact, profuse in their expressions of appreciation. Although the colony is so small it has been split into factions—a condition that seems to have been brought about by rivalry between some of the American women in regard to what is called the American Refuge (an orphan asylum supported by Americans).[34]

But the war was the all-absorbing subject in Russia at this time. Everyone in any position of responsibility was under the highest tension. Recruits were being drilled on the street in front of the Embassy.[35] This street is nearly 200 feet wide and paved with cobblestones which are not pleasant to walk upon, but the soldiers didn't seem to mind them. These soldiers often sang familiar Russian airs. They are plaintive but enchanting—so much so that one found the airs running through one's mind long after the songs had ceased. Soldiers were being sent out of the city by train

---

[32] Tsarskoe Selo, literally "Tsar's Village," a tiny town in the vicinity of Petrograd where Nicholas II had his residence from the time of the Russian Revolution of 1905. Now the city of Pushkin.

[33] At the moment, the American colony at Petrograd consisted of about two hundred people, mostly businessmen.

[34] American Refuge for Refugee Women and Children from the War Zone was established in 1915 under the honorable presidency of Marie Alice Marye, the US ambassador's wife. The refuge—located on Kamennoostrovsky Prospekt, 27—began its work with thirty beds for babies and their mothers. After Mrs. Marye left Petrograd in early 1916, it was presided over by Helen Meserve, wife of the representative of the National City Bank of New York at Petrograd. Another faction of the American colony sponsored an American hospital in Petrograd, established in 1914 under the honorable presidency of Ambassador George T. Marye. The hospital of the American colony had forty beds and operated almost entirely on donations from American residents of Petrograd. It was run by a committee, presided over by Consul General North Winship, with Commercial Attaché Henry Baker its secretary and the *Mayak* Society Secretary Franklin A. Gaylord its treasurer. The committee was assisted by the Ladies Aid Society. From November 1915, the hospital was located on Sergievskaya Street, 26.

[35] Furshtatskaya Street in the aristocratic Liteinaya section of Petrograd, which connected Liteiny Prospekt with the Taurida Garden.

loads, thousands daily, but no one knew where they were going except the general in supreme command.

The hatred of Germany was intense, just as the feeling in Germany toward England was exceedingly bitter. The merchants and all of the people seemed to feel that Germany had for a century or more been growing rich at the expense of Russia, and that during the Russian-Japanese War Germany took advantage of conditions to force upon Russia a burdensome treaty whereby Germany not only got advantage over other countries, but was enabled to exact tribute from all of her patrons in Russia. The Russian merchants, and in fact the nobility and even the Emperor himself, seemed determined that no other country should ever occupy the same relation to Russia that Germany did before the war. Such a position pleased me to a degree, as I had been fearful on account of the financial aid she was rendering to Russia that England might be planning to assume a position of superiority over other nations in her relations to Russia. I was not fully qualified as Ambassador until I had been received by the Czar. This was both an impressive and pleasant experience, which I described to Mr. Polk[36] in the following letter:

American Embassy,
Petrograd.
May 9th, 1916.

Dear Mr. Secretary:

I address you mainly for the purpose of making a report about my reception by the Emperor and Empress on Friday, May 5th,[37] advices of which I have cabled the Department.

The day before calling on the Emperor and Empress, accompanied by First Secretary Dearing, I called upon Baron Korff, Grand Master of Ceremonies,[38] and also upon Dame d'honneur Elizabeth Narychkine, Maitresse de la Cour Imperiale;[39] both of these calls were very agreeable, both officials responding promptly and cheerfully to my expressed desire of increasing the good feeling existing for so many years between Russia and the United States.

---

[36] Frank L. Polk (1871–1943), counselor for the Department of State, 1915–19; acting secretary of state, December 4, 1918–July 18, 1919. He headed the American commission to negotiate peace at the Paris Peace Conference of 1919.

[37] Francis and his staff were received by the emperor and empress on April 22 (May 5), 1916, in the Alexandrovsky Palace at Tsarskoe Selo.

[38] Baron Pavel P. Korf (1845–1935), graduate of Berlin University (DL), served at the Imperial Court from 1877 and was made grand master of ceremonies on December 12, 1912.

[39] Elizaveta A. Naryshkina (1838–1928), born Princess Kurakina, lady of the suite (Statsdame) and the mistress of the Imperial Court (Hofmeisterin).

The following day, Friday, accompanied by the Embassy staff and the Commercial Attache, I went to a special station on the railroad leading to Tsarskoe-Selo where a special train was waiting, which conveyed us to the Emperor's station, near the castle, after a journey of about 25 minutes. There we were met by the Master of Ceremonies and his staff all arrayed in gorgeous uniforms. It has been the custom of my predecessors, I am told, to wear uniforms on such occasions as this and on many other occasions, but I have not yet procured a uniform and don't know that I shall; my impression is that some of the Secretaries have them, but they are not permitted to wear them unless the Ambassador is so attired. We journeyed from the station to the palace in vehicles so rich in gilt finish that they had better be termed chariots. The one in which I was, was drawn by six horses with an outrider on the front lead horse. The only one who accompanied me in this carriage was a uniformed and titled attache of the Master of Ceremonies, whose name I do not recall.[40] In the second vehicle were Dearing and Mr. Peirce;[41] in the third were Second Secretaries White[42] and Sterling;[43] in the fourth were Third

---

[40] Master of Ceremonies Count Vladimir A. Musin-Pushkin (1868–1918).

[41] Peirce (often referred to as Pierce), Herbert Henry Davis (1849–1916), graduate of Harvard University and student of Royal School of Mines in London. He entered the Foreign Service as a non-career appointee in 1894 and was appointed secretary of the US legation at St. Petersburg. After raising the legation to embassy in 1898, he was appointed to first secretary and served at times as chargé d'affaires till 1901. Third assistant secretary of state, 1901–06; in charge of the arrangements for the deliberations of the Portsmouth peace conference, which ended the Russo-Japanese War of 1904–05. The first US minister to Norway, 1906–11. Appointed special agent of the Department of State with rank of minister plenipotentiary to assist the ambassador to Russia on February 1, 1915.

[42] John Campbell White (1884–1967), son of Ambassador Henry White, served as his private secretary in Rome and Paris, 1906–07. Graduate of Harvard University (1907, AB). Entered the Foreign Service in 1914, served at Santo Domingo. He was assigned to Petrograd as second secretary of the embassy on March 6, 1915, and appointed to Athens on May 25, 1916.

[43] Frederick Augustine Sterling (1876–1957), a native of St. Louis, MO, educated in Switzerland and graduated from Harvard University (1898, BA). Entered the Foreign Service and was appointed third secretary of the embassy at Petrograd on March 2, 1911, and second secretary on August 22, 1912. He was detailed to Santo Domingo in December 1913; served in China from February 1914; assigned to Petrograd as second secretary on July 14, 1915; assigned to the Department of State as acting chief of the Division of Western European Affairs on June 24, 1916.

Secretary Ryan[44] and Commercial Attache Baker;[45] in the fifth Lieutenant Riggs[46] and Captain McCully;[47] in the sixth was Captain Breckinridge of the Marine Corps,[48]—ten in all including myself. In each vehicle was a member of the retinue of Baron Korff. The drive to the castle was about half a mile; on arrival the doors were opened and there were more uniformed servants ready to receive us than I could count. After a very short delay I was conducted to a room where I found the Emperor awaiting me. The doors were closed behind me; the Emperor advanced and gave me a cordial handshake and accompanied me to a seat. The staff were all outside awaiting my return, and although

---

[44] John Latta Ryan (1889–?), graduate of Yale Law School. Entered the Foreign Service in 1915, appointed third secretary of the embassy at Petrograd on March 6, 1915; assigned to San Salvador on June 13, 1916.

[45] Henry Dunster Baker (1873–1939), graduate of Yale University, reporter and financial editor of the *Chicago Tribune*, *New-York Evening Post*, and London's *Financial Times*. He entered the Consular Service in 1907 and served in Australia, New Zealand, the Bahamas, and British India. He was appointed the first US commercial attaché to the embassy at Petrograd on October 12, 1914, and appointed consul at Trinidad (British West Indies) on October 27, 1916.

[46] E. (Elisha) Francis Riggs (1887–1936), Yale graduate (1909, AB), was traveling throughout the world visiting Italy, Montenegro, Turkey, Austria, Germany, France, Switzerland, Egypt, Morocco, Spain, and England. He entered the US Army in 1911; served at Hawaii and the Philippines; made a trip to Cuba, Jamaica, and the Panama Canal. Second lieutenant of the field artillery, appointed military attaché at Petrograd on December 31, 1915. Promoted to first lieutenant on July 1, 1916, and then to captain on May 15, 1917. Assistant military attaché from July 17, 1917; promoted to major on May 20, 1918. Promoted to lieutenant colonel on October 26, 1918, and headed special military mission to south Russia, March–May 1919.

[47] Newton Alexander McCully (1867–1951), graduate of the US Naval Academy. Lieutenant, naval attaché and official observer in Russia and Manchuria during the Russo-Japanese War of 1904–05. Captain, naval attaché to the US embassy at Petrograd; appointed on August 12, 1914; left Petrograd in August 1917. Served later in north and south Russia (see n. 44, p. 247).

[48] James Carson Breckinridge (1877–1942), son of the former US Minister at the Russian Imperial Court Clinton R. Breckinridge (1894–97). On service in the Marine Corps from 1898, he served in the Philippines, Panama, Nicaragua, Cuba, and Mexico. Captain, assigned to duty as assistant naval attaché at Petrograd on February 26, 1916. Promoted to major on June 12, to lieutenant colonel on August 29, 1916, and to temporary colonel on May 22, 1917. He was assigned to duty as naval attaché to Norway and Sweden with residence at Christiania on July 31, 1917, and was the only Marine Corps officer awarded during the World War with the Navy Cross for non-combat services and for "distinguished service in the line of his profession as Naval Attaché to the American legations at Christiania and Stockholm, Sweden, and for a time also at Copenhagen. At all of these points the service of information established and conducted was of great value to the United States and the Allied Powers." (Home of Heroes [website], "Navy Cross—Other Conflicts and Peacetime—1915 to 1926: Diplomatic Service (1916–1917): Breckinridge, James C," https://homeofheroes.com/distinguished-service-cross/service-cross-other-conflicts/navy-cross-recipients-other-conflicts/navy-cross-recipients-other-conflicts-1915-to-1926/.)

the conference lasted but about 35 minutes by the watch, as they were kept standing during this time, it must have seemed like hours to them.

After expressing to the Emperor my appreciation of the honor conferred by his receiving me, I handed him the sealed missive from the President and almost immediately proceeded to tell him that I had come to Russia mainly for the purpose of negotiating a new commercial treaty. He smiled and said that Russia was equally desirous to have a new treaty, and trusted there would be no difficulty in negotiating one. (As I later learned this was a very characteristic attitude. This unfortunate monarch was always trying to avoid difficulties.) At some stage of the conversation I congratulated him upon his vodka edict,[49] at which he seemed pleased, saying that when it was first issued the period for its operation was limited to 30 days, or during mobilization. The appeals from women, communities, and associations, however, were so numerous and importunate that it be extended for the duration of the war, which at that time doubtless no one thought would last more than a few months, that he prolonged the operation of the edict to make it contemporaneous with the war; as the war progressed and the benefits of the prohibition of the sale of vodka became more and more apparent, he issued formal edict making the prohibition perpetual.

He asked me with great interest about the relations between our country and Germany and I told him that the first official information received at the Embassy was in regard to treatment of merchant vessels by the Allied and Belligerent Powers, but that the newspapers contained reports to the effect that Germany's reply to the President's note suggested arbitration and that they further stated that the proposition had not been accepted. I also told him that our official advices from Washington which had been transmitted to the Foreign Office were not only a virtual reply to Germany's proposition to arbitrate, but an announcement to the world of the position assumed by the United States on the question so long discussed—a position our country meant not only to observe, but to enforce. His reply was, "Of course such matters cannot be arbitrated." I told him that as the representative of a neutral country, I should be discreet in my expressions concerning the great war in which Russia and most of Europe was engaged, especially as the United States was here looking after the interests of Germany and Austria. During this statement he was smiling and bowing his head affirmatively, and when later I told him that my personal sympathies were with the Allies and had been from the beginning and that my sentiments on the subject were well known in the community where I lived and also throughout the country, he

---

[49] The so-called "Dry Law" of 1914 prohibiting the retail trade of vodka in Russia. Originally the sale of vodka was suspended temporarily on July 19, 1914, for the period of mobilization. On August 22, the prohibition was extended to the end of the war.

smiled in a pleased manner, and said he was confident such was the case but was delighted to hear it from my own lips.

When I told him I was residing at the Embassy, he expressed satisfaction, but when I went further and told him that I planned to make an effort to induce my country to purchase a home for the Embassy in Petrograd, he was exceedingly pleased and said such action would be very gratifying to the Russian people.

At the end of the interview—I can't recall whether it was terminated by the Emperor or myself—upon arising I asked if I could present the Embassy staff. He replied, "Of course." As I approached the door a uniformed man who had been guarding it, threw the doors open and the staff entered. I presented them one by one to the Emperor who shook hands with each. I said something about each man and the Emperor also made some personal remark to each one.

After this ceremony which must have required ten minutes, I was conducted to another room in the castle where the Empress was waiting to receive me. She very gracefully advanced with extended hand and after a genuine American handshake, conducted me to a seat. Suffice it to say she was exceedingly gracious, and so interesting that when back on the way to Petrograd I was asked by the members of the staff how she was attired I was compelled to admit that she was so entertaining that I had forgotten to note how royalty dressed on such occasions. I am thinking of writing to the Mistress of the Robes to ask how the Empress was dressed, but shall not do so before being told whether that would be proper form,—of course, I have no curiosity myself in the subject, but all the ladies whom I meet seem to be very much interested and furthermore it would give an opportunity to state why I made the inquiry. This, however, is pleasantry. The special train conveyed us back to Petrograd where we arrived about 4:30 p.m. The Petrograd papers all stated that the Emperor and Empress had received me. I now am a fullfledged Ambassador; until my reception by the Emperor First Secretary Dearing was Charge d'Affaires and signed all the official communications to the Russian Government.

Upon my return to the Embassy I remitted 300 roubles to a member of Baron Korff's staff for distribution among the liveried men who drove and rode the horses and received me at the palace; I was told that such was the custom and such would be expected of me.

I have the honor to be, sir,
Your obedient servant,
David R. Francis.

As my conversation with the Emperor was drawing to a close my attention was attracted by a very fine life-sized portrait. I remarked to His Majesty that it was a very fine likeness of him. He smiled and replied, "It is not me at all, but my cousin, King George.[50] You are not the first one, however, who has mistaken that painting for a portrait of me."

The Emperor's domestic relations were ideal. He was devoted to the Empress and to his children, particularly the frail little Czarovitch.[51] Before his marriage to Princess Alix of Hesse-Darmstadt, he was said to have been devoted to Dshesinskaya, the ballet dancer;[52] who, until some weeks after the March Revolution[53] lived in a beautiful palace[54] across the River Neva from the American Embassy, and had charge of the Imperial Ballet. However this may have been, his love for the Empress and his faithfulness to her were never questioned.

I cannot better describe the relations between the royal couple and the character of each than by telling the following story as related by Dr. Dillon, the well-known British publicist and authority on Russia,[55] whose son was a member of my staff.

Once a nobleman of great experience and progressive tendencies was received in audience by the Czar. He laid before the sovereign the wretched state of the peasantry, the resulting general unrest and the strong necessity of remedying it by a modification of the political machinery of the Government. The Emperor, after listening very attentively and approvingly to his visitor, said, "I know. Yes, yes. You are right, quite right." The nobleman retired well satisfied with his interview and feeling certain that the monarch would mollify his policy. Immediately afterwards a great landowner, also a member of the nobility, was ushered in and he unfolded a very different

---

[50] King George V of Great Britain, 1910–36.

[51] Tsarevich, the title of heir to throne in Imperial Russia. At the moment it was the Grand Duke Aleksei Nikolaevich (1904–18).

[52] Matilda F. Kseshinskaya (1872–1971), a famous ballet dancer who reportedly had connections with some members of the imperial family.

[53] February Revolution in Russia, which occurred from February 23 to March 2 (March 8–15), 1917.

[54] Kseshinskaya's mansion was built in 1906 on Great Dvoryanskaya (now Kuibyshev) Street, 2. In March 1917, it was seized by the Bolsheviks, who headquartered the Petersburg Committee there and military organizations of their party, as well as other revolutionary organizations. On July 6, 1917, Kseshinskaya mansion was taken up by governmental troops. Now a residence of the Museum of Political History of Russia.

[55] Emile Joseph Dillon (1854–1933), British writer and journalist. Doctor of Philosophy (Leipzig University), Doctor of Oriental Languages and Literature (Catholic University of Leuven), and Doctor of Comparative Philology (Khar′kov University). Russian correspondent of *The Daily Telegraph*, 1887–1914; author of the best-seller *The Eclipse of Russia* (1918) and other books on Russian history and culture.

story. He sought to show that affairs were quite satisfactory with the exception of the leniency of the throne toward peasants. "What is needed, Sire, is an iron hand. The peasants must be kept in their place by force, otherwise they will usurp ours. To yield to them and treat them as though they were the masters of the country is a great crime." To this statement, Nicholas II, after giving an attentive audience, said, "Yes, yes, I know. You are right, quite right." The second visitor departed as pleased with his interview as the first had been. A side door opened, the Empress entered, and said to the Czar: "You really must not go on like this, Nicky. It is not dignified. Remember you are an autocrat. You should show a will strong enough to stiffen a nation of 150,000,000 people!"

"But what is it you find fault with, darling?"

"Your want of resolution and of courage to express it. I have been listening to the conversation you have just had. Count S., whom you first received, pleaded the cause of the disaffected. You assented to everything he advanced telling him he was 'right, quite right.' Then M.Y. was introduced. He gave you an account of things as they really are and you agreed with him in just the same way saying, 'You are right, quite right!' Well, now such an attitude does not befit an autocrat. You must learn to have a will of your own and assert it."

"You are right, dear, quite right," was the reply of the Czar.

I never met the Empress again, but I shall always remember her as a dignified, graceful and exceedingly handsome woman, with strong features and a pleasant expression. She was very proud and very jealous of the royal prerogatives of the Emperor. She was an absolute monarchist by birth, by nature and by training. She supplanted her mother-in-law, the Empress Dowager, in dominating the weak-willed Emperor who had such a dread of controversy that he would agree with anyone on any subject so long as they were in his presence.

Chapter II
GERMAN INFLUENCE IN RUSSIAN AFFAIRS

On July 22nd all Russia was startled by the sudden and unexpected resignation of Foreign Minister Sazonoff. Ten days later I wrote Secretary Lansing the following letter about this resignation:

Personal and confidential
Petrograd, July 25th, 1916.

Dear Mr. Secretary:

The resignation of Foreign Minister Sazonoff and the appointment of Minister of Interior Sturmer as his successor was announced in the papers Sunday morning, July 23rd, and was a great surprise to all classes of people and to every section of the country. On Monday, July 10th, upon which day I was expecting a conference with Mr. Sazonoff concerning a plan between the Allies and Belligerents whereby America could extend aid to Poland, etc., the Embassy was informed by telephone that the Minister had been called to the front to confer with the Emperor. Mr. Sazonoff returned to Petrograd the morning of Thursday, July 13th. I saw him that afternoon in company with Mr. Samuel McRoberts, of the National City Bank of New York,[1] who had asked to pay his respects, and to whom the Minister extended a cordial welcome because Mr. McRoberts had formed the American syndicate which loaned $50,000,000 to the Russian Government. Mr. Sazonoff complained of being tired and said that on the following day, July 14th, he would go to Finland[2] for a rest of two or three weeks. He was in Finland when his resignation was announced and is still there.

---

[1] Samuel McRoberts (1868–1947), a Missourian, vice president of the National City Bank of New York, 1909–19; director of American-Russian Chamber of Commerce, established in early 1916 at New York City. He visited Petrograd in the summer of 1916 to negotiate a loan with the Russian government.

[2] Finland was a grand duchy in personal union with the Russian Empire until the abdication of Nicholas II, and autonomous province of Russia after the February Revolution from March 7, 1917. The Declaration of Independence was proclaimed by Finland's Senate on December 6, and recognized by the Soviet government on December 18, 1917.

Universal regret is expressed at the retirement of Mr. Sazonoff, which he and the Emperor and all members of the Government attribute to ill health. At the same time there are rumors to the effect that his parting with the Emperor on July 12th was not only friendly but affectionate; the Emperor, it is said, kissed him three times and expressed the highest appreciation of his public services. The day after the Minister's departure the Empress joined the Emperor at his military headquarters, and two days later Mr. Sazonoff received a telegram asking for his immediate resignation. Whether this is true no one can say authoritatively. It is generally believed, however, that the Empress is very desirous of peace. She has long been suspected of German sympathies. One story was to the effect that when Minister Sazonoff was directed to submit to Russia's Allies proposals of peace suggested by Germany, he refused to do so, whereupon Mr. Sturmer said he would submit such proposals if the Foreign Minister declined to do so, and that thereupon Mr. Sazonoff resigned.

Mr. Sturmer is looked upon as a reactionary; in fact that is his record. Some charge him with being an opportunist and with having no convictions. He is not reputed to possess a keen intellect or an incisive mind; on the contrary he is said to be slow of comprehension, but stubborn and possessed of great courage. I have had two conferences with him, and must say that he did not impress me as a man with breadth of view or imbued with high ideals. He is of German origin, but his loyalty to Russia in this contest has never been questioned. As Minister of the Interior his jurisdiction has been very extensive and his power great.

This would indicate that the court party of the Empire is preparing to counteract what they fear will be a liberal movement on the part of the people after the close of the war. It is now charged that Russia is planning to make a separate peace with Germany. One report is to the effect that von Lucius, present Minister from Germany at Stockholm,[3] has recently made a secret visit to Russia and suggested terms of peace which are attractive to Russia and not objectionable to France, as they provide for ceding to France Lorraine, which has belonged to Germany since 1870. It is not fully known what concessions are proposed for England, but she is to be propitiated by being allowed to retain the German South African Colonies which she has captured. Japan will be appeased by being permitted to retain the territory she has captured in the Far East. It is said that Germany is willing to recognize the integrity of Belgium and to indemnify her for damage inflicted.

In the meantime Russia is marshaling the largest army ever assembled. She has already called 16,100,000 men, and in a call issued ten days ago

---

[3] Baron Helmuth E. F. Lucius von Stoedten (1869–1934), counselor of the embassy at St. Petersburg, 1911–14; minister at Stockholm, 1915–20.

increased this number by 2,500,000, making a total of 18,600,000. What an army! What a menace it would be to other countries if these men were armed and well organized! It may be that the supporters of an absolute monarchy in Russia are asking themselves what such an army, well disciplined and conscious of its strength, will do in Russia when there are no more foreign enemies to fight. These soldiers are as fine looking men as I ever saw carry a musket. I have seen thousands of them coming into Petrograd in obedience to a call, fresh from the fields, boys who had never before seen a village of over 2,000 inhabitants, with sunken chests, slip-shod gait and careless carriage. After three or four weeks of drill, equipped with military clothing, including boots of which they are very proud, they march singing through the streets with swinging gait, heads high in the air, chests out-thrown, and their very countenances manifesting pride in their country and consciousness of their own power. After arrival in their barracks they are given the most nourishing food, including meat which previously they had had not more than once a week,—soup and black bread having been their principal means of subsistence.

The last call, which comprised 2,500,000 men, was to have gone into effect July 15th-28th, but yesterday the date when the call was to be effective was postponed from July 15th to August 15th. This change of date may not have any significance, but it was determined upon the day after Sazonoff's resignation and Sturmer's appointment.

Minister Sazonoff was and is a bitter enemy of Germany. Von Lucius, present Minister to Stockholm, was Counselor of the German Embassy in Petrograd and its ruling spirit when the war began. He told me in Stockholm that he and Sazonoff were formerly friends, but that Sazonoff now dislikes him very intensely. Sazonoff told me on the other hand, that he had never liked von Lucius, never trusted him, and if he did not consider him crazy and irresponsible, would say he was a liar and a rascal.

You have probably seen before reading thus far that I am disposed to share in the belief that the resignation of Sazonoff was forced and that the promotion of Sturmer is a triumph for the party of reaction and for the champion of absolute monarchy in Russia, although the victory may be due in part to the strengthening of pro-German sentiment in the Empire.

I have the honor to be, sir,
Your obedient servant,
David R. Francis

In a later letter to the Secretary of State on the same subject, written August 14th, I said:

The new Minister of Foreign Affairs, Baron Sturmer, who is still President of the Council of Ministers, does not seem to have the respect of any of the prominent Russians whom I have met. His predecessor, Mr. Sazonoff, was looked upon as a statesman, but when I asked the president of a large bank in Petrograd, a man who is said to be the ablest financier in the Empire, what he thought of Baron Sturmer's appointment to the Foreign Office, he said, "It is just as appropriate as would be the appointment of a tailor to the place I occupy." It is generally believed that the reactionaries are in the saddle and were looking for an opportunity to unhorse Minister Sazonoff, who is looked upon as a liberal. Baron Sturmer is said to have remarked after learning of the first victories of General Brousiloff[4] in Galicia, "One or two more such victories and we can do away with the Duma." Whether these reports are true remains to be proven. There is no doubt, however, that the liberal or progressive element in Russia is greatly disappointed and chagrined at the removal of Sazonoff and the appointment of Sturmer. I think in a former letter I stated that while the loyalty of Sturmer had never been questioned, that he and the reactionaries generally were more disposed to sympathize with Germany than any other element in Russia. My view concerning the benefit to the plain people of Russia through their education and the broadening of their views by the war is stronger now than when expressed two or three weeks ago. I do not think there will be a revolution immediately after the close of the war; that would be premature, but if the Court Party does not adopt a more liberal policy by extending more privileges to the people and their representatives in the Duma, a revolution will take place before the lapse of even a few years.

In the meantime, not only are the Russian people acquiring more information concerning the resources of their own country, but it seems to me that the attention of the world is becoming directed or fixed more intently on Russia from day to day. European and American newspapers and periodicals all dwell upon the magnificence of this Empire, and its undeveloped wealth and immense possibilities. There will be a great competition for the trade of Russia after the close of the war. American enterprise is already looking with interested eyes on the mineral deposits, the great water power, and the opportunities for railroad construction which this country offers. Several Americans are going home by the steamer which takes this pouch, but there is

---

[4] Aleksei A. Brusilov (1853–1926), general of cavalry, commander in chief of the Southwestern Front, March 1916–May 1917 who led the notable Russian offensive in Galicia in the summer of 1916 (Brusilov breakthrough). Commander in chief of the Russian army, May 22–July 19, 1917.

not one of them that is not planning to return to Russia, as all think there is no field on earth to be compared with this. The National City Bank has decided to open a branch here,[5] and I think it is not only a good move for that institution but will prove highly beneficial to the commercial relations of the two countries. I have no intention or desire to violate the neutrality of America, but in my judgment American capital and ingenuity should be encouraged here in order to offset, if nothing more, the well-designed plan of England, and perhaps France also, to capture the trade of Russia after the war through the operation of the resolutions passed at the Economic Conference of the Allies held in Paris, June 17th-20th. There have been many Americans here, and perhaps there are some now, who are unwise enough to take advantage of the necessities of Russia to extort unreasonable prices for what they have to sell; that is short-sighted policy, however, and one which I am advising all Americans to void. Your cautions concerning the improper use of the pouch are timely and just, but all other embassies and legations here do not hesitate to use their respective pouches to promote commerce for their countries.

In a later letter written to my friend and business associate, Breckinridge Jones, President of the Mississippi Valley Trust Company, St. Louis,[6] I expressed my view of an Ambassador's opportunities and obligations regarding commercial relations—a view which longer experience has strengthened.

It has been the policy of our foreign representatives of the diplomatic service to eschew all commercial matters and refer them to the consuls. My judgment from the beginning was, and my experience of seven months has only served to strengthen that opinion, that friendly diplomatic relations could be engendered and fostered and promoted by close commercial relations. Consequently, from the beginning, since taking charge here April 28th last, I have devoted much thought and time to cultivating direct commercial relations between the United States and Russia. Several hints were given me soon after I came that I had too keen a scent for commerce to make an ideal diplomat; but such insinuations only served to amuse me and had no effect upon my plans. Very soon after I came an Economic Conference between the Allies was planned and held June 17th-20th. Immediately upon being advised of the resolutions there adopted, I called upon the then Minister of Foreign

---

[5] The Petrograd branch of the National City Bank of New York was opened on December 20, 1916 (January 2, 1917). It had its residence in the former Turkish embassy at Dvortsovaya Embankment, 8.

[6] Breckinridge Jones (1856–1928), president of the Mississippi Valley Trust Company, of which Francis was one of the directors. The company contributed significantly to the financing of the St. Louis World's Fair in 1904.

Affairs Sazonoff and told him that those resolutions, although ostensibly and professedly adopted to destroy the commercial prestige of Germany, would operate with almost equal effect against all neutral countries and could not be enforced. It was not long thereafter before Brice[7] and some other broad-minded Britishers expressed the same view. Those resolutions have never been confirmed by Russia either through the Duma or the Council of Ministers.

There is a limit, however, to promoting American commerce with Russia, beyond which it would be unwise for me or anyone to go, as there is a feeling more prevalent in England than in any other foreign country and more so in France than in Russia, but a feeling that is growing here, to the effect that America is being so enormously enriched by the prosecution of the war that she does not wish to end it. You can see without my going further into this subject that if I should ostensibly devote more time to the prosecution of commerce than to the diplomatic relations between the two countries, this feeling, which does great injustice to America, would be strengthened and might find expression in a way that would be not only disagreeable but offensive to me and to our countrymen. In England and to a less extent in France there is a feeling that the war now being waged is for the great principles in which America is as much interested as any other country, and consequently the United States, instead of holding aloof and getting enormous prices for what she furnished, should be participating in the conflict.

At about the same time (October 26th, 1916), in a letter to my friend, Hamilton Cooke, of St. Louis,[8] I wrote: "An American doctor who came here at the beginning of the war and tendered his services to Russia, Dr. Hurd,[9] who is now Surgeon-General of an army corps of 40,000 men, an American soldier of fortune about 6 feet 2 inches, and weighing 250 pounds, came to Petrograd from the front not a great while ago, and told me he had seen a Russian army advancing in which only every other man had a gun and the men without guns were told to seize the guns of their armed comrades when they fell."

I wrote in 1920, "the German people are continuing to show their appreciation of the resources of Russia by supporting the Bolsheviks in their efforts to dominate

---

[7] James Bryce (1838–1922), British historian and liberal politician well-known in America for his magisterial book *The American Commonwealth* (1888). He served as ambassador to the US, 1907–13; was made Viscount Bryce in 1914; and entered the House of Lords.

[8] Hamilton Cooke, manager with the New York Life Insurance Company.

[9] Eugene Hurd (1881–1941), surgeon from Seattle, member of the Washington State Legislature, 1913. He volunteered for the Russian army after the outbreak of the World War; was promoted to colonel in 1915; and directed a large field hospital near the front line. Left Russia for France in 1917 and served in the US Army Medical Corps.

Russia. The Bolshevik army is at present organized and disciplined by German officers and German commercial agents are the only ones permitted to enter Bolshevik Russia. Germany was threatened at one time by Bolshevik domination but checkmated the movement by forming a republic which is nominally socialistic but far from a Soviet Republic. The German mind works in various ways and by devious methods. It embraces any strategy to accomplish its end. Germany having been defeated in its effort to subjugate the world by force is resorting to other means and is pushing with unparalleled energy and activity her well-planned economic conquest of Russia and the world."

Although it had no connection with the loan referred to in the letter to Secretary Lansing, I believe it would here be appropriate to mention some of the facts and figures relative to Russia's wealth which I gathered about a year and a half later at the time I was recommending that our Government extend financial assistance to the Provisional Government of Russia. I found that aside from her public buildings and domiciles formerly occupied by the imperial family and state officials, Russia had millions upon millions of acres of tillable lands, forests of immeasurable extent, ore deposits both precious and base, to say nothing of vast water power. I talked with N. Pokrovsky,[10] former Comptroller of the Empire and former Minister of Foreign Affairs and then Chairman of the Commission engaged in appraising the value of Russia's property. I also talked with several of the leading business men and bankers of Russia, and they all said that Russia's wealth far exceeded that of any other country on the earth. I asked if two hundred billion roubles (a rouble is equivalent to 51 1/2 cents) would be an overestimate, to which the invariable reply was, "It's very much greater than that!" This property includes crown lands, but does not comprise land or property privately owned and upon which taxes are paid. It is similar to the public domain of the United States which was sold by the Government to actual settlers. I am of the opinion, therefore, that although the national debt of Russia is forty-one billion roubles, it might be doubled, or trebled or quadrupled without jeopardizing the interests of the holders of Russian bonds. The resources of the country owning between one-seventh and one-sixth of the dry land on the globe and having a population of nearly two hundred million, possessed of common sense and kindly instincts is, in fact, incalculable.

On September 23rd, 1916, I wrote Mr. Lansing regarding my efforts to improve commercial relations between Russia and America by securing a direct cable between the two countries. I said:

---

[10] Nikolai N. Pokrovsky (1885–1930), graduate of St. Petersburg University, lawyer, assistant minister of finance, 1906–14; the last minister of foreign affairs of the Russian Empire, November 17, 1916–March 2, 1917.

I took up with the Premier and Minister of Foreign Affairs the question of laying a cable to the United States, and also made calls in relation thereto upon the Minister of the Interior,[11] the Director-General of Posts and Telegraphs,[12] and the Minister of Finance,[13]—all of whom expressed themselves quite favorably toward the project. Finance Minister Bark was almost enthusiastic, and when I ventured to tell him of the complaints that had come to my hearing from American and Russian merchants as to the commercial domination of England, he bowed affirmatively and said that while not speaking officially it was personally distasteful to him. It has been reported in Petrograd several times that Minister Bark was to be removed because he was wholly under English influence. England is financing all of the Allies, who are no doubt depending upon her for such service, consequently they must accept the terms she imposes.

It is very desirable that American merchants should get a firm foothold in Russia while the opportunity is presented. It is, consequently, very important that this cable should be laid at once. As you have been advised in several other communications, I took up the subject with the Western Union Telegraph Company just before clearing from New York for Russia, and have since exchanged several letters with the President of the company, Mr. Newcomb Carlton,[14] and am in receipt of a cable from him which is confined to two words, "Six million." That is in reply to a letter of mine asking him the cost of laying such a cable and suggesting that he frame his reply so that no one would understand it except myself. I conclude, therefore, that the cable can be laid for $6,000,000, and so told Minister Bark. He expressed very great surprise that it would not cost more and said that he would recommend to the Council of Ministers that an appropriation to the amount of $3,000,000 be made and that the cable be owned half by our Government and half by his, and I cabled you to that effect.

Russia seems to have become aroused to her woeful want of transportation facilities and is planning the construction of many lines of railroads for which she will have to buy a large quantity of material. She has within her borders boundless forests and immeasurable deposits of iron, ore and coal, but the demands of the people are immediate and will have to be supplied to a great

---

[11] Alexander A. Khvostov (1857–1922), minister of interior, July 7–September 16, 1916.

[12] Vladimir B. Pokhvisnev (1858–1927), chief of general administration of Posts and Telegraphs, October 26, 1913–March 2, 1917.

[13] Peter L. Bark (1869–1937), assistant minister of trade and industry from August 10, 1911; manager of the Ministry of Finance from January 30, 1914; minister of finance, May 6, 1914–February 28, 1917.

[14] Newcomb William Carlton (1869–1953), president of Western Union Telegraph Company.

extent from other countries. We should be prepared to take advantage of the situation, and direct cable communication is essential to that end.

I trust that you will look favorably upon this project and will give it your potential personal and official support.

The Russian government carried out its part of the bargain and appropriated the $3,000,000, but our government declined to participate on the ground that it could not engage in business enterprises.

This Russia whose wealth, exclusive of private lands and property, is underestimated at 200,000,000,000 roubles, and whose population is almost 200,000,000, is the prize for which Germany has been contending for generations; first, through commercial penetration (which would have been complete and permanent within another decade); second, by war; and then by means of Bolshevism.

Chapter III
TREASON IN HIGH PLACES

In spite of what Foreign Minister Sazonoff had told me of Russia's unwillingness to negotiate any commercial treaty with any country until the future economic relations between Russia and her Allies had been definitely determined, such a treaty with Japan[1] was announced about sixty days later which must have been in process of negotiation at that time. In a letter written about this time, I commented in these terms on the situation thus created:

> Russia's position at this time is dangerous or certainly very serious. Japan took advantage of Russia's inability to protect her Eastern Border and dictated a Russian-Japanese Treaty, much to my regret, although I was unable to prevent it; however, I did express my disapproval of it to Sazonoff immediately after its promulgation.
>
> No one here outside of the Ministry, and not all of the Ministers, in my judgment, knew anything about this Japanese Treaty until it was promulgated, and I have never ceased to suspect that there are some provisions in the treaty which have never been made public. The Japanese Ambassador, Motono,[2] who negotiated the treaty, was immediately made a Viscount by the Mikado, and has since been called to Japan, where he was installed last week as Minister of Foreign Affairs. Japan had banquets, and bonfires and festivals in celebration of the treaty, but there has never been any expression of approval of it in Russia—in fact the people of this country in private conversation with me and with others have expressed very great regret that such a treaty was entered into. I believe, as stated above, that Japan forced that treaty upon Russia; of course, Japan is an ally of Russia in this war; she was far-seeing and adroit enough to declare war against Germany soon after Germany declared war against Russia. But if reports here are true, Japan

---

[1] The Russo-Japanese Agreement concluded in Petrograd on July 3, 1916, and consisted of public and secret parts. In the public convention, each government promised not to participate in any political formation directed against the other. The secret convention established a de facto military alliance.

[2] Motono Ichiro (1862–1918), baron, Japanese ambassador to Russia, 1906–16. Viscount, Japanese minister of foreign affairs, October 9, 1916–April 23, 1918.

made Germany believe not only that she would not join Germany's enemies but would become an ally of Germany, and Germany believed that Japan was honest in this intention until Japan secured a number of men-of-war and some great munitions of war which she had ordered from Germany, then she declared war against Germany in order to become the possessor of Germany's holdings on the Chinese coast. Japan is now making every effort to strengthen her foothold in China, and the United States should watch the progress of this effort diligently and jealously. The Japanese are not only unscrupulous, but bright and resourceful and intensely patriotic. China has a population of 400,000,000—twice that of Russia and four times that of the United States. If Japan secures control of China, she can form and discipline an army that will be even larger than the enormous one that Russia has now and then there will be a "Yellow Peril" indeed.

I never knew exactly what the terms of this Russo-Japanese Treaty were until it was published in December, 1917, by the Soviet Government together with the other secret treaties into which the Imperial Government had entered.[3] The first two articles of this treaty give its essentials. They read:

Article I.

Both the High Contracting Parties recognize that the vital interests of both of them require the preservation of China from the political mastery of any third Power nourishing hostile intentions against Russia or Japan—and, therefore, mutually bind themselves in future, whenever the circumstances demand it, to enter with each other into open-hearted communications based on entire confidence, in order to take together the measures that shall be necessary to exclude the possibility of such a situation of affairs arising (in China).

Article II.

In the event that, as a consequence of measures adopted by the common consent of Russia and Japan, on the basis of the preceding article, war were to be declared by any third Power, contemplated by the first article of this convention, against one of the Contracting Parties, the other Party, at the

---

[3] Many secret treaties of the World War era were published by the Soviet government at the end of 1917 and made a great sensation. Among the most important were the Treaty of Alliance between Germany and Turkey (1914); the Constantinople Agreement, by which the Turkish capital and Black Sea straits were promised to Russia (1915); Treaty of London, by which Italy joined the Entente (1915); the Treaty of Bucharest, by which Romania agreed to enter the war (1916); and the Russo-Japanese Agreement of 1916.

first demand of its ally, must go to her assistance; each of the high Contracting Parties hereby undertakes, in case such a, situation were to arise, not to make peace with the common enemy without first having received its ally's consent to do so.

On December 20th, 1916, M. Protopopoff,[4] who had been the Vice-President of the Duma,[5] was appointed by the Czar as Minister of the Interior. He was looked upon as a Liberal at the time of his appointment, but almost immediately on assuming this portfolio he became a Reactionary of the most extreme type. This sudden change of front was naturally bitterly resented by his former Liberal associates.

I never had any extended conversation with Protopopoff, the Czar's most hated Minister. He had been an unusually successful business man before he entered public life and had been highly respected in commercial circles. He was a member of the Russian delegation to the Economic Conference held in Paris in June, 1916. On his way back to Russia he was believed to have had a preconcerted meeting in Stockholm with agents of the German Government for the purpose of discussing the terms of a separate peace between Germany and Russia. It was freely asserted and generally believed that he owed his appointment to the Ministry to the monk Rasputin. A leading merchant in Petrograd told me that he thought his elevation to high office must have upset his reason. By way of illustration, he said Protopopoff had recently remarked to him, "Since I have come into contact with the Czar, I have changed my mind about him. I have really come to hold His Majesty in high esteem and I think he likes me, too."

Protopopoff was charged with deliberately making food scarce for the purpose of inciting uprisings among the people which would give him an excuse for their ruthless suppression and also make possible a separate peace with Germany. As Minister of the Interior, he controlled the police of the entire Empire. In order to make them his ready tools, he not only offered them material increase in pay, but promised to pay an honorarium of 2,000 roubles to the family of any policemen who should be killed. He deliberately deceived the Emperor and the Empress as to the state of public sentiment by arranging to have them receive scores of letters purporting to come from the peasants and the plain people in which the supposed writers affirmed their undying allegiance to the monarchy and advised the suppression with an iron hand of all outbreaks of the people. Each letter came from a different locality and alleged to give the

---

[4] Alexander D. Protopopov (1866–1918), member of the Union of October 17, deputy of the Third and Fourth State Dumas, assistant chairman of the State Duma from 1914; headed the Duma delegation sent to Great Britain, France, and Italy in 1916. The last minister of internal affairs of the Russian Empire, September 16, 1916–February 28, 1917.

[5] The State Duma (from the Russian verb *dumat'*—to think), a legislative body in the late Russian Empire that was created after the Russian Revolution of 1905. The First Duma was opened on April 27, 1906; the last was the Fourth Duma, November 15, 1912–October 6, 1917.

sentiment of that part of the Empire. He also had machine guns placed on the tops of the buildings, including even the Saint Isaac's and Kazan Cathedrals, with which to shoot down the people should they gather in crowds to defy the authorities.

When I left Petrograd, February 27th, 1918, Protopopoff had been transferred from the prison of the Saint Peter and Paul Fortress to an insane asylum. Whether he still lives I do not know.

In concluding a dispatch to the Secretary about November 7th, 1916, I wrote as follows:

There have been manifestations lately of unrest among the workers in the factories and also among the long lines of people waiting to be served small amounts of sugar or meat in the shops where such things are distributed. I have heard it rumored that these rumblings are instigated by German money, and I have also heard it charged by an intelligent man who gave the information to me in the most confidential way that the Government itself through its emissaries is attempting to bring about an uprising of the people in order to give Russia an excuse to negotiate a separate peace. Every Minister in the Government is solicitous about the tenure of his office. The Duma will meet in pursuance of adjournment on November 1st–14th. To-day's papers state that Prime Minister Sturmer will be unable to address the Duma because of illness. He is not seriously ill and the meeting is one week off. It would seem that he fears to go through the ordeal.

At a meeting of the Duma held a week or ten days later, the reason for Prime Minister Sturmer's reluctance to appear before that body was explained in a thunder-bolt oration by Professor Paul Miliukoff, the Russian scholar and statesman who is so well and favorably known in this country,[6]—which is—in my view, such a classic example of oratory and so suggestive of the old Hebrew prophets or of Cicero's attacks on Cataline that I am going to reproduce it in full.

Gentlemen:

We have all heard of funeral orations, sad affairs, yet they serve some purpose. Let us analyze these purposes.

---

[6] Pavel N. Milyukov (1859–1943), a prominent Russian historian and political figure. From 1903 to 1907, he delivered a set of lectures on Russian history in the US. He was the prime mover in the foundation of the Constitutional Democratic Party (Kadets) and its leader till 1918; deputy of the Third and Fourth State Dumas, 1907–17; member of the Provisional Committee of the State Duma, created during the February Revolution; and minister of foreign affairs in the first Provisional Government, March 2–May 5, 1917. Francis presented a rather free paraphrase of Milyukov's famous "Stupidity or Treason?" speech, delivered on November 1, 1916.

Firstly, we see such orations remind the relatives and friends of the deceased of some of his good qualities. Secondly, they may inspire a listener to imitation; and thirdly, they give the orator an opportunity to relieve his feelings, or, better still, to practice his oratorical power.

But have you noticed, Gentlemen, that whatever the aim of the oration it leaves the dead dead? What would you, I wonder, think of an individual who should attempt an oration to resurrect the dead—to revive the spirit which has passed and bring him back amongst the living! Mad? Yes, I agree; yet there are such occasions when such an endeavor would be permissible. Gentlemen, I am standing on this Tribune with this mad desire upon me. Like a fire this desire has burned into my very soul. I want to deliver an oration over the dead, to resurrect it, because we, the mighty Russian Empire, cannot think of leaving dead the most precious entity in a nation's possession. The corpse over which I, together with the bulk of Russian society, weep tears of blood must not remain lifeless. We must revive it. You and I must use superhuman effort, all our powers, magic, witchcraft, call it what you like—but it must be made to live. This highest inheritance of a nation—its honor—must not be buried. Tarry with me, have patience with me, I am a sorrowful mourner. Honor has died in Russia and before the world at large becomes aware of our dead we must bring it to life again.

Do you know that unless you act now, unless you do your very utmost, the name of Russia will stink in the nostrils of humanity? Even the most savage tribes of the world will turn aside on the approach of a Russian, because Russia is about to betray the trust of her Allies. Allies of whom she should be proud, like the gaolbird when he is received by the Mayor and Corporation. Allies to whom she ought to listen with respect and humiliation.

The oldest civilized countries in the world, the oldest democracies. Allies who are careful in the selection of their friends. Allies who have lowered their prestige to call us friends. Allies who have helped us. Allies who have worked for us. Allies who fight for us. Allies of blood's wealth. And these are to be betrayed. Judas has closed the bargain! Judas is the traitor amongst us. I quite understand your turmoil. I can read the terror in your eyes. Even the President's hand is quaking. He rings his bell nervously, but even the bell revolts; it strikes, but instead of its usual shrill note you hear it muffled—the funeral bell. No, it will not quiet me; its sound reechoes in my soul and urges me to further effort. I have here the evidence of Judas. Evidence in the cold figures—shekels, Gentlemen. The pieces of silver of betrayal. A new sound comes out of the bell; the jingle of silver, the blood money.

Either Russia is a fool or a knave. Which is it? Was it not madness to appoint as a Prime Minister a man with a name and a face apart from our sympathies and methods; a man of a race with whom we are at war! Is it a frolic in which our manhood from the lowest of peasants upwards is shedding its precious blood? Is it a money-making expedition into which we are sent? Are the trenches the steps towards riches for the Premier and his clique? Are the moans of the wounded, the groans of the dying, only the accompaniment of a festival—a carnival? Is it only another method of shedding Russian blood by German autocrats in Russia? Has it all been prearranged? Answer! Let your conscience, your soul, answer before you howl like a band of hooligans or starving wolves. What are we allowing to take place? Why are we silent? Yes, silence, our silence, is golden to Sturmer and his colleagues; but for us, for our generations to come, it is a crime, a terrible bloody crime; when honor is buried all we shall have to leave to our descendants is disgrace, an everlasting disgrace which even time will not efface. Awake, you sons of Russia, you representatives of the Russian people, and bestir yourselves to avert this, the greatest catastrophe!

Sturmer is in negotiation for separate peace.

Sturmer has betrayed Russia.

Sturmer is disarranging supplies for our brave sons and brothers in the trenches.

Sturmer is doing it for German money. I have here a document which shows every mark which he received from Germany from July, 1901, to July, 1916. Let him come and deny it, and, if I am allowed to live after this (though I'll gladly die if honor lives) I will bring witnesses to prove the truth.

Traitors and spies are amongst us.

No doubt, says Sturmer, separate peace will be beneficial to Russia when arranged by Sturmer, but what is Russia without honor? Rise up; dead Honor! Arise from thy Coffin, and let us see thee live! Come face thy high position! Accuse him in front of this Assembly; let thy voice thunder!

Yes, I am emotional, but where is the man who knowing all this can be cool—can be unmoved? Why look! There sits the Ambassador of an Allied Country, the coldest and calmest, and yet, though he follows me with difficulty, he is pale, he is perturbed.

I am cool in comparison with the crime with which I am charging Sturmer. I wish I were younger. I wish the spirit of 1905 were upon me—it would be practical emotion then. You accuse me of shouting, of being mad. I agree; but if you are sane after having heard what I have said, you also are traitors. All right. I withdraw; it is against the regulations to call you traitors; it is admittedly heated. I know you too well to even think it of you. On the contrary, I am standing on this Tribune only because you are honest men and true. You will not tolerate these things, now you know of them. You will, as I said in the beginning, resurrect dead honor and bring gratitude instead of contempt into the hearts of our children. Rachel, we are told, is crying for her children;

if you open your ears you will hear a heartbroken sob)—a sob which will fill you with horror. Do you know who is crying? Russia! The gallant Russia, the brave Russia, the Mother of us all, bad and good, is crying. Her heart is breaking. Are we to help her—we, her sons? This heartens me. This is the miracle I have been working for. The dead has come back to life. Your shouts of encouragement are its first signs of life.

Now with a live honor in our midst we can speak more calmly, we can deliberate.

As you know, our agreement with our Allies does not permit a separate peace—with one exception. This exception should have been known to our statesmen only, but it is known in Berlin. And Berlin has its friends here; what is easier therefore than to make the exception possible.

Now just take the trouble to analyze the activity of the Sturmer Ministry since its inception. What were all measures adopted for! What were they intended to produce? The oppression, the disorganization? What is the aim of all these acts? Dissatisfaction of the masses? What does such dissatisfaction produce? Revolution! Red, bloody revolution! And this is the exception to make separate peace possible.

No, Berlin does not pay money for nothing! Sturmer had to earn it and he did. He paved the way for a revolution as the means of separate peace. Must not the great Russian public be told of this and be warned to suffer and be patient? But were it not better to remove the cause of their suffering, their anxiety?

Gentlemen, this traitor, this German, must go. No matter what excuse be made for him. For the sake of honor, to reestablish the confidence of our Allies, Sturmer, nay, the whole German clique, must go.

Just a few words more, Gentlemen, these are history-making epochs. Russia's hope, Russia's life, is based on her alliances; these alliances depend on victory. The Russian Duma, though it has no power, must help to achieve it. The people stand helpless awaiting your lead, you the representatives of the people, are responsible. You must act.

Soon after the meeting in which this attack upon Sturmer was made, I wrote Secretary Lansing that in my judgment the Government was preparing to do two things: one to abandon to her fate her small Ally, Roumania, whom she had induced to enter the war through promises of support, and, second, to make a separate peace with Germany. I said that I believed this had been the underground plan of the Ministry ever since Sturmer became Prime Minister in July, and knowledge of these plans or plots reaching the Duma had caused the outbreaks of wrathful denunciation.

Attacks such as Miliukoff's upon the Prime Minister, instead of causing the Emperor to prorogue the Duma, as would have been the case a few years earlier, led him to dismiss Sturmer, who quickly disappeared into ignominious oblivion. He later died in prison in the Saint Peter and Paul Fortress, and his wife after an attempt to cut her throat is now in the insane asylum.

While the removal of Sturmer temporarily allayed public indignation, the appointment of M. Trepoff[7] as his successor was not reassuring. Trepoff, although opposed to a separate peace, was also a reactionary and was not satisfactory to the Duma. He was, moreover, a man with deep convictions and iron nerve, and on that account more dangerous than Sturmer, who was venal and with neither convictions nor strength. As I said at the time of his appointment Trepoff was a man who would not hesitate to demand that the Emperor dissolve the Duma if that body opposed him, and such action could hardly fail to result very seriously.

On November 18th, shortly after Sturmer's dismissal and Trepoff's appointment, I attended a turbulent and stirring session of the Duma. I was the only Ambassador in the diplomatic loge when the President called the meeting to order, but a few minutes later was joined by the Italian,[8] British[9] and French[10] Ambassadors successively. After a few remarks by the President, Premier Trepoff was introduced, advanced to the Tribune and tried to read a written speech. His voice was inaudible amid the taunts, shouts, clapping and stamping from the "Left." Three times he returned to the Tribune from his seat in the space at the right of the President, reserved for the Ministry. The President used bell in his efforts to keep order instead of a mallet as in other deliberative assemblies. Three times the Premier's efforts to be heard were drowned in the uproar. Finally after the expulsion of a half dozen of the most obstreperous disturbers, he got a hearing, read his address, and received perfunctory applause. He denied that Russia had sought a separate peace, and said that no peace would be concluded that did not give Russia control of the Dardenelles and added that Russia's Allies had agreed to this. At this point a number of the members looked curiously toward Sir George Buchanan, the British Ambassador, who sat next to me, but his expression showed no trace of dissent.

---

[7] Alexander F. Trepov (1862–1928), minister of ways of communication, October 30, 1915–December 27, 1916, and chairman of the Council of Ministers, November 10–December 27, 1916.

[8] Marquis Andrea Carlotti di Riparbella (1864–1920), Italian ambassador, February 13, 1913–November 17, 1917.

[9] Sir George William Buchanan (1854–1924), hereditary British diplomat. He entered the Foreign Service in 1876; served in Austro-Hungary and Italy; made a trip through the US en route to Japan; served in Switzerland, Germany, France, Bulgaria, and the Netherlands. Ambassador to Russia, December 1910–December 1917 (January 1918).

[10] Maurice Paléologue (1859–1944), French diplomat of Greco-Romanian origin; entered the Foreign Service in 1880; served in Morocco, China, Italy, and Bulgaria. Ambassador to Russia, January 12, 1914–May 3, 1917.

Several speakers followed the Premier, but the speech of General Purishkevich[11] was the only one which created a sensation. The General had been well known as an ultraconservative—a member of the "Right" and joined the "Left." He made specific charges that German influence had permeated not only Court and military circles, but banking and commercial affairs also. He accused some of the Russian Generals with inefficiency and indifference, if not actual treachery. He cited one General in particular who had used freight cars to transport mineral waters to his headquarters which should have been used to haul munitions and soldiers to Roumania—Russia's small and sorely pressed Ally. He made other definite charges against the army, of which he claimed to have documentary evidence and stepping to the Ministerial Bench he handed the Minister of War[12] a document. He was merciless in his criticism of the Ministry, saying that the Minister and Duma could not work together—one or the other must go. He singled out Minister of the Interior Protopopoff for his bitterest denunciation. Protopopoff had not stayed to hear what the General had to say about him.

He told of a movement to start a daily newspaper in Petrograd which should be under German influence and should advocate a separate peace between Russia and the Central Empires. He charged that ten prominent banks in Russia had agreed to subscribe 500,000 roubles, each, to this paper, but that seven of them on learning its real purpose had withdrawn their support. The three that remained were the International Bank of Commerce,[13] the Russian Bank of Foreign Trade[14] and the Azoff-Don Bank.[15] He stated that of the assets of the Russian Bank of Foreign Trade of 70,000,000 roubles only 20,000,000 was Russian capital, the remaining 50,000,000 being German. Further he said that of the 170,000,000 roubles representing the combined capital of the three banks, 50,000,000 only was Russian, the rest, or 120,000,000, being German.

---

[11] Vladimir M. Purishkevich (1870–1920), one the founders of the Union of Russian People and a popular deputy of the State Duma, who took part in the murder of Rasputin. During the war, he was chief of hospital train and was nicknamed "General."

[12] Dmitry S. Shuvaev (1854–1937), general of infantry, minister of war from March 15, 1916 to January 3, 1917.

[13] St. Petersburg International Commercial Bank was created in 1869. By the eve of the World War, it had become the second largest bank in Russia. A special building was constructed for it in 1896–98 at Nevsky Prospekt, 58.

[14] Russian Bank for Foreign Trade, established in St. Petersburg in 1871. A specially designed mansion was built for it in 1887–88 at Morskaya Street, 32.

[15] The Azov-Don Commercial Bank, one of the largest banking establishments in Imperial Russia, was created at Taganrog in 1871 and transferred to St. Petersburg in 1903. From 1908–13, prominent Russian architect Fyodor I. Lidval constructed a magnificent building at Morskaya Street, 3–5, which is regarded as one of the finest examples of Northern Modern.

When General Purishkevich took his seat he received a great demonstration of approval both from the members and from the spectators in the galleries.

On December 17th, O. S. 1916, all Russia was stirred by the report of the murder of Rasputin, the monk, who had exercised such a dominant influence over the royal family, particularly the Czarina. In January I wrote Counselor Polk a personal letter in which I gave him the most authentic version I could then obtain of the murder. I said:

> I have heard some of the particulars from a very authentic source concerning the killing of Rasputin—the monk or pretender who was killed because he was supposed to have too much influence with the Empress and was bringing disgrace on the royal family. You have no doubt read in the public prints of this man. He was uneducated and untidy in his dress, but had a wonderful eye and hypnotic influence. He undoubtedly had access to the Empress at all hours and through her was very potential with the Emperor. Consequently his assistance was sought by all aspiring to power and position. He was a man of extraordinary if not unprecedented sexual passions. He was very human in other regards, having an appetite for liquor and rich food, notwithstanding his obscure origin.
>
> On the night of the tragedy he was sent for to come to the house of Prince Usoupoff,[16] a fine palace on the Moika.[17] It appears there had been a dinner at this house attended by Russian ladies, who, however, had taken their departure before Rasputin arrived. After considerable drinking Rasputin began to boast of his power, claiming to have influenced a number of appointments to official positions, and even asserted that he had illicit intercourse with many women of high position, calling them by names. He went so far as to say that his next mistress would be a well-known young Grand Duchess of the royal family whose character is above reproach and who is very well thought of by all classes in Russia. When he made that statement, it is said that the host, Prince Usoupoff, drew his pistol and laid it down on the table in front of Rasputin, and told him that after making such a statement it was time for him to kill himself. Rasputin grasped the pistol but instead of firing it at himself, shot at Usoupoff, whom he fortunately missed, the bullet going through a door and attracting the attention of the police on the outside. The other members of the party then drew their weapons and began to fire at Rasputin, who tried to leave the room. The young noblemen continued to fire and Rasputin fell to the floor just before reaching the door, having been

---

[16] Prince Felix F. Yusupov (1887–1967), husband of Nicholas II's niece.

[17] Yusupov Palace is located at Moyka Embankment, 94. Now the Palace of Culture for Educators.

shot three times through the back. No one knows who fired the fatal shots—
in fact it is said that none of those present admitted having fired at all. My
information, however, is from a source which is said to be very reliable. Prince
Demitry,[18] a son of a Grand Uncle of the Emperor,[19] and Prince Usoupoff,
the son of one of the richest if not the richest nobleman in Russia, and General
Purishkevich are generally thought to have been the only ones present. After
Rasputin was killed an automobile was sent for, driven by the owner, another
nobleman, Count Pistelcorse,[20] connected by marriage with the Grand Duke
Paul—the Emperor's uncle. It came to the house, the body of Rasputin was
placed in it, and taken across the Neva to one of the bayous or inlets of that
river, where it was put through a hole cut in the ice. The body was discovered there in a few days after a thorough search by the police, was identified
and taken to a hospital on this side of the river. It is said that the Empress
went to this hospital herself, had the body removed to Tsarskoe-Selo, about
twelve miles out of the city limits, and that funeral services were held in the
Emperor's church and the body buried in the grounds of the palace. It is said
to be the intention of the Empress to erect a chapel over this body and to
locate its altar immediately over the grave. Whether these reports are true it
is difficult to say, but at any rate they are generally believed. Other accounts
of the killing of Rasputin have come to me since, but I do not know that they
are any more authentic than the version given.

It was thought for a day or two after Rasputin's death that nothing would
be done about it; everyone feeling that his removal would be beneficial from
every viewpoint. In fact the Emperor who was at the Front when the killing occurred is said to have been not displeased when the news reached him
and as especially talkative and good-humored when enroute from the front
to Tsarskoe-Selo. But in a few days a change came over the Emperor concerning the punishment of those who had killed Rasputin. Meantime the
Empress had herself signed an order for the arrest of Demitry and had given
it to a much beloved Russian General of advanced years whose name I don't
recall.

When the General presented the order of arrest to Demitry, the latter said
he was a member of the royal family and no one could order his arrest except

---

[18] Grand Duke Dmitry Pavlovich (1891–1942), first cousin of Nicholas II, son of Grand Duke Pavel Alexandrovich. After the murder of Rasputin, he was exiled to Persia to serve in the Russian Army Corps. After the 1917 revolution, he emigrated and married American heiress Audrey Emery in 1926.

[19] Grand Duke Pavel Alexandrovich (1860–1919), uncle of Nicholas II.

[20] Colonel Erich Gerhard von Pistohlkors (1853–1935). His former wife, Ol'ga V. Pistohlkors (later Princess Paley, 1865–1929), married Grand Duke Pavel Alexandrovich.

the Emperor himself. Thereupon the old General said, "If you don't observe this it will be the cause of my downfall, and I appeal to you through personal consideration for me to consider yourself a prisoner in your own house," to which Demitry consented. About two days after the Emperor's arrival, he ordered Demitry to military service in Persia and is said to have prohibited his return to Petrograd for a period of twelve years. He banished Usoupoff to his estates somewhere in Southern Russia. Purishkevich, a General in the Army, and the same who had made the bitter speech in the Duma against Protopopoff, had assembled a trainload of supplies for the relief of the Russian wounded which was waiting for him on a side-track in the suburbs of Petrograd. He joined it about daylight and went to the front where he is supposed to be now, distributing the supplies. It is probable, however, that some punishment has been inflicted upon him.

On January 1st, all the members of the royal family, including many Grand Dukes and Grand Duchesses, united in a "round robin" to the Emperor, asking his clemency for Demitry on the ground that his health is broken and that Persia where he has been ordered to special service on the staff of the commander of the Russian forces is a very unhealthy country. This "round robin" was signed by the Empress Dowager who is at Kieff where she has been ever since my arrival here. It is said that she is not permitted to return to Petrograd by order of the Emperor, and while a strong woman and exceedingly popular in Russia, she admits that she has no influence over her son who seems to have been prejudiced against her by his wife, the Empress. This "round-robin" was presented to the Emperor by the Queen Dowager of Greece, who lives in Petrograd.[21] The Emperor, however, was immovable and handed the petition back to the Queen Dowager of Greece, after writing on the reverse side that he was surprised such a petition should be presented to him, as he could not permit so heinous a crime to go unpunished. It is reported that the new count who drove the automobile which conveyed Rasputin's body from Usoupoff's house across the river was ordered to leave Petrograd for two months; that all of the signers of the "round robin" were informed that they would find it beneficial to their health to make a visit of from two to four weeks to their respective country places.

The Minister of the Interior, Protopopoff, was said to have gone into a trance when talking to the Empress a short time before the assassination and when he recovered himself to have said in answer to an inquiry that he had communicated with Jesus Christ, who had told him to follow the teachings of the Saint Rasputin.

---

[21] Olga Konstantinovna (1851–1926), Russian grand princess by birth, qween of the Hellenes from 1867, widow of King George I (1845–1913).

TREASON IN HIGH PLACES

In a letter to Frederick Sterling who had been Second Secretary of the Embassy when I arrived in Petrograd, and who was a St. Louisan, I wrote on January 8th, 1917:

> Not long before this murder both the Imperial Council and the Congress of Nobles had passed resolutions inveighing against "the invisible influences" surrounding the Government. The influences are commonly referred to as "dark forces." The Emperor has been undoubtedly very much provoked by all these hostile demonstrations, and in his appointment of reactionaries is showing a defiant attitude. Trepoff has resigned as Premier, and is said to have told the Emperor that he would not serve longer with Protopopoff. His resignation was accepted after an interval of about two weeks. Ignatieff, Minister of Education,[22] and Brobinsky, Minister of Agriculture,[23] have also both resigned for the same reason—namely, hostility to Protopopoff. Prince Golitzin[24] has been appointed to succeed Trepoff as Premier. He is a reactionary and is said to have been appointed through the influence of the Empress. He has had charge of her charities and relief work. Last Sunday, which was the Russian New Year's Day,[25] Rodzianko, the President of the Duma,[26] refused to shake Protopopoff's hand and told him that he desired to have no relations with him at any time or place. Protopopoff retorted, "If that is the case I will send you a challenge!" Rodzianko turned on his heel with the remark, "I hear you." Nothing has come of it however.

---

[22] Count Pavel N. Ignatiev (1870–1945), assistant minister of agriculture from 1912; acting minister of people's education from January 9, 1915; minister, May 6, 1915–December 27, 1916.

[23] Count Aleksei A. Bobrinsky (1852–1927), deputy of the Third State Duma; chairman of the Council of the United Nobility; marshal of St. Petersburg nobility; assistant minister of internal affairs, March 25–July 21, 1916; minister of agriculture, July 21–November 14, 1916.

[24] Prince Nikolai D. Golitsyn (1850–1925), chairman of the committee to render assistance to the Russian prisoners of war abroad and member of the State Council from 1915. The last chairman of the Council of Ministers of the Russian Empire, December 27, 1916– February 27, 1917.

[25] According to the Julian Calendar, which was used in Russia till January 31, 1918, the country began the new year thirteen days later than nations using the Gregorian Calendar. Therefore, January 1 (Old Style) was equivalent to January 14 (New Style).

[26] Mikhail V. Rodzianko (1859–1924), one of the founders and leaders of the Union of October 17; chairman of the Third and Fourth State Dumas, 1911–17; chairman of the Provisional Committee of the State Duma, February 27–October 6, 1917.

In a letter to Mrs. Francis,[27] January 15th, 1917, New Style, I wrote:

It has long been the custom in Russia for the Emperor to receive the Diplomatic Corps on the Russian New Year's Day, which is our January 14th. There was no reception January 14th, 1916, because the Emperor was at the front. It was generally understood there would be no reception this year, but the Embassy was notified by the Master of Ceremonies January 10th that the Emperor would receive the Diplomatic Corps at 4 p.m., January 1st–14th at Tsarskoe-Selo, and that a special train would be provided for them leaving Petrograd at 2:35 p.m., and leaving Tsarskoe-Selo for the return at 5:30 p.m. I was in Moscow when this notice was received, and Counselor Wright[28] was requested by the Master of Ceremonies to wire me and state that it was expressly desired that I should be present at the reception.

Accompanied by my staff I left Petrograd on the special train at 2:35 p.m., arriving at Tsarskoe-Selo about thirty minutes later. Each Ambassador was conveyed from the station to the castle,[29] a distance of about one verst[30] or two-thirds of a mile, in a separate carriage; the Ministers and Staffs of the Embassies and Legations followed in carriages and sleighs loaded to their respective capacities. Upon arrival at the castle the Diplomatic Corps was conducted to a large room about 120 feet long and about 40 feet wide, richly furnished in gold and red and lighted by hundreds of electric lamps. When all were assembled each head of a mission took position in his proper order, accompanied by his staff, who stood two paces in the rear. A few minutes later the Emperor entered, accompanied by the Grand Master of Ceremonies and by the Marshal of the Court and also by twenty or thirty members of His Court. The Emperor advanced first to the British Ambassador, whom he engaged in conversation for five or six minutes. The Ambassador read a paper to His Majesty, the contents of which were not made known to the other missions. The conversation between the Emperor and the Ambassador was not audible more than three or four feet away. I have not learned the contents of the paper read by Sir George Buchanan, but conclude that as I was not

---

[27] Jane Francis (née Perry), the ambassador's wife (1854–1924).

[28] Joshua Butler Wright (1877–1939), graduate of Princeton University (1899, BS), was engaged in banking in New York City and farming and stock-raising in Wyoming. He entered the Foreign Service in 1909; served in Honduras, Belgium, and Brazil; assigned to the Department of State as acting chief of the Division of Latin American Affairs in 1915; designated as counselor of the embassy at Petrograd on October 2, 1916; assigned to the Department of State on May 14, 1918.

[29] Great (or Ekaterininsky) Palace at Tsarskoe Selo.

[30] Versta, an ancient Russian unit of measurement of distance, a bit more than one kilometer.

consulted that the Ambassador did not presume to speak for my Government. At the end of the conversation between the Emperor and the Ambassador, the suite of the British Embassy, consisting of about fifteen men, were presented to the Emperor, each man shaking hands with His Majesty. After a few words addressed by the Emperor to the members of his suite, His Majesty advanced to the Italian Ambassador where the same proceedings were enacted; the Italian Ambassador, however, did not have any paper in his hand and the conversation appeared to be of an informal character. The Emperor next advanced to the French Ambassador, with whom he held conversation in an undertone for a few minutes and then the members of the French suite were presented—they were nine in number.

The Emperor then advanced to myself and after shaking hands cordially recalled my presentation to him last May. I remarked that I had learned a great deal more about his country and his people than I knew when I saw him last and had found much in both to admire and much to interest me. He expressed gratification, talking all the time in excellent English (I think his conversation with the Italian and French Ambassador and the Spanish Ambassador[31] and, perhaps, with all of the other heads of the missions except Sir George Buchanan and myself was in French) and when I said to him that I had been endeavoring to promote closer relations between Russia and America he smilingly and responsively replied: "Yes, I have heard of your actions in that line and think considerable progress has been made." After a few more words of casual conversation and with sincere expression by me of New Year's Greetings, I presented the nine members of my Staff[32] to His Majesty and took occasion to say some word of commendation or explanation about each member. We were all impressed with the cordiality of His Majesty's manner, by his poise and his apparent excellent physical condition, as well as by the promptness of his utterances. After leaving the American Embassy, the Emperor next conversed with the Spanish Ambassador and then with the heads of all of the other missions, ending his very trying ordeal, which occupied about an hour and twenty minutes, in a talk with the Charge d'Affaires of the Japanese Embassy.[33] The Emperor was attired in a Cossack uniform, with an overcoat extending to within a few inches of his ankles. He is a man of medium stature and gave appearance of having supreme confidence in himself. During this hour and twenty minutes the members of the Diplomatic Corps all retained the positions to which, they were first assigned.

---

[31] Marquis Luis Valera y Delavat de Villãsinda (1870–1926), Spanish diplomat and writer; served in China, Morocco, and Portugal; ambassador to Russia from August 22, 1916.

[32] Actually ten (see n. 34, p. 46).

[33] Counselor of the Japanese embassy Marumo Naotosi.

The Emperor after leaving the Japanese Embassy, proceeded to the door and, turning with a dignified and graceful bow, saluted the entire Diplomatic Corps and then took his departure, accompanied by his suite.

The Diplomatic Corps numbered over eighty persons; the chief of every mission was in uniform except the American; seven members of the American mission were in full dress suits with white vest, white tie and white gloves—the two Naval Attaches and the Military Attaché were, of course, in their dress uniforms.[34] After a light luncheon we were driven from the castle to the station in the same order and in the same vehicle that conveyed us from the station. The special train arrived in Petrograd at the Imperial Station a few minutes after six o'clock.

This entire ceremony was very impressive. The scene in the magnificent room was brilliant indeed. The Emperor appeared to me as taking advantage of the occasion to impress his royal personality upon all present.

On the same day the Emperor announced the new members of the Imperial Council; the names of these members are said to be nearly or quite all those of Reactionaries. If so, that is but another indication that His Majesty is not yielding in the slightest degree to the liberal sentiment which expressions in the Duma and in the Imperial Council during the past month, indicate has been spreading throughout the Empire.

Little did any of us who were present at this reception know that we were witnessing the last public appearance of the last ruler of the mighty Romanoff dynasty.[35] And as I look back on it I am convinced that just as little did the central figure, the Czar of all the Russians, realize that within sixty days he would be compelled to abdicate the throne of his ancestors. In fact he made the impression upon me and upon every member of my staff that he was more at his ease and felt more secure in his position than he did when I presented to him seven months earlier my letters from the President of the United States. This complacent monarch had no premonition of the storm that was brewing. This weak ruler had no idea that he was standing on a volcano whose eruption within seven short months was to bury himself and his dynasty.

---

[34] Counselor J. Butler Wright; First Secretary Sheldon Whitehouse, Third Secretaries Norman Armour and Livingston Phelps; Commercial Attaché William C. Huntington; Special Assistants to the Ambassador Basil Miles and William F. Sands; Naval Attaché Captain Newton A. McCully and his assistant Lieutenant Colonel James C. Breckinridge; Military Attaché First Lieutenant E. Francis Riggs.

[35] The Romanovs, tsarist and imperial dynasty, reigned 1613–1917.

Chapter IV
RUMBLINGS OF REVOLUTIONS

On December 23rd, 1916, I delivered to Foreign Minister Pokrovski President Wilson's communication to each of the Belligerents requesting them to state the terms upon which they would be willing to make peace and stop the terrible slaughter.[1] A few days before I had delivered to the Minister the overtures for peace of the Central Powers which I had received from the State Department.[2] These I handed him without comment. I had told Minister Pokrovski at that time, however, that I would shortly present to him a communication from the President of the United States, but that such message not only was not inspired by the note of the Central Empires, but was being prepared before it was known that the Central Powers were to make any overtures. I read the President's note to the Minister and then delivered the original to him.

Almost exactly a month later I delivered to the Foreign Minister a copy of President Wilson's speech to the Senate in which he outlined the terms and conditions under which the United States might be willing to join with the other Powers for the preservation of the peace of the world after the close of the war—the celebrated fourteen points.[3] The reaction to this message at the time can perhaps best be suggested by giving here an account of a dinner given to some of my colleagues of the Diplomatic Corps representing the Neutral countries and sent to the Secretary immediately afterwards. I said:

---

[1] Woodrow Wilson's failed offer to mediate peace made on December 18, 1916.

[2] On December 12, 1916, the German government proposed to negotiate peace with the Allies through the US charge d'affaires at Berlin. It declared readiness to begin negotiations immediately but did not formulate any definite conditions.

[3] Actually, Francis meant Wilson's message "Peace Without Victory," delivered to the Senate on January 22, 1917. Wilson's "Fourteen Points" were presented on January 8, 1918.

I gave a dinner in the Embassy last evening which was attended by the Ministers of Sweden,[4] Norway,[5] Denmark,[6] Holland,[7] China,[8] Siam[9] and Serbia.[10] There were eighteen plates but only six ladies as most of the members of the Diplomatic Corps are either unmarried or unaccompanied by their wives. The general subject of discussion was the President's message as I anticipated it would be. It is not surprising that the representatives of these smaller countries should be in entire sympathy with the President's desires, but all of them expressed doubt and fear lest his views might be so impractical as to prevent their being put into operation. I told them that they should bear in mind that this utterance of the President of the United States was not addressed to the Belligerents nor to the Neutrals, but to that branch of his own Government to which, in connection with himself, was entrusted the direction of our foreign relations; that the message gave the conclusions of the President after mature deliberation as to the kind of a peace which in his judgment would prove lasting and for the preservation of which he would be willing to see our Government enter into a League with other nations. I reminded them that no revolution in the history of the world and in fact no reform had ever been broached or agitated or consummated that had not been the result of a moral conviction in the minds and hearts of men and that invariably the first expression of such conviction had appeared to the supporters of the "old order" as a Utopian dream which society was unprepared to put into effect and that in most instances those advocating such changes had been charged with insincerity and accused of being moved by selfish objects. Of course, there were no speeches at this dinner and this conversation was a mutual interchange of views concerning the President's message and its bearing upon conditions which are unprecedented in the world's history. Every one of these ministers was prompt to avow his belief in the purity and unselfishness of the President's motives, while expressing the fear that his plan for peace would not be realized in connection with the end of the present war.

---

[4] Lieutenant General Edvard Brändström (1850–1921), Swedish minister to Russia from 1906.

[5] Nikolai Prebensen (1850–1938), Norwegian minister from 1906.

[6] Harald Scavenius (1873–1939), Danish minister from 1912.

[7] Baron Arthur Martin Désiré Sweerts de Landas Wyborgh (1862–1944), Dutch minister from 1906.

[8] Liu Tszin Jen, Chinese minister from 1912.

[9] Visan Botchanakan, Siamese minister from 1913.

[10] Miroslav Spalajković (1869–1951), Serbian minister from 1913.

The criticism of the President's message most frequently heard is of that expression that a peace based on victory of either side will not be a lasting peace. While admitting that a cessation of hostilities as the result of a war of conquest would result in a peace characterized by bitterness and resentment, the general feeling seems to be that Germany merits punishment and should be taught a lesson for the violation of her agreements and because of the policy which has characterized her prosecution of the war, which it is charged has been in defiance of all international law and of all of the instincts of civilized society.

Discussion of this speech was, however, soon terminated by our breaking off of diplomatic relations with Germany on February 4th. I gave a statement to the newspapers concerning our rupture of diplomatic relations with Germany immediately after the receipt of a cable from the State Department officially informing me of the act. This was necessary in order to give the Russian people a clear idea of what the United States had done. Otherwise they would have thought we had declared war. In a letter to Secretary Lansing written at this time, I said:

The Russians are very much pleased with the stand we have taken and are already beginning to treat us as Allies. The French are delighted also and according to telegraphic reports there have been demonstrations of an enthusiastic nature in Paris.

I don't like the position of England, or rather that of the British Embassy here. Neither the British Ambassador nor the French nor the Italian has called nor have I met any one of them since Bernstorff[11] was given his passports—it seemed to me that it would not have been improper for those Ambassadors to call and express gratification at least that our diplomatic relations with the arch-enemy of their countries had been severed. The Belgian Minister, de Buisseret,[12] did call and expressed himself as being much pleased with the stand we had taken. The Siamese Minister called yesterday and stated that his Government had instructed him to ascertain what reply the Neutral countries had made or would make to the suggestion of President Wilson that they take similar action to ours. I told him that no official information

---

[11] Count Johann Heinrich von Bernstorff (1862–1939), German ambassador to the US, 1908–17.

[12] Count Conrad Marie Joseph Leonce de Buisseret Steenbecque de Blarenghien (1875–1927), Belgian diplomat; minister at Washington, 1909–11; minister at St. Petersburg/Petrograd, 1912–17. Left Petrograd on September 5, 1917, and was replaced by socialist Jules Destrée (1863–1936). In 1896, while serving as secretary of the Belgian legation at Washington, he married Caroline Sherman Story (1870–1914), daughter of Major General John P. Story (1841–1915).

had been received on the subject, and all I knew concerning it was what had appeared in the public prints. He told me he had called upon me first, but proposed to call upon the Ministers of the other neutral countries, and that when he left the Embassy he would go to the Norwegian Legation.[13] I requested him to telephone me the result of his conference with Minister Prebensen, which he did later and informed me that the Scandinavian countries had come to no conclusion other than an agreement to confer and make a joint reply. Meantime I had telephoned to the Chinese Minister and called at his Legation[14] where he informed me of the action by his government. (China had followed President Wilson's advice and also severed diplomatic relations with Germany.) He seemed very much pleased and I was exceedingly so. I informed the Siamese Minister of the action taken by China and strongly urged him to recommend his government to do likewise—he virtually promised to do so.

It is the practise in the diplomatic service for all Ambassadors and Ministers to submit their resignations at the close of a Presidential term. Accordingly on February 25th, I cabled mine to the President paraphrased in the following terms:

> Understand that it is customary for Ambassadors to tender their resignations at the beginning of a new term. Mine is herewith presented. Am thoroughly reconciled to return or perfectly willing to remain, or would cheerfully serve in any position where you thought I could be more effective. In this critical juncture personal interests and inclinations should be subordinated to country's welfare.

I also requested that if agreeable to the President it be published in the American papers. My object in desiring its publication was to indicate that I had no sympathy with the obstructionists in the United States who were seeking to keep us out of a just and inevitable war—particularly did I wish it understood that I entirely disagreed with Senator Stone of Missouri, my own State. In this connection, I might say that after I had served five months in Russia and had established not only pleasant, but friendly relations with the Russian Government, I was told by some of my friends among the Russian officials that I had originally been supposed to be pro-German in my sympathies and that my appointment was thought to have been brought about by pro-German influences in America. This rumor was strengthened by my hailing from St. Louis, where the German element was supposed to predominate.

---

[13] The Norwegian legation was located on Potemkinskaya Street, 3.

[14] The Chinese legation was located on Sergievskaya Street, 22.

On March 9th there had just occurred several demonstrations of dissatisfaction by the working people, especially the women. These were caused by the ever-increasing difficulty in getting food. Long bread lines were constantly seen, one of them being just across the street from the Embassy; the women formed these at four or five o'clock in the morning and sometimes waited for hours with the thermometer 8 or 10 degrees below zero, and then on reaching the point of distribution, after enduring such hardships for so long, they were told there was no more bread or no sugar. That state of affairs prevailed for several weeks when finally there was no more black bread even. The women became clamorous, the men refused to work in the factories and the inevitable consequence was a congregation of boisterous crowds on the streets demanding provisions, bread, and in some instances crying for peace. An assemblage of several thousand hungry people on a street near the Embassy was dispersed by the Cossacks, who did not, however, treat the people with cruelty or even harshly. The city is fortunately separated into sections by canals and by the River Neva, upon each side of which are large and compactly built areas. Communication between these sections is by bridges only. On these bridges Cossacks were stationed to prevent all suspicious-looking characters from crossing. It was suspected and charged that this scarcity of food was the result of design on the part of some of the members of the Government in order that internal dissensions might justify Russia in concluding a separate peace with the Central Empires. (Under the terms of Russia's agreement with her Allies she could only enter into a separate peace if obliged to do so by internal revolutionary disturbances.) The Cossacks who had always obeyed the Emperor's orders implicitly, regardless of consequences, were said to be advising the people, while dispersing them, to demand bread or the cessation of the war.

When in the face of these critical and dangerous conditions, the Emperor prorogued the Duma, instead of enlarging its powers as he had solemnly promised his apprehensive Ministry he would do, one can readily understand that the effect was like throwing a burning match into a powder magazine.

In the midst of this critical situation Baron Uchida, Japan's present Minister of Foreign Affairs, arrived in Petrograd as the new Japanese Ambassador.[15] Soon after his arrival he called upon me and I promptly returned his call.[16] I found that he felt particularly friendly toward the United States because he had served on the staff of the Japanese Embassy in Washington, while the Baroness was a graduate of Bryn Mawr College. Consequently our relations speedily became unusually close.

Only four days before the outbreak of the March revolution when the desultory street firing which preceded the outbreak had actually begun, I gave a dinner at the

---

[15] Baron Uchida Kosai (1865–1936), Japanese diplomat; served in China and Austro-Hungary; ambassador to the US, 1909–11; minister of foreign affairs, 1911–12; ambassador to Russia, 1917–18; minister of foreign affairs from September 30, 1918.

[16] The Japanese embassy was located on the Frantsuzskaya Embankment, 14.

Embassy for the Baron and Baroness Uchida, which was the last function of its kind to be attended by Ministers of the Russian Empire.

When bidding my guests good night, I expressed the hope that they would reach their homes safely. As they departed they made jesting references to the disturbances and were inclined to accept my solicitude about their safety as a conversational pleasantry.

Chapter V
THE MARCH REVOLUTIONS

The gathering storm of Revolution soon broke. The American Embassy was in the midst of the fighting. Many of the chief encounters could be seen from the Embassy. More could be heard.

In a dispatch to the Department, I gave the following description of the situation:

> As I have written you from time to time, there has been considerable unrest in Russia for the past several months. I cabled you about two weeks ago that I had asked for a military guard to be placed at the Austrian Embassy which contains the office of the Second Division of the American Embassy, and where 12 or 15 of the Embassy employees live. (We had taken over the Austrian Embassy building when we took over Austrian interests in Russia.) Although the Foreign Office promised to send the guard immediately, six days elapsed before any guard made its appearance and then only two soldiers were sent; that guard was increased to 18 about a week ago. The Austrian Embassy is on Sergiuskaia Street[1], which is the next parallel street to Fourstatdskaia Street on the West. The Embassy is, as you know, at No. 34 Fourstatdskaia and faces South; the block is perhaps 1,000 to 1,200 feet long; the street on the West is Liteiny, which is about 1,000 feet distant;[2] on the East is Voskresensky which is about 200 feet away.[3] There are tram cars on both streets, but no cars have been operating for two or three days. On Friday, March 9th, crowds visited a number of factories and ordered the men to stop work, which they promptly did. Yesterday, Sunday, there were soldiers in the streets and perhaps 50 people were killed or wounded, but most of the firing was with blank cartridges. Yesterday evening the order was given that no persons or vehicles should go on the streets to-day. About ten o'clock this morning a regiment of 1,000 to

---

[1] Sergievskaya Street.

[2] Liteiny Prospekt, the main avenue of the Liteinaya section of Petrograd connecting Liteiny Bridge with Nevsky Prospekt. It crosses Sergievskaya and Furshtatskaya streets, where two divisions of the US embassy were located. In February 1917, the prospect itself and the adjoining streets turned into an epicenter of revolutionary events.

[3] Voskresensky Prospekt.

1,200 men stationed in barracks about two blocks from the Embassy mutinied and, according to reports, killed their commanding officer because he would not join them.

At 11:30 a.m., Mr. Miles[4] phoned me from the Second Division in the Austrian Embassy that some of the mutineers accompanied by many revolutionists had visited the munition factory adjoining the Austrian Embassy; had killed the officer in command there, and had ordered the men to quit work; that many of the employees and one lieutenant had come into the Austrian Embassy, crawling through the back windows to seek protection from the angry crowd. Mr. Miles said that he was at the time endeavoring to prevent more employees from entering the Embassy and fearing that the crowd might learn that the Embassy was being used as a refuge he called me up and requested an additional guard. I telephoned to the Foreign Office and was assured that the guard would be strengthened if possible, but that it must be done by the War Department or General Staff, with which the Foreign Office would immediately communicate. That was the last communication I had with the Imperial Foreign Office.

This is written at 8 p.m. For four or five hours there have been crowds on the Liteiny which is the most frequented thoroughfare in this section of the city, and Secretary Bailey[5] who came to the Embassy from his apartment at about 3:30 p.m. reported that he had seen four dead and five wounded men lying on Liteiny. Within one hour thereafter many of the mutineers were seen walking on Fourstatdskaia in front of the Embassy, some with guns and some without. There also marched by the Embassy in the roadway a body of about one hundred men in citizens' clothes who carried muskets but observed no order of marching and appeared to have no commanding officer. During this

---

[4] Basil Miles (1877–1928), graduate of the University of Pennsylvania (AB) and Oxford University (BLitt). He served in St. Petersburg as private secretary to Ambassador George von Lengerke Meyer, 1905–06, and afterwards continued as third secretary of the embassy, August 24, 1906–May 21, 1907. He was in charge of the Washington office of the US Chamber of Commerce, 1908–16; appointed special assistant to the ambassador at Petrograd on August 25, 1916; headed the Second Division of the embassy. He was made special assistant to the ambassador with rank of minister plenipotentiary on January 4, 1917; appointed secretary of the Root Mission on May 14, 1917; ordered for duty in the Department of State in connection with Russian Affairs on October 16, 1917; turned out to be the founder and first acting chief of the Division of Russian Affairs.

[5] James G. Bailey (1868–?), studied law in Northern Indiana University of Law; was a member of Kentucky Legislature, 1895–97; served in the US Census Office, 1900–01. He entered the Foreign Service in 1901; served in Central America, Sweden, Mexico, Switzerland, the Netherlands and Luxembourg, and Portugal; was appointed first secretary of the embassy at Petrograd on December 6, 1916; and assigned for duty in the Russian section of the Division of the Near Eastern Affairs in the Department of State on June 24, 1918.

hour, from 4 to 5 p.m., there also passed in front of the Embassy a number of motor cars filled with soldiers with guns, but in every car there were some citizens or men in citizens' clothes who were no doubt revolutionists. About this hour the Embassy was informed by telephone that the Duma had been dissolved or prorogued until about the middle of April. I heard later that this order was issued yesterday afternoon but as there have been no newspapers for the past two days it was not known until the hour for the Duma's assemblage, and I suppose the members were ignorant of it until they went to the hall for the meeting.

At about 6 p.m., Captain McCully, the Naval Attache of the Embassy, who had left for his apartment[6] about 5, telephoned that in his walk from the Embassy to his apartment, a distance of over a mile, he had seen neither police nor soldiers who acknowledged fealty to the Government, but had passed a thousand or more cavalrymen riding quietly toward the Neva and abandoning the streets of the city to the mutineers and revolutionists. About 6:30 p.m. the telephone connection of the Embassy was severed. Between 7:30 and this writing, 9:30 p.m., many rumors have come to the Embassy through the Secretaries and other attaches. Mr. Basil Miles, Director of the Second Division, took the women employees from the Austrian Embassy to the Hotel de France,[7] where they are quartered for the night. The city seems entirely quiet but absolutely under the control of the soldiers who have mutinied, and of the revolutionists. It is reported that six regiments have joined the revolutionists and the Government seems to have abandoned all effort to curb the revolution. One rumor is to the effect that the Duma, after being dissolved, assembled notwithstanding the royal decree, and declared the Ministry deposed and made the President of the Duma, Rodzianko, the President of the Council of Ministers. The President of the Imperial Council, a Reactionary, is said to be under arrest. Another rumor is to the effect that Grand Duke Nicholas has been made Commander-in-Chief of all the Russian forces to supplant the Emperor. I cannot vouch for the truth of any of these rumors, but the Duma has certainly been prorogued until the middle of April, and the order to that effect is said to have been signed by the Emperor several days ago.

---

[6] McCully resided on Great Konyushennaya Street, 15.

[7] Hôtel de France, a residence of the Fox Mission in 1866 and one of the oldest and most fashionable Petrograd hotels. It was located near the Palace Square, on Morskaya Street, 6/ Moyka Embankment, 51.

I had a telephonic talk with Moscow today about noon and Consul-General Summers[8] reported that everything was quiet in that city; the treatment of the Duma, however, will arouse every section of the Empire. No one can foretell what to-morrow will bring forth. It is said that the Ministers of State have all left their respective houses for fear the revolutionists will arrest them. One theory is that the city has been abandoned and will be subjugated by being starved out.

Everything depends upon the Army. If the Grand Duke Nicholas, who is known to be very antagonistic to Pro-German influences, which are said to be dominating the Emperor through the Empress, should assume command of the Army it would be very likely to rally to his appeal. The Emperor, however, has many friends, and it is not likely that he will yield without a struggle.

The antagonism to the Minister of the Interior, Protopopoff, is bitter and quite general as he is charged with being the creature of Rasputin and is also suspected of German sympathy and of having assisted in bringing about the scarcity of food in order that the resulting unrest might justify Russia in making a separate peace.

During this same eventful day the Countess Nostitz,[9] who lives near the Embassy, called me up and told me that an army officer had just died in the lazaret on the first floor of her house, having been shot because he refused to give up his sword to the revolutionists. When I put up the receiver I ordered the "dvornicks"[10] and employees of the Embassy who were standing on the the sidewalk "rubbering," to come into the house and lock the gates.

At about midnight my secretary, Mr. Johnston,[11] and I started out for a walk to see what was "doing." When less than a block from the Embassy door we saw a group of men on an intersecting street and heard rifle shots. Concluding that a walk in that direction would be indiscreet we started back toward the Embassy. Just as we turned

---

[8] Maddin Summers (1877–1918), a former bank clerk in Nashville, TN. He entered the Consular Service in 1899; served in Spain, Bolivia, Serbia, Brazil, and in the Latin American division of the State Department (1916). On August 18, 1916, he was detailed to Moscow to take charge of the office during the absence of the consul general and assumed charge on November 1, 1916. He was appointed consul general on April 21, 1917, and died at the post on May 4, 1918. He married a Moscow lady, Natalia Goriainova, who was appointed clerk in the State Department on October 15, 1918.

[9] Countess Nostitz ("Countess from Iowa," 1875–1967), a former American actress; original name Lilie Bouton, stage name Madeleine Bouton. She married colonel (later general) of the Russian army Count Grigory I. Nostitz, her married name was Lidiya P. Nostitz. She patronized the American hospital located in their mansion on Sergievskaya Street, 26.

[10] *Dvornik* is a yard-keeper or janitor in Russian households.

[11] Earl M. Johnston (1890–?), a Missourian, Francis's private secretary from November 1916.

the corner we came upon about fifteen soldiers carrying guns, but not in formation and evidently under the influence of liquor. As we passed one of them held his gun in very uncomfortable proximity to my secretary's stomach. We heard no further disturbances during the night. The twelve or fifteen members of the staff who lived in the Austrian Embassy after two or three unsuccessful attempts to reach that building, which is only three blocks away, decided to spend the night with us.

The next morning there was still firing in the streets and many people were killed, a few accidentally. Many citizens, as well as the revolutionary soldiers, had arms. They paraded the streets and when they met an officer demanded his sword. If he refused to give it up they shot him. They showed a particularly unrelenting hatred of the police whom they shot on sight. The Commercial Attache's cook when two blocks from the Embassy saw a policeman's head severed from his body by a saber. The cook had hysterics for several hours afterwards. The police tried to disguise themselves in soldiers' uniforms and in citizens' clothes. Some of them placed minute guns on the roofs of houses and fired into the crowds as they marched by. They also fired into the crowds from windows of houses and even from hospitals in which they had hidden. When this happened soldiers and students would raid the houses and kill all the police they could catch. In some cases they would lead them out into the street and then shoot them.

I remained in the Embassy during the day. By 5:30 in the afternoon the shooting had become so incessant and so wild that for the first time I ordered the flag raised over the building. The Italian Embassy had raised three flags during the forenoon.[12] Just before the flag was raised two soldiers had called at the Embassy and asked if there was an automobile in the building. The "dvornick" who opened the door, replied that there was one but that it was a small one and not a very good one (referring to my "Ford" which I had bought with which to go to and from the golf course), and he added "This is the American Embassy."

At that the soldiers replied, "Why didn't you raise your flag?" and went away. During the day a crowd of soldiers and citizens visited the French Embassy[13] with a band which played the Marseillaise, and one of the attaches came out and made a non-committal speech.

During all of this time the Duma was in session, having refused to obey the Emperor's order to dissolve. They were striving to organize a Provisional Government. From time to time they issued orders and manifestoes signed by the President of the

---

[12] The Italian embassy owned the former Prince Liven mansion on Morskaya Street, 43.

[13] The French embassy rented the former Colonel Pashkov mansion on the Frantsuzskaya Embankment, 10.

Duma, as Chairman of the Provisional Government Commission.[14] The streets were filled with bands of soldiers who in many instances were led by students who as a class were very enthusiastic revolutionists.

During the night the firing was continuous, some of it by mitrailleuse. A barricade was made at the intersection of Liteiny and Serguiskaia, a corner of the block in which the American Embassy is located, and there were placed three cannon pointing toward the Nevsky Prospect—the most frequented avenue in Petrograd. On this day also Lieutenant-General Stackelberg was shot.[15] He was a veteran of the Russo-Turkish and the Russo-Japanese Wars and had served as Military Attache with various Russian Embassies. For several months he had been the Military Commander of all the Russian hospitals in Petrograd. I had made his acquaintance in connection with the exchange of a German and an Austrian officer. I had seen him several times, highly respected him and also liked him very much. A band of soldiers demanded admission to the General's apartment. When the porter refused to admit them they fired on him and killed him after he had killed two of them. The General then came to the door with his revolver, and after killing several more of the soldiers, tried to escape. He was killed, however, after eleven of his assailants had fallen. The remaining soldiers then mutilated his body, rode their horses over it; and, according to one report, severed his head from his body, put it on a spike and used it as a target.

On Wednesday, the 14th, the firing on the streets continued and desultory parties of from two to a dozen armed men wandered about without restraint of any kind. They were fired at from windows and from housetops as they passed, supposedly by policemen, and whenever this occurred the bands would fire back wildly. The Duma in the Tauride Palace[16] was the place to which soldiers and revolutionists both armed and unarmed reported and to which they took such prisoners as they did not kill. Irresponsible soldiers, and citizens who had taken arms from the police or the

---

[14] The Provisional Committee of the State Duma, officially called the "Committee of Members of the State Duma for establishing order in the capital and for dealings with persons and institutions"; also known as Executive Committee of the State Duma. Created under the chairmanship of Mikhail V. Rodzianko on February 27, 1917, as transitional governing board which, along with the Petrograd Soviet, set up the Provisional Government of Russia on March 2, 1917.

[15] Count Gustav E. Stackelberg (1853–1917), chief of military-medical establishments during the World War. He was killed on March 1, 1917, near his home on Millionnaya Street, 16, and beheaded by mutinous soldiers.

[16] The Taurida Palace was built in the 1780s for Catherine the Great's favorite, Grigory A. Potemkin, who had the title of prince of Taurida (antique name for Crimea). It was situated at Shpalernaya Street, 47, in the vicinity of the US embassy. The palace was a meeting place of the State Duma, 1906–17. After the February Revolution, it was a residence of the Provisional Committee of the State Duma and of the Provisional Government (till July), and the Petrograd Soviet (till August 1917), as well. The only session of the All-Russian Constituent Assembly also convened there on January 5, 1918.

armories, arrested, sometimes with and sometimes without orders, all the Ministers of the Imperial Government whom they could find except Pokrovsky, the Minister of Foreign Affairs, and Grigorovitch, the Minister of the Admiralty.[17] On arriving at the Duma the captives were turned over to tribunals which were often self-constituted and were locked up in rooms of the Palace. Ex-Premier Sturmer was among those captured and after being confined for some time in the Palace was taken across the Neva to the prison of St. Peter and Paul Fortress. The arch-offender, Minister of the Interior, Protopopoff, could not be found, but finally went voluntarily to the Duma and approaching a student said, "Are you a student?" On receiving an affirmative reply, he said, "I am Protopopoff and I have come to give myself up." He was taken before one of the tribunals and had he not been protected would have been killed on the spot. He too, was confined in the prison of St. Peter and Paul. Another hated character, Sokomlinoff, ex-Minister of War, was brought to the Duma and when the enraged soldiers were prevented from killing him they demanded that he be led down a hall some 300 feet long, so that they might have opportunity to tell him to his face their opinion of his treachery. He, too, was at length locked up in St. Peter and Paul Prison. Many army officers from Lieutenant Generals to Lieutenants were also seized and taken to the Duma. Among these was General (Count) Nostitz,[18] a wealthy nobleman whose wife is an American and who was in the entourage of the Emperor. Two other high Russian officers married to American women, Prince Belloselsky,[19] who married a Miss Whitman of New York, and Baron Ramsai,[20] whose wife was a Miss Whitehouse, obeyed the summons of the Duma and took the oath of fealty to the new Government. The number of such officers finally became so great they could not all get in the Tauride Palace, whereupon they were directed to go to the Officers Club

---

[17] Ivan K. Grigorovich (1853–1930), admiral; the last naval minister of the Russian Empire, November 19, 1911–February 28, 1917.

[18] Count Grigory I. Nostitz (1862–1926), major general, military attaché at Paris, 1908–12; chief of staff of the Guard Corps, 1912–15; major general of the Imperial Suite, served in the general staff from August 1915; discharged on September 11, 1917. He married former American actress Lilie Bouton (see n. 9, p. 56).

[19] Prince Sergei K. Belosselsky-Belozersky (1867–1951), lieutenant general, commanded the Caucasus Cavalry Division during the World War. In 1917, he was appointed to the staff of Lieutenant General Karl Mannerheim, who led the White forces in the Finnish Civil War of 1918. He married Susan Tucker Whittier (1874–1934), the eldest daughter of the Brevet Brigadier General Charles Albert Whittier of Boston.

[20] Baron Konstantin A. Ramsay (Constantin Johan Axel Edvard Ramsay, 1868–1939), former master of ceremonies at the Imperial Court. He married Frances Sheldon Whitehouse (1874–?), sister of the embassy secretary Sheldon Whitehouse, and later served as a liaison officer between the Russian War Ministry and the US Military Mission.

on the Liteiny,[21] about two blocks from the Embassy, and to register their allegiance. As I said in my report to the Department:

> During the day, March 14th, the Duma Commission headed by its President, Rodzianko, made considerable headway toward asserting its authority and restoring order. That commission was empowered by the Duma to name a Ministry, the composition of which was announced the following day. The members of that Ministry are men of education, of good records, some of them possessed of great wealth, and their selection does great credit to the judgment of the Commission by which they were chosen.
>
> About midnight, it became known that a body of armed men, the Gens d'Armes, who were supposed to be loyal to the Emperor, were to arrive at the Baltic station[22] to suppress the revolution. Revolutionary representatives were sent to the station to meet them and to persuade them to join the revolution; armed bodies were also sent to the station to resist the new-comers in the event they could not be persuaded or converted. Upon arrival, however, these supposedly loyal men also joined the revolution. It had been reported during the day that the garrison at Tsarskoe-Selo, the palace where lived the Empress, her four daughters and one son, had also gone over to the revolutionary party. The report proved to be true, as the Empress telephoned to Rodzianko and asked for protection. At about 12:30 at night I walked, accompanied by my secretary, Johnston, around two or three blocks adjoining the Embassy. We met a body of armed men, two or three hundred in number, marching quietly down Sergiuskaia, and apparently commanded by non-commissioned officers. Firing was kept up during the night, but was not so frequent as during the preceding nights. As we were returning to the Embassy we were stopped by two very alert soldiers and asked who we were. Our reply appeared unsatisfactory and they called the non-commissioned officer commanding them. Upon his approach, I advanced toward him and pointing to myself said in Russian: "Amerikanski Pasol"—"American Ambassador." Thereupon he saluted me, motioned Mr. Johnston and myself to proceed and directed the two soldiers to pass on. In the light of subsequent events I must admit that these midnight walks of Tuesday and Wednesday were more reckless than discreet.

---

[21] The Officers' Assembly of the Army and Navy was opened in 1898 and had its residence in the specially constructed building on the corner of Liteiny Prospekt and Kirochnaya Street.

[22] Baltic Station—one of five Petrograd railway stations, providing communication with Peterhof and Oranienbaum.

THE MARCH REVOLUTIONS

March 15th.

During this day comparative quiet prevailed. The abdication of the Emperor was authoritatively announced and his manifesto published in circular form and distributed on the streets—no newspapers had been published since the morning of Saturday, March 10th. Later in the day, Grand Duke Michael,[23] in whose favor the Emperor had abdicated, was summoned to the Duma and issued a manifesto accepting the authority transferred to him on condition that the people of Russia so desired, and pledged himself that if the people desired it he would exercise the functions of the office under the control and advice of the representatives selected by the people. Meantime several manifestoes or proclamations and some orders had been issued by a committee calling itself "Commission of Workingmen and Soldiers' Deputies";[24] these publications were violent in tone and tended to alarm all law-abiding citizens, as they advised the soldiers, of whom there were thousands walking the streets, that they were not compelled to salute their officers and that they could by a vote select their own commanders. This commission is still professing or attempting to exercise authority and is in almost continuous session in the Duma building—in fact, they were meeting in the Duma hall last evening when I went to the Duma building unofficially, accompanied by my secretary and colored valet, Philip Jordan. This visit was made incognito, but in order to gain admission to the building I was compelled to reveal my identity to the guard, and upon doing so was shown every courtesy. I was asked whom I wished to see and although there was disappointment when I said "no one" and it was learned that I was only a sightseer, there was always a soldier or student at hand who spoke English and very courteously conducted me through the building. This was my second visit to the Duma building. On my first visit, the large white hall, called Catherine Hall, was filled with two regiments who were enroute from Siberia to France, but who on arriving in Petrograd had joined the revolution. On the second visit we were conducted to a door of the Duma hall where we saw a large audience composed of soldiers and agitators or workingmen's delegates listening to a speaker in the Tribune who wore a soldier's uniform.

---

[23] Grand Duke Mikhail Alexandrovich (1878–1918), the younger brother of Nicholas II.

[24] The Petrograd Soviet of Workers' and Soldiers' Deputies. It was created on February 27, 1917, as the Petrograd Soviet of Workers' Deputies, with Soldiers' Deputies joining it on March 1. The Petrograd Soviet was functioning as a rival governing body alongside the Provisional Government, which created the situation of the so-called "dual power" in the Russian capital. At first, the Soviet was in conference in the Taurida Palace, but on August 4 transferred to the Smolny Institute. Its first chairman was the Menshevik Nikolai S. Chkheidze, who was replaced on September 9, 1917, by the Bolshevik Lev D. Trotsky.

March 16th.

On this day there were still a few parties of armed men walking the streets and an occasional shot was heard but the new Ministry had assumed authority and issued a proclamation appealing to the reason and patriotism of the people and calling upon them to observe order and support the Provisional Government which had succeeded the detested Administration of the Imperial power exercised by Protopopoff and his hated police. On this day the new Ministers assumed charge of their respective Departments and made some progress toward administering the affairs of the Government, a new Prefect of Police had been appointed and was endeavoring to suppress the irresponsible soldiers and armed civilians who had been walking the streets for five days without restraint. Reports came to Petrograd from Moscow, Kieff and other cities to the effect that the authority of the Provisional Government was being accepted and its representatives installed without bloodshed or opposition of any kind. On the afternoon of this day the newspapers were again issued. The commanders of two of the Russian fronts under whom were hundreds of thousands of soldiers publicly announced their allegiance to the new government and it began to appear as if the revolution was successful in every respect. Reports of the unfortunate and unprovoked killing of some of the naval commanders even after they had acknowledged allegiance to the new government produced depression but the Imperial Government and its friends had been so completely over-awed that they made no attempt to resist the new order. In fact, all who were opposed to anarchy had about arrived at the conclusion that the only way to avoid such a reign was to yield willing allegiance to the new Ministry if not to support it aggressively.

March 17th.

On this day the abdication of the Emperor for himself and son was officially promulgated. The authority of the new Ministers who had taken charge of their respective Departments was generally recognized. The soldiers and students and the unreasonable revolutionists seemed to be exhausted and willing to rest and take stock of the surrounding conditions. By this time all thought of the Imperial Party attempting any opposition to the new Ministry was abandoned. The program of the Duma began to be discussed. The plan was a most comprehensive one and eminently wise. The Duma, a committee of which had named the Ministry, had practically abdicated and all governmental authority was vested in a Council of Ministers, the personality of whose members seemed to meet with universal satisfaction, and in fact commendation. Meetings of the "Commission of Workingmen's and Soldiers"

Deputies" were continued in the Duma. Soldiers in uniform and armed were marching in the streets and although they had few commissioned officers they were keeping step, observing discipline and making efforts to enforce order. The revolutionists were divided in judgment or preference as to whether the Provisional Government should be succeeded by a republic or a constitutional monarchy. There was no difference of feeling, however, concerning the wisdom of respecting the authority of the Provisional Government. That was the condition at the end of six memorable days during which the extent and the marvelous success and the comparatively bloodless consummation of a widespread revolution had surprised and stunned even its projectors and most ardent champions.

The day before I had said in a letter to Madden Summers, Consul-General at Moscow:

Whitehouse and Riggs have just brought into the Embassy a report which seems authentic to the effect that the Czar has abdicated for himself and for the Czarevitch in favor of his brother Michael. And just before W. and R. met the man with whom they were talking and from whom they got this information, Schidloffsky, one of the Duma Committee of Twelve,[25] a telegram had been received from Grand Duke Michael also abdicating. These men reported that there was great excitement in the Duma and that Schidloffsky told them there was only one thing determined and that was that no Romanoff should succeed to the throne. The workingmen's party have been joined by some soldiers, I don't know how many, and they have a committee called "Committee of Workingmen's Party and Soldiers' Deputies"; this committee has issued a number of proclamations—I think several daily—and these pronunciamentos have been filled with rot. That organization demands a republic.

The Ministry selected seems to be composed of good men whose selection reflects credit on the judgment of the authorities by whom they were chosen. I am much pleased to hear that the President of the Ministry, Lvoff,[26] is a first cousin of your mother-in-law and that other members of the Ministry

---

[25] Sergei I. Shidlovsky (1861–1922), deputy of the Third and Fourth State Dumas, 1907–17; leader of the Octobrist faction of the Duma; chairman of the Bureau of the Progressive Block from September 4, 1915. After the February Revolution, a member of the Provisional Committee of the State Duma ("Duma Committee of Twelve").

[26] Prince Georgy E. Lvov (1861–1925), graduate of Moscow University, lawyer, Constitutional Democrat. Chairman of the All-Russian Zemstvo Union from 1914; chairman of the United Committee of the Union of Zemstvos and Union of Towns from 1915. The first minister president of the Provisional Government and minister of internal affairs, March 2–July 7, 1917. He visited the US in the fall of 1918 as representative of the Siberian government.

are connected with your family and that you know many of them personally. I have been of the opinion that it would be unwise to attempt to establish a republican form of government in Russia just now, but if such men as these are put at the helm, it is possible they may be able to steer through the breakers that beset its course. The Duma party favors a vigorous prosecution of the war, but the utterances of the Workingmen and Soldiers Deputies Committee declare in favor of concerted action on the part of the proletariat of the belligerent countries in putting an end to a war which they say is waged in the interest of capital at the expense of labor and the laboring classes.

There is a rumor this afternoon that Emperor William has been deposed and there have been rumors extant for several days to the effect that there is a revolution in Germany. One report is that there was a bread riot in Berlin, and that the people went to the Imperial Palace en masse and demanded bread of the Emperor, who replied by turning the hose on them, and that thereupon the mob demolished the palace. There are so many rumors, however, that one does not know which to credit if any.

I have since realized that these rumors of a German revolution and all similar rumors were deliberately circulated by the radical leaders in order to make their plan for a world revolution appear feasible.

In a dispatch to the Department, of March 15th, in commenting on the revolution, I said:

This is undoubtedly a revolution, but it is the best managed revolution that has ever taken place, for its magnitude. The Duma is assuming control and is exercising its authority in Petrograd with rare good judgment. Its President, Rodzianko, is head of the provisional government and is called "Chairman of the Commission." Bulletins are issued, although no newspapers are published, giving official information concerning events. This one that came to the Embassy this morning gives the names of a new Cabinet of Ministers—in some cases two or more are appointed instead of one as heretofore. The Emperor was stopped on his way to Tsarskoe-Selo—from the front—and there are rumors about his being forcibly detained; in fact, one of the Assistant Ministers of Foreign Affairs, Polotsoff,[27] made this statement to Mr. Miles yesterday afternoon.

Upon the whole Russia is to be congratulated in my judgment on the prospect of getting through an important change in government with so little bloodshed and without material interference with the war she is waging with

---

[27] Alexander A. Polovtsev (1867–1944), assistant minister of foreign affairs, October 1916–March 14, 1917.

powerful antagonists. One cause of this revolution is a suspicion on the part of the army and of the people who call themselves true Russians, that the Empress and those surrounding her have been planning a separate peace with the enemy and that the Emperor has yielded too often and too completely to her influence.

In a circular letter addressed to my colleagues in the American diplomatic service, I commented thus upon the outcome of the revolution:

At this writing, Saturday, March 24th, orderly quiet prevails and every day it continues strengthens the present government. The Government is the Ministry which is in absolute control and its authority is loyally recognized by the army and navy and by every municipality and province in Russia so far as known. The duty and prerogative of this Ministry is to call a constituent assembly, or a convention as we would designate it, the members of which are to be chosen by universal suffrage, including women. That assembly will be empowered to determine the kind of a government Russia will have, whether a republic or a constitutional monarchy. In the wise plan worked out by the Duma, through the Committee appointed to select the Ministry, care was taken that the Imperial succession should not lapse, and thus a claim of any member of the royal family to the throne by virtue of blood succession was barred. That was done by having the Emperor abdicate for himself and the Czarevitch in favor of his brother, Michael, and then Michael was "persuaded" to accept the transferred crown on condition that the people of Russia so desired, and when and if so accepted to exercise its functions under the advice or control of a law making body elected by, and representative of, the people.

In a dispatch to the Secretary of State sent the next day, March 25th, I touched upon the vulnerable spot in the new Government—the point at which entered the poison which eventually destroyed the entire governmental organism. I said:

As to present conditions, the situation is very remarkable. While the authority of the Ministry is recognized throughout Russia the Ministers very candidly tell me that of the troops in Petrograd, numbering from 100,000 to 150,000, a majority are on the side of the workingmen and are influenced more (if not absolutely) by the Committee of Workingmen's Party and Soldiers' Deputies than by the Ministry itself. The policemen, who were so bitterly hated by the people, and who were pursued so mercilessly during the three days of rioting, are all in confinement and are to be sent to the front. The patrol of the city is still under an officer called the "Grande Archalnick,"[28] who was selected by the Ministry with the approval of the Workingmen's and Soldiers' Deputies. The patrol is composed of soldiers who walk the streets in companies of two or four, and by what is called the "city militia"—a body composed mostly of students, armed with guns and patrolling generally in groups of the same size. It speaks highly for the spirit of this revolution that notwithstanding the want of respect for authority, order is so well preserved—there are very few disturbances. On the first day of the revolution the prison doors were opened and the inmates liberated. The incentive to this action was the desire of the populace and the revolutionary soldiers to liberate the political prisoners, but they failed to make distinction when they opened the prison doors, with the result that hundreds of hardened criminals were released to prey upon the public. Some of these criminals dressed in soldiers' uniforms went to private residences and demanded admittance to search for firearms and while in the houses committed thefts. The present police authority is attempting to arrest these fugitive criminals, and very few of them are still at large—many of them, in fact, are reported to have returned voluntarily to their prisons.

An assistant to the Prefect of Police called at the Embassy Monday or Tuesday and said he desired to send a guard of seven soldiers to protect the Embassy. I had seen no occasion for a guard, but thinking it unwise to refuse and fearing the Prefect knew more of the danger of the Embassy than I did, I consented. Seven soldiers with guns and fixed bayonets appeared the following day. One was stationed at the front door, the other at the gateway, and quarters were provided for the remaining five; these soldiers were given by the Embassy two roubles (Rs.2.00) per day each for their subsistence. Yesterday, March 24th, the Embassy was notified that there was no longer occasion for a guard and the soldiers left about 5 o'clock in the afternoon.

It is marvelous that there doesn't seem to be as much scarcity of food as there was before the revolution began, notwithstanding that the transportation lines have been crippled and fewer trains have been operated. Indeed the cause of the outbreaks was that the people believed that food was not half as scarce as the dealers or the Government supply station professed.

During the first two or three days of the revolution, March 12th-14th, the bread lines disappeared and I have neither seen nor heard of any during the past four days. Sugar which could not be obtained for three roubles (90c) per pound, I understand, is now on sale at eighty kopeks (24c) per pound, and it is the same with butter.

---

[28] To say correctly, "Grande Nachalnik" ("Great Commander"). Actually the commander in chief of troops of the Petrograd military district. From March 2 to April 29, 1917, the post was occupied by Lieutenant General Lavr G. Kornilov; from May 22 to July 14 by Major General Peter A. Polovtsev (1874–1964), a brother of the above mentioned diplomat.

THE MARCH REVOLUTIONS

An eye-witness has described the abdication of the Czar and the events immediately preceding it in an account written for a Russian newspaper.

It seems that on the night of March 14th, 1916,[29] the Emperor's train, preceded by a train under command of Major-General Tsabel, Commandant of the Railway Regiment,[30] was on the way from Staff Headquarters to Tsarskoe-Selo whither Nicholas had been summoned by the Empress. With the Emperor on the Imperial train were the feeble old Count Fredericks,[31] the celebrated Admiral Niloff,[32] former Commander of the Marines of the Guard and the Commandant of the Palace, Voeikoff.[33] The Emperor's companions were drinking heavily and Admiral Niloff kept urging the Emperor to drink.

At this time the Emperor had not been informed of the situation in Petrograd and Voeikoff and Niloff were afraid lest he should learn the truth. At one o'clock General Tsabel became excited and told Voeikoff he must tell the Emperor, otherwise he, Tsabel, would tell him himself. Voeikoff agreed but told the Czar a much modified story. Later, the Emperor called Niloff and asked him what was going on in Petrograd. Niloff answered that though there were great disorders, a telegram had just come stating that 700 knights of St. George[34] were then on their way to Petrograd and that these brave soldiers could quickly put down all revolt.

At this point General Tsabel entered the train and said:

"All this is a lie! Your Majesty, they are deceiving you. Here is the telegram. See, it reads, 'Petrograd, Commandant of the Nicholas Railway Station, Lieutenant Grekoff.[35]... Hold at Station Vishera Train No. A, and when you dispatch it send it to Petrograd and not to Tsarskoe-Selo.'"

---

[29] 1917.

[30] Sergei A. Tsabel (1871–?), military engineer, major general, commanded His Majesty's Railway Regiment, 1914–17. After the October Revolution, he joined the Red Army.

[31] Count Vladimir B. Frederiks (1838–1927), general of cavalry, minister of the Imperial Court and Household, 1897–1917.

[32] Konstantin D. Nilov (1856–1919), admiral, general adjutant of the Imperial Suite, flag captain of Emperor Nicholas II, 1905–17.

[33] Vladimir N. Voeikov (1868–1947), major general of the Imperial Suite, commandant of the Winter Palace, 1913–17.

[34] Cavaliers of the Georgian Cross, which was the highest military decoration for lower ranks of the army for "undaunted courage" and distinction in combat. They divided into four classes; those awarded with the crosses of all classes bore the honorary title "Full Georgian Cavalier." During the World War, about 1.2 million soldiers and officers were awarded with the Georgian Cross of the fourth class and about 33,000 of the first class. The Union of Georgian Cavaliers was established in 1916.

[35] First Lieutenant Konstantin F. Grekov, Socialist Revolutionary, commandant of the Nikolayevsky Railway Station, February 28–March 5, 1917. Later commandant of the

The Emperor jumped up.

"What's this? Revolt! Lieutenant Grekoff commands Petrograd?"

Tsabel replied:

"Your Majesty, in Petrograd there are 60,000 soldiers with their officers at their head that have already gone over to the side of the temporary Government. Your Majesty has been declared dethroned. Rodzianko has proclaimed to the whole of Russia that a new order has come to hand. You cannot go ahead; Deputy Bublikoff is running all the railroads."[36]

In extreme surprise, perplexity and anger the Emperor cried:

"Why have you not told me anything about this sooner? Why are you telling me only now, after all is over?"

But after a minute with calm despondency he said:

"Well, thank God! I'll go to Livadia.[37] If the people want me to, I'll abdicate and retire to Livadia to my garden. I love flowers."

At the station of Dno, they came up with the train of General Ivanoff,[38] who reported to the Emperor all that had happened in the capitals and said:

"The revolutionists have got the power in their hands. The only salvation now is to go to the army."

One of those present belonging to the Emperor's suite affirms that at this moment General Voeikoff cried:

"Only one thing remains to be done now. Open the Minsk front to the Germans and let the German armies come in and put down this rabble!"

Drunk as he was, Admiral Niloff grew indignant and said:

"That would hardly do any good, for they would take Russia and they would not give it up again to us."

Taurida Palace and Smolny Institute. The Nikolayevsky Station, the main railway station of Petrograd, was situated on Znamenskaya Square. Now the Moscow Station.

[36] Alexander A. Bublikov (1875–1941), engineer of ways of communication, deputy of the Fourth State Duma, vice chairman of the Central War Industrial Committee. During the February Revolution, he was appointed commissar of the Provisional Committee of the State Duma to the Ministry of Ways of Communication. He gained control over the Russian railway and telegraphic network, playing a crucial part in the success of the revolution, and also took part in the arrest of the imperial family. Left Petrograd for Paris in September 1917, later went to the US, and died in New York City.

[37] Imperial residence in Crimea.

[38] Nikolai I. Ivanov (1851–1919), general of artillery; commander in chief of the Southwestern Front during the World War; was replaced by General Brusilov and appointed to the Imperial Suite in March 1916. He was appointed commander of the Petrograd military district on February 27, 1917, with the order to suppress the revolution but, having no reliable forces, failed to do so. After the October Revolution, he joined the White Army in south Russia.

Voeikoff kept on urging his plan, however, assuring the Emperor that, according to what Princess Vassilchikoff[39] had reported, Emperor William was making war not on Emperor Nicholas but on Russia with its antidynastic tendencies.

To this the Emperor replied:

"Yes, Gregory Ephimovich (Rasputin) often talked to me along this line, but we would not listen to him. This could have been done when the German armies were in front of Warsaw, but I never would have betrayed the Russian people."

So saying, the Emperor wept.

Then, after a moment's silence, he added:

"If only my wife and children have been saved, I shall go to Livadia and pass the rest of my life there in peace and quiet. Let Michael rule the best he can. By the way, he is liked."

The Emperor had left Tsarskoe-Selo for Moghileff[40] early Friday morning, March 9th, after being persuaded by the Empress and Protopopoff to destroy the decrees which he had promised the Ministry to issue to the Duma, extending the powers of the Duma, and promising a new Constitution to Russia. These decrees had been drawn up by the Council of Ministers and sent by Protopopoff to the Palace at Tsarskoe-Selo for the Emperor's signature. When the Empress saw them she was very indignant, and, seconded by Protopopoff succeeded in convincing the Emperor that he was making a mistake in adopting such a liberal policy. Nicholas II. in his weakness yielded to the arguments of his wife, ably and aggressively seconded by the Minister of the Interior, who assured the Emperor that he could suppress any uprising of the people. It was a fatal moment for the Czar when he yielded to this appeal of the Czarina. If he had been firm and had complied with his promise to the Council of Ministers the Revolution could at least have been deferred. Before a week had elapsed the Emperor had abdicated the throne which he had inherited from his ancestors and the Romanoff Dynasty was no more. If he had signed the liberal decrees prepared for him and which he had pledged himself to sign, the result would have been far different. Russia would have probably continued in the war until its successful ending and hundreds of thousands of lives of the youths of the Allies would have been spared.

Rodzianko had telegraphed the Emperor once Monday the 12th and twice on Tuesday, but the telegrams had not been delivered to the Emperor until Tuesday evening, when the Russian officer had threatened to communicate their contents to the Emperor himself if General Voeikoff, Commandant of the Palace, did not deliver them to His Majesty.

---

[39] Maria A. Vasilchikova (1859–1934), maid of honor at the Imperial Court. After the beginning of the World War, she was interned in Austria, and released in the fall of 1915 on condition of delivering German peace proposals to the Russian imperial family. Instead, she lost her court title and was exiled from Petrograd.

[40] Mogilev, the Belorussian town where the Stavka (Headquarters of the Commander in Chief of the Russian Army and Navy) was located.

The Emperor at once decided to go to Petrograd, but his advisers persuaded him to go to Tsarskoe-Selo first and call a meeting of his Ministers. The special train was hastily prepared, and the Emperor started from Moghileff for Tsarskoe-Selo. During the night the train was stopped and upon Voeikoff being informed that the road was blocked he changed the route and the train proceeded. The next morning the Imperial Party arrived at Pskoff where it was held by the Superintendent of the Station to await the arrival of the two deputies of the Provisional Government, as related in the article quoted above. These two deputies were Goutchkoff[41] and Shulgin[42] who had been sent by the Provisional Government to demand the abdication of the Emperor. He received them courteously and upon being informed of their business calmly said he was ready to abdicate in favor of Grand Duke Michael not only for himself but for his son also. Retiring into his private room he came out a few minutes later with a typewritten document which he submitted to Goutchkoff and Shulgin, and upon their approving, promptly signed his abdication. It was witnessed by Count Fredericks, the Mareschal of the Imperial Court, who had served the Crown loyally for nearly forty years. This occurred late Wednesday evening, March 14th, and the Emperor in a private wire conversation with the Empress the next morning did not tell her of his abdication. The first knowledge she had of it was on the afternoon of Thursday, on the arrival of an officer with a guard, who informed her that she was under arrest. When she asked where the Emperor was, he told her that he had abdicated. She retorted, "It is a lie, I talked to him this morning and he did not tell me of it." What must have been her feelings when she was convinced of the truth of the abdication! Did she realize she was responsible for it? Both the Emperor and the Empress have long since paid the penalty of their follies. Upon abdicating the Emperor asked of the delegates of the Provisional Government what disposition they proposed to make of him, and they replied that he could return to Headquarters if he so desired. He did return to Moghileff, and remained there four days, during which time he was visited by the Empress Dowager, who endeavored to comfort him, but from all accounts she was more perturbed than he was. The Emperor did not seem to realize what had happened. At the end of four days when he was ordered to Tsarskoe-Selo Palace he went quietly and calmly while his mother, the Empress Dowager, in bidding him good-by was overcome with emotion.

---

[41] Alexander I. Guchkov (1862–1936), founder and leader of the Union of October 17; chairman of the Duma Committee on Imperial Defense; chairman of the Third State Duma, 1910–11; head of the Central Military-Industrial Committee, 1915–17; minister of war and navy in the first Provisional Government, March 2–May 5, 1917.

[42] Vasily V. Shulgin (1878–1976), one of the leaders of the Russian national movement; deputy of the Second, Third, and Fourth State Dumas, 1907–17; leader of the Progressive group of nationalists; member of the Provisional Committee of the State Duma in February 1917. He returned to his native city Kiev in July 1917; led the campaign against violent Ukrainization; later took active part in the White movement in south Russia.

Upon his arrival at Tsarskoe-Selo he was received by the Empress, whose spirit had not been broken. Her children were seriously ill with the measles and had absorbed her attention. A few days later Kerensky, the Minister of Justice of the Provisional Government,[43] visited the Emperor and had an hour's conference with him. Toward the end of the conversation, the Empress is said to have entered the room and upon the Emperor presenting Kerensky to her, the latter kissed her hand and drawing up a chair invited her to be seated. Straightening her queenly figure, she remarked, "I do not need to be offered a chair in my own palace." This to the man to whom she was probably indebted for her life and the Emperor's. Kerensky had during the first days of the Revolution exerted his potential influence with the violent workmen and soldiers to prevent them from committing excesses. Too much credit cannot be given Kerensky for his conduct during the first week of the Revolution.

The Emperor and Empress were permitted to have private conversation during the first two days after the Emperor's arrival, but they were separated during the remainder of their stay at Tsarskoe-Selo, only being permitted to see each other at meals when there was always a representative of the Provisional Government in attendance. When someone in authority was asked why the Emperor and Empress were not permitted to enjoy each other's society, the reply was, "He is too weak and she is too strong."

Upon the occasion of Kerensky's visit to Tsarskoe an incident occurred relating to the Czarevitch. The story is told that when Kerensky emerged from the conference he was approached by the Czarevitch, who, after making known his own identity, asked Kerensky if he was the Minister of Justice of the Provisional Government.

"Yes," said Kerensky, "I am."

"I want to know," said the Czarevitch, "if my father had any right to abdicate for me when he abdicated for himself."

Kerensky's reply is not recorded. Another instance of children asking questions which learned and wise men were unable to answer.

---

[43] Alexander F. Kerensky (1881–1970), graduate of St. Petersburg University; lawyer; one of the most outspoken members of the State Duma in late Imperial Russia; member of the Labor group (Trudovik). After the February Revolution, a member of the Provisional Committee of the State Duma and assistant chairman of the Petrograd Soviet; joined the Party of Socialists-Revolutionaries. Minister of justice, March 2–May 5; minister of war and navy, May 5–September 25; minister president of the Provisional Government, July 8–October 26, 1917.

Chapter VI
AMERICAN RECOGNITION OF THE PROVISIONAL GOVERNMENT

In the absence of instructions from the Department of State I did not feel authorized to have any official communication with the Provisional Government. Realizing, however, that the Embassy was confronted by conditions with which the Department was unacquainted, I determined to take advantage of personal acquaintanceship in order to advise myself authoritatively for the purpose of communicating with the Department and giving my opinion if not making an outright request for authority to act. By telephone I made an engagement with Michael Rodzianko, President of the Duma, whom I knew personally and who was the man who had officially promulgated the decrees of that body which, by refusing to obey the decree of the Emperor ordering its adjournment, had commanded the attention and in fact the admiration and respect of all opponents of autocratic government. He received me cordially at his residence[1] and in a conversation of about half an hour I learned from an authoritative source the plans of the leaders of this remarkable uprising which had met with such universal approval among all classes of Russia's immense population. I told Mr. Rodzianko that I was making an unofficial call upon him in order to learn the truth concerning the state of affairs so that I could cable the same to my government and could base thereon my judgment as to future developments.

Rodzianko had been President of the Fourth Duma since its organization and had made a satisfactory presiding officer; impartial in his rulings and prompt in his decisions. He was a large man, over six feet in height and very heavy, weighing almost three hundred pounds. I had met him several times—in fact he had dined with me previous to the Revolution. He was an eloquent speaker and had a great voice that could reach thousands of auditors in the open air, and it was a familiar saying among Russians that Rodzianko's voice "on a still day could be heard a verst"—which is about two-thirds of a mile. He was a constitutional monarchist by conviction and a large landowner, but very liberal in his views; I don't think he acknowledged allegiance to any party. He spoke English fairly well and was very affable and approachable. He received me in his study or library and when I stated the object of my call seemed very much interested. At the time of my call the Revolution had been in progress six days

---

[1] Rodzianko rented apartment 9 on Furshtatskaya Street, 20, in the vicinity of the US embassy.

and during all that time he had been in the Duma building, and my recollection is that he told me the preceding night was the only night he had stayed at home since the Sunday night before. He was not as clear in his statements concerning the plans of the Provisional Government as was Miliukoff and before I suggested calling on Miliukoff as I had intended, he advised me to do so and made the engagement for me. The President of the Duma while much respected for his character and oratorical ability was not considered the strongest man in that body. At the time of my call he was on the top wave of his popularity; he was President of the Commission of Twelve appointed by the Duma to select a Ministry for the Provisional Government, and his speaking qualities had made him quite prominent during the previous six days in addressing soldiers who left their barracks and marched to the Duma in bodies of a thousand or more, and in addressing the crowds that assembled in the building and adjacent grounds. I never learned whether it was the President that made the suggestion to the Duma to adjourn sine die but always thought that adjournment was a mistake. The Commission of Twelve, of which Rodzianko was made Chairman, was vested with full power to select a new Ministry and as an extra precaution was instructed by the Duma to cease functioning when the Ministers had been named. This was also a mistake in my judgment. The Duma was the most representative body in Russia at the time of the Revolution and if it had not been dissolved by its own vote could have remained in session notwithstanding the decree of the Emperor ordering its dissolution. Furthermore, it could have directed the Commission of Twelve to report to it and would have thereby strengthened the Provisional Government. However, the Workmen's Party under the leadership of Chidzi[2] was exercising authority in the Duma building, and increased its power by giving to the soldiers representation in their organization after which it was named Workmen's and Soldiers' Deputies; later by adding representation for the Peasants it came to be known as the "Workmen's, Soldiers' and Peasants' Deputies." The members of the Duma no doubt reasoned that if they continued in session it would provoke a contest with the Workmen, Soldiers and Peasants; furthermore the Clergy and Monarchists constituted a potential faction in the membership of the Duma. A stronger man in the President's chair might have perpetuated the Duma and made of it a potential factor in the situation, but Rodzianko was not equal to that undertaking.

Rodzianko remained in Petrograd most of the time during the eight months' existence of the Provisional Government but after the Bolsheviks came into power he lived in retirement if not in hiding. There was a rumor in Petrograd a few days after

---

[2] Nikolai S. Chkheidze (1864–1926), leader of the Social Democrats-Mensheviks, deputy of the Third and Fourth State Dumas. After the February Revolution, he was a member of the Provisional Committee of the State Duma; chairman of the Executive Committee of the Petrograd Soviet, February 27–September 6, 1917; chairman of the First All-Russian Congress of Soviets of Workers' and Soldiers' Deputies; chairman of the All-Russian Central Executive Committee of Soviets, June–October 27, 1917.

the Bolsheviks came into power that they were looking for ten or twelve men and Rodzianko's name headed the list. The day after this report was circulated I received a note from him introducing its bearer as his friend and a man to whom I could talk freely. The bearer of this note told me that Rodzianko and he had been friends from their youth. When I asked him where Rodzianko was at that time he replied that he was in his apartment a short distance from the Embassy. He said that Rodzianko was in hiding and when I asked if I could see him replied, "Of course, if you will come to my apartment." I went and had a talk with him. He said his life was in danger and asked if he could take refuge in the American Embassy. I replied that it would be unsafe for him to come there but my secretary, Earl Johnston, was living in an apartment with a special investigator of the Department of Commerce[3] and that both young men could be trusted and, as they were occupying a commodious apartment, would be glad to furnish him a refuge. This proved satisfactory to Rodzianko and he expressed the intention of availing himself of the hospitality of the young men provided it would be agreeable to them. After consulting them I advised Rodzianko that the young men would be glad to receive him and care for him as long as he desired to stay with them, but he did not avail himself of the considerate offer and I heard nothing more from him for several days. I afterwards learned that after remaining at his friend's house for five or six days unmolested he went to Novo Russisk[4] and joined Kaledin[5]—so I was informed by his friend whom I asked, "How was Rodzianko disguised?" He replied, "As a woman," and when I expressed doubt about the possibility of successfully disguising the huge figure of Rodzianko as a woman he replied he had had a telegram reporting that Rodzianko had arrived safely at Novo Russisk. When I asked him how the telegram got through he said it was prearranged that the signature should be in an assumed name and the telegram should state only "She arrived safe."

From the satisfactory interview which I had with Rodzianko, I returned to the Embassy where I had invited to luncheon Baron and Baroness Nolde.[6] Baron Nolde had been connected with the Foreign Office for many years as its judiciary adviser, having retained that place through many changes in the Ministry. He, however,

---

[3] Probably Edward B. Thomas (1891–?), commercial agent of the Department of Commerce, attached to the office of the Commercial Attaché in Russia. On May 8, 1918, he was appointed vice consul at Moscow.

[4] Novocherkassk, the capital city of All-Great Don Host. Now a city in Rostov Oblast.

[5] Aleksei M. Kaledin (1861–1918), general of cavalry, ataman of All-Great Don Host from June 18, 1917, and head of the Don Host government. Refused to recognize the Provisional Government; headed the first abortive anti-Bolshevik mutiny. Resigned on January 29, 1918, and committed suicide.

[6] Baron Boris E. Nolde (1876–1948), graduate of St. Petersburg University, lawyer, professor of international law, Constitutional Democrat. Division director in the Ministry of Foreign Affairs, 1914–17; assistant minister of foreign affairs, March–May 1917. Married Alexandra A. Iskritskaia.

could give me little information as he had remained in the Foreign Office during the entire week, devoting himself to his official duties. Meantime, after learning from Rodzianko that Miliukoff possessed the confidence of himself and his colleagues as Foreign Minister, I had made by telephone an appointment to make an unofficial call upon that Minister with whom the heads of all the foreign missions had the closest relations. I learned from Dr. Miliukoff, with whom I had no difficulty in getting telephonic communication, that he could not receive me at his residence before 11:30 p.m. but that if I would come to the Foreign Office he would be pleased to grant me an interview. I went to the Foreign Office promptly, was cordially received by the new Minister and learned from him the plans of the Provisional Government as I had from Rodzianko, but Miliukoff stated them more clearly.

I had met Dr. Miliukoff soon after my arrival in Petrograd, having sat beside him at a function given to me by the Russo-American Society,[7] of which Baron Rosen, formerly Ambassador to the United States, was President.[8] Miliukoff was emphatic in his assurance that the Provisional Government was firmly established and would administer affairs until the meeting of the Constituent Assembly[9] which, would determine the form of Government for all the Russias. He was so well equipped to be Minister of Foreign Affairs that no other man had been spoken of for the place. Miliukoff had lectured in America and was well known in the United States as an eminent scholar and patriotic Russian. He was supposed to be the owner of the Ryetch[10] (in English "Voice"), a Petrograd daily newspaper whose columns were ably edited. Dr. Miliukoff had visited several of the universities of this country and was personally acquainted with many American scholars. He was looked upon in Russia, as in all other countries, as a statesman who had the courage of his convictions and

---

[7] The Society for Promoting Mutual Friendly Relations between Russia and America was created in Petrograd in 1915. Its membership included such prominent Russian figures as Mikhail V. Bernadsky, Nikolai V. Chaikovsky, Pavel N. Milyukov, Andrei I. Shingarev, as well as American businessmen and diplomats Henry D. Baker, M. McAllister Smith, David B. Macgowan, and Herbert H. D. Peirce. The society had its headquarters at Nevsky Prospekt, 59. A luncheon in honor of Ambassador Francis was given by the society's council on June 28, 1916, at the fashionable restaurant Dodon.

[8] Baron Roman R. Rosen (1847–1921), Russian diplomat who served as consul general in New York City from 1884, and chargé d'affaires in Washington, 1886–90 (with intervals). Ambassador to the US, 1905–11; was the second Russian representative at the Portsmouth peace negotiations, which ended the Russo-Japanese War of 1904–05. Chairman of the Society for Promoting Mutual Friendly Relations between Russia and America, 1915–18. Emigrated to the US in 1919, died in New York City as a result of a street accident.

[9] The All-Russian Constituent Assembly convened on January 5, 1918, but was dissolved the next day by the Soviet government, despite the protest of non-Bolshevik parties.

[10] *Rech'* (Speech), daily political paper, organ of the Constitutional Democratic Party. Published in Petrograd from February 1906 to October 1917.

withal possessed of a high degree of culture. He was a thorough linguist, speaking English, French, German and Polish fluently. His attack on Sturmer in the Duma in the preceding November had attracted attention throughout Russia. He had aroused the revolutionary spirit of the country and unquestionably had been a potential factor in bringing about the first Revolution. He had been for a long time the leader of the Cadet Party[11] which was the popular designation for constitutional Democrat; he had lead that party with a firm hand and had been fearless in his denunciations of the oppressions of the Monarchy. He had long been in disfavor with the monarchial or reactionary party when the Revolution began. He appeared to be about fifty-three years of age, and his manner and speech, although decided, was courteous. He had a smooth face with the exception of a slight mustache and was about five feet eleven inches in height, muscular and active with no surplus flesh. He was never at a loss for words with which to express his thoughts, and was a facile writer and logical thinker. He impressed me when I called upon him that Sunday, March 18th, as a man who realized his responsibility and would not shirk it.

As I looked at him and heard his prompt replies to my questions, the thought passed through my mind that here was the real leader of the Revolution; here was a deep thinker and a genuine Russian patriot. His philippic on Sturmer had shown his high sense of honor when he appealed to the Duma and to the country to uphold at any cost the pledges of Russia to her Allies. I left him more convinced than ever that the rule of the Romanoffs was ended and that those entrusted with the administration of the new Government were right-thinking, sincere and determined Russians who would prosecute the war fearlessly regardless of its cost in blood and treasure and would advocate the form of government which they thought would best serve the interest of their country.

Miliukoff took a leading part in the Council of Ministers; he was outspoken in his defense of what he believed to be the right policies regardless of consequences. He had no patience with the pronunciamentos of the Workmen's and Soldiers' Deputies. He had precipitated the Revolution by charging Sturmer and Protopopoff and the Court with negotiating for a separate peace with Germany and thereby breaking faith with Russia's Allies, and he foresaw that the predominance of the principles championed by the Workmen's and Soldiers' Deputies would lead inevitably to a separate peace with the Central Empires. He was a bitter opponent of socialism and had often locked horns with Kerensky in the Duma. Kerensky was at this time Minister of Justice and performed an essential part, and performed it well in preventing excesses by the radical revolutionists. Kerensky probably had more influence during the first days of

---

[11] The Constitutional Democratic Party (Kadets), which was created during the Russian Revolution of 1905 and adopted the additional name "People's Freedom Party" the next year. Liberal historian Pavel N. Milyukov was the party leader throughout its existence. After the February Revolution, Kadets dominated the Provisional Government from March to May 1917. The party was suppressed by the Soviet government on November 28, 1917.

the Revolution than any other Minister of the Provisional Government and possibly more than any other Russian. Therefore when Miliukoff differed with Kerensky concerning the retention of Constantinople by Russia in the event the Central Empires should be defeated in the World War and when these two distinguished Russians clashed concerning the provisions of the secret treaties between Russia and her Allies, Miliukoff was not only in the minority in the Council of Ministers, but decidedly in the minority with the Russian people. Notwithstanding this situation, and Miliukoff understood it better than anyone, he stood by his guns.

According to the plans, as explained to me by both Rodzianko and Miliukoff, the supreme authority of the Government was vested in a Ministry under the Presidency of Prince Lvoff, who is perhaps the most highly respected citizen of Russia, who had been President of the Union of Zemstvos[12] which Protopopoff several months before had prohibited from continuing their meetings notwithstanding the very efficient and excellent service they had performed in furnishing supplies to the army and to the large cities of Russia. It was the duty of this Council of Ministers, in addition to administering the affairs of the government in these troublous times and during the progress of a terrible war, to arrange for a meeting of a Constituent Assembly at as early a date as practicable; the prerogative and duty of such assembly would be to adopt a form of government for Russia; that form when adopted would be binding upon the whole people because the membership of the Assembly was to be chosen by direct vote of the people at an election held on a date to be fixed by the Ministry and at which every citizen and soldier of Russia would be permitted to vote. The success of this wise and comprehensive plan depended upon many contingencies but, however problematical the outcome might be, the best if not the only promise of organized government, the maintenance of order and the protection of life and property lay in the administration of a Ministry composed of patriotic men who had character and ability and who were inspired by high motives. Such a government merited the support of all good citizens and was entitled to the recognition of all foreign governments that favor law and order and especially of that government represented in Russia by me.

After these conferences I was so thoroughly imbued with the conviction that it was wise for the Government of the United States to recognize the Provisional Government, that upon returning to the Embassy I retired to my private apartment with my secretary, denied myself to all callers and prepared the following cable to the Secretary of State:

The six days between last Sunday and this have witnessed the most amazing revolution in history. A nation of two hundred million people who have lived

---

[12] The zemstvo (from Russian *zemlia*–soil) was a form of limited local self-government instituted in the course of the Great Reforms of the 1860s. The All-Russian Union of Zemstvos was set up in 1914.

under absolute monarchy for more than a thousand years and who are now engaged in the greatest war ever waged have forced their Emperor to abdicate for himself and his heir and have induced his brother, to whom he transferred the Imperial authority, to accept it on condition that a Constituent Assembly of the people so request and when so accepted to exercise its functions under authority of the Government framed by that Assembly. This is official information obtained by my personal unofficial calls to-day on Rodzianko at his residence and Miliukoff, Minister of Foreign Affairs, at his office. There is no opposition to the Provisional Government, which is a Council of Ministers, appointed by a Committee of Twelve named by the Duma. Quiet prevails here and throughout Russia so far as known. Rodzianko and Miliukoff both assure me that the entire army accepts the authority of the Provisional Government and all appearances and advices confirm the same. The plan of the Provisional Government is to call a Constituent Assembly or convention whose members will be elected by the whole people and empowered to organize a government. Whether that will be a republic or a constitutional monarchy is not decided but the conclusions of the Assembly will be accepted universally and enforced by the army and navy. There has been no concerted action in the Diplomatic Corps; no meetings have been held or called. It has been customary for British, French and Italian Ambassadors to call daily together at the Foreign Office and they called upon Miliukoff Friday, yesterday and to-day but have not formally recognized the Provisional Government. Miliukoff: tells me confidentially that Buchanan, the British Ambassador, has authority from his government for recognition but is waiting until the Italian and French Ambassadors are likewise authorized. I request respectfully that you promptly give me authority to recognize the Provisional Government, as the first recognition is desirable from every viewpoint. This revolution is the practical realization of that principle of government which we have championed and advocated—I mean government by consent of the governed. Our recognition will have a stupendous moral effect especially if given first. Rodzianko and Miliukoff both assure me that the Provisional Government will vigorously prosecute the war. Furthermore, upon Russia's success against the Central Empires absolutely depends the salvation of the revolution and the perpetuity of the government it establishes. The third of the eight principles in the manifesto issued announcing the new Ministry and signed by the President of the Duma and all of the Ministers is "abolition of all class, religious, and national limitations." Answer.

On March 19th, one week after the Revolution began, and the day after I sent my cable to the Department, I called on Goutchkoff, the Minister of War. When I handed my card to the officer in charge of the outer room I was told that the Minister was in conference with delegates from the Workmen's and Soldiers' Deputies, but the officer sent in my card. Goutchkoff came out promptly and after receiving me courteously conducted me to a private room. I saw that he was in a nervous state and, knowing that he had excused himself from a delegation to see me, lost no time in stating the object of my visit. I asked him if recognition by my Government would strengthen the Provisional Government of Russia. He replied with alacrity that it would and asked if it could be done on the following day. I told him "No," that I had only sent the cable the preceding evening and could not expect a reply before the 22nd or 23rd. With much agitation he expressed doubt as to whether the Provisional Government could survive until that time. I asked him how many soldiers he had in Petrograd. He replied about one hundred and twenty-five thousand, but expressed the fear that the Government could not rely upon more than twenty-five thousand of these soldiers being loyal to it, while the remainder would side with the Workmen's and Soldiers' Deputies. I expressed regret at my inability to recognize the Provisional Government without authority from my Government. Goutchkoff was about fifty-five years of age. He is of medium height with keen gray eyes and close cropped iron gray whiskers. His eye and the set of his jaw gives evidence of decided courage. He is a member of a distinguished Russian family, an elder brother having been a popular and efficient Mayor of Moscow[13] who was at the time of our interview a leading manufacturer of that city who had married a Miss Tertiakoff, the daughter of the man who gave to Moscow the celebrated gallery bearing his name.[14] I had visited Moscow in January, 1917, and had been shown through the Tertiakoff Gallery by this brother. Goutchkoff was the leader of the Octobrist Party[15] and was the man who, in company with Shulgin, had visited the Emperor at Pskoff as the representative of the Provisional Government to demand his abdication. He had joined the Boer Army

---

[13] Nikolai I. Guchkov (1860–1935), Moscow city head, 1905–12; chairman of the Russian-American Chamber of Commerce, established in Moscow in 1913. He married Vera P. Botkina (1862–1916), whose two nephews married Tretyakov's daughters.

[14] Pavel M. Tretyakov (1832–98), a Russian textiles manufacturer, patron of art, and philanthropist who donated his own and his brother's art collections to the city of Moscow. The "Moscow City Art Gallery of Pavel and Sergei Tretyakov" was opened on August 15, 1893. The gallery was equal in importance to the largest museums of Russia and turned out to be the foremost depository of Russian fine art in the world. On June 3, 1918, it was nationalized by the Soviet government and renamed the State Tretyakov Gallery.

[15] The Union of October 17 was created in 1906 and named after the Imperial Manifesto of October 17, 1905, which established something resembling constitutional order in Russia. The party's main object was transforming the Russian Empire into a constitutional monarchy. It was banned by the Soviet government after the October Revolution, which made the very name of the party meaningless.

in the South African War in 1899,[16] where he had made a brilliant record. When I called upon him I was not aware that the celebrated General Order No. 1 to the Army had been issued.[17] This was the order that contributed more than anything else toward the demoralization of the superb Russian army because it demoted all the officers to the ranks and permitted the army organizations down to the smallest units to elect their commanding officers. The Workmen's and Soldiers' Deputies had sent this order out without the knowledge of the Minister of War and when he learned of it he found himself powerless to countermand it. This caused him great distress as he had been trained as a soldier and believed in strict discipline.

On March 22nd, four days after the dispatch, I received a sweepingly favorable reply to my cable. That was a record time both for the cable service and for the State Department. I subsequently learned that on its receipt it had at once been submitted by the Secretary to the President and by him had been brought up at a Cabinet Meeting.

I immediately called up the Foreign Office, secured an appointment and an hour later told Foreign Minister Miliukoff the contents of the cable he had had sent for me and of the favorable reply. I said that as Ambassador I formally recognized the Provisional Government, but that I desired to be presented to the President, Prince Lvoff, and to present to him my eight Secretaries and Attaches and my Military and Naval Attaches in full uniform as I thought it important to make the recognition as formal as possible. He not only agreed but suggested that I make the formal recognition not merely to President Lvoff, but to the entire Council of Ministers. I told him that would be very gratifying to me, and he at once arranged for me to meet the Ministry at the Marensky Palace[18] at 4:30 that afternoon.

At that hour I accordingly appeared before the Ministry, having driven up the Nevsky Prospect with my coachman in full livery on the box and the chasseur also in full livery standing behind me. I was accompanied by the Counselor, the

---

[16] The Anglo-Boer War (1899–1902) between Great Britain and the union of two tiny Boer states, the Orange and South-African (Transvaal) republics, in which a number of foreign volunteers, including Russians, fought against British troops.

[17] The first Order of the Petrograd Soviet, issued on March 1, 1917. It was addressed to the Petrograd garrison, which played a crucial part in the February Revolution. The Soviet directed soldiers and sailors not to obey their officers if their orders would contradict its own decrees. The order decreed elections of soldiers' and sailors' committees in each military unit to run their affairs instead of officers, and placed all weapons under their control. Order No. 1 paved the way for the "democratization" of the Russian army, which resulted in a crash of military discipline and the army's disintegration.

[18] The Mariinsky Palace was built in 1839–44 in St. Isaac's Square, 6, for Nicholas I's daughter Grand Princess Maria Nikolaevna. It was rebuilt in 1906–07 as a residence for the State Council of the Russian Empire. After the February Revolution, it was used by the Provisional Government.

four Secretaries, the Military and Naval Attaches in full uniform, the Commercial Attaché and two Attaches on special mission.[19] Upon being presented to Prince Lvoff I made the formal recognition in these words:

> Mr. President of the Council of Ministers:
> I have the honor as American Ambassador, and as representative of the Government of the United States accredited to Russia, to hereby make formal recognition of the Provisional Government of all the Russias and to state that it gives me pleasure officially and personally to continue intercourse with Russia through the medium of the new Government. May the cordial relations existing between the two countries continue to obtain and may they prove mutually satisfactory and beneficial.

After a brief speech of appreciation by Foreign Minister Miliukoff, the short but impressive ceremony concluded. Two days later, with like ceremony, the British, French and Italian Embassies made formal recognition of the new Government to the Council of Ministers.

Important as I felt this recognition of the Provisional Government by the United States to be I did not at the time fully realize its significance. It should be borne in mind that at the time of this recognition our country was still neutral as we did not enter the war until fifteen days later. This recognition undoubtedly had a powerful influence in placing America in a position to enter the war backed by a practically unanimous public opinion. There can be no doubt that there would have been serious opposition to our allying ourselves with an absolute monarchy to make war no matter in what cause. President Wilson recognized this by his eloquent reference to Russia in his soul-stirring address to the Congress made April 2nd.[20]

Moreover this recognition of the Provisional Government, followed as it was within forty-eight hours by like action on the part of the British, French and Italian Governments, undoubtedly gave strong moral encouragement to the new Government, which, as the above account of my interview with Goutchkoff, Minister of War, shows, was in a situation of extreme peril. It was menaced on the one side by forces desiring the restoration of the Monarchy and on the other by the threat of the Workmen's and Soldiers' Deputies to take the administration of affairs into their own

---

[19] Counselor J. Butler Wright; first secretaries James G. Bailey and Sheldon Whitehouse; third secretaries Norman Armour and Livingston Phelps; military attaché First Lieutenant E. Francis Riggs; naval attaché Captain Newton A. McCully and his assistant Lieutenant Colonel James C. Breckinridge; commercial attaché William C. Huntington; special assistants to the ambassador Basil Miles and William F. Sands.

[20] President's message to the extraordinary session of Congress, delivered on April 2, 1917. Four days later, Congress passed the War Resolution, which brought the US into the World War.

hands. If either of these hostile elements had succeeded an armistice with the Central Empires would have followed immediately and consequently Germany would have sent her hundred-odd divisions from the Eastern to the Western front almost a year sooner than they were sent and at a time when the Allied Armies were particularly ill prepared to resist them.

Chapter VII
THE COUNCIL OF WORKMEN AND SOLDIERS' DEPUTIES

My recognition of the Provisional Government described in the preceding chapter had taken place just eleven days before President Wilson delivered his memorable message to the Joint Session of Congress recommending that a state of war be declared to exist with Germany.

I addressed the following letter to Miliukoff on April 5th:

Excellency:

I am just in receipt by cable of the following noble sentiment eloquently expressed by President Wilson in his address to Congress delivered the evening of April 2nd to the two houses in joint session.

A steadfast concert for peace can never be maintained except by a partnership of democratic nations. No autocratic government could be trusted to keep faith within it or observe its covenants. It must be a league of honor, a partnership of opinion. Intrigue could eat its vitals away. The plottings of inner circles who could plan what they would and render account to no one would be a corruption seated at its very heart. Only free peoples can hold their purpose and their honor steady to a common end and prefer the interests of mankind to any narrow interest of their own. Does not every American feel that assurance has been added to our hope for the future peace of the world by the wonderful and heartening things that have been happening within the last few weeks in Russia? Russia was known by those who knew her best to have been always in fact democratic at heart, in all the vital habits of her thought, in all the intimate relationships of her people that spoke their natural instinct, their habitual attitude towards life. The autocracy that crowned the summit of her political structure long as it had stood and terrible as was the reality of its power, was not in fact Russian in origin, character or purpose, and now it has been shaken off and the great generous Russian people have been added in all their native majesty and might to the forces that are fighting for freedom in the world, for justice and for peace. Here is a fit partner for a league of honor.

I thought this would be of interest to you and hasten to communicate it. In my judgment it is not only thrilling and impressive but should be an inspiration to the Russian people and prompt them to a patriotic support of the Government which you and your Colleagues are so ably and faithfully administering.

With assurances of personal and official esteem, I am,
Yours sincerely,
David R. Francis

This same day I also forwarded to the Minister to use as he saw fit this wise message to the workingmen of Russia from Samuel Gompers:[1]

Washington, April 2, 1917. N. S. Tschedzi,[2] Petrograd, Representative of working people of Russia. Accept this message to the men of labor of Russia. We send greeting. The established liberty of Russia finds a warm response in the hearts of America's workers. We rejoice at the intelligence, courage and conviction of a people who even while concentrating every effort upon defense against foreign aggression have reorganized their own institutions upon principles of freedom and democracy, but it is impossible to achieve the ideal state immediately.

When the right foundation has been established the masses can daily utilize the opportunities for progress, more complete justice and greater liberty. Freedom is achieved in meeting the problems of life and work. It cannot be established by a revolution only. It is the product of evolution. Even in the Republic of the United States of America, the highest ideals of freedom are incomplete, but we have the will and the opportunity. In the name of America's workers, whose watchwords are Justice, Freedom and Humanity, we plead that Russia's workers and masses shall maintain what you have already achieved, and practically and rationally solve the problem of to-day and safeguard the future from the reactionary forces who would gladly take advantage of your lack of unity to reestablish the old regime of royalty, reaction, tyranny and injustice. Our best wishes are with Russia in her new opportunity.

Samuel Gompers,
President American Federation of Labor

In a dispatch to the Secretary of April 17, 1917, I made the following observations on some of the initial experiences of the new Government in its efforts to consolidate its power:

---

[1] Samuel Gompers (1850–1924), founder and first president of the American Federation of Labor, 1886–1924.

[2] Chkheidze (see n. 2, p. 73).

For a week or ten days after our recognition of the Provisional Government the tension continued very great, as the Council of Ministers or Provisional Government was trying to establish itself but was so fearful of the consequences of a test of strength with the Workingmen and Soldiers' Deputies that it proceeded very cautiously. The soldiers were permitted to parade with banners and bands throughout the city and the workingmen if returning to work at all were making unreasonable demands as to wages and hours and in some or many instances were selecting their own foremen. There has been, however, no contest between these two authorities up to this time and I think there is likely to be none.

The Provisional Government or Council of Ministers has been gaining strength from day to day; they have made two visits in a body to the front and at this writing the entire situation is much better than it has been at any day since March 12th, when the first regiment mutinied.

Representatives of the Workingmen's Party and of the Soldiers' continue in session daily at the Duma or Tauride Palace, and I think meet in the Duma Hall. On Friday last, April 13th, this body passed by an overwhelming majority a resolution favoring a vigorous prosecution of the war to a successful issue and either the same day or the day after adopted another resolution endorsing the Provisional Government.

The general impression is that Rodzianko is in favor of a Constitutional Monarchy and that Miliukoff is also so inclined, but that Minister of Justice Kerensky, who is a Social Revolutionist,[3] and who has conducted himself most admirably, favors a republic.

It has been my effort, and in such effort there has been no cessation, to impress upon all the importance of a vigorous prosecution of the war and to subordinate thereto all questions as to the rights of races or the recognition of classes.

The Jews have undoubtedly been subjected to many injustices and unjust restrictions in Russia, and all fair-minded people are pleased that most if not all of such restrictions have been removed. The prejudice against the race, however, has by no means been eradicated; it pervades the peasants to a won-

---

[3] A member of the Party of Socialists-Revolutionaries (SRs), which was a major political force in the early twentieth century and a key actor in the Russian Revolution of 1917. Founded in 1902, it was largely a peasant party; it stood primarily for distribution of land property and made use of political terror as a weapon of struggle. Kerensky was a member of the labor group in the State Duma and joined the SRs after the February Revolution. Until the autumn of 1917, the SRs were the most influential party for many Soviets and won the majority in the November election for the All-Russian Constituent Assembly. In the summer of 1917, a faction of Left SRs emerged inside the party—which created an independent party on December 2, 1917, and shared power with the Bolsheviks until July 1918—while the mainstream SRs strongly opposed the Bolsheviks from the very beginning and fought them in the Civil War.

derful extent and that prejudice will be fanned into flame by opponents of the present regime if any reason therefor is given or can be charged with any appearance of truth.

In reply to your cable concerning a separate peace, received the 14th, I cabled the result of a conference with Miliukoff. While I was talking with him in the Foreign Office, delegations of British and French Socialists[4] were awaiting an audience and subsequently he phoned me that they had come to Russia for the purpose of advising Russian Socialists to push the war vigorously and to give no thought of a separate peace as the Socialists of Germany and Austria-Hungary were more devoted to their respective countries than they were to socialistic doctrines, or at least were pursuing the policy of achieving a victory for the Central Empires first.

The people of Petrograd learned of America's entrance into the war before I received official notification thereof.

The President's address delivered on April 2nd, 1917, to the Joint Session of Congress not only aroused great enthusiasm in America but electrified all of Europe. There had been no doubt in my mind about America's coming into the war since President Wilson had severed diplomatic relations with Germany and given Bernstorff his passports.

Our declaration of a state of war existing with the German Empire, coming as it did ten or fifteen days after the Russian Revolution, and our recognition of the Provisional Government of Russia was not only hailed with delight in Russia but was vastly strengthening to the Provisional Government, and served to dissipate all fear of the restoration of the monarchy.

There were many assemblages of people throughout the country and wherever they were held there were demonstrations of great joy. There were some" doubting Thomases," as there were in our own country, as to the extent of the part we would perform, and some of these pointed to Japan's course after she had declared war against the Central Empires, but the great bulk of the Russian people were aroused to a high state of enthusiasm; if they had thought that America would perform so important a part in the war as to bring the Central Empires to their knees within eighteen months Russia would no doubt have remained in the war to the end.

I was frequently called upon to make speeches, and being well acquainted with the American spirit, predicted on every occasion that America having finally entered the conflict would prosecute it to a successful finish. Our people not only surprised

---

[4] Both delegations of pro-war socialists arrived in Petrograd on March 31, 1917. The British delegation included such prominent labor leaders as members of Parliament James O'Grady (1866–1934) and Will Thorne (1857–1946). The French delegation consisted of socialist deputies of the National Assembly Marcel Cachin (1869–1958), Ernest Lafont (1879–1946), and Marius Moutet (1876–1968).

and astonished the people of Europe by the rapidity and magnitude of their operations but even surprised themselves.

On Sunday evening, April 22nd, while I was entertaining some guests at the Embassy my colored valet, Philip Jordan, came to me and said that the police official in charge of the district had called up to warn me that an anarchist mob was gathering with the intention of attacking the Embassy. Their object was to avenge themselves upon the American Ambassador for a death sentence which had been passed upon one "Muni" in San Francisco.[5] I had never heard of "Muni," and did not know what it was all about. I instructed Jordan to reply to the police officer that I thanked him for his warning, but considered that it was his duty rather than mine to protect the Embassy. I then told him to load my revolver and bring it to me. In a few minutes the police official who had telephoned arrived at the Embassy with a squad of police. Revolver in hand I went to meet the police officer, and told him to station his men at the Embassy gate, with instructions to shoot anyone who tried to enter the building without my permission. I stated I would take my stand inside prepared to shoot anyone who attempted to cross the threshold.

The mob never reached the Embassy although they started for it. Reports also differed as to how they were dispersed and why they did not carry out their intention. One explanation was that while they were gathering on the Nevsky in front of the Kazan Cathedral, some Cossacks happened by and, attracted by the crowd as Russians always are, joined in and inquired what was on foot. When told that the crowd was going to attack the American Embassy because a socialist was to be hung in America, the Cossacks replied, "Not if we know it," or words to that effect, and began attacking the mob which scattered in all directions.

I later learned with amusement that some of my friends had circulated a very much more sensational version of this episode. According to this version, the angry mob did reach the Embassy where I met them with a threat to shoot the first man who crossed the threshold and thus violated American territory, and that thereupon the mob slunk away. When in Paris on my way home I found this was the version of the story which had been circulated in the Peace Conference circles. I tried to correct it, but with little success. Everyone seemed to prefer the more sensational story, so I suppose I shall have to resign myself to this heroic role. It, at any rate, truthfully represents my intentions. All I lacked was the opportunity to carry them out.

Two days afterwards the Spanish and Japanese Ambassadors and the Chinese Minister came to express their solicitude and regrets at the threatened indignity to the Embassy and myself. The same day the Minister of Justice, Alexander Kerensky, called and expressed the sympathy of the Government and their indignation at the threat to which I had been subjected.

---

[5] Thomas J. Mooney (1882–1942), an American labor leader and socialist activist who was wrongly convicted of the San Francisco Preparedness Day bombing of July 22, 1916, and spent twenty-two years in prison before finally being pardoned.

Alexander Kerensky performed noble, patriotic and effective service in this critical stage in the life of the Provisional Government.

I met Kerensky at the time I formally recognized the Provisional Government. He was a young man, thirty-four years of age, with a smooth-shaven face, not over five feet ten inches in height, and of extremely nervous temperament. He had been the leader of the Socialist Revolutionists in the Duma, where he had shown eloquence of a high order; his speeches always commanded attention, because they were logical and delivered in a good voice, and they were always characterized by a vehement opposition to the Czar's government. Consequently the Workingmen's and Soldiers' Deputies had more confidence in Kerensky than in any other member of the Provisional Government.

Numerous instances of his influence with the Workingmen's and Soldiers' Deputies and with the populace were told me.

Baron Rosen, who had been Russian Ambassador at Washington, one day came to the American Embassy fresh from one of these scenes. He told me that he had seen a mob on the point of killing an officer, when Kerensky rescued the doomed man, and speaking to the angry crowd said he was the Minister of Justice and as long as he held that office no man should be deprived of life except after conviction in a fair trial.

The Ministry of the Provisional Government frequently called upon Kerensky to exert his influence at this time, and had it not been for his efforts and the recognition by America of the Provisional Government, it would have been deposed and the revolution which took place the following November, eight months later, would have occurred in March, 1917.

Kerensky, whom I came to know well, and with whom I had close relations during the regime of the Provisional Government, did such valiant work that we should not be harsh in our condemnation of his subsequent mistakes. When Goutchkoff resigned as Minister of War, Kerensky succeeded him. Kerensky was responsible for the decree abolishing the death penalty in the army, and although he issued a later decree, at the instance[6] of Korniloff,[7] reinstating the death penalty, his heart was too soft to command an army.

I well remember being present when Kerensky was addressing a large audience in the Miransky Theater.[8] He was interrupted three times by a man in the gallery,

---

[6] Probably insistence.

[7] Lavr G. Kornilov (1870–1918), lieutenant general, commander in chief of the troops of the Petrograd military district, March 2–April 29, 1917. Promoted to general of infantry on June 27, 1917; commander in chief of the Russian army, July 19–August 29, 1917. He led the patriotic movement to save Russia from revolutionary chaos, which culminated in the so-called Kornilov Affair, August 25–31, 1917. After the October Revolution, he took part in the formation of the Volunteer Army in south Russia and headed it until his death on April 13, 1918.

[8] The Mariinsky Theater was built in 1859–60 at Theater Square, 1, and named in honor of Alexander II's wife Empress Maria Alexandrovna. Now the Theater of Opera and Ballet.

to whom he paid no attention at the first two interruptions. The audience was spellbound, but the man in the gallery insisted on interrupting the speaker the third time, calling out, "What about restoring the death penalty?" Then Kerensky, pointing in the direction whence the voice came, remarked, "Wait until I order a man put to death," thereby demonstrating that his feelings were still with the decree abolishing the death penalty.

After he became War Minister he made several visits to the Eastern front, and at one time took command of the army and ordered an advance which was successful. But he never countermanded Order No. 1, which demoted all officers to the ranks and permitted the soldiers to elect their own officers, and made provision for the officers so elected to be removed by the soldiers when they saw fit.

I was lunching with Kerensky in Terestchenko's[9] apartment one day when Nekrassoff,[10] Bakhmatieff,[11] Ambassador of the Provisional Government at Washington, and others were present.

Terestchenko's apartment faced the Quay, along which a procession was passing. As we watched the parade I asked Kerensky if Lenin and Trotzky[12] were not both

---

[9] Mikhail I. Tereshchenko (1886–1959), graduate of Leipzig and Moscow Universities, lawyer, major landowner, banker, and sugar magnate. Assistant chairman of the Central Military-Industrial Committee, 1915–17; minister of finance, March 2–May 5, 1917; minister of foreign affairs, May 5–October 26, 1917.

[10] Nikolai V. Nekrasov (1879–1940), Constitutional Democrat, deputy of the Third and Fourth State Dumas, assistant chairman of the Duma from November 6, 1916. Member of the Provisional Committee of the State Duma in February 1917; minister of ways of communication in the Provisional Government from March 2; assistant minister president from July 8 and minister of finance in the first Kerensky cabinet from July 24; governor-general of Finland from September 4, 1917.

[11] Boris A. Bakhmetiev (1880–1951), graduate of the Institute of Engineers of Ways of Communication; spent one year in the US studying American methods of hydraulic construction, 1904–05; Doctor of Engineering, 1911; professor of the St. Petersburg Polytechnic Institute. From October 1915 to November 1916, he was a representative of the Central Military-Industrial Committee at the Russian Purchasing Commission in America. Assistant minister of trade and industry in the first Provisional Government, March–April 1917; headed the Russian extraordinary mission sent to the US in June 1917 (Bakhmetev Mission); Russian ambassador in Washington, July 5, 1917–June 30, 1922.

[12] Lev D. Trotsky (Bronstein, 1879–1940), one of the main organizers of the October Revolution and Soviet state along with Vladimir I. Lenin. A non-factional Social Democrat after the split of the RSDWP in 1903; chairman of the St. Petersburg Soviet of Workers' Deputies in the fall of 1905. He emigrated abroad after the Russian Revolution of 1905; went to the US in December 1916; returned to Russia in May 1917; joined the Bolsheviks; was elected chairman of the Petrograd Soviet on September 25, 1917. People's commissar for foreign affairs in the first Soviet government, October 1917–March 1918; headed the Soviet delegation at the Brest-Litovsk peace negotiations from December 22, 1917 to February 10, 1918. People's commissar for military and naval affairs from March 13, 1918.

Jews. Trotzky I knew was, and I had heard that Lenin's mother was of Jewish descent. Kerensky promptly replied that he went to school with Lenin, and that Lenin was of pure Russian blood. He said his first recollection of political life was of being in Lenin's father's house at the age of six when the house was searched for Lenin's elder brother,[13] who had made an attempt upon the life of Alexander III.[14] The brother was afterwards arrested and shot.

This reminds me of a report which was current in Petrograd at the time Kerensky escaped. It was said that Kerensky could have apprehended Lenin when the attempted revolution of July 16th and 17th, 1917,[15] occurred. Trotzky was arrested at the time and imprisoned, although later released. Lenin was never arrested by the Provisional Government although he was continually trying to undermine it. During the Bolshevik Revolution of November, 1917,[16] all the other Ministers were arrested and imprisoned in Saint Peter and Paul Fortress, but Kerensky escaped. It was rumored that Lenin and Trotzky permitted Kerensky to escape in return for his having permitted Lenin to escape in the previous July.

The next day after the threatened attack of April 22nd, on the Embassy, a delegation of one hundred or more school children called and through one of their number made a little speech condemning the threatened action of the mob. I had learned meantime that the "Muni" for whose death sentence the mob proposed to make me vicariously responsible was Mooney, the labor leader, who had been convicted of responsibility for the bomb outrage in California. I explained to all my Russian visitors that while I was not familiar with the details of this particular case that in America persons were condemned to death for two causes only—murder and treason. That free speech and free press were permitted. That if any person so used

---

[13] Alexander I. Ulyanov (1866–87), member of the terrorist group Narodnaya Volya (People's Will); took part in a failed plot to assassinate Alexander III and was executed.

[14] Alexander III (1845–94), emperor of Russia from 1881, father of Nicholas II.

[15] The July Crisis or July Munity, a crucial turning point in the Russian Revolution of 1917. It was provoked by the failure of Russia's June Offensive and by ministerial crisis, which resulted from the Kadet ministers' withdrawal from the Provisional Government in protest against recognition of Ukrainian autonomy. During the "July Days" of 1917 (July 3–5), mass demonstrations of armed revolutionary soldiers, sailors, and workers under strong anarchist influence and with limited Bolshevik participation marched through Petrograd with the slogan "All Power to the Soviets." Order was restored by government troops called from the front line. The failure of the mutiny meant the end of the so-called "dual power" shared by the Provisional Government with the Soviets and resulted in a temporary decline of Bolshevik influence. The political outcome of the crisis was the resignation of the Prince Lvov's cabinet and the formation of a new Provisional Government under the chairmanship of Alexander F. Kerensky.

[16] Another name for the October Revolution, which occurred on October 25–26 (November 7–8), 1917.

these privileges as to menace the safety of other individuals, of the Government, or of society he was bound over under bond to keep the peace if an American citizen, and if an alien he was deported to the country whence he came. On May 1st, I said in a letter to my son Perry:

> Today is labor day throughout Europe and is a very strict holiday. The guests in the hotels were told yesterday that no meals would be served today. The streets were and are now practically deserted but the crowds have congregated at several places listening to speeches, some of which are sensible and some otherwise. Many allowances, however, must be made for people who have been living under an absolute monarchy all of their lives and who have never been permitted the liberty of free speech, which everyone has in our country.
>
> This government is still doing a great deal of constructive work but it has not yet asserted its authority with any force. There are daily meetings of the Committee representing the Workingmen's and Soldiers' Deputies and the membership of that Committee, I am told, is over two thousand. An ultra-Socialist named Lenin has been doing a great deal of foolish talking and has advised his hearers to kill all people who have property and refuse to divide. We are living somewhat in suspense. Lenin's followers are an unknown quantity. We occasionally hear rumors of violence being planned. One up-rising was said to be fixed for today, but at this hour, 5 p.m., it has not materialized. My relations with the Ministers are very close, and I feel justified in stating that the American Embassy never stood so well in Russia as it does today.

In the huge Labor Parade which was the feature of the day there were many banners bearing the inscription "Peace with Victory but without Annexation or Contribution."

Two days later, on May 3rd, Foreign Minister Miliukoff issued the following statement on Russia's war aims[17] apropos of America's entrance into the conflict.

> I never doubted that the United States could join only the powers of the Entente. In the definition of the objects of the war by President Wilson and the statesmen of the Continent, there never appeared any diversity of opin-

---

[17] The Milyukov note to the Allied powers—dated April 18 (May 1), 1917—was devoted to an explanation of the Provisional Government's war declaration of March 27 (April 9). It confirmed the Russian obligation to continue the war alongside her allies. Publication of the note caused the governmental crisis (April Crisis), which resulted in the resignation of Milyukov and War Minister Alexander I. Guchkov and led to the creation of the first coalition Provisional Government with greater socialist representation.

ion. As President Wilson, so also Briand,[18] Asquith[19] and Grey[20] recognized as the fundamental object of the war—the prevention of war; that is to-day, the finding of peaceful means for the settlement of conflicts and the creation of a new and equitable organization of nations, founded on the triumph of justice in international relations. The best pledge of America's entering the ranks of the Allied Powers was undoubtedly this accord of views in the domain of the conception of the war. Assuredly the formula "Peace without Victory,"[21] proposed by President Wilson is unadmissible for the Allies, but it must be noticed in this connection that the logical development of all the ideas on which are founded the President's statements imperiously demands the continuation of the war by the Allies to a victorious end. Only victory is able to give the powers of the Entente the possibility of solving those broad international questions, the settlement of which President Wilson himself recognizes as necessary for the good of humanity. It must not be forgotten that in her declarations concerning her efforts for peace Germany remains true to her policy, wishing to march ahead of a pacified universe. The only obstacle to the development of normal international relations has always been found in German presentations to world domination, to the enslavement of peoples and to the transformation of all Europe according to the law of the Prussian mailed fist. Without victory over Germany the establishment of the ideal international order of which President Wilson dreams is an utopia impossible of realization.

The concurrence of the views of the Allies with the fundamental tenets of President Wilson is not only apparent in the definition of these ideal aims of the war, but also of those entirely concrete objects, the attainment of which is to lead to an international organization of the universe. Not one of the Allies can be reproached with pursuing a policy of encroachment. The program of the Entente powers consists in the realization of the leading idea of President Wilson concerning the satisfaction of all national aspirations, the restoration of crushed nations and trampled rights. The Entente powers must fix the map of Europe on lines that will include every possibility of a new international catastrophe. I repeat it: none of the Allies is pursuing encroaching aims; the

---

[18] Aristide Briand (1862–1932), French prime minister and minister of foreign affairs from October 1915 to March 1917.

[19] Herbert Henry Asquith (1852–1928), British prime minister, 1908–16.

[20] Sir Edward Grey (1862–1933), baronet of Fallodon; Viscount Grey of Fallodon from July 1916; secretary of state for foreign affairs, 1905–16; later ambassador to the US, 1919–20.

[21] Wilson's message to the Senate, January 22, 1917, which might be considered the first approach to his fantastic plan to lay "foundations of peace among nations" with active American participation and in accordance with American principles.

Allies consider necessary only the restitution of what was forcibly amputated or the settlement of national historical questions. Under these circumstances it is possible to speak of "peace without annexations" only under the condition that by the word "annexation" is meant a conquest. The fixing of frontiers in accord with national endeavors must in no wise be considered a conquest. In general the formula "peace without victory" must be treated with great precaution, this formula having been launched by the Allies of German social democracy as corresponding to German interests only.

Starting from the principle of the liberation of nations put forward by President Wilson as well as by the Entente Powers, the fundamental task of the Allies tends toward the liquidation of Turkish rule over oppressed nations beginning with the Armenians, who, after the victory, must be under the care of Russia, and toward the radical reorganization of Austria-Hungary. One of the natural consequences of this transformation will be the uniting of the Servian territories; another—the creation of a Czecho-Slovak state—bulwarks against Germany's plans of conquering non-German lands. Hungary and German Austria must contract within their ethnographical frontiers in order to restore Italians to Italy, Roumanians to Roumania, and the Ukrainian provinces to Ukrainia.

All these ideas are entirely conformable to the ideas of President Wilson. The same concurrence of views is also noticeable in the Russian endeavors to command the Straits. As it is known, President Wilson on the question of the Straits did not only take the position of their possible neutralization, but also of their transfer to Russian control. In the establishment of Russian domination over the Straits there must be in no wise seen a manifestation of tendencies of conquest, but exclusively the existence of a national object—the necessity of commanding the gate to Russia without which it is impossible to guarantee the safety of the Black Sea. When this gate shall have been firmly fortified, we shall not be obliged to increase the defenses of the shores of the Black Sea, or to maintain a powerful battle fleet. As far as the neutralization of the Straits is concerned, this solution of the question would give access to the Black Sea to foreign battleships, which is precisely the consideration impelling Russia to prefer to a neutralization the retention of the Straits in the hands of a weak power. Occupying Constantinople as mere parasites and ruling by the sole force of conquest the Turks cannot, in opposition to the Russian aims, allege their national rights.

This statement, although only a reiteration of the declaration made by the Provisional Government on April 10th, proved to be a bombshell. I had known for some time that a serious difference of opinion in the Cabinet was threatened on the question of annexation or foreign policy at the close of the war. I knew that Miliukoff, as stated in this interview, claimed that Russia must be given Constantinople in accordance with the promise of the Allies to the Imperial Government before the Revolution. Kerensky, however, demanded the neutralization of the Dardanelles and was opposed to any annexations to Russian territory as a result of the war. I knew that the Ministry had been about equally divided between these two positions, but had understood that the matter had been decided in favor of Kerensky's position—that is against annexations. The British Ambassador, Sir George Buchanan, had told me a few days before that he could say nothing because the Allies had promised Constantinople to Russia before the Revolution, when Russia's policy with regard to Constantinople was well defined and well known. He added, however, that he personally hoped and believed that the result would be the neutralization of the Dardanelles.

Miliukoff gave out this statement without consulting that self-appointed branch of the Government, the Workmen's and Soldiers' Committee. This they bitterly resented and instigated hostile demonstrations against him. As I wrote the Secretary at the time:

> The offense seems to have been that the Provisional Government presumed to make a statement without consulting with and obtaining the consent of the Workingmen's Committee. In the midst of these hostile demonstrations I called upon Miliukoff, who was in a meeting of the Council of Ministers in the War Department, and told him and Goutchkoff, the Minister of War, in effect that having risked my judgment in asking my Government to recognize the Provisional Government and having done all I could to assist the Ministry, I felt considerable official and personal responsibility concerning a stable government in Russia and that if more satisfactory evidence was not given of such government, I should feel compelled to advise my Government not to extend the aid which I have been continuously recommending.

I was endeavoring to secure from our Government a credit to the Provisional Government of Russia and had fair prospects of success. I was also seeking to have a practical railroad man sent to Vladivostok to relieve the congestion at that point and generally to make the Siberian railroad[22] more efficient. I had also made public addresses urging support of the new government and continuation of the war to a

---

[22] Trans-Siberian Railway (Great Siberian Route), the longest railway line in the world, built in 1891–1916. It comprised the Trans-Manchurian line via Harbin—officially called the Chinese Eastern Railway—which provided a shorter route from the Russian mainland to Vladivostok. The railway was seized by mutinous Czecho-Slovak troops in May 1918 while Vladivostok and the eastern part of the line were occupied by the Allied and American Expeditionary Forces.

successful conclusion. I had spoken thus at a great rally[23] at the City Duma[24] only a week or so before. I spoke with the Ministers of Foreign Affairs, Finance, Commerce and Industry[25] and Ways and Communications. The huge hall was crowded to overflowing and the enthusiasm great. When I was introduced as the first Ambassador to recognize the Provisional Government, I received an ovation.

Goutchkoff seemed very much pleased at the statement and asked if I would make it public, but before I could answer Miliukoff remarked that he trusted there would be no occasion for me to do so and added that he expected hostile demonstrations against himself at the meeting of the Ministry to be held that evening, May 3rd, at the Marinsky Palace at 9 o'clock, when there would be a conference with the Executive Committee of the Workingmen's Committee; that his friends had desired to make a counter demonstration but he had advised against it. The conference did take place and at about 10 p.m. a large crowd, including some soldiers in uniform and armed, appeared in front of the Marinsky Palace, but the friends of the new government were there also and in larger numbers than its opponents. In response to loud calls for Miliukoff, Nekrassoff, Minister of Ways and Communications, appeared and addressed the crowd, stating that the Government was confident of its position and would continue to direct affairs according to its best lights; that Miliukoff was in the meeting and was at that moment engaged in conference, but would address the assemblage in a few minutes. Miliukoff soon appeared and was given an ovation; he spoke with more confidence and firmness than on previous occasions and was very much gratified at the reception his remarks met with. On his return to the Foreign Office after midnight, he found a crowd assembled there and made another talk. How much influence my talk with the Ministers had upon their assuming for the first time a rather independent position I cannot say, but the report has gained circulation and credence that the stand taken by the Ministry was inspired if not demanded by the American Ambassador. I give you this for what it is worth and must rely upon your knowledge of my discretion in whatever I did or said. It seemed to me there was a crisis in the situation and I endeavored to meet it in the most effective manner. The

---

[23] The public meeting convened at the Petrograd City Duma on April 10, 1917, by the Society for Promoting Friendly Relations between Russia and America, on the occasion of the US entering the war.

[24] The St. Petersburg City Duma was established in 1786 as an administrative body of limited local self-government. It was reformed in the early 1870s in the course of the Great Reforms, renamed the Petrograd Central City Duma after the February Revolution, and dissolved on November 16, 1917. The City Duma building is located on the corner of Nevsky Prospekt, 33, and Dumskaya Street, 1.

[25] Alexander I. Konovalov (1875–1949), textile manufacturer, member of the Fourth State Duma, 1912–17; member of the Provisional Committee of the State Duma during the February Revolution; minister of commerce and industry, March 2–May 18, and September 25–October 26, 1917.

following day, Friday, the hostile demonstrations continued for a few hours; in fact, I passed one of these demonstrations on the Nevsky where there was a procession of workingmen, some of whom were armed, and there was one black flag with an inscription anarchistic in tone. I communicated with Miliukoff by phone, congratulating him on his success the previous evening, and was informed by him that an agreement had been reached with the Workingmen's Committee, which would be promulgated within a few hours. As the day wore on, friends of the new government and opponents of the anarchistic and extreme socialistic expressions of Lenin, gained courage to such an extent that whenever a Lenin banner appeared on the streets it was captured and torn to shreds. On Friday evening late it became known that an agreement had been reached and the Saturday morning papers contained an explanatory note from the new government and also a proclamation from the Workingmen's Committee advising its friends to refrain from congregating in crowds and carrying arms. That proclamation contained only one objectionable paragraph and that was a statement that no troops other than the small squads for police duty could appear upon the streets without the written consent of the Workmen. The result, however, was that the streets then became extremely quiet; the Provisional Government expressed great satisfaction with the situation, and was entirely confident of the observance of its authority.

In a letter to my son David,[26] written the same day, I said in commenting on the same events that when the Ministry asserted itself it found, to their gratification if not surprise, that the overwhelming sentiment of the people of Petrograd was in favor of the new Government and against the anarchistic doctrines which had been preached from every street corner by an extreme Socialist named Lenin and his followers. I am inclined to the opinion that Lenin is in the pay of the German Government and this Government thinks so too.

This opinion formed in the early Spring of 1917, when Lenin was a mere agitator who had come to Russia from Switzerland, traveling through Germany, I have held ever since and hold to-day.

Not long after Lenin reached Russia through Germany, Leon Trotzky arrived from the United States. Neither one would have been allowed to enter Russia under the Empire. Both were taking advantage of the democratic hospitality of the new Government. The way they used that hospitality is an interesting study.

While these events were taking place in Petrograd, conditions were going from bad to worse throughout Russia as I learned from reports received from the Consuls and other official sources throughout the country as well as from the press. Perhaps one such report will serve to indicate the tenor of them all; it was from Consul-General Summers of Moscow, and read in part as follows:

---

[26] David Rowland Francis, Jr., the ambassador's second son (1879–1938).

While, under your guidance, we are duty bound to do everything possible to encourage a free government here, yet there is a limit to everything, and this is being reached rapidly. The soldiers are plunging the country headlong into anarchy and civil war, and the army as a fighting force no longer exists. This is the unanimous opinion of everyone who returns from the front. The situation in the provinces is still worse. Estates are being sacked and the owners beaten and murdered. Drunkenness is rampant and the soldiers are plundering everywhere. In Moscow no one dares keep anything of value in the house. Robberies are of daily occurrence and no one protests. The Commanding General of the District resigned yesterday, and he stated he could do nothing with the troops who absolutely refused to obey his orders. The entire garrison of the city spends its time riding over the city in the tram cars, refusing to pay their fares and generally behaving in a disorderly manner.

In every province there are riots and murders daily. The landowners dare not go to their estates and many of them will not be able to raise crops this year as the peasants, who are being inflamed by the soldiers, refuse to allow them to cultivate the land. Everywhere the soldiers and peasants are threatening the landowners with death and confiscation of their property. The managers of large factories report that the workmen are doing what they please and that they are managers in name only. The food supply of the city is rapidly diminishing, and it is with the greatest difficulty that one can provide a meal. Servants must stand all day in the bread, milk, and meat lines and then return with very little.

The local authorities here are desperate and make heart-rending appeals to the people, but the soldiers are bent on their destructive work and there is no hope of improvement.

The time has come when strong representations will have to be made to avoid one of the bloodiest situations in history. God grant that it may pass over, but we must be prepared for the worst.

I then suspected and now feel confident that all this disastrous disintegration of Russian society was largely accomplished by Lenin and Trotzky and a host of similar agitators, liberally provided with German money. They worked, in so far as they could, through that potential but irresponsible branch of the Government, the Council of Workmen's and Soldiers' Deputies, over which body they finally secured control.

Chapter VIII
SIGNIFICANT CHANGES IN THE MINISTRY

In a letter to my son Perry of May 15th, 1917, I remarked: "The first change in the Provisional Government took place Sunday when Goutchkoff, Minister of War, resigned. Other changes were made last evening and to-day, and you will no doubt hear of them long before you receive this letter. At this time these changes appear to me to be wise as they will divide the responsibility with that socialistic element representing the workmen and the recalcitrant soldiers who have never acknowledged unreservedly the authority of the new government."

In a letter at about the same time to John F. Stevens,[1] the Chairman of the Railroad Commission[2] which was then about to land at Vladivostok, I commented on the Ministerial changes in these words:

> The situation in Russia at this writing has just undergone a very material change. There have been two powers exercising authority—one the Provisional Government, composed of ten ministers all of whom are able, patriotic and courageous; the other a self-constituted Committee of forty or fifty who represent the workingmen and the soldiers and do not recognize the authority of the Provisional Government. I say self-constituted in the sense that no provision was made by the Duma for such committee. I think they have been elected by the workingmen and soldiers whom they claim to represent. However that may be, this Committee has been almost supreme in Petrograd and has claimed the right to veto all of the decrees of the Provisional Government including those given by the Minister of War to the army. For

---

[1] John Frank Stevens (1853–1943), a prominent railroad engineer, former general manager of the Great Northern Railroad and chief engineer of the Isthmian Canal Commission. Chairman of the Advisory Commission of Railway Experts to Russia, 1917; president of the Inter-Allied Technical Board of the Siberian Railways, 1919–22.

[2] The Advisory Commission of Railway Experts to Russia (Stevens Commission) was created by President Wilson in May 1917. It consisted of five noted engineers: John F. Stevens, chairman; William L. Darling; George Gibbs; John G. Greiner; and Henry Miller. They arrived at Petrograd via Vladivostok on May 30 (June 12), 1917, and worked in Russia during the Revolution and Civil War, operating primarily on the Trans-Siberian and Chinese-Eastern Railroads.

this reason the Minister of War, Goutchkoff, resigned two days ago. I have just heard that Kerensky who has been Minister of Justice since the beginning of the Revolution has been appointed Minister of War but he has not yet been installed. Professor P. N. Miliukoff, who was looked upon in America as the leading spirit of the Revolution, and who has been Minister of Foreign Affairs since the organization of the Government, has also resigned his portfolio but I understand will take another portfolio in the Government—probably that of the Department of Education. Terestchenko who has been Minister of Finance from the beginning of the Government has been made Minister of Foreign Affairs. I am also sending with the Commission, my military attaché, Lieut. E. Francis Riggs. You may talk freely with Lieut. Riggs who is familiar with the military situation on the Russian front and also in Petrograd. Lieut. Riggs, however, is a military man and consequently is not as sanguine about the outcome of the present situation as I am. All army and navy officers are naturally pessimistic concerning present conditions because the soldiers and sailors have treated their officers with little respect and some people think that discipline cannot be restored for a long time if at all in the Russian army.

In commenting on the same situation to a business associate, Mr. William H. Lee,[3] I said:

The part we are performing in this war is of the utmost importance especially in Russia, where the Government and the people seem to look to America for guidance and assistance and I may say for leadership. An Englishman said a few days ago that when America entered the war Russia left it. That may not be entirely true but the situation here at this writing is by no means satisfactory. The Provisional Government which I so heartily endorsed at a critical time more than two months ago has grown in strength from that time to this, but yesterday the Minister of War, Goutchkoff, one of the ablest and strongest men in the Government, resigned. He has never been popular with the Workmen's and Soldiers' Deputies Committee because he was looked upon as an aristocrat, being a man of property, and furthermore having had considerable experience as a soldier, he had little patience with the position assumed by the soldiers of the left to elect their own officers, and never could listen for a moment to the claim of the Workmen's Committee to vise his military orders. The fraternizing at the front between Russian and German soldiers has always been objectionable to him.

---

[3] William H. Lee of the Merchant Laclede National Bank, St. Louis, MO.

Upon hearing of Goutchkoff's intended resignation, I had attempted to find him for the purpose of remonstrating with him and telling him he should not forsake the Provisional Government, and that in my judgment such an act would be cowardly. I telephoned to the War Office and to his residence also and sent a note by messenger to his house. He could not be found, however, and when I finally saw him Kerensky had already been appointed as his successor and installed in the office.

I met Goutchkoff several times after his resignation, and learned from him that he abandoned his office because he could not endure the dictation of the Workingmen's and Soldiers' Deputies to which he was subjected.

The next to leave the Provisional Government Ministry was Miliukoff, who resigned. At a private meeting of the members of the Duma, Miliukoff stated that he left the Government as a large majority of his former colleagues were against him. He expressed as his opinion that the new foreign policy, adopted by the Socialists, was the result of theoretical speculations supported by the minorities of socialistic parties abroad, and that the realization of this policy would be dangerous for the Entente, and that therefore he, Miliukoff, could not take upon himself the responsibility to conduct such policy. However, he said he hoped that the new Government would succeed in obtaining real authority and bringing about a change for the better in the army. Therefore he stated that all parties should support the new government.

When Miliukoff resigned, Terestchenko, the Minister of Finance in the Provisional Government, was transferred from the Department of Finance to the Foreign Office. He was a young man, only thirty-one years of age, descended from Cossack ancestors. His family was rich; his mother[4] was a widow and universally beloved for her charities.

I recall that while Terestchenko was dining with me at the American Embassy, his eye fell upon an engraving of Rapine's celebrated painting, "The Cossack's Reply to the Sultan of Turkey."[5] "One of these Cossacks," he said, "was my ancestor." He was a "Radical" in politics, but the party to which he belonged had only a small membership. He was reported to have given 5,000,000 or 10,000,000 roubles to assist the Provisional Government. He spoke English, French, German and Polish. His father died long before the war began, and the young man had gained much credit by applying himself to the preservation of his father's estate, which owned several large sugar refineries. His mother purchased a yacht for him before the war began at a cost of 500,000 roubles, and when Russia entered the war he gave that yacht to the Government. He was a close student and a sincere lover of his country. The Provisional Government was fortunate in having a man so well qualified to fill Miliukoff's place.

---

[4] Elizaveta M. Tereshchenko (Sarancheva, 1860–1923).

[5] Ilya E. Repin (1844–1930), a prominent Russian artist. Francis meant one of his most famous paintings: *Zaporozhtsy are writing a letter to the Turkish Sultan* (1878–91).

Shortly after he became Minister of Foreign Affairs, I made an arrangement to see him at a fixed time each day; this resulted in our becoming close friends. Terestchenko was loyal to Kerensky, whom he greatly admired up to within two or three weeks of the Bolshevik Revolution. I did not know, indeed, that he ever lost confidence in Kerensky until Terestchenko visited me incognito in the latter part of October, 1918, at Archangel.

When, after the fall of the Provisional Government and during the Bolshevik regime, the Germans approached within twenty-five miles of Petrograd, which caused the departure of all of the Allied Missions from the city, Terestchenko and the other former Ministers were released from the St. Peter and Paul Fortress. After living in seclusion for some weeks, Terestchenko managed to get through the lines to Sweden, and told me when he arrived in Archangel that he had spent the summer of 1918 on a farm in Norway belonging to a former employee of his. He said he had come with the intention of joining Kolchak[6] if he could get through, but that if he could not make his way through the lines, he wished to go to America. I told him I would give him a passport to America, but he was loath to abandon his plan to join Kolchak, and was still in Archangel when I left that city November 6th, 1918. He did not come to America but during my stay in London, I heard that he was in Stockholm. I have heard nothing from him since I parted with him in Archangel the day before I was borne on a stretcher aboard the cruiser *Olympia*;[7] suppose he is somewhere in Scandinavian country, awaiting the restoration of established order in Russia when he will return to his beloved country.

Shortly after Terestchenko's assuming the Foreign Office portfolio, he issued to the Russian press the following statement of his policy:

> You ask what is my program? You can read it in the declaration of the new Provisional Government called to power by Free Russia. This program is short, but significant, namely, the reestablishment as early as possible of universal peace. A peace which aims neither at domination over other peoples,

---

[6] Alexander V. Kolchak (1874–1920), Russian naval officer and polar explorer. During the World War, he fought in the Baltic Sea, was promoted to vice admiral, and then appointed commander of the Black Sea Fleet on June 28, 1916. He was relieved of command on June 6, 1917, and returned to Petrograd with Rear Admiral John H. Glennon of the Root Mission. He headed the Russian naval mission to the US, September 10–October 25, 1917. In the fall of 1918, he returned to Russia and, with British support, was made the war minister of the Provisional All-Russian Government at Omsk. The government was overthrown in a British-sponsored coup d'état, and Kolchak was proclaimed supreme ruler of Russia from November 18, 1918 to January 4, 1920.

[7] The USS *Olympia*, a protected cruiser built in 1895, which received fame as the flagship of Commodore Dewey at the Battle of Manila in the course of the Spanish-American War of 1898. It operated in the North Russian waters during the Allied intervention in 1918, and is now preserved as a museum ship in Philadelphia.

nor a seizure of their national patrimony, nor a taking by force of foreign territories, a peace without annexations or indemnities, based on the principle of the rights of peoples to dispose of themselves, a peace concluded in close and indissoluble union with the allied democracies. Free Russia, like every country which has made a great renovating revolution, is moved by two motives profoundly idealistic. The first is an aspiration to give a just peace to the entire world, not to injure any nation, not to create after the war a hatred, an estrangement which remains always when one nation comes forth from the struggle enriched at the expense of the other nations, when the latter are crushed and obliged to accept humiliating conditions of peace. We have seen a sad example of that in 1870. The wounds dealt to France by Germany remained open for forty-five years. The hope of the people of Alsace-Lorraine for a better future is not dead up to the present and they have now a right to hope for the realization of their ideal. Outrage and injustice are not forgotten, violence creates hatred. Liberated Russia does not wish that either for herself, or for others.

The second motive is the consciousness of ties with the allied democracies, consciousness of the duty which these ties have imposed on her. Revolutionary Russia cannot and ought not to break these ties sealed by blood; for her it is a question of revolutionary honor which is so much the more precious to her now. The great revolution which stirred the public ocean to its greatest depths could not but influence the army, which was unable to immediately accommodate itself to the suddenly changed state of affairs. At the same time, the democracy of the west continued to accomplish with tenacity its war-like work which was for us a powerful aid. The allied armies of whom the great mass is composed, as with us, of peasants and workmen, carried on without stopping the struggle against the enemy, diverting his strength and by their heroic effort are saving the Russian revolution from an external defeat. The success of the Russian revolution is also bought by their blood; it is with a sentiment of profound satisfaction that I must state that in Free Russia, in spite of a divergence of opinions of the democratic parties, there has not been a single party, a single organization as there was in reactionary Russia, which would have made a propaganda for a separate peace. I know, however, that there exists a question capable of stirring the emotions of the numerous groups of the Russian democracy, that is the question of the treaties concluded by the old Russian regime. This question stirs up the passions. But I believe nevertheless that I ought to touch upon this question, expressing my entire and true opinion, for the Russian people have the right to expect and expects that the Provisional Government should only tell it the truth. The Russian democracy is afraid that bound by these old treaties it will be made to serve purposes of annexation which are foreign to it. This disturbs its revolutionary confidence, diminishes its spirit and enthusiasm. That is why demands for the immediate publication of all the treaties concluded by the old regime are being made. I think that in this case the sentiments which bring forth these demands are highly humanitarian, but I am convinced that the question is raised in an entirely erroneous manner and that should be understood by the Russian democracy.

It ought absolutely to understand that in the name of the safety of the Russian revolution and the Allied democracies, the immediate publication of the treaties is equivalent to a rupture with the Allies and will result in the isolation of Russia. Such an act will necessarily bring on a separate situation and for Russia will be the beginning of a separate peace. But it is exactly this which the Russian people repudiates with all its force and not only by a feeling of honor. It understands that the international war can only be ended by an international peace. It is only this peace which could guarantee this justice, this right of the people to dispose of themselves which is ardently desired by liberated Russia, Other ways must be chosen, for new Russia must look forward and not backward. Now the world at war is confronted by some new facts, namely, the great Russian revolution and the entry into the war of the Great American Republic, which hailed with enthusiasm the Russian revolution and has united itself without hesitation to the Allies after the disappearance of Russian absolutism. We must start from these facts and these facts cannot but be counted on by the Allied democracies. Personal intercourse with representatives of the western democracies, as for example Mr. Thomas,[8] makes near and clear to all the aims which are now placed before Russia and before the world as a result of the Russian revolution. In basing oneself on this intercourse, I notice the growth of a reciprocal confidence with the Allies which will permit the Russian Government to undertake preparatory measures for an agreement with the Allies on the basis of the declaration of March 27th–April 9th,[9] and I will apply every effort to hasten the process of approachment of mutual understanding and agreement. But to attain this aim with success Free Russia must prove that she is accomplishing faithfully her fundamental engagement that she has taken towards the Allies, the engagement of united struggle and mutual help.

She must inspire an unlimited confidence in herself and prove that her idealism is not derived from weakness and that she renounces annexations

---

[8] Albert Thomas (1878–1932), French socialist, minister of munitions, 1915–17. He visited Russia on special mission, April 9–June 1, 1917.

[9] Declaration of War Aims, issued on March 27 (April 9), 1917, by which the Provisional Government promised to keep Russia in the war in close union with the Allies and to fulfill all accompanying obligations.

not because she cannot realize them but because she does not desire them. It is precisely the reason why in the name of the demands of the democracy, in the name of a peace rapid and just, it is necessary to re-create the military power of new Russia, to strengthen it by all the force of her revolutionary enthusiasm and to prove really the existence of this force. The Russian army proved its heroism, its great self-denial even when it was sent to the field of battle by the old regime. At present being subjected only to a discipline freely accepted it must understand and understands that it is struggling for what it holds most dear, for the integrity and the safety of its freed country aspiring to a new life. It understands also that a defeat will annihilate this liberty and this new life. And that ought to be the only aim to animate it. It is ridiculous in fact to speak at the present moment of the annexationist plans of the Allies as of a real menace to peace, just when Russia, Belgium, France and Servia are themselves occupied in whole or in part by the enemy. Now it can only be a question of an active defense with a view to defending the national independence and liberty. As for the future the Allied democracies in their ever growing confidence must count with the desire and tendency of all. It is not for nothing that Russian liberty comes to the world and that its consequences and influences are spreading in a large and powerful wave across the civilized world. That is all that I can say for the moment in regard to what will serve me as a basis for my activity and the measures that I propose taking.

The reader will note how radically this statement differs from the pronouncement on the same subject issued by Terestchenko's colleague and predecessor, Miliukoff, only a few weeks before. In fact there is scarcely any similarity except on the fundamental points of the necessity of winning the war and remaining loyal to Russia's Allies. It was the insistence on these fundamentals which made it possible for me to continue my cooperation with the Government.

The Provisional Government, with which I had close relations, was surrounded at this period by many difficulties. I saw the Minister of Foreign Affairs daily, and attempted to keep my Government advised concerning the situation.

Terestchenko, Kerensky and Lvoff, the latter two of whom I saw frequently, told me that they did not need men but supplies and credit, in order to equip and feed and clothe the Russian army. Soon after America entered the war a credit was extended to the Provisional Government, on my recommendation, by the United States of $100,000,000 on condition that the entire amount be disbursed in America. After

SIGNIFICANT CHANGES IN THE MINISTRY

the arrival of the American Commission,[10] Senator Root[11] and I joined in a recommendation that $15,000,000 of this $100,000,000 and if the entire $100,000,000 had already been obligated, an additional credit amounting to $15,000,000 be extended in cash for the purpose of paying the Russian army in Finland. Finland had an agreement with Russia by which the former was to pay the latter 20,000,000 roubles annually, and in return Finnish citizens were not subject to conscription for service in the Russian army. The government of Finland had informed the government in Petrograd that the Russian soldiers in Finland threatened to mutiny in default of their pay, which was overdue.

The Government of the United States followed the recommendation of Senator Root and myself and placed $15,000,000 to the credit of Russia in the Bank of England, in accordance with an agreement made with the Bank of Finland, with which the Russian soldiers in Finland were promptly paid.

Finland had long desired her independence; in fact a number of the richer classes sympathized with Germany from the beginning of the war. Germany was continuously propagandizing in that country with a view of creating an uprising of the Finns. During this period I realized the importance of maintaining the Russian army on the Eastern front, and was well acquainted with the trials and tribulations of the Ministry. America had entered the war ninety days previously; and, in my opinion, it would require at least one year for her to land troops in France or Belgium that would be of material assistance to the Allied cause. It was, therefore, of vital importance that the Russian army should maintain the Eastern front, so that Germany and Austria

---

[10] The Special Diplomatic Mission of the United States to Russia (Root Mission) was commissioned by President Wilson on May 14, 1917. It consisted of nine members with diplomatic ranks. Additionally, Colonel William V. Judson was appointed as "military attaché to the special diplomatic mission"; Basil Miles was made its secretary; and Major Stanley Washburn its assistant secretary. Concerned that the Provisional Government would reach a separate peace with Germany, the Root Mission was to assess conditions and needs in Russia, assure the Russian government of US support, and confer on how the US could best cooperate in the prosecution of the war. The mission visited Petrograd from May 31 to June 26 (June 13–July 9), and submitted its final report on August 19, 1917.

[11] Elihu Root (1845–1937), a prominent American lawyer and statesman, Republican, former secretary of war and of state, former US senator from New York, and Nobel Peace Prize winner of 1912. In the summer of 1917, he headed the Special Diplomatic Mission of the United States to Russia with rank of "ambassador extraordinary of the United States of America on special mission." (*FRUS, 1918, Russia*, vol. 1, 109.)

could send no assistance to their armies in France. Hindenburg[12] and Ludendorff[13] were advancing their lines in France and Belgium; consequently, this was a critical juncture of the world war.

This situation, in my opinion, not only justified but demanded activities on my part to assist the Russian Government to keep the Russian armies fighting which under ordinary circumstances would have been not only unusual but improper for an Ambassador to undertake.

About this time I said in a letter to my eldest son:

I have not lost faith in Russia coming out of this ordeal as a republic and with a government which will be founded on correct principles. My constant effort is to keep her in the war as her withdrawal would throw the bulk of the burden of the defeat of Germany upon our country. I realize the magnitude of my responsibility but at the same time feel fortunate that it has fallen to my lot to play such an important part in occurrences which are determining not only the future of our country and of Russia but of all international relations and in fact of society itself.

On May 31st, I received the following confidential report on the experiences of Kerensky at the front:

Kerensky is still continuing his inspection of the front, and is met everywhere with the greatest enthusiasm. The reception given him at the Frontal Congress at Odessa and Sevastopol is characteristic of this enthusiasm. Kerensky entered the Assembly Hall in Odessa at the moment when, at the chairman's call, the soldiers were handing over their decorations and medals for the needs of the war, whereas those who had none, handed over money. Young women in the audience came forward and laid on the chairman's table their jewelry. Kerensky, as usual, was met with enormous enthusiasm. In his speech, he mentioned amongst other things: "We have gone through a period of destruction, but now we must understand that this cannot be continued or repeated, but we must commence the positive work of construction. Enemies

---

[12] Paul von Hindenburg (1847–1934), general of infantry, fought successfully during the World War on the Eastern Front against Russia. He was appointed chief of the German General Staff on August 29, 1916, and became actual military leader of Germany in the last years of the World War. Later president of the Weimar Republic, 1925–34, who appointed Adolf Hitler Reichchancellor.

[13] Erich von Ludendorff (1865–1937), fought successfully during the World War on the Eastern Front against Russia along with Paul von Hindenburg. He was appointed quartermaster general on August 29, 1916, and promoted to general of infantry; became the closest Hindenburg associate in military leadership until his resignation on October 27, 1918.

SIGNIFICANT CHANGES IN THE MINISTRY

of Russian freedom dare not go against us openly. They choose the path of deceit and to the famine-stricken masses, corrupted by the old regime and inspire them "to demand everything immediately," and they whisper words of mistrust against us, who have, all our lives, struggled for freedom against Tzarism. There are also, amongst us, idealists, who, much too stubbornly, look towards the skies, and lead us to the precipice of anarchy. We must say to them: "Stop!" Do not shake the new foundations. It is easy to criticize and destroy, but the Russian Revolution demands other things of its sons, wise statesmanship, and demands that one does not play on the cords of the fatigue of the people and of the dullness inherited from the old regime. All that we have conquered is in the balance. If the Russian people, and especially the Russian army, cannot retrieve its bravery and courage, if it cannot again put on its steel armor of discipline, we shall be lost, and the whole world will despise us, and besides us, will despise the ideas of Socialism, in the name of which we made the Revolution." Kerensky ended his speech with the words: "I have come to you, not to blush for the Russian army, but in order to, together with you, accomplish an heroic action, and forgetting the damnation of the past, rush forward in the name of freedom, equality and fraternity." The speech called forth great ovations, and all present swore a solemn oath, to go forward and only forward. The whole audience shouted: "Lead us and we will follow you."

In the midst of our apparently successful efforts for the revival of Russia's military power this disquieting report among many others was received at the Embassy.

Under the influence of the Bolsheviks, the Council of Workmen's and Soldiers' Deputies of Cronstadt had by a vote of 210 to 40 decided to take all power into its own hands and to repudiate the Provisional Government. The local representatives of the Government had been dismissed and replaced by the Council's own appointees. In order to keep in touch with the rest of the country the Cronstadt Council had opened communications with the Petrograd Council of Workmen's and Soldiers' Deputies.

Chapter IX
THE DIPLOMATIC AND RAILWAY COMMISSION

President Wilson appointed a Commission to visit Russia of which Honorable Elihu Root was Chairman. The other members were General Hugh Scott,[1] Admiral Glennon,[2] Charles R. Crane, present Minister to China,[3] James H. Duncan, Vice-President of the American Federation of Labor,[4] S. R. Bertron,[5] John R. Mott, Executive Secretary of the Young Men's Christian Association,[6] and Charles E. Russell, at one time Socialist candidate for President.[7]

Upon the arrival of this Commission at Vladivostok there was a hostile demonstration on the part of some unfriendly spirits, at the instigation of Russians living on the East Side of New York City, but it was suppressed and the Commission proceeded upon its way. When it arrived in Petrograd I met it at the station and escorted it to the Winter Palace, where provision had been made for its accommodation and where the Commissioners were the guests of the Provisional Government during their stay in

---

[1] Hugh Lenox Scott (1853–1934), major general, chief of staff of the US Army, November 17, 1914–September 22, 1917. A member of the Root Mission with the title "military representative of the President of the United States of America, on special diplomatic mission, with rank of minister." (*FRUS, 1918, Russia*, vol. 1, 109.)

[2] James Henry Glennon (1857–1940), commandant of the Washington Navy Yard, promoted to rear admiral on August 10, 1916. A member of the Root Mission as "naval representative of the President of the United States of America, on special mission, with rank of minister." Other members of the Root Mission had the title "envoy extraordinary of the United States of America on special mission."

[3] Charles Richard Crane (1858–1939), a prominent Chicago businessman and promoter of Russian-American rapprochement. Minister to China in 1920–21.

[4] James Duncan (1857–1928), second vice president of the American Federation of Labor.

[5] Samuel Reading Bertron, Jr. (1865–1938), a prominent New York banker.

[6] John Raleigh Mott (1865–1955), a founder and general secretary of the World Student Christian Federation, 1895–1920. General secretary of the International Committee of the American Young Men's Christian Associations, 1915–28.

[7] Charles Edward Russell (1860–1941), a popular American journalist, "muckraker," activist of the Socialist Party. Francis missed Cyrus Hall McCormick, Jr. (1859–1936), president of International Harvester Company.

Russia. The Ministry held a special session to receive the Commission, which I had the honor of introducing. In the presentation of the Commission to the Ministry I said among other things that the Commission represented all the interests in our country, and had come for the purpose of welcoming Russia to the sisterhood of republics, furthermore, that the Commission was composed of men eminent in America, who were serving without compensation, and who had left their avocations at great personal sacrifice; that they represented a country whose institutions were based upon the great principle that all just powers of government are derived from the consent of the governed, and whose superstructure was universal education, and the crowning arch equality of opportunity.

Chairman Root spoke eloquently on behalf of the Commission, and to him Minister Terestchenko made a fitting reply. The Commission remained in Petrograd about six weeks, visiting Moscow in the meantime, and General Scott went to the front, while Admiral Glennon reviewed the Black Sea Fleet.

I entertained the members of the Commission at luncheons and dinners, inviting to meet them at one time Rodzianko, at another time Miliukoff; Kerensky, who was then Minister of War and Minister of Marine also, was invited to meet General Scott and Admiral Glennon. Messrs. Mott and Bertron lunched or dined at the American Embassy, and had long talks with the Ministers of Commerce and Industry. Messrs. Duncan and Russell had discussions at the American Embassy on several occasions with Tchernov,[8] who was Minister of Labor. The American Society of Petrograd honored the Commission by giving it a dinner on July 4th in celebration of our Independence Day and Minister Terestchenko gave visiting Americans an elaborate luncheon at the Department of Foreign Affairs.

The Commission took its departure from Petrograd on the 8th of July, 1917, just nine days before the July Revolution, which attempted to overthrow the Provisional Government. Felicitations between the Commission and the Provisional Government were hearty and sincere.

The Commission in parting jointly and severally expressed their gratitude to the American Ambassador, complimenting him on his relations with the Provisional Government, and his standing with the Russian people, which they attributed to the opportune recognition of the Provisional Government by our Government.

I had recommended the sending of a railway commission to Russia. The Allied Missions of England, France and Italy by agreement had assigned the transportation systems of the Provisional Government to the American Ambassador. When I was advised of the commission appointments, I was pleased to hear that so eminent

---

[8] Viktor M. Chernov (1873–1952), a founder and leading theorist of the Party of Socialists-Revolutionaries. After the February Revolution, assistant chairman of the Petrograd Soviet; minister of agriculture in the Provisional Government, May 5–September 25, 1917. Chairman of the All-Russian Constituent Assembly, January 5, 1918. He emigrated abroad after the October Revolution, went to the US in 1941, and died in New York City.

an engineer as John F. Stevens had been named as its head. The State Department had cabled me that Mr. Stevens would be appointed Chairman if I did not object, to which cable I made prompt reply that if I had had the selection of a chairman I did not know of any man I would have preferred to Mr. Stevens. I knew Mr. Stevens personally and esteemed him highly. The other members of the Commission were: George Gibbs, a mechanical engineer of experience formerly connected with the Pennsylvania Railroad;[9] Henry Miller, who had served the Wabash and made a fine record as General Manager;[10] W. L. Darling, a civil engineer of repute,[11] and John E. Greiner, Consulting Engineer of the Baltimore and Ohio.[12]

The Commission arrived in Vladivostok in June, 1917. I sent the Commercial Attache of the Embassy, E. Francis Riggs,[13] to meet them, with the following letter of greeting:

> My dear Stevens: I was more than pleased when advised by the State Department that you had been designated to come to Russia as the head of a commission of experts whose mission is to relieve the congestion at Vladivostok and to improve generally the transportation facilities of the Siberian railway. My understanding is that you will be given absolute control at Vladivostok, and I hope to have that control extended throughout the entire length of the Siberian railway. I have not asked the latter at this time because it is impolitic to do so. The railroad engineers of Russia are highly educated men and claim to be exceedingly practical. They are jealous to a degree of any reflection upon their ability and qualifications, and consequently they must be handled diplomatically as I know you are capable of doing.

When the Railroad Commission arrived in Petrograd, they reported to me that they had inspected the Trans-Siberian and had begun the erection of an assembling plant near Vladivostok. I promptly secured quarters for the Commission in the Department of Ways and Communications. Mr. Stevens was taken ill soon after arriving in Petrograd and was confined to the hospital for about two months. In the meantime, Darling and Greiner had left for America, via Sweden. Gibbs departed soon after and reported from Vladivostok that the assembling plant was making satis-

---

[9] George Gibbs, consulting engineer of the Pennsylvania Railroad.

[10] Henry Miller, president of Missouri & Illinois Bridge & Belt Railroad.

[11] William Lafayette Darling (1856–1938), consulting engineer with residence at St. Paul, MN, and associate member of the Naval Consulting Board.

[12] John Edwin Greiner (1859–1942), expert in bridge building, founder of the J. E. Greiner Company of Baltimore (1908), honorary Doctor of Science (1917).

[13] Riggs was a military attaché.

factory progress. I requested Mr. Stevens—when he recovered from his illness—and Mr. Miller to inspect the Donetz system of railroads. They had just completed this work and had reached Moscow on their return when the Bolshevik Revolution took place. Mr. Stevens wired me from Moscow that his mission was completed and that he would await further orders at Moscow. This telegram was received the Sunday after the Bolshevik Revolution began. I replied suggesting that the party remain at Moscow until the situation cleared up, or as long as it was safe to remain in that city, and then come to Petrograd, where I would protect them. I don't know whether Mr. Stevens ever received this telegram or not, but I learned from other sources that he had attached his private car to the Siberian Express bound for Vladivostok.

In the meantime there had been assembled for Russia, in accordance with the request of the Railroad Commission, endorsed by myself, a party of over 200, consisting of railroad operating men, engineers and interpreters, under the command of George Emerson,[14] which planned to leave Seattle November 19, 1917. I cabled the Department to allow this party to come on to Russia, stating in the cable that I had no confidence in the survival of the Soviet Government, but regardless of whether it survived or not there would be some government in Russia, and that that country, which was our ally in the war, would accept gladly whatever assistance we could render in its transportation. I did not calculate on Russia agreeing to an armistice and signing the Brest-Litovsk Peace which resulted in Russia withdrawing from the war.[15]

These railroad men did arrive in Vladivostok and there met Mr. Stevens. There were frequent changes in the Department of Ways and Communications under the Bolsheviks, but I had made the acquaintance of several subordinates in this department, with whom I kept in close touch. The railroad men after landing in Vladivostok, concluded to reembark and go to Nagasaki, Japan, where they remained some months.

When at Vologda, I wired Mr. Stevens to send me twenty railroad engineers, and cabled the Department of State that I had so wired. Mr. Stevens promptly replied that the instructions would be followed. The Department cabled to know what I wished with these railroad men, to which inquiry I replied that it was my intention to improve the transportation facilities of Russia, with a view to assembling all supplies at Archangel and Murmansk to prevent the Germans from capturing them. The Department seemed satisfied and cabled that Emerson was leaving with ten engineers

---

[14] George H. Emerson (?–1950), general manager of the Great Northern Railway. A colonel in the US Army, he commanded the Russian Railway Service Corps in the Far East, 1917–20.

[15] A peace treaty between Soviet Russia and Germany and her allies signed at Brest-Litovsk on March 3, 1918, and ratified by the Extraordinary Fourth All-Russian Congress of Soviets on March 15. It was denounced by Germany on November 5 and by the Soviet government on November 13, 1918. Another Brest-Litovsk peace treaty was concluded by Germany and her allies with the Ukrainian People's Republic on January 27 (February 9), 1918.

from Harbin,[16] via Vladivostok. Mr. Emerson did not arrive at Vladivostok, however, until the 12th of May, when it was too late for them to reach Vologda on account of the fighting between the Czecho-Slovaks[17] and the Red Army along the line of the Trans-Siberian Railroad.

The Bolshevik Revolution prevented the consummation of the well-laid plans of these railroad experts.

---

[16] The administrative center of the Chinese Eastern Railway Zone in Manchuria. Now the capital of the Chinese province Heilongjiang.

[17] The soldiers of the Czecho-Slovak Legion. It was volunteer military force comprised predominantly of Czech and Slovak prisoners of war from the Austro-Hungarian army; created in 1917, it numbered about 40,000 by 1918. After Russia's withdrawal from the World War, the decision was made to evacuate the legion by way of Siberia to the Western Front, but in May 1918, Czecho-Slovaks revolted, joined the Russian White forces, and became the powerful party in the Russian Civil War. They were supported by the Allied Powers, which used the Czecho-Slovak mutiny as pretext for military intervention in Russia.

Chapter X
THE JULY REVOLUTION

Lenin and Trotzky had not belonged to the same faction of International Socialists, but they soon saw after arriving in Russia that they had the same ulterior object, which was world-wide social revolution, and that it could be best promoted by their joining forces. Lenin was the stronger intellect of the two. Trotzky was the abler executive. Lenin led a simple life; Trotzky was fond of display and luxury. Whenever the two disagreed, Lenin dominated because he had the stronger will and the greater following. These two men soon became the recognized leaders and drove the moderate Socialists out of the organizations which they dominated. Both believed in "direct action," that is, they scrupled at no means by which their ends could be accomplished. In other words, they believed in force rather than argument. Plekahnov,[1] at whose feet Lenin had imbibed the principles of Socialism, also returned to Russia after the first Revolution; he had championed Socialism and internationalism, but believed in putting them into practical operation by peaceful means, contending that if the people were educated in the principles of Socialism, they would all become its supporters. Lenin claimed that the education of the masses in Russia was too slow a process. He had been the leader of the "Defeatists"[2] at the beginning of the war, and had advocated the defeat of Russia—his own country—as the surest and quickest means whereby the Russian Monarchy could be overthrown, and a world-wide revolution promoted.

Lenin was living in Switzerland when I arrived in Petrograd, but when the Provisional Government, soon after its installation, issued a degree pardoning all political offenders, whether in prison or in exile, he returned through Germany in a special car, and immediately set to work to demoralize the Russian army. Trotzky, who had been banished from France, was eking out an impecunious existence on

---

[1] Georgy V. Plekhanov (1856–1918), veteran of the revolutionary movement and the first Marxist theorist in Russia. He lived in Switzerland from 1880 and headed the Social-Democratic Edinstvo (Unity) group from 1914 to 1918, which supported Russian participation in the World War on the Entente side. After thirty-seven years of exile, he returned to Petrograd on March 31, 1917, but failed to find his place in the new Russian reality.

[2] Followers of the socialistic doctrine of defeat of their own nations in imperialist war, which, in their opinion, must turn into a civil war and lead to the proletarian revolution ("revolutionary defeatism").

the East Side in New York by contributing articles to radical socialistic publications. When he attempted to return to Russia the steamer upon which he sailed touched at Halifax, and Trotzky was taken ashore by force, after refusing to obey the commands of the inspection officer and detained in Halifax for several weeks. He was later, at the request of the Provisional Government, permitted by the British Government to proceed on his way to Russia.

Lenin on arriving in Petrograd immediately began to disburse money which was supposedly furnished by Germany. He was disregarded by the Provisional Government, and for some time the Workingmen's, Soldiers' and Peasants' Deputies denied alliance or cooperation with him. Lenin was persistent, however, and gradually gained influence with the enemies of the Provisional Government.

Across the Neva on the Petrograd side[3] was the palace, a beautiful structure, of an influential ballet dancer named Dschinskaia,[4] who was reputed to have been the Emperor's mistress before he married. This palace was pointed out to all visitors as having been the gift of the Emperor to the dancer. She had subsequently become the mistress, according to current rumor, of two Grand Dukes with royal connections. Her word was still law with the ballet, which was subsidized by the Imperial Government, and upon rare occasions she participated in its performances. Soon after the Revolution she fled from her palace, and it was taken over by the Workingman's, Soldiers' and Peasants' Deputies. Just across the street from this palace was the Circus Moderne,[5] which had a seating capacity of from 6,000 to 10,000. In the same neighborhood was the St. Peter and Paul Fortress, which continued under the control of the Provisional Government.

The Circus Moderne was the place of assemblage of all the radical elements in Petrograd. Here they came to listen to orators, whose themes were opposition to the government, the dictatorship of the proletariat and the division of all property. Lenin took possession of the Dschinskaia palace, but at what time or by whose authority was never known. There was in the corner of the grounds a circular pagoda, or band stand, from which Lenin and other orators addressed the crowds which congregated day and night. Lenin and Trotzky, whose followers were continually increasing in numbers, decided upon a "peaceful demonstration" on the evening of July 16th, 1917.

So it was that on Monday evening, July 16th, according to the Bolshevik schedule, demonstrations took place all over the city. Parades were everywhere formed.

---

[3] Petrogradskaya Storona, the part of Petrograd comprising Petrogradsky Island as well as Aptekarsky, Petrovsky, and Zayachy Islands.

[4] Kseshinskaya (see nn. 52 and 54, p. 20).

[5] The Circus Modern was built in 1909 on Petrogradskaya Storona in Kronverksky Prospekt, 11, near the Kseshinskaya Palace, as New Circus; it was renamed Circus Modern in 1911. It accommodated about five thousand people and was one of the main centers of Bolshevik agitation in 1917. It was destroyed by fire in early 1919.

Thousands of peasant soldiers, for the most part unarmed, formed in lines carrying banners—"Let Us Go Home and Harvest the Crops Then We'll Fight!" and "All Power to the Workingmen's, Soldiers' and Peasants' Deputies!"—"All Power to the Soviets!" They marched by the thousands to the Smolny Institute.[6] There were also gathered hundreds of Kronstadt sailors and amongst the masses gathered around the buildings of the Smolny Institute were three-inch field pieces with caissons and other equipment. All during the evening speeches were made inciting the people against the Government and turning them to the Soviet by advocating the alluring slogans proclaimed on the banners.

The Government took no active measures against these meetings preferring to await the results and then arrest the ringleaders.

The next day, however, the Government finally decided to permit no more demonstrations of this character and accordingly called upon the Cossacks with armored cars to keep the crowds dispersed and prevent such demonstrations.

Tuesday evening about 7:30 I received a telephone call from Frederick Holbrook, of Holbrook, Cabot & Rollins, of Boston,[7] saying that there was going to be trouble in the city and that he was coming to the Embassy. About the time he arrived the trouble began all over the city. The fighting nearest the Embassy took place about 300 yards away on the Liteiny Prospect, when a calvacade[8] of Cossacks riding toward Liteiny Bridge[9] across the Neva River four blocks from the Embassy, with the intention of controlling the bridge and preventing communication between the different organized bands of provocateurs and agitators met with resistance. When they rushed the crowd with their horses, however, the mob broke and ran in all directions. But a new and unlooked-for factor now showed itself. An automobile truck loaded with Kronstadt sailors appeared on the scene with a machine gun on the rear, which they turned upon the Cossacks and opened fire. They poured a deadly and disastrous fire into the ranks of the Cossacks. They were mown down without any chance to defend themselves. Horses and drivers fell together and, although there was a driving rain

---

[6] The former residence of the Imperial Educational Society of Noble Maidens, which was commonly called the Smolny Institute after the neighboring Smolny Cathedral. Built in 1806–08, it was situated at Lafonskaya Square, 4. It was the residence of the All-Russian Central Executive Committee of Soviets and the Petrograd Soviet from August 4, 1917; headquarters of the Military-Revolutionary Committee during the October Revolution; afterwards a residence of the Council of People's Commissars and Central Committee of the Bolshevik Party till their removal to Moscow in March 1918.

[7] Frederick Holbrook (1861–1920), engineer and contractor, organizer, and vice president of Holbrook, Cabot & Rollins Corporation of Boston (1894).

[8] Cavalcade.

[9] The second constant bridge across the Neva, built in 1874–79, connects the two city districts of Vyborgskaya Storona and Liteynaya Section. The Liteyny Bridge was the nearest bridge to the US embassy.

a half hour afterward when I visited the scene, the street was literally and actually running with blood.

Bodies were scattered for four blocks along the street from the bridge to the Kirochnaya,[10] while those responsible had driven rapidly away with their death-dealing machine. What a catastrophe to the Government an what shouts of triumph broke exultingly from the Bolshevik leaders when informed of this coup! Where were the armored motor cars of the government? With the same speed with which the Bolsheviks had fled after the encounter the Government's armored cars, the only real aid which might have saved the Cossacks, had been rushed to a different section of the city where they thought they might be more needed and by the time communication had been established with them the scene was quiet save for the bodies and the blood in the street and the ever curious crowds who gathered as always to talk and talk and talk.

Although the government won a technical victory that night, as a survey showed that 450 Bolsheviks had paid the penalty and about 70 Cossacks, nevertheless it was by so close a margin as to presage their ultimate downfall unless new and radical means were adopted.

While the July Revolution showed the Bolsheviks that their time had not quite come, it showed the Government that while they were not helpless yet they still were being surely undermined; and it showed the Allied Diplomats that unless conditions changed and changed radically Russia would soon be out of the war with all of the uncertainties and dangers which that would mean not alone for Russia, but for the world.

Lenin is believed to have fled to Kronstadt disguised as a sailor. Trotzky was arrested the following day but was soon freed upon demand of the Soviet. Soon after this temporary inconvenience he was allowed to proceed with his work of undermining the democratic government without hindrance of any kind.

Following is a statement by Prince Lvoff which appeared in the "Bourse Gazette"[11] of July 4th–17th, concerning this July Revolution:

---

[10] Kirochnaya Street, a block away from Furshtatskaya, where the naval attaché Walter S. Crosley resided (8).

[11] *Birzhevye Vedomosti* (Stock Exchange News), influential business newspaper. Founded in 1880, circulated daily from 1885, closed in October 1917.

The crisis in the Provisional Government, which developed in connection with the Ukrainian question,[12] was somewhat unexpected. Certain members of the Provisional Government supposed that certain misunderstandings and even disorders might be produced by this question, but at all events not in such an acute form. The cause of the crisis is properly not the Ukrainian question. This is only the pretext; the cause lies considerably deeper. It lies in the difference of the Socialist and bourgeois standpoints. Through their resignation from the Provisional Government the Cadets added the last touch to a sufficiently difficult situation: Owing to their resignation the impression is produced that the best organized portion of the Bourgeoisie, the spokesmen of which are the Cadets, is in opposition to the whole Government. There cannot be any question of discussing the persons who shall take place in the new Ministry. The program for immediate action of the new Government must be made clear and only thereafter would it be possible to call those individuals.

Rumors of the entire breaking up of the Provisional Government, which are agitating the population, are entirely unfounded. The Provisional Government, notwithstanding the resignation of some of its members who belong to the party of national freedom, continues to exist. The Provisional Government is animated only by its former endeavors to realize all the main lines of the Revolution and to bring the country to the Supreme Constituent Assembly which will settle the destiny of the country and the people. The agitation among the troops and the excesses that have taken place during the evening and the night will, I am convinced, cease by morning. Entire calm will very soon be restored. The majority of the garrison is on the side of the Provisional Government, and this is a guarantee that order will speedily be reestablished. The armed demonstration of military bodies is shameful and sad, and is not the result of the resignation of the Cadets from the Provisional

---

[12] The Ukrainian question arose after the February Revolution, when the Ukrainian Central Rada was created in Kiev on March 4, 1917, and demanded autonomy for the southwestern provinces of the former Russian Empire. On June 10, 1917, the Rada declared regional autonomy, which was recognized by the Russian Provisional Government with important reservations. This decision caused the July governmental crisis, which resulted in replacing Minister President Georgy E. Lvov with Alexander F. Kerensky. After the October Revolution, the Ukrainian People's Republic was proclaimed in Kiev on November 7, 1917, as part of the Russian federated state. The alternative Ukrainian Soviet Republic was created in Kharkov on December 12, 1917. On January 9, 1918, the Rada declared complete independence from Russia—but on January 27 (February 9), it signed a separate peace treaty with Germany and its allies at Brest-Litovsk, after which the country was occupied by German and Austro-Hungarian troops and actually turned into a German protectorate. After Germany's defeat in the World War, the Ukrainian Socialist Soviet Republic was established while the western part of the country was annexed to Poland.

Government. The immediate cause for these demonstrations must be sought in the fermentation produced among the troops of Petrograd by the reformation of the Regiment of Grenadiers. The crisis of the Provisional Government will be closed by the formation of a new coalition Cabinet.

During the outbreak some automobiles, armed with machine guns, went to the Warsaw station.[13] The soldiers sitting in them stated that they had been ordered to arrest the Minister of War. The soldiers, however, were too late. The train which carried the Minister of War to the front had left the station fifteen minutes before their arrival.

Other incidents of the Revolution reported by the Bourse Gazette were as follows:

At 9:40 p.m. an automobile armed with machine guns, with six armed and four unarmed men, drew up to Prince Lvoff's door. The men demanded the surrender of all the Ministers in the apartment, and stated that they requisitioned all the automobiles of the Provisional Government. This information was carried to the Ministers in session, Prince Lvoff, Tseretelli,[14] Chernou[15] and Nekrasoff. Tseretelli expressed the desire to speak with the men, but while he was going to the door the armed automobile disappeared. At ten o'clock the automobile reappeared and the Ministers could not be informed of it as one of the two automobiles of the Provisional Government standing by the door was seized and removed. It turned out to be the one belonging to Minister Tseretelli. To the porter who said that Tseretelli had asked that the motor should not be touched, they answered, "One automobile will do for me,"—During the evening Bolshevik soldiers requisitioned all the automobiles of the members of the Provisional Government, as well as all the motors in the garages of the former palace.

Late at night the Minister of Justice was informed that the printing presses of the Novoe Vremya[16] had been seized. The Minister of Justice applied for

---

[13] One of five Petrograd railway stations that provided communication with the western border. Before World War I, the Warsaw Station was the European gate of the Russian capital.

[14] Irakli G. Tsereteli (1881–1959), Georgian Social Democrat-Menshevik standing on a program of "revolutionary defensism." One of the most influential figures in the Petrograd Soviet, March–September 1917; minister of posts and telegraphs, May 5–July 24, 1917. After the October Revolution, he returned to Georgia, then emigrated abroad, went to the US in 1940, and died in New York City.

[15] Chernov (see n. 8, p. 109).

[16] *Novoe Vremia* (New Times), influential and widely read conservative daily newspaper published in St. Petersburg/Petrograd from 1868–1917.

assistance to the Commander of Troops, who replied, "The military authorities are powerless to take any measures."

Had the Provisional Government at this time arraigned Lenin and Trotzky and the other Bolshevik leaders, tried them for treason and executed them, Russia probably would not have been compelled to go through another revolution, would have been spared the reign of terror, and the loss from famine and murder of millions of her sons and daughters.

Prince Lvoff resigned from the Presidency of the Provisional Government shortly after this attempted revolution. He was not forced out, but broken-hearted and in despair over his country's plight, probably on account of the failure of his colleagues to mete out due punishment to Lenin and Trotzky and their like. The government may not have felt that it had the strength to do this, or may have feared the effect of executing Lenin and Trotzky would be to make martyrs of them and so strengthen their hold on their followers. Whatever may have been their reasons, I am persuaded now, as I felt at the time, that the government showed decided weakness. In fact, I so expressed myself at the time to the Minister of Foreign Affairs, Terestchenko. Drastic action might have precipitated the revolution which took place in the following November, but I am convinced in the light of subsequent events that whatever the immediate result, the consequences of executing Lenin and Trotzky would have been of benefit to Russia in the long run and would have produced less unrest than now prevails throughout the world. The Russian army was not then so demoralized as it became four months later. Korniloff and Alexieff[17] and Brousiloff and other brave soldiers were then living and the Intelligencia and Bourgeoisie had not been so decimated by famine and slaughter as they soon were.

Furthermore, I doubt whether two more as strong characters as Lenin and Trotzky could have been found among the Bolsheviks of the entire world.

---

[17] Mikhail V. Alekseev (1857–1918), general of infantry, chief of staff of the commander in chief of the Russian army, August 18, 1915–April 1, 1917; army commander in chief, April 1–May 21, 1917; chief of staff, August 30–September 9, 1917. After the October Revolution, he took part in the formation of the Volunteer Army in south Russia. He died on September 25, 1918.

Chapter XI

THE PROVISIONAL GOVERNMENT AND THE FORCES OF DESTRUCTION

Even though Lenin and Trotzky and their fellow conspirators had not been shot as traitors as they should have been, Lenin was a fugitive and was supposed to have fled to the ever-ready protection of Germany while Trotzky was under arrest. The Provisional Government had asserted itself even though all too feebly, had put down open insurrection, and restored a semblance of order. The most reassuring act of the Ministry, at least in my view, was the appointment of General Korniloff as Commander-in-Chief of all the Russian forces. He immediately began to restore discipline.

On August 7th, 1917, I wrote to Charles K. Moser, American Consul at Harbin, China,[1] a letter in which I commented on the new government in these terms:

> It is a Coalition Government in which all political parties are represented. Kerensky in addition to being President is also Minister of War, but under him Savinkoff is the Executive Head of the War Department[2] and Lebedev is Executive Head of the Navy.[3] Nekrasoff is nominal Minister of Finance,

---

[1] Charles Kroth Moser (1877–1968), businessman, journalist, lawyer. He entered the Consular Service in 1909 and served in Aden and Ceylon. He was appointed consul at Harbin (Manchuria) on June 24, 1914; assigned to Tiflis on September 8, 1919, and served there until March 1921.

[2] Boris V. Savinkov (1879–1925), one of the leaders of the Fighting Organization of the Party of Socialists-Revolutionaries; a war correspondent in France during the World War. He returned to Russia in April 1917; was assistant minister of war and navy, July–August 1917. After the October Revolution, he headed the Union for the Defense of the Motherland and Freedom, which led the struggle against the Bolsheviks.

[3] Vladimir I. Lebedev (1884–1956), graduate of a Russian infantry school; served in the Foreign Legion in France during the World War; lieutenant of the French army; military aide to Kerensky from May 1917; acting manager of the Navy Ministry from June 13, 1917. One of the organizers of the People's Army of the Samara government in 1918. After the Civil War, he emigrated abroad, went to the US in 1936, and died in New York City.

but the Director of the Department is Bernatsky, a University Professor,[4] and the Assistant Minister is a practical banker named Glasberg, a Jew of good standing.[5] So that there are fifteen Ministers and three additional executives. Kerensky, Nekrasoff and Terestchenko are all supposed to represent no parties. Of the remaining fifteen three are Social Democrats,[6] four are Social Revolutionists, two are National Socialists,[7] four are Cadets[8] and two are Radical Democrats.[9] I have not the time to explain the difference between these parties—don't think I could if I had the time. Of the fifteen Ministers, however, nine are Socialists and six are non-Socialists.[10]

Lenin is now a fugitive and is supposed to be in Germany. The Bolsheviks gave a so-called "peaceful demonstration of power" July 16th and 17th on the streets of Petrograd in which four hundred people were reported killed,

---

[4] Mikhail V. Bernatsky (1876–1943), professor of political economy, Constitutional Democrat, deputy of the Petrograd City Duma. Business manager of the Finance Ministry from July 24, 1917; minister of finance in the last Provisional Government from September 25, 1917. During the Civil War, he served as minister of finance in the governments of Generals Denikin and Wrangel.

[5] Valentin N. Glasberg.

[6] Members of the Russian Social Democratic Workers' Party. It was founded in 1898 but split in 1903 into two major factions—the Bolsheviks and the Mensheviks—which in the course of political strife developed into two independent parties. Members of the Provisional Government were Social Democrats-Mensheviks.

[7] Members of the Labor People-Socialist Party. It was created in June 1917 by way of merging the People-Socialist Party, which had split away from the Party of Socialists-Revolutionaries in 1906 with the Labor group of the State Duma, which had emerged the same year as a parliamentary faction.

[8] Kadets, members of the Constitutional Democratic Party.

[9] Members of the short-lived Russian Radical-Democratic Party, which was formed in mid-1917 by progressive deputies of the State Duma under the chairmanship of Ivan N. Efremov (1866–1945).

[10] The second coalition Provisional Government was formed on July 24, 1917, under the chairmanship of Alexander F. Kerensky. He himself was a Socialist Revolutionary along with Minister of Internal Affairs Nikolai D. Avksentev and Minister of Agriculture Viktor M. Chernov. Minister of Finance Nikolai V. Nekrasov was a Radical Democrat, as was Minister of State Charity Ivan N. Efremov. Social Democrats-Mensheviks were represented by Minister of Labor Matvey I. Skobelev and Minister of Posts and Telegraphs Aleksei M. Nikitin. Minister of People's Education Sergei F. Oldenburg, Minister of Ways of Communication Peter P. Iuren´ev, Ober-Procurator of the Most Holy Governing Synod Anton V. Kartashev, and State Controller Fyodor F. Kokoshkin were Kadets. Minister of Justice Alexander S. Zarudnyi and Minister of Provisions Aleksei V. Peshekhonov were National Socialists. Only Minister of Foreign Affairs Mikhail I. Tereshchenko and Minister of Trade and Industry Sergei N. Prokopovich represented no party.

of which seventy were Cossacks, but exactly the number of casualties has never been ascertained. The Bolsheviks are now in great disfavor, and their leaders are being arrested—one, Trotzky, was arrested yesterday; he was an exiled Russian Jew, who returned from America two or three months ago and immediately set his mouth going since which it has never ceased to operate. If we could keep such men in America they could be handled much better than they can be in Russia at the present time. Tseretelli, a well-poised Socialist who has been in the Ministry, has resigned and it is feared will be the leader of the Workingmen's and Soldiers' and Peasants' Deputies who are likely to oppose the new Government.

Kerensky is unquestionably the most influential man in Russia; some of his own people say he has it in mind to be a second Napoleon, consequently effort is being made to undermine him. He is only 34 years of age and if his head is not turned by the adulation he is receiving he is indeed a wonderful man. He is now living in the Winter Palace and sleeping in the bed of Alexander the Third, which is not good politically to say the least. He addressed last night the all-Russian Congress of Peasants[11] and when he told them he was appointed their President as Minister of the Interior they applauded him vigorously. Then he said: "I continue as President or Premier of the Government," whereupon the applause was terrific. I will make no prophecies concerning the future, which is uncertain. In Russia now it is presumption to prophesy in the forenoon what will occur in the afternoon.

Food is very scarce here and if at any time you can find a man who will bring me fifty pounds of breakfast bacon I would appreciate it and will promptly remit you not only the cost but will send you a souvenir in addition if you will tell me what there is in Petrograd you would like to have — always provided it is obtainable, as most of the stores here now are closed and those remaining open have very depleted stocks.

In a long letter written to my son David a week later, which was really a diary of four or five weeks of this critical period, I said:

The Minister of Foreign Affairs, Terestchenko, told me on his return from the front a few days ago, when I asked him about General Korniloff, the new Commander-in-Chief of the Russian Army, some most absorbing experiences of his. General Korniloff is a Cossack, a man of about 50 years of age, rather small of stature and not robust in appearance but with an iron constitution. He speaks seventeen languages and is thus able to address each

---

[11] The First All-Russian Congress of Soviets of Peasants' Deputies was held in Petrograd on May 4–28, 1917; the second one on November 26–December 10, 1917. There was no Peasants' Congress in July or August.

division and brigade and even each regiment in its own tongue. This makes him exceedingly popular. The Cossacks follow him around and are ever on the alert to protect him against possible danger or to do whatever they think will please him. If his constitution is iron, his will is steel. Soon after taking command he had one hundred deserters shot and their bodies stood up by the roadside with a placard on each reading, "I was shot because I ran away from the enemy and was a traitor to Russia.' When advised that several German and Austrian officers had surrendered, his suspicions were aroused and he ordered their knapsacks and effects searched. Literature in Russian was found, which had been printed in Germany, and advocating a separate peace along the lines of Bolshevik preachments which were demoralizing the army and which had for many weeks disturbed Petrograd and other cities throughout Russia. He ordered all of those officers shot and had their bodies stood up by the roadside also. General Korniloff was wounded in 1915 and taken a prisoner by the Austrians. When he recovered he put on the uniform of a private Austrian soldier and escaped. He walked 800 versts, about 600 miles. His linguistic accomplishments enabled him to talk to all the people whom he encountered in their own tongue. One night when he was being guided by an Austrian shepherd they both climbed a tree while a company of cavalry was passing. The shepherd showed General Korniloff a circular in the shepherd's language describing Korniloff, stating he had escaped from an Austrian prison, and offering fifty thousand Austrian crowns for his capture. The shepherd said that he would like very much to capture General Korniloff and get the fifty thousand crowns.

I met General Korniloff the day he resigned the command of the Petrograd Military District, of which he had been in charge since the first day of the Revolution. He told me in English that he did not like his position and was going to resign to go to the front. The papers next morning stated he had resigned. Upon going to the front he was given command of a brigade, but rapidly rose to be a divisional commander then a corps commander, next an army commander, and finally to be the Commander-in-Chief of all the Russian forces, which number at least ten million men. Russia has called into service over sixteen million men, but three or four million of them have been killed, are in hospitals or have deserted.

There was a meeting yesterday afternoon at the Narodni Dom, the largest auditorium in Petrograd.[12] All of the Ambassadors were invited to take loges,

---

[12] The People's House, a kind of popular educational institution often used for mass entertainments and political rallies. There were about twenty People's Houses in Petrograd in the early twentieth century. The largest was Narodny Dom, opened in 1900 at Alexandrovsky Park on Petrogradskaya Storona, which was able to accommodate about five thousand people. Attractions in the Dom's pleasure garden included a roller coaster and a railway train made

but the Japanese Ambassador and myself were the only ones in attendance. I arrived accompanied by my Naval Attache, Commander Crossley,[13] an hour or more after the exercises had begun and after Kerensky had spoken from his loge. After some difficulty experienced by the Russian officer who conducted me, I was shown to mine, whereupon Kerensky saluted me, and immediately came in a white uniform, with his aide, from his loge to mine and thanked me for attending. Very few in the immense audience knew me, but all of them knew Kerensky and when he pointedly made his way through the crowd to greet me the curiosity of the audience was aroused as to my identity. Kerensky only remained a few minutes and then left the building. Some minutes later Miliukoff was called to the platform, and made in Russian what I was told was an eloquent speech. During his talk he alluded to America's part in the war and pointed to the American Ambassador, whereupon there was great applause, the entire audience rising and continuing the ovation for several minutes. I arose and acknowledged the compliment and bowed but made no speech. There was a call for the American hymn but the band was compelled to admit it knew no distinctive American air....

Mrs. Pankhurst, the English Suffragist,[14] came to Petrograd about five or six weeks ago not for the purpose of fighting for votes for women, as suffrage had already been thrust upon the Russian women without any effort or expressed desire on their part, but for the purpose of counteracting the Bolshevik or separate peace influence and to infuse some courage into the Russian army which had been threatening to cease fighting and was opening debating societies not only at every front but in every division and brigade, and even in

---

in New York City. In the course of the 1917 Revolution, the Dom was used for great public gatherings, including the First All-Russian Congress of Peasants' Deputies. Francis visited the Dom on July 31 (August 13), 1917.

[13] Walter Selwyn Crosley (1871–1939) was assigned to duty as naval attaché at Petrograd on March 20, 1917, and arrived at the post on May 7 (April 24) with his wife Pauline S. Crosley. He was promoted to temporary captain on August 31, 1917. He left Petrograd on February 24, 1918, for Stockholm via Finland, where he gathered around him a group of American citizens fleeing from Russia. He was awarded with the Navy Cross "for distinguished service in the line of his profession as Naval Attaché at Petrograd, and for conducting a party of Americans out of Russia in April, 1918, under difficult and trying conditions." (Home of Heroes [website], "Navy Cross—WWI—US Navy A to C," https://homeofheroes.com/distinguished-service-cross/service-cross-world-war-i/navy-cross-world-war-i/navy-cross-wwi-navy/navy-cross-wwi-navy-a-to-c/.)

[14] Emmeline Pankhurst (1858–1928), a prominent English suffragette. She visited the US in 1916 and 1918 urging American support of the Allies against Germany. In between she visited Russia, trying to convince Russians to continue the war in British interests, June–September 1917.

every regiment. Mrs. Pankhurst held a meeting at Hotel Astoria,[15] where she was stopping, which was presided over by Mrs. McAllister Smith,[16] an American lady who had interested Lady Georgina Buchanan, the wife of the British Ambassador;[17] Mrs. Butler Wright, the wife of my Counselor,[18] and several other ladies. I attended the meeting as did the Italian Ambassador and the Roumanian Minister.[19] Mrs. Pankhurst was talking when I entered the room and quietly took a seat in the audience. I soon became interested in her remarks which were extremely sensible, being attracted by the intonations of her voice, by her easy delivery and most of all by her excellent choice of words.

Several days before the formation of the Coalition Ministry Mrs. Pankhurst, assisted by Mme. D. C., a Russian lady[20] (I would give her name but as she is still in Petrograd it might cause her trouble), obtained an audience with Kerensky[21]—Mrs. Pankhurst had requested me through a third party to secure this audience but I inquired why she did not have her own Ambassador do it and was told that she had asked Sir George Buchanan to secure the audience but he had refused, whereupon I declined also. Immediately after the audience this Russian lady came to the American Embassy and in a very nervous and excited manner, told me that Kerensky, in talking to herself and Mrs. P. (who could understand no Russian and K. could speak no English and very indifferent French), threatened to resign and she feared he would and become the leader of the Bolsheviks; that he said he would resign and let someone act who loved Russia more than he, if they could find any one. I asked my informant what she wished me to do. She replied: "Send

---

[15] Hôtel Astoria, the most luxurious and modern hotel in Petrograd, which opened at the end of 1912 on the corner of Morskaya Street and St. Isaac's Square. In the fall of 1915, it was sequestered and turned into the Petrograd Military Hotel. On February 28, 1917, the hotel was wrecked by the mutinous troops, and in the course of the October Revolution, seized by Bolshevik forces.

[16] Mercedes Lee Smith, wife of the representative of Guaranty Trust Company of New York in Russia.

[17] Born Lady Georgina Meriel Bathurst (1863–1922), daughter of Allen Bathurst, sixth Earl of Bathurst. She married Lord George W. Buchanan in 1885.

[18] The second wife of J. Butler Wright, born Harriet Rodman Southerland, who married him on May 27, 1916.

[19] Count Constantin Diamandy (1868–1931), Romanian diplomat, entered the Foreign Service in 1892 and served in Bulgaria and Italy; minister to Russia in 1913–18.

[20] Matilda de Cramm, Francis's acquaintance in Petrograd with a dubious reputation due to suspicion that she was a German spy.

[21] Kerensky received two ladies on July 21 (August 3), 1917.

for Miliukoff." I said he had no influence with Kerensky by whom he was forced out of the Ministry; she replied that she was aware of that, but that at an informal meeting of Duma members, Miliukoff had valiantly and ably defended Kerensky. I thereupon agreed to telephone Miliukoff and ask him to come to the American Embassy. He came and I related to him what I had heard and told him the source of my information; he listened attentively and after remarking that he was going to Moscow at 7:30 p.m. that evening (it was 6 p.m. when I was talking to him), he said he was not surprised at my narrative, as K. had arrived at the parting of the ways, and that if he remained as President of the Council of Ministers he must break with his old associates, and he was in consequence nervous and overwrought. I asked him if K. should resign who would form the ministry. He replied that K. was the only man to select a cabinet and the only one who could save Russia from a Bolshevik government. I mentioned Nekrasoff who was Vice-President of the Ministry, and Terestchenko Minister of Foreign Affairs, and Tseretelli a member of the Ministry, and holding the portfolio of the Interior, I think, and Tchernof,[22] Minister of Labor, but he said no one of those could cope with Lenin and Trotzky. "Well," I said to him, "you must postpone your Moscow trip and attend the meeting at the Winter Palace tonight." Whereupon M. consented to do so; in my judgment he was the real leader of the First Revolution, as I have said heretofore, and a sincere and zealous lover of Russia.

Miliukoff left the Embassy about 6:30. I went to the Foreign Office at 7, according to appointment with Terestchenko, and upon arrival was told that Kerensky had resigned about an hour and a half previous, and that the Council of Ministers would meet at 9 o'clock to act upon his resignation. The resignation was presented, and the Council of Ministers decided to call a conference of the leaders of all parties to confer about the situation. This meeting assembled in the Winter Palace about midnight and continued in session until 7:30 the next morning. Miliukoff was present and spoke several times—in fact seemed to be the guiding spirit of the meeting. The outcome assumed no definite shape but resulted in Kerensky being appealed to form a new Ministry. In the meantime Kerensky had left the city and only a few of his closest friends knew where he had gone or when he would return, if at all. By this time it was the morning of Saturday, August 4th. Kerensky returned to the city Sunday morning and began the formation of a new Ministry which was perfected about 4 p.m., Monday, August 6th, and announced in the papers the next morning. That is the present Ministry which met with general favor and has been growing in strength from that day to this. Having

---

[22] Chernov (see n. 8, p. 109).

confidence in this Ministry, I have recommended to my Government that an additional credit of sixty million dollars be extended to Russia.

It is impossible to tell to what extent this course of events was affected by the interview of Mrs. Pankhurst and this Russian lady with Kerensky. If, however, I had not seen Miliukoff he would probably have gone to Moscow as he had planned; Kerensky might possibly in that case have declined to form a Ministry and another less able and less worthy Government might have come into power.

It may be admissible to add here a few observations which I made in a letter written about this time in regard to the effect which it seemed to me the war was bound to have upon the position of women and of labor and in class distinctions. Obviously whatever interest these observations may have is derived chiefly from the fact that they were made in 1917 rather than in 1919. I said:

The experience of the past two and one-half years in the countries engaged in war has taught them many lessons valuable indeed, although in some instances very costly. I think this war has done more for woman than anything which has occurred since the birth of Christ. The teachings of the lowly Nazarene did more for woman than had ever been done in the history of the world up to that time. The demonstration made by woman of her ability to aid her country in difficulty and strife and in accomplishing a worthy end has been demonstrated in this war and hereafter whatever kind of peace may be negotiated, woman will be given more consideration and will be a more potential factor not only in the affairs and development of the government to which she owes fealty but in international affairs also. Woman has not had a position anywhere in the world that will compare with that which has been accorded her in America and in England. In Russia heretofore women have been treated as chattels merely, while in Germany they have been looked upon almost as beasts of burden, who were compelled to do not only common labor but the lowest forms of such labor and at times were obliged to work side by side with the dogs.

In the next place I think another result of this war will be to dignify labor of all kinds; every country has had to reckon with the labor interests whose rights as human beings many people have been disposed to ignore. In my judgment also another effect will be the abolition of class distinctions in countries where such distinctions still exist. There have fortunately never been any titles of nobility in America; Jefferson prevented that by his fight against the law of primogeniture, but they have survived in most European countries, and are not only a great injustice to all children after the first but preserve classes of nobility, the representatives of which are by no means worthy of the preeminence and good fortune that falls to their lot. After this war every man and every woman must by service show why he or she is given the privilege of living.

Chapter XII
THE BREAK BETWEEN KERENSKY AND KORNILOFF

Not long after the formation of the Coalition Ministry there were two Congresses held at Moscow—one the All-Russian Cossack Congress[1] and the other the All-Russian Congress of Soldiers and Workmen.[2]

When I mentioned these approaching Congresses to Minister of Foreign Affairs Terestchenko he said they would result in nothing except talk, but that the Government had nothing to fear from them. The forecast of the Minister seems to have been correct as far as it went, as indicated by the following comments on the Congresses and attendant conditions in Moscow received by me from Consul-General Summers at the time:

> The political situation here is interesting. General Korniloff arrived yesterday and there is much guessing at what he will do. The speech of Kerensky seems to have fallen flat, as he laid out no program nor did he make any new declarations. There was absolutely no disorder, and the local papers content themselves with giving the speeches of the orators. Only Korniloff's arrival appeared to interest the public. He was preceded through the main streets with an escort of twenty or thirty automobiles full of picturesque Cossacks and officers of the St. George Cavaliers. He was applauded everywhere. All day the streets were crowded with well-groomed soldiers and officers of the St. George Cavaliers. They were shown sympathy everywhere.

---

[1] The Second All-Cossacks Congress was held in Petrograd on June 7–19, 1917. It supported the Provisional Government and continuation of the war.

[2] The First All-Russian Congress of Soviets of Workers' and Soldiers' Deputies was held in Petrograd on June 3–24, 1917. It was dominated by Socialist Revolutionaries and Mensheviks, who led the majority for support of the Provisional Government. The congress created the All-Russian Central Executive Committee of Soviets, which was headed by Menshevik Nikolai S. Chkheidze. The only important gathering held in Moscow during the summer was the so-called Political Conference convened by the Provisional Government on August 12–15, 1917. In the opinion of one of its delegates, the conference demonstrated that "Russia is governed by unrealizable dream, ignorance, and demagogy." (*Gosudarstvennoe sovešanie.* (*Stenografičeskij otčet*). (Moskva-Leningrad: Gosudarstvennoe izdatel'stvo, 1930), 255.)

There can be no cooperation with the radical element on the part of the intelligencia of the country as long as all rights and opinions are trampled down. A man is not going to give up without a struggle all that he has and for which he has labored. There can be no cooperation between two parties one of which is doing its level best to destroy instead of construct all that stands for liberty, freedom and rights of men. Nor can there be any hope for a party which stands, for a moment, and more particularly at the present time, for any semblance of anarchism or insubordination. Who is it that is giving their lives at the present to their country? It is the body of officers constituting the conservative, patriotic backbone of the country, and not the anarchist who seems to have the upper hand at Petrograd. There is a wave of disgust at the manner in which the Government has been conducted up to the present, and to the incompetency and insincerity of the radical cabinets. This feeling is rapidly growing and is penetrating all soberly thinking people who do not now hesitate to organize against a further continuance of such comedies as have been pulled off at Petrograd. The Moscow people have received the conference with a coldness to be expected. The papers give the speeches of the politicians without a remark. The people themselves consider that the Moscow industrial and conservative element only can save the situation. They have no patience with empty words and misgovernments.

The foreign newspaper correspondents are of the opinion that the conferences have fallen flat and that the situation is just what it was before, or even more serious, as nothing has been done in the way of laying down a program. The Council of Workmen and Soldiers remained seated when the General-in-Chief of the Army arose to speak. This is considered here as a challenge to the military code of discipline.

Miliukoff's speech was not considered what it might have been or what the excited feelings of his party might have led one to believe that he would make. Korniloff's speech also was not considered as containing a challenge. There was, in summing up the whole matter, nothing done of any importance, each side only feebly declaring what a terrible state the country was in without giving the sick man any medicine. Moreover, as a Russian said to me this morning, it was a case where the sick man was being attended by disagreeing doctors. Woe to him, especially as the doctors are young and inexperienced in their profession.

Although both Congresses passed resolutions endorsing the Government these resolutions were so restrained and were carried with such lack of enthusiasm as to amount to "damning by faint praise."

The outlook in Russia at this time was indeed dark and had been growing steadily worse for several months. There was fraternization and mutiny at the front with strikes, pillage, robbery and famine in the rear. As if the situation was not in all conscience bad enough a tragic break between General Korniloff and Premier Kerensky, the two main pillars, upon whom what hope there was left for the salvation of Russia rested, occurred a few weeks later. By this added complication this stricken country was simultaneously threatened by ruthless foreign invasion, smoldering internal revolution and open civil war.

I have subsequently learned that the Kerensky-Korniloff break occurred in the following manner: V. N. Lvoff,[3] former Procurator of the Holy Synod[4] (who should not be confused with Prince Lvoff, former President of the Ministry), after several conversations with Kerensky, went to General Korniloff and proposed to him that he and Kerensky combine against the constantly and alarmingly growing power of the Bolsheviks, who were working through the Council of Workmen's, Soldiers' and Peasants' Deputies. While Lvoff did not specifically state to Korniloff that he represented Kerensky it is nevertheless probable that he allowed him to gain that impression. As a matter of fact, Kerensky had not authorized him to represent him, or to make such a proposal. He was acting entirely on his own responsibility. General Korniloff replied that he would enter into such an undertaking with Kerensky provided he, Korniloff, were placed at the head of the Government; that he would have no objection to Kerensky occupying his former post as Minister of Justice or to Savinkov being Minister of War.

Kerensky, amazed at this sweeping proposal, which came without warning or provocation as far as he was aware, called General Korniloff on the long distance telephone at his Military Headquarters and inquired whether Lvoff was his representative and authorized by him to make the proposal he had just made. Korniloff without even taking the precaution to ask Kerensky to state the proposal made by Lvoff replied in the affirmative. Kerensky, his pride wounded and greatly incensed, ordered Lvoff placed under arrest and notified General Korniloff that he was relieved of his command and should regard himself as under arrest. Korniloff, enraged at this reception of his reply to the proposal which, as he believed, had been sent him by Kerensky, retaliated by issuing a proclamation in which he announced his intention of marching his army against Petrograd and seizing the governmental power.

This action had the effect of leading Kerensky to turn to the Workmen's and Soldiers' Deputies for the support of his threatened Government and led him to make his final and fatal blunder of distributing arms and ammunition to the workingmen of Petrograd, in order that they might help to defend his tottering regime

---

[3] Vladimir N. Lvov (1872–1930), graduate of Moscow University, member of the Union of October 17, deputy of the Third and Fourth State Dumas. Member of the Provisional Committee of the State Duma, created during the February Revolution; ober-procurator of the Most Holy Governing Synod, March 7–July 24, 1917.

[4] The Most Holy Governing Synod, the highest administrative body of the Russian Orthodox Church from 1721 to 1918.

against Korniloff and his advancing army. In other words, he found himself in the predicament where he had to arm one group of virtual enemies of his Government in order to prevent its overthrow by another and more immediately threatening hostile group. After things had been brought to this pass the position of the Kerensky Government was hopeless. Its overthrow was only a matter of time. Had Lvoff been a wise and strong man instead of the meddlesome rattle-brain that he was, and had Kerensky been big enough to place his country's welfare above his own pride and seek some middle ground upon which he and Korniloff might have worked against the Bolsheviks—their common enemies—they might between them have rescued Russia and the world from the curse of Bolshevism; and have given the Constituent Assembly, the time for convening of which had already been fixed, a chance to establish a government based upon the consent of the governed, instead of upon force as was the Czar's government, and as is that of Lenin and Trotzky.

In the conferences held by the Allied Ambassadors in reference to the Kerensky-Korniloff embroglio[5] I steadily maintained, and succeeded in persuading my fellow diplomats to accept my view, that we should preserve a neutral attitude. I argued that should Korniloff be successful it would not mean a restoration of the Monarchy, but merely a new administration and a more vigorous prosecution of the war. If, on the other hand, as I said in my letter to Judge Priest,[6] Russia should be forced out of the war through Kerensky's failure to restore discipline in the army, the Allied diplomats would receive and deserve severe censure for having aided Kerensky to eliminate Korniloff. If, on the contrary, we were to support Korniloff and he should fail we would obviously find ourselves in an impossible position with relation to the Kerensky Government.

In a letter written at the time to Judge Henry S. Priest, of St. Louis, I commented thus on the situation:

> We are now in the midst of a counter-revolution which appears to have failed. By counter-revolution I do not mean a restoration of the monarchy but the reaction against the present Provisional Government which many think is Socialistic in its spirit if not in its policies. General Korniloff who has been Commander-in-Chief for about two months past made demands of the

---

[5] Or Kornilov Affair, the armed movement led by Commander in Chief of the Russian army Lavr G. Kornilov against the Provisional Government on August 25–31, 1917. Its aims were to restore strong government, rehabilitate discipline in the army, and bring Russia out of the revolutionary crisis. Minister President Alexander F. Kerensky approved the program unofficially, but in the midst of events changed his mind, proclaiming Kornilov a mutineer and dismissing him from the post. The outcome was the fatal decline of Kerensky's authority and new rise of influence of the Bolsheviks, who played an active part in resisting the Kornilov forces.

[6] Henry Samuel Priest (1853–1930), a judge of the US District Court for the Eastern District of Missouri, 1894–95.

Provisional Government for powers which were not granted him although they should have been as they were essential to the restoration of discipline among the soldiers who are still maintaining committees and "commissaires," as they are called, who interfered with the orders of the Commander-in-Chief and with the sentences of courts martial. You would inveigh against these conditions if you were in my place much more vigorously than I have, and I am feeling to-night as if some expressions I have made to the Government within the past few days might possibly result in my being looked upon as persona non grata. Being over six thousand miles away from Washington with very irregular cable connection and most unreliable and uncertain mail communication I am often compelled to act solely upon my own judgment. I always cable to the Government what I have done but sometimes act without instructions.

To-day at a meeting in the Foreign Office of the British, Italian, French[7] and American Ambassadors with Terestchenko, Minister of Foreign Affairs, I took issue on a matter concerning which the four others agreed, but requested the British Ambassador, as Dean of the Diplomatic Corps, to call a meeting of the Allied representatives or the heads of Missions representing the governments of the Entente. They are eleven in number and had met last Monday afternoon and agreed upon an expression of their views and a tender of their services to the Government in its controversy with General Korniloff. The British Ambassador presented this expression to the Foreign Office and phoned me about noon yesterday that it would be given to the afternoon papers. It did not appear and at 9:30 p.m. I received an autograph note from the British Ambassador that the Minister of Foreign Affairs had concluded not to publish the action of the Allied representatives because such action put General Korniloff on a "par with the Government," but that he would publish a statement in the morning papers giving our position and our efforts "to clear the situation." When I reached the Foreign Office at 12:30 to-day I found those three Ambassadors in conference with the Ministers and learned they had agreed upon a statement for the press in which they wished my concurrence. It was in French and, although I understood it, I told them I wished to consider it before giving assent to its publication, and suggested to the British Ambassador that he should call another meeting of the eleven Allied representatives by whom the expression of the Allies was originally framed. By this time it was after one o'clock and the British Ambassador asked me if I could attend a meeting at half past two. I replied that I could attend immediately, but he said that he must have his luncheon (English, wasn't it?).

---

[7] Joseph Noulens (1864–1944), French politician, minister of war, 1913–14; minister of finance, 1914. Ambassador to Russia, 1917–19. Arrived in Petrograd on July 2 (15), 1917.

I went to the British Embassy[8] at 2:30 p.m. and found there only the British, Italian and French Ambassadors and upon inquiry was told that no others had been invited. I then stated my position, which was that we should insist upon the Minister of Foreign Affairs giving to the press the expression originally framed by the Allied representatives. I was met with the argument that these are the days of censorship and that if the Russian Government refused to give our statement to the press we should have no redress. I replied that we could have in any case the satisfaction of stating our views, and by this and other arguments finally induced my colleagues to insist upon the Minister of Foreign Affairs giving to the press the conclusions of the Monday meeting, omitting merely the word "mediation"' which did not lessen or impair the force of the statement. Sir George Buchanan said he would call upon the Minister of Foreign Affairs and ask the publication of the original statement. We also instructed Sir George to inform the Minister that if he did not give out this statement for publication we would.

My objection to being misrepresented in addition to the principles involved was that the statement which Terestchenko wished to give out concerning our action placed us in the position of aiding the Provisional Government to suppress Korniloff, which we had not done.

Korniloff phoned at 3:30 this morning that he would surrender, consequently the Provisional Government is stronger than it was before. If, however, it does not immediately restore discipline in the army, Russia's part in this war will be henceforth ineffective and in fact absolutely futile. In such event the causes leading to such condition will become known and will be viewed with a critical eye. If the Allied representatives should permit the impression that they aided the defeat of Korniloff to prevail they would receive and merit severe censure. I used these and other arguments with my colleagues to-day, and although the position taken may produce strained relations with the Kerensky Government, I prefer such situation to the credit of aiding the Provisional Government to condemn as a traitor, and perhaps to convict, a brave soldier and patriot whose mistake was making demands before public sentiment was sufficiently strong in their favor to force their acceptance.

I have not yet lost all hope for Russia, as the Provisional Government can still save the situation if it takes prompt and decisive steps to restore the discipline of the army and navy. I remained with the Minister of Foreign Affairs to-day after my colleagues had left and had with him a very plain talk. In answer to his statement that Russia or any sovereignty would object to the interference of any outside governments in their internal affairs I stated that

---

[8] From 1863, the British embassy had its residence at the mansion of Prince Saltykov in the Dvortsovaya Embankment, 4/Millionnaya Street, 3.

while such a position would be tenable under ordinary circumstances the situation in Russia at this time is peculiar. Russia is one of a number of Allies who are fighting a common enemy and Russia is asking and receiving very material assistance. I furthermore stated that I felt the responsibility of keeping my Government advised concerning the conditions in the country to which I am accredited and of giving my best judgment as to the proper policy to pursue.

It is unnecessary, however, to tire you any longer with this narrative, as I have just received a note from the British Ambassador saying that the Minister has complied with our request and given to the press for publication to-morrow morning the exact expression formulated by the Allied representatives September 10th.

In a letter written my son Perry the next day, I said:

By a telephone talk with Terestchenko, Minister of Foreign Affairs, I learn that the report received an hour ago of an agreement between the Government and General Korniloff is untrue. The Minister claims that a division ordered by General Korniloff to attack Petrograd has abandoned the General and is giving allegiance to the Government. My Military[9] and Naval Attaches contend, however, that Korniloff will undoubtedly dominate the situation. The Provisional Government has been weak in that it has failed to restore discipline in the army and has given too much license to the ultra-Socialistic sentiment whose champions are called "Bolsheviks."[10]

---

[9] William Voorhees Judson (1865–1923), graduate of the US Military Academy, served in the Corps of Engineers of the US Army; captain, US military observer on the Russian side during the Russo-Japanese War, 1904–05. He was promoted to colonel on May 15, 1917, and designated military attaché to the Root Mission. On June 26 (July 9), 1917, he was assigned to duty as military attaché to the US embassy at Petrograd as well as "chief of the American Military Mission to Russia, observer in connection with military operations in which Russia is engaged, and the military representative of the United States Government in all matters connected with the supply to Russia of materials and personnel for use during the war." (Neil V. Salzman, ed, *Russia in War and Revolution: General William V. Judson's Accounts from Petrograd, 1917–1918* (Kent, OH: Kent State University Press, 1998), 43–44.) He was promoted to temporary brigadier general of the National Army on July 23 (August 5), 1917; left Petrograd for Washington on January 10 (23), 1918.

[10] Members of the Bolshevik Party. Originally it was a faction of the Russian Social Democratic Workers' Party (RSDWP), which split from the rest of the party at its second congress in 1903. Its members were labeled "Bolsheviks," from a Russian word meaning "majority," because they received the support of the majority of the delegates. The opposing faction was called the Mensheviks, from a Russian word meaning "minority." Under Lenin's leadership, the Bolsheviks turned into a party of "professional revolutionaries." In 1912, they declared themselves a separate party, the RSDWP(b), which was commonly referred to as the Bolshevik Party. In March 1918, it was renamed the Communist Party.

I further commented upon this complicated situation in a letter written at the time to American Consul Mosher[11] at Harbin, China, in which I said:

> The air is full of rumors and general fear is entertained of a Bolshevik outbreak. The British Embassy and Consulate are said to have given notice to all British subjects to leave Russia. It is also reported that the Scandinavian Legations have given all of their subjects advice to do likewise. Many Americans are frightened and that condition prevails somewhat in the Embassy and in the Consulate also. I do not partake of it in the slightest degree, as I feel no concern about my personal safety, nor do I anticipate that the Embassy itself will be attacked. In compliance with the repeated appeals of some members of the Embassy Staff, and of other members of the Colony, I have, however, chartered a small steamboat upon which Americans who so desire can take refuge in the event disturbances should occur. I shall remain in Petrograd as long as the Government does, and perhaps longer, as there is some doubt expressed as to the survival of the present Government. The failure of General Korniloff's attempted overthrow of the Government has resulted in strengthening Kerensky, and the appointment of Alexieff as Commander-in-Chief inspires us with hope, however faint it may be, that the Provisional Government will make some effort to put the army again in fighting condition. At this writing General Korniloff is said to be demanding terms for the surrender of himself and his Chief of Staff, Lukomsky.[12] The whole situation may be changed to-morrow or before night. I was informed by the Foreign Office yesterday noon that General Korniloff had phoned at 3:30 a.m. on the 12th to know to whom he should surrender. Russia is certainly going through a severe ordeal, and if she should go out of the war the whole burden of the contest will fall upon the United States and would cost untold millions of treasure and probably millions of American lives.
>
> The movement of General Korniloff resulted in failure because it was ill advised, inopportune and was against the only recognized constituted authority in Russia. General Korniloff's reasoning that the Government was under Bolshevik influence was denied by its president, Kerensky, who immediately ordered Korniloff to relinquish command of the army and directed Alexieff, his successor, to arrest him. The present status is that Korniloff is under arrest

---

[11] Moser (see n. 1, p. 120).

[12] Alexander S. Lukomsky (1868–1939), lieutenant general, chief of staff of the commander in chief of the Russian army, June 3–August 29, 1917. Along with Generals Alekseev and Kornilov, he took part in the formation of the Volunteer Army and fought the Bolsheviks in south Russia till February 1920.

THE BREAK BETWEEN KERENSKY AND KORNILOFF

awaiting trial. Alexieff has resigned and a new Minister of War, Verkhovsky,[13] has been installed, whose policy is broad and liberal, and whose expressions have convinced the Soviet of his devotion to the cause of the Revolution and have resulted in the lessening of the hold of the Soviet over that large portion of the army which was a menace not only to the Government but to the preservation of order. After the failure of Korniloff this is the only policy that contains any hope for the salvation of Russia and her continuance in the war. It may be that the Korniloff fiasco was a blessing in disguise. Verkhovsky is a young man, 34 years of age, who was a Lieutenant-Colonel in command of the Moscow District when Korniloff defied the Government and threatened the arrest of all the Ministers. Korniloff sent for Verkhovsky and gave him orders to that effect, but he defied Korniloff and said that he would be loyal to the Provisional Government. Kerensky, who is President of the Council of Ministers and Commander-in-Chief of the Army, has issued orders putting into effect the policies of Verkhovsky.

In a letter to Judge Priest already quoted, I said of this period:

It is my intention to remain in the Embassy and if the Russian Government cannot protect me and the residence of the representative of the Government which is extending such moral and material aid to Russia, then I shall defend myself and the property of my country from the mob. Don't understand me as meaning that I shall go on the street and defy a bloodthirsty pillaging crowd, but I shall remain in the Embassy, and if the doors are broken in in face of my remonstrance I shall not attempt to escape.

The National Democratic Conference was called to meet in Petrograd on December 25th.[14] It was not recognized by the Government, but Foreign Minister Terestchenko told me that the Government had no fear of this Congress which was called by the Soviet for the purpose of forming a Government to administer the affairs of Russia pending the meeting of the Constituent Assembly.

---

[13] Alexander I. Verkhovsky (1886–1938), Socialist Revolutionary, colonel, commanding officer of the Moscow Military District from May 31, 1917. He was promoted to major general and appointed minister of war on August 30, but resigned on October 20, 1917. He later joined the Red Army.

[14] The All-Russian Democratic Conference was convened by the All-Russian Central Executive Committee of Soviets on September 14–22, 1917.

In a letter of September 24th to my friend, Walter Williams, of Columbia, Missouri,[15] I said of the then prevailing conditions:

> The greatest menace to the present situation is the strength of the Bolshevik sentiment which, intoxicated with its success (attributable in no small degree to the failure of the Korniloff movement), may attempt to overthrow the present Provisional Government and administer affairs through its own representatives. If such condition should eventuate, failure will undoubtedly ensue in a short time, but meanwhile there may be bloodshed, of which there has been remarkably little since the beginning of the revolution, when taking into consideration all of the circumstances. Another menace of which I have evidence while dictating this letter is the scarcity of food in Petrograd; just across the street is a bread line of several hundred people, who stand for hours and are sometimes told thereafter that the supply is exhausted. In walking yesterday afternoon we overheard a woman whom we passed, and who was talking with considerable emphasis, say, "I have asked for bread so often and have been refused it that now I am going to demand it." These manifestations indicate bread riots. There is no scarcity of food in Russia but very imperfect, inadequate and insufficient transportation facilities.

As I said also at the time in a dispatch to the Secretary:

> Food is very difficult to procure here now and is commanding exorbitant figures; in front of the Embassy I counted to-day about 200 people in a bread line, many of whom after waiting four to six hours were told the supply was exhausted. This is one of many such in every section of the city.

About this time hand bills, of which the accompanying is a copy, were widely distributed throughout the city. They read:

---

[15] Walter Williams (1864–1935), journalist, newspaper editor, founder and the first dean of the School of Journalism at the University of Missouri (1908). It was the first institution of its kind in the world, so Walter Williams is considered the "Father of Journalism Education."

THE BREAK BETWEEN KERENSKY AND KORNILOFF

PROTEST MEETING

(Free) America wants to execute a Russian emigrant, Revolutionist, Alexander Berkman.[16] All the Soldiers and Workers of Petrograd must attend a Mass Meeting which will be held in Circus Moderne on Sunday, September 17th (30th), at 7 p.m., to find out how this (free) country deals with its revolutionists.
Admittance free.

I sent a representative to this meeting who made this report on what took place: A resolution was passed to the following effect:

The Soldiers and Workers of Petrograd, assembled on the 17th of September, at the Circus Moderne, having received reports of the state of things in the United States, energetically protest against methods of the so-called "free" republic of North America in its repressive measures against true friends of the liberation movement, and fighters for the peace of all nations.

The Soldiers and Workers of Petrograd send their fraternal greetings to the revolutionists Goldman[17] and Berkman and all those who in "free" America fight for the social revolution, and they demand in the name of free speech and free press, which are supposed now to be the foundation of free society, the immediate release of our revolutionist friends, and the abolition of all provocative measures of the United States Government against internationalist measures which remind one of the best days of Russian Tsardom. This meeting addresses itself to the Council of Workmen and Soldiers as well as to the Central Committee of the Councils, requesting it to send effective protest to the American authorities against persecution of men and women whose only crime is doing in their country, against autocracy, what Russian workers have done here against autocracy....

There were about six thousand present at the meeting, counting 200 for each of the sixteen sections of the amphitheater and 3,000 for the arena. In

---

[16] Alexander Berkman (1870–1936), a Russian-born political activist who emigrated to the US to become one of the leading figures in the American anarchist movement. He opposed the US entry into the World War, was arrested, found guilty of conspiring to obstruct the operation of the selective service law, and sentenced to two years in jail. In 1919, he was deported to Soviet Russia together with Emma Goldman. Disappointed with Soviet reality, he returned to America in 1922.

[17] Emma Goldman (1869–1940), a Russian-born political activist who emigrated to the US to become one of the leading figures in the American anarchist movement. She opposed the US entry into the World War, was arrested with Alexander Berkman, convicted of conspiring to obstruct the operation of the military draft, and sentenced to two years' imprisonment. In 1919, she was deported to the Soviet Russia together with Berkman, but was disillusioned with Soviet experiment and left Russia in 1921.

addition to this there were a great many people coming and going, so that it would probably not be wrong to say that 8,000 saw all or part of the meeting.

Shotoff, an anarchist and former agitator in America,[18] was the chief speaker.

I have reason to believe that John Reed[19] brought over the story of the proposed execution of Berkman (as far-fetched a tale as has ever been made the subject of an appeal to the mob). Also that he obtained exclusion of the Associated Press from the democratic congress on the ground of their "capitalistic" character. I have also learned that he has been expelled from England and France and from Russia under the old regime.

The Kronstadt sailors, 11,000 in number, passed a resolution similar to the one above.

A petition to request immediate action on the case of Berkman will be presented to the Soviet and the American Ambassador.

The John Reed referred to had come to the Embassy about a month before this time with a letter of introduction from a prominent federal official of New York:

New York, August 17, 1917.

Dear Mr. Ambassador:

I want to present to you my old friends, Mr. and Mrs. Jack Reed,[20] both of whom are of the American newspaper world and are visiting Russia with a view to studying conditions.

---

[18] Vladimir S. Shatov (1887–1943), Russian revolutionary who emigrated to the US in 1906 and joined the Industrial Workers of the World. He returned to Russia in July 1917 and became one of the leaders of the Union of Anarcho-Syndicalist Propaganda. A member of the Military-Revolutionary Committee, he took an active part in the October Revolution and closely cooperated with the Bolsheviks afterwards.

[19] John Reed (1887–1920), American journalist and socialist activist, war correspondent in Europe during the World War. He arrived in Petrograd in September 1917 with his wife, fellow journalist Louise Bryant, to report upon developments in the Russian Revolution. He became an eyewitness of the fall of the Winter Palace and victory of the October Revolution. After returning home, he grew agitated with Soviet power. He arrived back in Russia by the end of 1919, died in Moscow, and was buried at the Kremlin wall.

[20] Louise Bryant (born Anna Louise Mohan, 1885–1936), an American journalist and writer who married John Reed in 1916. She visited Russia as a representative of the Bell Syndicate to report on the war and revolution "from a woman's point of view."

Any courtesy at any time which you and the gentlemen of the Embassy may extend to them will be deeply appreciated by,

                                  Yours faithfully,

                                  "———"

On October 1st, I sent the following cable to the Secretary of State in reference to Reed:

Sept. 18/Oct. 1, 1917.

Secstate,
Washington,
    Reliably informed that John Reed, holder of American Passport No. ———, cordially welcomed by Bolsheviks whom he apparently advised of his coming. Lost pocketbook soon after arrival which found delivered Consulate containing letter from Hillquit[21] introducing Reed to Huymans,[22] Secretary of the Stockholm Conference.[23]

    Think Bolsheviks' information concerning Berkman obtained through Reed and William Shotoff. Understand Reed secured passport upon affidavit was not going Stockholm Conference. Presented personal letter to me from ——— (a prominent federal official), presenting "my old friends, Mr. and Mrs. Jack Reed" and bespeaking courtesies. Endeavoring to ascertain inspiration of Protest Meeting. Shotoff been in America much past twenty years. Returned Russia recently is now Secretary of some Soviet Committee. Please give record of both.

The lost pocketbook referred to contained the following letter of endorsement:

---

[21] Morris Hillquit (1869–1933), a Russian-born labor activist, one of the founders and leaders of the Socialist Party of America.

[22] Camille Huysmans (1871–1968), Belgian socialist politician, secretary of the International Socialist Bureau of the Second International, 1905–22.

[23] An informal international socialist gathering, which was inspired largely by the February Revolution in Russia. It was called by the Petrograd Soviet and Dutch-Scandinavian Organizing Committee to discuss "socialist peace." Invitations were formally issued by the All-Russian Congress of Soviets in June 1917. The intended conference actually degenerated into a series of meetings of socialist delegates, who arrived in Stockholm in September 1917.

Stockholm, Sept. 9, 1917.

Hellano Scandinavian Socialist Committee,[24]
I beg to recommend to you very warmly the citizen John Reed, member of the Socialist Party of the United States, editor of the socialist publication, *New York Call.*

He is recommended to me especially by the citizen Mr. Hillquit, delegate of the United States to the International Socialist Bureau.[25]

Huymans,
Secretary of the Stockholm Conference.

The personal note also contained in the pocketbook was addressed to "Dear Sally" and the whole enclosed in an envelope addressed to Mrs. ——, —— Croton-on-Hudson, New York, and read in part:

There may be a possibility for me to make money here, so tell —— not to send me any more money until I cable, but then to do it quick or whatever else I ask him to do with it. I do not think my benefactors are going to lose much on this trip of mine.

After these disclosures I naturally regarded Mr. Reed as a suspicious character and had him watched and his record and acts investigated. To an agent of mine he expressed these views and made these statements:

Says —— "He is Socialist. Believes that the Workmen can manage the factories themselves. Some works are being run by them with a great deal of success. The newspapers only mention the failures. Barring the Cadets—the Bolsheviks are the only Party with a program. The other factions of the Socialistic Party are at sea in regards to a policy and program. Though the Russian workman has not reached the same high standard of efficiency of the American—he is farther advanced in politics and in political thought."

Says —— "That if the workmen were paid in proportion to their labor they would get all the profits. Instead of shutting down, the works should be compelled to furnish the material, or to turn the factories over to the workmen." Was at the all-night session of the Democratic meeting held in the Alexander

---

[24] Organizing Committee of the Stockholm Conference, a Dutch-Scandinavian committee that consisted of socialists from neutral states.

[25] Permanent executive body of the Second (Labor) International established in 1900 with the secretariat in Brussels.

Theater.[26] Seemed to know all about what took place there. Says that if the Bolsheviks get control of the Government the very first thing they would do would be to kick out all the Embassies and all those connected with them. Vesey's[27] paper (*The Russian Daily News*, printed in English) is liable to be closed any day as he is playing up to the American Embassy and in favor of the Cadets. The Embassies are interfering too much with the internal politics of the country. Mentioned the Marx theory. Apparently knows a great deal about all the Socialistic factions here.

Thus at this time were the American Bolsheviks coming to the aid of Russian Bolsheviks in their efforts to overthrow the democratic government of Russia just as now the Russian Bolsheviks are coming to the aid of American Bolsheviks, in their efforts to overthrow our democratic government. In a letter of October 13th to my son Perry, I said:

The air is always full of rumors here concerning plots of the Bolsheviks, but the outbreaks that are prophesied seem never to occur—it is only the unexpected that happens here. I heard a few days ago that the Bolsheviks had made a list of people whom they intended to kill, and that, while the British Ambassador heads the list, I am not many removes from the top. I do not believe this and consequently I am not regulating my actions or movements accordingly.

And in a later letter I observed:

The Bolsheviks are said to be armed and organized for a demonstration, which means "shooting up the town" in our western vernacular. I may be in danger but do not feel so any more than I did when that mob on the Nevsky, with a black flag, was advancing to attack the Embassy.

---

[26] The Alexandrinsky Theater near Nevsky Prospekt was built in 1828–32 and named after Empress Alexandra Fyodorovna, Nicholas I's wife. Now the Drama Theater, named after Alexander S. Pushkin.

[27] Harry Custis Vezey (1873–1939), businessman from Philadelphia and importer of American goods into Russia. Private secretary to Ambassador George von Lengerke Meyer, 1905–07; secretary to the American delegation to the Second Peace Conference at The Hague, 1907; vice and deputy consul general at St. Petersburg, 1908–14; later translator and unofficial adviser for the embassy. He was removed to Harbin in 1918.

Chapter XIII
THE BOLSHEVIKS OVERTHROW THE GOVERNMENT

On October 11th, O.S., 1917, Kerensky issued this his last appeal to the Russian people to support his Government and its policies until the Constituent Assembly could be convoked:

> Great confusion has once more been brought into the life of our country. In spite of the swift suppression of the revolt of General Korniloff, the shocks caused by it are threatening the very existence of the Russian Republic.
>
> Waves of anarchy are sweeping over the land, the pressure of the foreign enemy is increasing, counter-revolutionary elements are raising their heads, hoping that the prolonged governmental crisis, coupled with the weariness which has seized the entire nation, will enable them to murder the freedom of the Russian people.
>
> Great, boundless is the responsibility of the Provisional Government, on whom devolves the historic task of bringing Russia to a state where the convocation of the Constituent Assembly will be possible. The burden of this responsibility is alleviated only by the deep conviction that, united by the common desire to save the fatherland and to protect the achievements of the Revolution, the representatives of all classes of the Russian people will understand the necessity for cooperation with the Provisional Government in establishing a firm governmental power, capable of realizing the urgent demands of the country, and bringing it, without further upheavals, to the Constituent Assembly, the convocation of which, it is the deep conviction of the Provisional Government, cannot be postponed for one day.
>
> Leaving to the Constituent Assembly, the sovereign master of Russia, the final solution of all great questions on which the welfare of the Russian people depends, the Provisional Government, the personnel of which has now been completed, holds that only by carrying out energetically a series of resolute measures in all spheres of the life of the State, will it be able to fulfill its duty and satisfy the urgent needs of the nation.
>
> In the firm conviction that only a general peace will enable our great fatherland to develop all its creative forces, the Provisional Government will continue incessantly to develop its active foreign policy in the spirit of the demo-

cratic principles proclaimed by the Russian Revolution. The Revolution has made these principles a national possession, its aim being to attain a general peace—a peace excluding violence on either side.

Acting in complete accord with the Allies, the Provisional Government will, in the next few days, take part in the conference of the Allied Powers. At this conference the Provisional Government will be represented, among other delegates, by one who particularly enjoys the confidence of the democratic organizations.

At this conference our representatives, together with the solution of common questions and military problems, will strive towards an agreement with the Allies on the ground of the principles proclaimed by the Russian Revolution.

Striving for peace, the Provisional Government will, however, use all its forces for the protection of the common, Allied cause, for the defense of the country, for resolute resistance to any efforts to wrest national territory from us and impose the will of any foreign power on Russia, and for the repulsion of the enemies' troops from the borders of the fatherland.

For the purpose of securing for the revolutionary authorities close contact with the organized public forces and thus imparting to the Government the necessary stability and power, the Provisional Government will in the next few days work out and publish a decree establishing a Provisional Council of the Republic, which is to function until the Constituent Assembly convenes. This Council, in which all classes of the population will be represented and in which the delegates elected to the Democratic Conference will also participate, will be given the right of addressing questions to the Government and of securing replies to them in a definite period of time, of working out legislative acts and discussing all those questions which will be presented for consideration by the Provisional Government, as well as those which will arise on its own initiative. Resting on the cooperation of such a council, the Government, preserving in accordance with its oath, the unity of the governmental power created by the Revolution, will regard it its duty to consider the great public significance of such a council in all its acts up to the time when the Constituent Assembly will give full and complete representation to all classes of the population of Russia.

Standing firmly on this program, which expresses the hopes of the people, and calling upon all for immediate and active participation in the preparations for the convocation of the Constituent Assembly in the shortest period of time, the Provisional Government presumes that all citizens of Russia will now rally closely to its support for concerted work, in the name of the basic and paramount problems of our time, the defense of the fatherland from the foreign enemy, the restoration of law and order and the leading of the country to the sovereign Constituent Assembly.

A. Kerensky,
Prime Minister.

As if in brazen response to this appeal appeared the announcement by the Bolsheviks, Volodarsky[1] and Maninef,[2] of the formation of a Military Revolutionary Committee organized to seize the power of the Government.[3]

On the 19th of November, 1917, following the downfall of the Provisional Government and upon the usurpation of control by the Bolsheviks, I issued this address:

To the People of Russia:

I address you because there is no official in the Foreign Office with whom I can communicate, and all of the members of the government or ministry with which I had official relations are inaccessible, being in flight or in prison, according to my best information.

When, on March 5th–18th, 1917, six days after your memorable revolution began, and three days after the Provisional Government was named, and before I had received official notice of its appointment, I cabled to my Government earnestly requesting authority to aid the revolution by recognizing the new government at a critical juncture of its existence. I had no thought that within the short period of seven months you would be engaged in civil strife as you are to-day, and so divided that the liberty for which you had striven and suffered for so many generations would be so endangered as it is at present. Within four days I received instructions from Washington to recognize the Provisional Government, and did so promptly and in the most impressive manner I could command, on March 9th–22nd.

Fifteen days thereafter (March 20th–April 4th) President Wilson sent a message to the American Congress, recommending that a state of war be declared to exist between the United States and the imperial government of Germany. That immortal message electrified the people of my country and

---

[1] V. Volodarsky (Moisei Markovich Goldstein, 1891–1918), Jewish-Ukrainian revolutionary, emigrated to the US, 1913–17; member of the American Socialist Party. Returned to Russia in May 1917, elected to the Petrograd City Duma and Petrograd Soviet, joined the Bolsheviks in July, led propaganda work in Petrograd. Killed by an SR terrorist in June 1918.

[2] Probably Vyacheslav M. Molotov (1890–1986), chief of the Agitation Division of the Petrograd Military Revolutionary Committee.

[3] An extraordinary body of the Petrograd Soviet created in mid-October 1917 to facilitate the revolutionary defense of Petrograd. Used by the Bolsheviks and their allies for the overthrow of the Provisional Government in the course of the October Revolution.

thrilled the lovers of liberty throughout the world—especially in Russia—by its deeply-moving allusion to the heart of the Russian people.

The Congress promptly responded to the appeal, and very soon thereafter I cabled my Government urging the extension of a credit of $500,000,000 to Russia, to enable her the more vigorously to prosecute the war against Germany whose success would mean the loss of the dearly bought freedom of the Russian people. Up to the beginning of the present revolution, credits had been extended to Russia to the extent of $256,000,000 by the United States Government, and a cable sent by myself two days before the beginning of the present revolution recommended an additional advance of $100,000,000.

Almost immediately, President Wilson appointed a diplomatic mission to Russia under the chairmanship of Honorable Elihu Root, to express the good will of my country, and to extend encouragement to the Russian people in the bold stroke they had made for liberty. The factories of the United States, subordinating domestic needs to the necessities of Russia, at once devoted their energies and resources to the manufacture of munitions, railroad equipment and other requirements of your country. Soon thereafter American Red Cross missions were dispatched to Russia and Roumania[4] to minister to the sufferings of a people enervated by years of struggle and, for this voluntary offering, no compensation or reward was asked and none is expected. A railway commission of distinguished experts also came from America to Russia to render what assistance they could toward improving your transportation facilities, to the end that your magnificent food productions might be so distributed as to relieve the famine which seemed to prevail in some sections. This commission has already achieved great results, but its work has hardly begun.

America's motives in entering the war and the objects thereof have been set forth clearly and impressively by President Wilson in his message to Congress,[5] in his note to the Provisional Government on the coming of the diplomatic mission, in his flag-day speech, in his reply to the Pope,[6] and in many other

---

[4] The American Red Cross Mission to Russia, which consisted of about forty members commissioned as military reserve officers, arrived in Petrograd on July 25 (August 7), 1917, and established its headquarters in the Grand Hotel Europe. The ARCM was headed officially by Colonel Frank G. Billings (1854–1932), a noted Chicago physician, but actually by its business manager Colonel William B. Thompson (1869–1930), a Montana copper magnate and Wall Street financier. From November 1917 to May 1918, it was headed by Lieutenant Colonel Raymond Robins. Lieutenant Colonel Henry Watkins Anderson (1870–1954) headed another ARCM sent through Russia to Romania.

[5] Wilson's War Message of April 2, 1917.

[6] Benedict XV, 1914–22. In August 1917, he presented an unrealistic peace plan, which was rejected by both sides.

eloquent utterances, all of which show that my country has entered this war desiring and expecting no annexations and no indemnities, but has unselfishly assumed a stupendous task in the interests of humanity, to enable all peoples to dispose of themselves, to make the world safe for Democracy...

If reports received daily are to be credited, even partially, the Russian people are engaged in fratricidal strife and are paying no attention to the approach of a powerful enemy who is already on Russian soil. There is no power whose authority is recognized throughout Russia; your industries are neglected and many of your people are crying for food. This need can be supplied if you will permit the American railway commission to continue its helpful work, as there is sufficient food in Russia to feed all her people if properly distributed. An able and experienced railroad operator is clearing from America to-day with three hundred and forty engineers, skilled mechanics, and operatives, for Vladivostok, in accordance with an agreement between the Department of Ways and Communications and the American Railway Commission. I have cabled my Government urging that your internal conditions be not permitted to prevent the coming of this assistance. The men are coming to Russia for a temporary stay only and they will not take the places of any railroad men now employed. Food conditions or the scarcity of bread is the greatest menace confronting you at this time, and America is making every effort to improve the situation.

I have not lost faith in the ability of the Russian people to solve their own problems. On the contrary, I believe that your patriotism, your pride, your sense of right, and your love of justice will remove the difficulties that beset your pathway. But the time you have therefor is extremely limited. A powerful enemy is at your gates. A desperate foe is sowing the seeds of dissension in your midst. A hostile, unscrupulous, imperial government is maintaining a well-organized espionage throughout the land. Your liberties are threatened. Your beloved land is in danger. Your unapproachable resources may pass into unfriendly hands. Eternal vigilance is required to preserve for your descendants the rich heritage you now hold. Neglect of present opportunity may entail upon your children a commercial slavery worse than serfdom. I appeal to you to be watchful of your true interests, and I make this appeal on behalf of my Government and my people, with whom you have ever borne friendly relations, and who cherish a sincere, deep interest in your welfare. I make this appeal also for myself. I have lived in your midst for more than a year and a half. I have studied your character, and admire your many excellent traits. I think if you are now mindful of your true interests your future will be more glorious than your most sanguine expectations.

Your Constituent Assembly, upon which your minds and hearts are centered, is less than nine days distant. That august body is empowered to formulate a government for Russia. What preparations are you making for its assembling? Can it be representative of the soul of Russia if her sons are daily shedding the blood of each other?

It may be true that you are tired of war and desire peace, but what kind of a peace can you expect from a Government not only imperialistic in form but the greatest enemy of Democracy? You are dissipating your power and weakening your spirit, and wasting your energies, by family dissensions.

My country has no secret treaties in connection with this war. We are bound to our Allies in a league of honor. Our forefathers, the founders of the American Republic, warned us against entangling alliances with foreign powers, but they also taught us that a government which fails to fulfil its obligations to live up to its agreements, cannot command the respect of civilization and neither merit nor receive the loyal support of its own citizens, and consequently cannot survive.

I appreciate your friendly feeling for my country, and your considerate treatment of myself during my official stay among you. If by this candid expression of thought and feeling I forfeit your friendship, I shall regret it sincerely. My hope is that what I have said may make you stop and think. If so, it will inure to your profit.

Instead of rallying to the support of the Provisional Government the troops in Petrograd acknowledged allegiance to the Bolshevik Revolutionary Committee. This meant the overthrow of the Provisional Government just as surely as had the defection of these troops eight months before meant the downfall of the Czar.

"It is reported that a Bolshevik uprising or 'demonstration' is beginning on the other side of the river. The immediate cause is the suppression of the four Bolshevik newspapers, one of them Maxim Gorky's.[7] These papers have been advocating a separate peace and supporting extreme socialistic doctrines..." This I said in concluding a letter to my eldest son on November 6th, 1917.

On the same day I had a long talk with Terestchenko at the Foreign Office. After a brief discussion of routine matters I went to a window from which we could see a thousand or more soldiers drilling in the open space between the Foreign Office and the Winter Palace. We were both under great tension, but Terestchenko was more nervous than I was. We were alone and neither had spoken for some minutes when he said, "I expect a Bolshevik outbreak to-night."

"If you can suppress it, I hope it will occur," I commented.

"I think we can suppress it," the Minister said with apparent calmness; but when he abruptly added, "I hope it will take place whether we can or not—I am tired of

---

[7] Maxim Gorky, pseudonym of the writer Aleksei M. Peshkov (1868–1936), who published the moderate Social-Democratic newspaper *Novaia Zhizn'* (New Life), April 1917–July 1918.

this uncertainty and suspense," I realized to the full, the terrible strain under which this young man was living.

He was the richest man in the Government and had been reared in luxury, but unlike most men so reared he had never wasted his time. Beside his own language he knew English, French and German. He had been a student both of political economy and of Russian history. Having lost faith in his chief, Kerensky (a fact which I did not know at the time), he undoubtedly felt that the chief responsibility for saving his country from the terrible fate that threatened her rested upon his shoulders chiefly.

"Whose soldiers are those?" I asked.

"They are ours," the young Minister replied as he turned wearily to his desk, and I took my departure feeling hopeful that he was justified in his belief that the Government would be able to defeat any effort the Bolsheviks might make.

As I stepped into my victoria, drawn by two gray horses with small American flags attached to the rosettes of their bridles, I directed my coachman to drive by the soldiers who had stacked arms and were talking in little groups. I saluted as I passed and the men under their non-commissioned officers promptly came to attention and returned my salute with all proper military precision. I wanted to impress these men with the fact that America and her Ambassador were back of the threatened Provisional Government.

The next morning I was called up from the Foreign Office and told that because of pressing matters the Minister could not receive me at one o'clock that day. That was the hour of my daily call upon the Foreign Minister.

Shortly after receipt of this message Secretary Whitehouse[8] rushed in in great excitement and told me that his automobile, on which he carried an American flag, had been followed to his residence by a Russian officer, who said that Kerensky wanted it to go to the front. Whitehouse and his brother-in-law, Baron Ramsai, who was with him, accompanied the officer to General Headquarters in order to confirm his authority for making this amazing request. There they found Kerensky— the Headquarters are across the square from the Winter Palace, where he lived surrounded by his staff. Everyone seemed to be in a high tension of excitement and all was confusion. Kerensky confirmed the officer's statement that he wanted Whitehouse's car to go to the front. Whitehouse asserted, "This car is my personal property and you have (pointing across the square to the Winter Palace) thirty or more automobiles waiting in front of the palace." Kerensky replied, "Those were put out of commission

---

[8] Sheldon Whitehouse (1883–1965) was educated at Eton College (England), Yale University, and New York Law School. He served as private secretary to the US Ambassador to Great Britain Whitelaw Reid; entered the Foreign Service in 1909, and served in Venezuela, France, Turkey, and Greece and Montenegro. Assigned to Petrograd on May 25, 1916, as second secretary of the embassy and promoted that same year to first secretary. Assigned to Stockholm on January 8, 1918.

during the night and the Bolsheviks now command all the troops in Petrograd except some who claim to be neutral and refuse to obey my orders."

Whitehouse and Ramsai, after a hurried conference, came to the very proper conclusion that as the car had virtually been commandeered they could offer no further objection. After they had left the Headquarters Whitehouse remembered the American flag, and returning, told the officer who had originally asked for the car that he must remove the flag before using the car. He objected to doing this and, after some argument, Whitehouse had to be content with registering a protest against Kerensky's use of the flag, and left to report the affair to me.

On hearing the story I approved Whitehouse's action, but gave orders that no mention should be made of the occurrence to anyone. A rumor reached me later that Kerensky had left the city in an American Embassy automobile and under the American flag, but the rumor had a very limited circulation and was, I think, for the most part disbelieved. At any rate no point has been made of the manner of Kerensky's escape other than the fact that he deserted his colleagues.

He told Whitehouse to inform me that he was going to the army and would return within five days with a sufficient force to liquidate the situation. He did attempt to return at the head of 3,000 to 5,000 Cossacks, but his troops were repulsed about fifteen miles from the city by a force of about 20,000 men of whom 4,000 to 6,000 were armed workmen. It is not improbable that their arms had been furnished by the order of Kerensky himself when he armed the workmen of Petrograd in order that they might aid in repelling Korniloff's army. On Friday, November 16th [sic], there came to the Embassy after dark a young man whom, although dressed in civilian's clothes, I recognized as Captain Kovanko, Kerensky's naval aide.[9] He said he had left Kerensky the morning of the previous day after his defeat and had returned with papers from him for friends in Petrograd. He said Kerensky had told him to see me and advise me of the situation. He said that General Krasnoff,[10] commanding the Cossacks, had called Kerensky's attention to the German tactics of the Bolshevik army, and that both General Krasnoff and Kerensky believed that the Bolshevik army was commanded by German officers. It may be that he invented the story of Kerensky's sending him to me, as he again appeared after dark the next day and told me he was anxious to go to America. Naturally I could do nothing for him in that direction. The following day he was arrested and imprisoned in St. Peter and Paul Fortress.

---

[9] Lev E. Kovanko (1891–1938), senior lieutenant of the Russian navy, aide to the navy minister from June 1, 1917.

[10] Peter N. Krasnov (1869–1947), lieutenant general of cavalry. After the October Revolution, he commanded the Cossack forces, which were sent by Alexander F. Kerensky to recapture Petrograd but failed to do so. Elected Ataman of All-Great Host of Don on May 16, 1918, and with German support fought Soviet troops in the Don region. He was forced to resign in February 1919 and went abroad.

On November 7th, the day of Kerensky's flight, his colleagues of the Provisional Government held a meeting at the Winter Palace. Late in the afternoon the Palace was surrounded by Bolshevik troops and Red Guards[11] who demanded its surrender, which was refused. Thereupon the Bolsheviks opened fire assisted by the man-of-war, *Aurora*,[12] which lay in the river and by the guns of St. Peter and Paul Fortress across the river—the Winter Palace fronts on the River Neva and the Fortress is almost directly opposite. The Palace was defended by cadets, commonly known as "Junkers"[13] (youths corresponding to our West Pointers) of whom there were several hundred, and by a battalion of women soldiers.[14] At 2:10 a.m., November 8th, the Palace was surrendered. The Ministers were captured and compelled to walk, under guard and subjected to many indignities, to the Fortress two miles distant, where they were imprisoned. The four Socialist Ministers were subsequently released, but kept under surveillance. The other Ministers were said to be well treated, but their friends and relatives were in constant fear that they would be killed, which seemed to me not improbable. According to one report the Ministers were stood up in line to be shot when the commander of the prison intervened.

Madame Terestchenko,[15] the mother of the young Foreign Minister, called upon me at the Embassy a few days after her son's arrest. She was obviously in deep distress of mind and told me that her son's guards, as indeed those of all the former Ministers, were being changed from soldier cyclists to Kronstadt sailors by order of young Rothschild, the President of the so-called "Kronstadt Republic."[16] These

---

[11] Volunteer detachments created after the February Revolution for the protection of the Soviet power consisting mainly of factory workers. The first Red Guard units were organized in Petrograd by the end of April 1917. The Kornilov Affair gave an impetus for mass formation of the Red Guard detachments, their strength being about 20,000 by October. Red Guardsmen turned into the main fighting force of the Bolshevik Party and took an active part in the October Revolution.

[12] Built in 1903, the *Aurora* was a protected cruiser of the Russian navy. It took part in the Tsushima battle of 1905 and afterwards was interned by the US authorities in Manila, the Philippines. On the evening of October 25, 1917, a blank gunshot from *Aurora* signaled the start of the storm of the Winter Palace, which resulted in the overthrow of the Provisional Government. The cruiser is preserved as a museum ship on the Neva to the present day.

[13] Junkers were cadets in Russian military schools.

[14] The First Petrograd Women's Battalion, which was formed in June 1917 and took part in the defense of the Winter Palace during the October Revolution. It should not be confused with the First Russian Women's Battalion of Death, which was created in May 1917 and sent to the front.

[15] See n. 4, p. 100.

[16] Kronstadt was labeled "the Kronstadt Republic" in the second half of May 1917 when the local Soviet proclaimed itself the only authority in the city. There was not a person named Rothschild in the leadership of this "republic." The most active figure was the local

Kronstadt sailors had threatened to kill all the former Ministers. She added that her son could be released on the payment of 100,000 roubles to the Soviet Government—an amount which she would gladly pay, but that he refused to accept his liberty and leave his colleagues in prison. I explained to the distressed mother as best I could how gladly I would help her if I could, but that unfortunately any interest I might show in her son would simply lead the Bolsheviks to deal more harshly with him.

In a letter to Secretary Lansing written November 20th, 1917, I said of this period:

> On the night of November 7th, the Petrograd Council of Workmen and Soldiers, which is mainly Bolsheviks, and the National Soviet, of which a congress has been called in Petrograd,[17] named a new ministry calling it a "Commissaire" and appointed as commissaires of the people Lenin as President and Trotzky as Minister of Foreign Affairs, and ten or fifteen others whose names are immaterial. The Mencheviks[18] in the Soviet Congress thereupon withdrew, and also a few of the Bolsheviks. The second day thereafter the right wing of the Socialist Party, including the above Soviet-seceders, the Social Revolutionists, and a majority of the Internationals and most of the Peasant Deputies, held a conference and attempted to agree upon a compromise ministry. Dan,[19] speaking for the Social Revolutionists, stated they would not participate in any government with Bolsheviks and that the Peasants and Railway Union,[20] who have become a power in the situation,

---

Bolshevik leader Semen G. Roshal (1896–1917) who, along with his fellow Bolshevik Fyodor F. Raskolnikov (1892–1939), reached a compromise with the Provisional Government.

[17] The Second All-Russian Congress of Soviets of Workers' and Soldiers' Deputies was held in Petrograd on October 25–27, 1917. The congress legalized the results of the October Revolution, promulgated the Decree of Peace and Decree of Land, created the first Soviet government (Council of People's Commissars) headed by Vladimir I. Lenin, and elected the new All-Russian Central Executive Committee of Soviets dominated by the Bolsheviks.

[18] Originally a faction of the Russian Social Democratic Workers' Party, which had emerged after the 1903 party congress in opposition to the Bolshevik faction. Its members were labeled Mensheviks, from a Russian word meaning "minority," because their position was supported by a minority of the delegates. The two factions finally divided in 1912 when the Bolsheviks established their RSDWP(b). The Mensheviks created RSDWP (united) in August 1917 and restored the original party name RSDWP in April 1918. The Menshevik Party was suppressed by the Bolsheviks in the early 1920s.

[19] Fyodor I. Dan (Gurvich, 1871–1947), graduate of Dorpat University (Estland), physician, one of the leaders of the Social Democrats-Mensheviks. He was exiled from Soviet Russia, emigrated to the US in 1940, and died in New York City.

[20] The All-Russian Executive Committee of the Railway Trade Union (Vikzhel) was created in August 1917. It was dominated by Socialist Revolutionaries and Mensheviks and strongly opposed the Bolshevik government. In January 1918, it was abolished by the All-Russian Railway Congress.

were of the same mind. Later this decision appears to have been altered to the effect that a Bolshevik representation would be permitted provided neither Lenin nor Trotzky should be selected. Of course, Lenin and Trotzky objected, and that is the present situation. An adjourned meeting for the selection of a compromise ministry was planned but for some reason was not held. In the meantime, Lenin and Trotzky are administering whatever government there is, outside the City Duma, from the Smolny Institute, an educational building which has been headquarters of the Petrograd Council and the Bolsheviks since they were put out of the National Duma in order that it might be prepared for the Constituent Assembly. The military, or that portion of them which recognizes the Lenin-Trotzky government, is commanded by a revolutionary military committee.

A Colonel Mouravief,[21] whose reputation is not good, was appointed commander of the Petrograd District, and assumed charge of the Petrograd military headquarters. He issued an order, No. 1, in which he acknowledged in a complimentary way the supremacy of the Revolutionary Military Committee and the Red Guard. It appears that the British,[22] French[23] and American Military Attaches called on Mouravief and asked him to protect the foreign Embassies and Legations. I was not aware of this until after it was done, and when informed of it expressed my displeasure and gave orders that nothing should be done by anyone connected with the Embassy or subject to my control that could be construed as a recognition of the Lenin-Trotzky Government.

A few days before the revolution began—perhaps a week, the Provisional Government had sent to the Embassy seven Junkers or cadets as guards. I had not so requested, but gave them quarters and provided some of their food, until they were ordered to return to their school, which order they received November 12th or 13th, a day or two before the Junkers had made open resistance to the Bolshevik soldiers. I consented to their leaving, and have since

---

[21] Mikhail A. Muraviev (1880–1918), lieutenant colonel of the imperial army, Left Socialist Revolutionary, commanded the Soviet forces that defended Petrograd after the October Revolution against the Kerensky-Krasnov troops. After the mutiny of the Left SRs in July 1918, when he commanded the Eastern Front, he led his own coup d'etat in Simbirsk and was killed in the course of his arrest.

[22] Major General Sir Alfred W. F. Knox (1870–1964), attaché to the British embassy from 1911 to 1917. Headed the British military mission in Siberia, 1918–20; helped to establish the Kolchak government in Omsk.

[23] Colonel Jean Guillaume Lavergne, attaché to the French embassy from 1916. Promoted to brigadier general in 1917, appointed chief of the French military mission in Russia in March 1918.

heard that they arrived safely at Nikolai School.[24] The Red Guard has been killing the Junkers on the streets and on sight without warning, a species of unsurpassed brutality. On or about November 9th a telephone message was received at the Embassy asking whether I desired a guard of Polish soldiers.[25] I replied in the negative, but the Polish soldiers, ten in number including a lieutenant, arrived next day and were also given quarters and food. General Judson, the Military Attache, thought it unwise to keep the Polish soldiers in the Embassy, as they were known to be unfavorable to the Bolshevik government, and recommended that they be replaced by Bolshevik guard. I assumed the position that, while I was willing for the Polish soldiers to leave, I would not accept a guard from the Revolutionary Military Committee, nor from the Bolshevik Headquarters.

I have just had a call from Skobeleff,[26] whom you remember as a delegate appointed to accompany Terestchenko to Paris. He was accompanied by Tchaikovsky.[27] They both stated voluntarily that the present government is no government at all and that if it is not soon succeeded by a representative ministry anarchy will prevail throughout Russia, and this country will be disrupted and will disappear from the face of the earth as one of the Great Powers. They said they represented the committee of national defense[28] of which Avksentieff is chairman,[29] but he is not in Petrograd at this time

---

[24] Nikolaevskoe Cavalry School, named in honor of Nicholas I.

[25] Soldiers of the Polish Corps of the Russian army, which was formed in mid-1917 on the basis of the Polish Riflemen Division. In the course of the Civil War and struggle for Polish independence, the Corps turned their weapons against the Bolsheviks.

[26] Matvey I. Skobelev (1885–1938), Social Democrat-Menshevik, deputy of the Fourth State Duma, 1912–17. Assistant chairman of the Petrograd Soviet, March 12–September 6, 1917; minister of labor, May 5–September 5, 1917; assistant chairman of the All-Russian Central Executive Committee of Soviets from June 1917.

[27] Nikolai V. Chaikovsky (1850–1926), veteran of the Russian revolutionary movement. Graduate of St. Petersburg University, active member of one of the first revolutionary organizations in Russia (Circle of Tchaikovtsy), lived in the US in the 1870s. He visited the US once again in 1906–07 to collect money for arms in order to organize a revolutionary uprising in Russia. After the February Revolution, he was a deputy of the Petrograd Soviet; later the chairman of the Northern Government (see n. 7, p. 227).

[28] The short-lived Committee for the Salvation of the Motherland and the Revolution, headed by a prominent Socialist Revolutionary Abram R. Gotz (1882–1940), led anti-Bolshevik resistance in the first days after the October Revolution.

[29] Nikolai D. Avksentev (1878–1943), leader of the Party of Socialists-Revolutionaries; chairman of All-Russian Soviet of Peasants' Deputies and the First All-Russian Congress of Peasants' Deputies; minister of internal affairs in the Provisional Government, July 24–September 28, 1917. Became chairman of the Provisional All-Russian Government, which

because he and his friends thought it unsafe for him to remain here. They believed the situation could be saved if the Allies would agree to call a conference for the purpose of defining their aims in continuing the war. They asserted the soldiers and everybody in Russia were asking what the Russian army is fighting for and that the army could only be held together by an announcement of war aims by the Allies. If such announcement should be made and not accepted by Germany, then the army could be reorganized and solidified and would at least hold that part of Russia which is not now in the possession of the Germans. I am cabling you this proposition to-day. Skobeleff and Tchaikovsky said they had just left Sir George Buchanan, and that he had promised to cable their suggestion to his government with a recommendation that it be followed. It was their opinion that such a conference should not be held in Petrograd nor in Russia. I told them there was no objection on our part to such a conference as our aims in this war had been stated before we entered it and had been repeated by President Wilson several times since.

The situation here is extremely critical. The army is without bread, and many of the soldiers are likely to come to Petrograd in quest of food. When they arrive, it is possible they may indulge in excesses.

I have a strong suspicion that Lenin and Trotzky are working in the interests of Germany, but whether that suspicion is correct or not, their success will unquestionably result in Germany's gain. As I cabled you several days ago, it is believed by many that there are German officers here in touch with the commanders of the Bolshevik regiments. I have also cabled you concerning the German propaganda at the front, in Moscow and elsewhere. You do not need to be impressed with what it means to us for Germany to get possession of Russia.

Your cable of November 16th, 3 p.m., to Morris[30] was received by me to-day. You can readily see that cables between the Department and the Embassy have been willfully intercepted, especially when I call your attention to the fact that unimportant cables have come through unmolested. I appreciate your concern about the safety of the members of the Embassy and also about American citizens, but as I have cabled you several times, no American has been injured either in Petrograd or in Moscow.

---

was created on September 23, 1918, in Ufa (Ufa Directory) and was soon removed to Omsk. He was exiled abroad after the Kolchak coup d'etat in November 1918, emigrated to the US in 1940, and died in New York City.

[30] Ira Nelson Morris (1875–1942), the US minister to Sweden, July 13, 1914–April 3, 1923.

The day after the overthrow of the Provisional Government, I wrote in a letter to Consul-General Summers at Moscow:

> The streets are quiet to-day but some of them are barricaded. The principal point of interest is the telephone headquarters on the Moskaya,[31] which was taken by the Bolsheviks night before last. Some cadets attempted to recapture it yesterday afternoon but were repulsed.
>
> The Foreign Office in reply to my inquiry, phones this morning that it does not know where the Minister of Foreign Affairs is, and that no one representing the new power has appeared at the Ministry, consequently all of the officials there are folding their hands. An official of the Department of Agriculture called at the Embassy this morning and told me that the Ministry was closed as it was impossible to do any business with the Ministers in prison. I have just received word, however, from the Ministry of Ways and Communications, that a telegram I sent there to be forwarded to John F. Stevens would be promptly transmitted, consequently I conclude that the Department is transacting business.
>
> It is reported that the Petrograd Council of Workmen and Soldiers has named a cabinet with Lenin as Premier, Trotzky as Minister of Foreign Affairs, and Madame or Mlle. Kollontai as Minister of Education.[32]
>
> Disgusting!—but I hope such effort will be made, as the more ridiculous the situation the sooner the remedy. It is reported also and generally believed that Verkhovsky, late Minister of War, is at the Smolny Institute and directing the military affairs of the Bolsheviks. I am inclined to believe the report.

In a later letter, I said:

> There has been little fighting here on the streets. Last Sunday the Junkers (the cadets) captured the telephone office and held it about six hours, when they were compelled to surrender. They thought Kerensky's forces would enter Petrograd Sunday and they are said to have been promised that the three

---

[31] The Petrograd Central Telephone Station was located on Morskaya Street, 22. Morskaya Street was one of the most fashionable streets in Petrograd, connecting Palace Square with St. Isaac's Square, and bore this name from 1902 till 1920. Before 1902 and since 1993, it was/is called Great Morskaya Street.

[32] Alexandra M. Kollontai (Domontovich, 1872–1952), originally non-factional Social Democrat, joined the Bolsheviks in 1915; during the World War, she visited the US twice on party business. She returned to Russia after the February Revolution and was elected to the Executive Committee of the Petrograd Soviet. Appointed people's commissar for state charity on October 30, 1917; resigned in March 1918 in protest against the Brest-Litovsk treaty and was sent to organize Bolshevik propaganda in Crimea.

Cossack regiments here would attack the Bolsheviks, provided they were given an armored motor. The Junkers had heard on Saturday that their arms would be taken from them on Sunday, consequently on Saturday night they entered the garage where the motors are stored, and after binding and chloroforming the guards captured eight armored motors. About ten o'clock the next morning they captured the telephone office, and were engaged in more or less street fighting during the day. The Bolshevik soldiers and Red Guards took the Vladimir School[33] across the river, and, after almost demolishing it with artillery, captured the inmates, who had offered resistance, and are said to have practiced horrible cruelties on those who surrendered. During Sunday and Monday whenever a Junker was seen on the street he was shot by a Red Guard or a Bolshevik soldier without being questioned.

On the night of November 8th, after the fall of the Winter Palace, the Petrograd Council of Workmen and Soldiers, and the National Soviet, or what is left of it, after several factions had withdrawn, passed a decree dividing among the people all the land in Russia except that belonging to the Cossacks. They then adopted peace resolutions and recommended a three months' armistice, for their consideration, and ordered the resolutions sent to the army and by wireless to all belligerent and neutral countries.

The Embassy has never received any official notice that there has been any change in the government, but the departments are all closed or operating only partially and without chiefs. The Lenin-Trotzky Ministry has not sent any written or oral communication to the Embassy. In fact, I have not heard of its functioning at all except to demand the secret treaties from the Foreign Office, which were not forth-coming, and to take possession of the State Bank. The private banks have been closed notwithstanding Lenin's order to them to keep open for at least two hours daily. The National City Bank tells me it would open for the accommodation of its customers but it has no money outside the State Bank and can get none from there. Quiet prevails here notwithstanding there is no government.

When a government is formed and I am officially advised, I shall confer with the heads of the Allied Missions and the Department upon a course of action. Of course, we would not, or I would not, recognize any Ministry of which Lenin is Premier or Trotzky Minister of Foreign Affairs.

---

[33] Vladimirskoe Military School—originally St. Petersburg Military School, renamed in honor of Grand Duke Vladimir Alexandrovich after his death in 1910—was located on the Petrogradskaya Storona. Its Junkers took part in the anti-Bolshevik uprising on October 29, 1917, which was suppressed by Soviet troops with demonstrative cruelty. The school building was destroyed in 2007.

THE BOLSHEVIKS OVERTHROW THE GOVERNMENT

In a letter to my son Perry written November 26th, I thus commented upon later phases of the Revolution:

There has been no firing on the streets of Petrograd for the last three days except occasionally. Killing and robberies are much more frequent than anyone knows, however, because they are not given to the press, and for the further reason that all evidence of such crimes are rapidly removed. I never knew of a place where human life is as cheap as it is now in Russia. You can, however, become accustomed to murders and robberies. About ten days ago when I was returning to the Embassy in a Ford automobile, driven by Phil, my attention was attracted by a crowd congregated on the corner of this block, which is about 1,200 feet long, with the Embassy within 200 feet of one end of it. Phil was inclined to stop, but as I had an engagement at the Embassy I told him to drive on, but his curiosity was so strong that after leaving me at the Embassy he drove back to the corner and about half an hour later came into my office and told me the crowd was in front of a branch post-office, the woman in charge of which, a 19-year-old girl, had been killed and the office robbed of 82,000 roubles. It seemed incredible, but I have become so accustomed to such outrages that I only remarked that I was sorry and that the scoundrel who did it should be shot, and continued to dictate to the stenographer.

The Department has given no instructions concerning recognition of the Lenin-Trotzky government, nor have I made any recommendation looking toward such recognition. The Constituent Assembly will be convened day after to-morrow, but no one can foretell its political complexion or its action. I am still having the Embassy guarded nightly by two of its employees, who sit in the vestibule from 2 a.m. until 7, as I never go to bed until 2 o'clock, or haven't since the Revolution began.

In a letter to my wife written on Monday, the 12th, I commented:

We have had no government here since Thursday. Most of the government offices are closed as the employees have refused to work under Bolshevik Ministers. Some departments have been visited by the new Ministers but some have not. I understand all of those called upon to do so have declined to recognize the Bolshevik government and those not called upon have ceased to operate for want of authority.

On November 24th, Consul-General Summers wrote me a letter in which he thus described the Revolution as it affected Moscow:

We were for a week in the center of the fighting zone and for four days I could not get out of the house on account of the firing on the streets both of artillery and musketry. All the houses at the corner near our house were shelled and burned. I was very anxious about the Consulate where Poole, Macgowan[34] and Bullard[35] were sleeping, having been cut off from their homes. The Consulate is only about 400 yards from my home—in the direction of the National Hotel, and the heaviest fighting in Moscow was between us. Fire broke out the second night as the result of the heavy artillery fire directed against the buildings. Numerous persons were killed or burned to death. The Dom Gagarin, the property of my wife's aunt, was the stronghold of the Bolsheviks. It controlled the entrance to the Kremlin by the Nikitzkaya and was hotly contested until the last moment when shells set it and the surrounding buildings afire. Our house was struck several times by bullets and shrapnel, but we were not injured or even worried.

The Consulate was shot up a little but on the whole was respected as much as could have been desired. A large building in the yard, however, is torn to pieces by shell fire. All Americans are safe, although several at the Hotel Metropole, which is a partial wreck, have lost their baggage. The number of dead is not yet known, though it is very large. Last night thirty-five dead bodies were removed from the Dom Gagarin, nineteen were taken from a burning house in front and all over the city funerals are taking place. The morgues are full of Junkers and Bolsheviks. The dead of the latter are being buried to-day. Disorders are expected in the afternoon, though I think that the terror of the past week has cowed resistance.

The most horrible atrocities are known to have been perpetrated by the Bolsheviks. Large numbers of young students from ten to sixteen years of age have been murdered because they were cadets, the word Cadet being confused with the political party. Junkers were thrown into holes made in the ground and buried without funerals. Many of them were subjected to

---

[34] David Bell Macgowan (1870–1960), American journalist and consular officer. Took courses at universities in Halle and Berlin, served as correspondent of *The Associated Press* and the *London Standard* in St. Petersburg, 1901–08, and as correspondent of *The Associated Press* in Petrograd in 1915. Entered the Consular Service and was detailed as vice consul at Moscow on December 20, 1915. He was on special detail to investigate the arming of German and Austro-Hungarian prisoners of war in Siberia, 1918. Detailed to Vladivostok in June 1918; appointed to Riga on August 21, 1922.

[35] Arthur Bullard (1879–1929), American journalist. In 1904 he went to Switzerland, where he got acquainted with Russian political emigrants, and then went to Russia to write on the revolutionary movement for American magazines. Secretary of the American Society of Friends of Russian Freedom, 1905–07. Arrived at Petrograd as unofficial representative of the Committee on Public Information in July 1917; headed the American Press Bureau in Russia in the fall of that year.

THE BOLSHEVIKS OVERTHROW THE GOVERNMENT 161

unheard-of cruelties. The French Consul-General from Warsaw was brutally treated and the Roumanian officers at the Metropole were little less than executed. Concrete cases of looting, murder and other rapacious acts are not wanting. Immediately after the firing was stopped and the Consular Corps could be gotten together, a meeting was held at my home. All were present except the English Consul-General, who informed me that he did not propose to adopt any definite line of action until he received instructions from the Embassy. It seems to me that on occasions of this sort, when the life and property of foreigners is at stake, the first duty of a Consular officer is to see that every protection is given them, regardless of who has assumed the power. I have carefully studied this question at other times when the question of recognition of governments, created by revolution, was concerned, and find that representations to a body which has forcibly come into power and de facto occupies the government, in regard merely to the matter of protection of citizens and their properties, is not only in order, but is obligatory on Consular officers.

We have carefully given them to understand that we were merely treating with them on matters of the protection of our citizens. After long and rather strong arguments were employed, the representatives of the War Revolutionary Committee called at the Swedish Consulate on myself and the Swedish Consul-General, who in the meantime had been selected by the Consular Corps to represent them, and we succeeded in forcing them to place their seal on certain certificates of citizenship and residence which we prepared which would at once protect each foreigner, and insure his house against search except in the presence of a Consular officer. We insist on a strict compliance with the laws of the nations in the treatment of all foreigners and warned them of the consequence of any infringement of such laws.

I think in the end we have secured to all foreigners here a speedy and effective method of protection. Everyone seems to be contented, though there was a great panic the first days. The American Red Cross was making every possible effort to get out before anyone else, and annoyed the Consulate-General no little by taking up our time when we were busy trying to secure to our colony all due protection. I confess that it aggravated me not a little to have to stop this work to get special cars for them to get away. I realized that if all of them left precipitately as they wished to do there would be a panic here, and I told them that if they did, even though it cost me my post, I would telegraph the President what they were endeavoring to do and its effect at this serious moment.

I am glad to say they have all gone and sincerely hope they will not return. I am not by any means done with this matter, as I have many things in connection with the entire work of this body which I will bring to the attention of the government. Some of them are earnest men and others are little less than curiosity seekers who avail themselves of the official nature of the body to make nuisances of themselves and of the Red Cross, quite contrary from the Y.M.C.A.[36] which has done splendid work, as I have cabled the Department.

The colony is all quiet and quite untouched. We are making all due preparation for them in case we have to leave. As far as myself and family are concerned and all the staff of this office, we shall stay here until we are forced to leave. Like yourself I have no fear of these people and feel strongly that we should fight the thing to the end.

In reply to the question that is often asked me, "Why did the Kerensky Government fail?" I reply there are many reasons, among which these might be mentioned: The great mass of soldiers in the Russian army were ignorant peasants who had only the vaguest idea what they were fighting for. They had fought long, had lost enormous numbers, had been betrayed by some of their leaders, and in many cases their families were destitute. Lenin and Trotzky and their numerous agents came among them and promised them peace and land. They longed for peace! To gain possession of the land upon which they worked had been their ambition for generations. Under these conditions, to keep these peasant soldiers fighting and at the same time build up a democratic government in a land that had known only despotism for hundreds of years was a task for a leader with the iron nerve of Cromwell and the far-seeing wisdom of Lincoln. Not such a man was Kerensky! He was first and foremost an orator. He was also, in my belief, a patriotic Russian with the welfare of his country at heart. But he was weak, and twice in the brief tenure of his power he blundered fatally; first, when after the attempted Revolution of July, he failed to execute as traitors, Lenin and Trotzky. Second, when during the Korniloff episode, he failed to seek to conciliate General Korniloff and instead turned to the Council of Workmen's and Soldiers' Deputies and distributed arms and ammunition among the workingmen of Petrograd. By this singularly inept stroke he alienated his own army and armed his enemies.

In a private letter written from Vologda on June 23rd, 1918, I told of this incident of Kerensky's departure from Russia.

---

[36] Young Men's Christian Association. The American YMCA began its work in Russia in 1900, when the Society for Moral, Intellectual and Physical Development of Young Men—called *Mayak* (Lighthouse)—was established in St. Petersburg with the financial support of philanthropist James Stokes. Until the fall of 1917, it was directed by Franklin A. Gaylord (1856–1943), a former pastor of Trinity Church in New York City. During the World War, the YMCA launched its relief work in the prisoner-of-war camps, which culminated in 1917–18 with many dozens of the YMCA's secretaries operating throughout Russia. The YMCA headquarters in Petrograd—headed by Archibald Clinton Harte (1865–1946)—was situated in the Zinger House (Nevsky Prospekt, 28).

Kerensky was in Moscow four weeks ago after reports had stated he had settled in Norway, and I think the Government was aware of his presence there, but don't know such to be the case. The Ministers of the Provisional Government, who were kept in the St. Peter and Paul Fortress for four months, have all been released. Shingarieff, who was an ex-minister,[37] was killed in a hospital to which he had been transferred when the feeling against the Provisional Ministers was very bitter. His murderers have never been punished.

I was informed a few days ago that Kerensky might possibly apply for admission to the United States, whereupon I cabled the Department recommending that he be granted permission to enter. I received a few days ago authority to grant him admission. Meantime he has gone to Murmansk, by the Murman railroad, disguised by a full growth of whiskers, and wearing the uniform of a Serbian officer. He arrived safely at Murmansk, and while dining on a British man-of-war was so completely disguised that he was not recognized by all of his hosts, but one of them did recognize him. During the dinner when the British officers were talking about Russian affairs, one of them mentioned Kerensky in a very uncomplimentary manner, and said if Kerensky had had the courage and wisdom to perform his duty, and had shot Lenin and Trotzky when he could have done so, after the outbreak of July 17th and 18th, 1917, Russia and he Allies would have been spared much trouble and expense and loss of life. You can imagine Kerensky's feelings, and the embarrassment of the officer who had recognized him.

Kerensky was in England when I arrived there but did not call upon me. He was occupied in writing his book. I understand that, at this writing, he is in Paris and attends meetings of the Russians there who have organized an anti-Bolshevik association.

---

[37] Andrei I. Shingarev (1869–1918), graduate of Moscow University, a prominent figure in the Constitutional Democratic Party, deputy of the Second, Third, and Fourth State Dumas, 1907–17. Minister of agriculture from March 2, 1917; minister of finance, May 5–July 2, 1917. Arrested after the October Revolution and killed in the hospital by anarchist sailors on January 7, 1918, along with Fyodor F. Kokoshkin.

Chapter XIV
THE CONSTITUENT ASSEMBLY DISPERSED BY ARMED BOLSHEVIKS

Immediately after the Czar's abdication on March 15th, the Provisional Government had issued its address to the "citizens" of Russia. It declared the policy to be based on principles, one of which was as follows:

> To proceed forthwith to the preparation and convocation of a Constituent Assembly based on universal suffrage which will establish a stable governmental regime.

The members of the Provisional Government took oath of office immediately. Entering the great hall of the First Department of the Senate, the Ministers with Prince Lvoff at their head took their places in the center of the hall at a table, and each repeated this oath, following the text as pronounced by the President of the Senate, S. B. Brasski:[1]

> According to my duty as a member of the Provisional Government, established by the will of the people on the initiative of the Imperial Duma, I promise and swear before God Almighty and my conscience to faithfully and truly serve the people of the Russian State, sacredly protecting its liberty and rights, its honor and dignity, inviolably observing in all my actions and my orders the foundations of civil liberty and civil equality, and in all measures at my disposal to suppress all attempts, directly or indirectly aiming at the reestablishment of the old regime. I swear to apply all my intelligence and all my strength to entirely fulfill all the obligations which the Provisional Government has assumed before the whole world. I swear to take all the measures for the earliest possible convocation of a Constituent Assembly on the basis of universal, direct, equal and secret suffrage, to transfer to it the plenitude of authority which I am temporarily exercising together with the other members of the Government and to submit to the will of the people expressed through this assembly concerning the form of government and the fundamental laws of the Russian State. So help me God to fulfill my oath.

---

[1] Stepan B. Vrasky (1844–1922), senator from 1898.

Of like interest, bearing upon the purposes of the Constituent Assembly, was the order issued by Minister of War and of the Navy, Goutchkoff, on the 23rd of March.

> Officers, soldiers and sailors, trust one another. The Provisional Government will not permit a return to the past; having laid the foundation of the new order of Government, it seeks to quietly await the convocation of the Constituent Assembly. Do not aid agitators who sow among you dissension and lying reports. The will of the people will be strictly fulfilled, but the peril has not passed.

In a subsequent address to "citizens," the Provisional Government declared:

> While taking measures indispensable for the defense of the country against a foreign enemy, the Government will consider it its first duty to grant to the people every facility to express its will concerning the political administration, and will convoke as soon as possible the Constituent Assembly on the basis of universal suffrage, at the same time assuring the gallant defenders of the country their share in the Parliamentary Election. The Constituent Assembly will issue fundamental laws, guaranteeing the country the immutable rights of equality and liberty.

The Petrograd Soviet, describing their organization as "Russian Workingmen and Soldiers, united in the Petrograd Soviet of Workers' and Soldiers' Deputies," declined to join the cabinet of ministers composing the Provisional Government, in March, but issued a proclamation addressed to "Comrades, Proletarians and all Laboring People of all Countries." In this proclamation the Soviet did not oppose the proposed Constituent Assembly, but endorsed it. The Soviet said:

> The people of Russia will express their will in the Constituent Assembly, which will be called as soon as is possible on the basis of universal, equal, direct and secret suffrage. And already it may be said without a doubt that a Democratic Republic will triumph in Russia.

Stecklov, who was a member of the Executive Committee of the Petrograd Soviet,[2] said that following the establishment of the Provisional Government:

> The Soviet decided to limit itself to presenting to the Provisional Government definite political demands, and without influencing directly the composition

---

[2] Yuri M. Steklov (Nakhamkis, 1873–1941), originally non-factional Social Democrat, joined the Bolsheviks in the summer of 1917; editor of *Izvestiia*, 1917–25.

of the cabinet, which means without recommending directly desirable candidates for ministers, to confine itself to the right to veto those candidates who are definitely undesirable and definitely opposed and dangerous to the revolution.

The foregoing statement of the policy of the Soviet appeared in their organ, *Izvestia*.[3]

Even the imperialistic element gave apparent support to the proposed Constituent Assembly. The Grand Duke Michael Alexandrovitch, in whose favor the Czar abdicated, announced March 3rd-16th his refusal to accept without adherence to the plan of the Constituent Assembly:

> I have firmly decided to accept the supreme power only in case it is the will of our great nation, which through its representatives in the Constituent Assembly will decide upon a form of Government and the new laws of the Russian Empire. Calling God's blessing, I request all citizens of the Russian Empire to submit themselves to the temporary government created by the Imperial Duma and which has the full power until the time when the Constituent Assembly which shall be called upon the basis of general, direct, secret and equal suffrage, shall decide upon the new form of government.
>
> (Signed) Michael.

When the Provisional Government was reorganized in May, two months after the first organization, six Socialists were given places in the Cabinet, Prince Lvoff remaining as Prime Minister. Again the Provisional Government issued an address promising an early assemblage of the Constituent Assembly:

> Leaving it to the Constituent Assembly to decide the question of transfer of land to the toilers and making the requisite preparation for this, the Provisional Government will take all necessary measures to secure the greatest production of grain, in order to satisfy the needs of the country and to regulate utilization of land in the interests of the country's economic welfare and the needs of the toiling masses. The work of introducing and strengthening the democratic organizations of self-government will be continued with all possible assistance and speed. The Provisional Government will in like

---

[3] *Izvestiia* (News), the main Soviet daily newspaper. Its first issue appeared on February 28, 1917, as *Izvestiia Petrogradskogo Soveta Rabochikh Deputatov*. In the course of revolution, the newspaper changed its title according to the changes in the names of Soviet bodies. From March 12, 1918, it was published in Moscow, and soon gave up its position as the main Russian newspaper to the Bolshevik *Pravda*.

THE CONSTITUENT ASSEMBLY DISPERSED BY ARMED BOLSHEVIKS

manner make every effort to convoke the Constituent Assembly in Petrograd as soon as possible."

These expressions of the purposes of the Provisional Government and of the Soviet in the spring of 1917 seemed to justify a general feeling of hopefulness that Russia was about to create an established government of the people, but it was not until November 25th that the elections to the Constituent Assembly were held, and it was not until January 18th that the Constituent Assembly convened. In that long delay to fulfil the early promises and expectations, Russia's opportunity for a stable government by consent of the governed was lost. From time to time the Provisional Government sent out urgent appeals to stay the political disintegration and to establish harmony:

> Citizens of Russia! The fate of our country is in your hands. Without you the Government is helpless. Together with you it will with courage and determination lead the country toward its great future. Remember that it is impossible to observe freedom without authority and that in the new order the authority is set up and guarded by you yourselves, by your inner discipline and your free obedience. Gathering around the authority you have erected, and putting it in a position to use in point of fact the entirety of the rights you have conceded to it, you will give it force and power to overcome all the difficulties and dangers which stand in the country's path, and to bring Russia's freedom entire and untouched to that great day when the nation itself, in the person of the Constituent Assembly it will have elected, shall stand at the helm of government.

Following the attempted revolution led by Lenin and Trotzky in July, the Provisional Government issued another proclamation on the subject of the Constituent Assembly:

> The Provisional Government will take all measures for the election to the Constituent Assembly to take place at the appointed time (September 17th) and for the preparatory measures to be concluded in time to guarantee the uprightness and freedom of the votes.

The Bolsheviks made much capital out of the delay in calling the Constituent Assembly. They insistently demanded that the elections be held. They charged that the Provisional Government was purposely postponing these elections in order that it might remain in power.

They called attention to the luxurious style in which Kerensky was living. And all of the time they went on with plans to set up their own experiment in government.

Claiming to be for a Constituent Assembly, they organized "The National Congress of the Councils of the Deputies of the Workmen and Soldiers."[4] In a communication addressed to the American Embassy the Bolsheviks announced "a new government of the Russian Republic under the form of the Councils of the Commissaries of the People."[5] The communication sent to the Embassy stated that "the President of this government is Mr. Vladimir Ilyich Lenin, and the management of the foreign policy was entrusted to me as Commissary of the People for Foreign Affairs." This document was signed by "Leon Trotzky."

Only a few days before this notice was sent to the Embassy Trotzky had publicly charged Kerensky with conspiring to prevent the convocation of the Constituent Assembly. The date for the election had been postponed from September to November, which gave Trotzky additional ground for his oft-repeated claims that the Provisional Government did not at heart sincerely favor a Constituent Assembly. The Bolshevik government was now in power, but it elected only 168 of the 703 deputies to the Constituent Assembly. There were 81 election districts, but in only 54 of them were elections held. The returns showed that the Social Revolutionists were in the large majority. They had polled 20,893,734 votes against 9,023,963 for the Bolshevik candidates. The total vote cast was 36,257,960.

As soon as the results of the election were known the Bolshevik leaders began to plan for absolute control of the Assembly by their small minority. Through the Executive Committee of the Soviet, they put forth a declaration that where a majority of the voters were dissatisfied with the men they had chosen as deputies, writs for new elections might be issued.

The Constituent Assembly had been called to meet on the 12th of December. Pending the plans of the Bolsheviks to overcome the majority the meeting of the Assembly was postponed until January 18, 1918. The scheme of new elections failing, the Bolshevik leaders, through their newspaper organ, demanded that the Constitutional Democrats who had been elected to the Assembly be arrested and brought to trial before the revolutionary tribunals. The Council of Peoples' Commissaries by a decree announced that this would be done. Miliukoff and other Constitutional Democrats were threatened with arrest. Some arrests were made. Deputies were held in confinement until after the Constituent Assembly had met and had been dispersed by force. Then they were set free. The arrests were purely arbitrary acts on the part of the Bolsheviks to overawe the majority in the Constituent Assembly.

---

[4] The Second All-Russian Congress of Soviets of Workers' and Soldiers' Deputies, October 25–27, 1917 (see n. 17, p. 145).

[5] Council of People's Commissars, the official name of the first Provisional Workers' and Peasants' Government created by the Second All-Russian Congress of Soviets on October 26, 1917. It was made a permanent body by the Third All-Russian Congress of Soviets on January 18, 1918, after the dissolution of the All-Russian Constituent Assembly.

THE CONSTITUENT ASSEMBLY DISPERSED BY ARMED BOLSHEVIKS

Lenin, a short time before the meeting of the Assembly, printed an argument that the election had not given clear indication of what the people wanted. Briefly Lenin's position was:

> The Soviet Republic represents not only a higher form of Democratic institutions, but it is also the sole form which renders possible the least painful transition to Socialism.

A part of Lenin's argument was that the division of the Social Revolutionists Party into Right Wing and Left Wing after the election showed that the people had not acted with definite purpose.

The Social Revolutionists had the largest body of delegates in the Constituent Assembly. The Right Wing was composed of the Conservative Social Revolutionists, and the Left Wing was composed of the Radical Social Revolutionists. In various ways the Bolshevik leaders were preparing local sentiment in Petrograd so far as might be for the forcible dispersal of the Constituent Assembly.

The Assembly met at last on January 5th–18th, 1918. The day before the assemblage of the Constituent Assembly, January 4th–17th, I had a meeting of the Diplomatic Corps, of which I was Dean,[6] in the American Embassy. I proposed to them that we all attend in a body the meeting of the Constituent Assembly, but they objected, saying they were not invited. I said no one was invited. I insisted on going but as no one would accompany me, I did not go alone. The Italian Ambassador, Torretti,[7] afterwards mentioned it to me in Paris about thirteen months later and regretted that he had not gone. If we had gone, the presence of the Diplomatic Corps, representing Russia's Allies, might have had a pacifying effect on that assemblage.

There were stationed in and about the hall during the session sailors and Lettish soldiers[8] armed with rifles and grenades and machine guns. Very soon after the opening of the session, the Bolshevist delegates presented an ultimatum to the Constituent Assembly. Among other things they demanded the adoption of this decree:

> Supporting the Soviet rule and accepting the orders of the Council of Peoples' Commissaries, the Constituent Assembly acknowledges its duty to outline a form for the reorganization of society.

---

[6] Francis became doyen of the Diplomatic Corps after the departure of British Ambassador Sir George Buchanan on December 25, 1917 (January 7, 1918).

[7] Marquis Pietro Paolo Tomasi della Torretta (1873–1962), head of the Italian commercial delegation to Russia in early 1917 with rank of minister; manager of the Italian embassy from November 1917 to March 1919.

[8] Soldiers of the Latvian Riflemen Division of the Russian army, formed in 1916 and numbering about 40,000.

The Constituent Assembly refused to adopt this, whereupon the Bolshevik delegates withdrew. The meeting of the Assembly was attended by many disorders and much street fighting. There was violent but scattered opposition to the Bolshevik program. The Bolshevik newspapers claimed that the Bolshevik soldiers were fired on by mobs. The soldiers then fired into the crowds. Uritzky, one of the Bolshevik leaders,[9] was among the wounded in this street fighting. He was afterwards assassinated and the Bolshevik government shot 513 people as a reprisal for this deed.

One of the organs of the Bolsheviks stated the next day that the Constituent Assembly began well, but that when the Right Social Revolutionists began to assert themselves its fate was sealed. "It is now necessary to work on the enlightenment of the masses."

The *Dielo Naroda*[10] was compelled to suspend publication. The *Nova Vremya* was also suspended, and its editors committed to trial for publishing a statement that a motor lorry containing Red Guards and Lett rifles fired on the barracks of the Ismailov and Petrograd regiments. The Red Guard confiscated and destroyed all non-Bolshevik newspapers.

A delegation of the Looga Workmen's and Soldiers' Council visited Lenin and handed him a resolution of their Council supporting the Constituent Assembly. Lenin expressed his surprise at this resolution. The delegation replied that not all the Democracy was in favor of the Council government and that only the Constituent Assembly could unite it. Lenin answered that he had in his pocket a decree disbanding the Constituent Assembly, and that orders had been given to allow no one to enter the Tauride Palace. The delegation asked what would happen if the Constituent Assembly opened in another place. Lenin replied no one would support the Constituent Assembly, and that it would be disbanded. Instead a convention would be called which would be formed by the forthcoming Congress of Workmen's, Soldiers' and Peasants' Deputies.[11]

---

[9] Moisei S. Uritsky (1873–1918), graduate of Kiev University, lawyer, originally Social Democrat-Menshevik. He joined the Bolsheviks in the summer of 1917; was a member of the Military-Revolutionary Committee during the October Revolution; chairman of the Petrograd Emergency Commission for Combat with Counterrevolution and Sabotage (Cheka) from March 10, 1918. He was killed by a terrorist on August 30, 1918.

[10] *Delo Naroda* (People's Cause), daily newspaper published in Petrograd by the Central Committee of the Party of Socialists-Revolutionaries from March 15, 1917 to January 14, 1918.

[11] The Third All-Russian Congress of Soviets of Workers', Soldiers' and Peasants' Deputies. It was opened on January 10, 1918, as the Congress of Soviets of Workers' and Soldiers' Deputies and merged with the Third All-Russian Congress of Peasants' Deputies on January 13. The united Congress approved the dissolution of the All-Russian Constituent Assembly; made the Council of People's Commissars the permanent government, and suggested to Russia her new name—Russian Socialist Federative Soviet Republic (RSFSR), which was officially fixed on July 19, 1918, by the first Soviet Constitution.

THE CONSTITUENT ASSEMBLY DISPERSED BY ARMED BOLSHEVIKS

At 1:30 a.m. following the first day's session of the Constituent Assembly, the Central Executive Committee of the Council of Workmen's, Soldiers' and Peasants' Deputies issued the decree referred to by Lenin disbanding the Constituent Assembly. The decree said:

> The Constituent Assembly, opened on the 5th of January (18th), gave, owing to circumstances known to all, a majority of the Right Social Revolutionists Party—the party of Kerensky, Avksentiev, and Tchernov.[12] Naturally this party refused to consider the absolutely definite, clear, unmistakable proposal of the supreme organ of Council Government, the Central Executive Committee of the Councils: to acknowledge the program of the Council Government; to acknowledge "the declaration of Right of the Laboring and Exploited People"; to acknowledge the October revolution and the Council Government. By this act the Constituent Assembly broke all connections between itself and the Council Republic of Russia. The withdrawal from such a Constituent Assembly of the Maximalist[13] and Left Social Revolutionists Party, which now compose the great majority of the Council and have the confidence of the workmen and of the majority of the peasants, became unavoidable.
>
> Outside the walls of the Constituent Assembly the majority party of the Constituent Assembly—the Right Social Revolutionists and Minimalists,—carry on open war against the Council Government in their papers calling for the downthrow of it, thus indirectly supporting the resistance of exploiters and the transfer of lands and factories into the hands of the laborers.
>
> It is obvious that the remaining part of the Constituent Assembly can only in view of this play the rôle of masking the struggle of the bourgeois—counter-revolution to overthrow the Council Government. Therefore, the Central Executive Committee resolves the Constituent Assembly is disbanded.

Adjournment of the Constituent Assembly at the close of its first and only session was enforced in the most brutal manner. A drunken sailor[14] said to the deputies: "I am tired and want to go to bed. If you don't get out, I will turn out the lights."

---

[12] Chernov (see n. 8, p. 109).

[13] The Union of Socialists-Revolutionaries Maximalists, which split off the Party of Socialists-Revolutionaries in 1906 and represented the most radical wing of the SRs, fighting for immediate implementation of the "maximum program" of socialist revolution. The Union of SR-Maximalists re-emerged in October 1917, and in the course of the revolution, acted mostly in accord with the Bolsheviks, Left SRs, and anarchists.

[14] Anatoly G. Zheleznyakov (Viktorsky, 1895–1919), Baltic sailor, deserter during the World War, anarchist-communist. Commander of a semi-criminal gang of revolutionary sailors; commanded the guard on the opening session of the All-Russian Constituent Assembly on

On the morning of the 19th of January guards were stationed at the entrance of the palace to prevent the entrance of the deputies or delegates, and that was the end. The Constituent Assembly, forecasted with such promise and hope just ten months previously, never met again. Bolshevism, although in the minority and representing only one-fourth of the votes cast for deputies, was in power by force.

Anarchy quickly found opportunity in the success of Bolshevism. It is interesting to note that coincident with the forcible usurpation by the Bolsheviks the Anarchists[15] became boldly aggressive. Three or four days before the Constituent Assembly was dispersed, four Russians,—two sailors, a workman, and an anarchist orator—presented to the Embassy a resolution passed by a group of anarchists on the yacht *Polar Star*.[16] This resolution was addressed, "To the Envoy of the United States of North America," and was as follows:

> We, sailors, soldiers and workmen of the town of Helsingfors,[17] having become acquainted from all sides with the fact of the persecution by the Government of the United States of North America of our comrade Alexander Berkman, all of whose guilt lies only in the fact that he has devoted his whole life to the cause of serving the working and disinherited class, demand the immediate liberation of our comrade Alexander Berkman. In the contrary event we openly announce that we shall hold the representatives of the Government

---

January 5, 1918; was pressing its closure on the grounds that "the guard was tired." Killed in the course of the Civil War.

[15] The year 1917 marked the high point of the anarchist movement in Russia. Russian anarchists were divided on two main currents—anarchist-communists and anarcho-syndicalists. The latter were strongly influenced by former emigrants who returned from America after the February Revolution. The Union of Anarcho-Syndicalist Propaganda gained control of a number of trade unions in Petrograd, demanded the replacement of state with a federation of syndicates, and encouraged workers to take over factories. The Petrograd Federation of Anarchist-Communists called for a full-scale social revolution, overthrow of the Provisional Government, and establishment of a union of local communities instead of the centralized state. Anarchist-communists were of great influence among soldiers and sailors, particularly in Kronstadt. The majority of anarchists supported the Bolsheviks in the course of the revolution and helped them to overthrow the Provisional Government. Anarchists disagreed with the Bolsheviks on the question of the Brest-Litovsk treaty and issues of state-building, so in the spring of 1918, most of the anarchist organizations were disbanded. Some of them, labeled "Soviet anarchists" or "anarcho-Bolsheviks," joined the Bolshevik Party.

[16] The imperial yacht, built in 1890, where the Central Committee of the Baltic Fleet headquartered from June 1917 to March 1918.

[17] Historical Swedish name of Finland's capital, now Helsinki.

of the United States personally responsible for the life and liberty of the revolutionary and champion of the cause of the people, comrade Alexander Berkman.

> The President: S. Krylov.
> The Secretary: K. Kutzy.
> Seal of the Helsingfors group of anarchists.

No attention was paid by the Embassy to the resolution further than to send a copy to the Secretary of State at Washington, with this explanation:

> Delegation of four anarchists just visited Embassy; after stating they were anarchists said they represented sixty per cent of the Baltic Fleet and all the workmen and soldiers of Helsingfors, and requested to see the American Ambassador. I sent interpreter Secretary Phelps and Private Secretary Johnston to ascertain their mission. Delegation presented resolution in Russian, of which following is translation. Upon hearing the resolution I directed the two attaches above mentioned to say I was engaged and would not see them whereupon they asked that the resolution be presented to the American Government. The delegation was told this would be done and advised that no definite time could be fixed for reply as cable service was irregular and unreliable. The delegation also said a copy of resolution was being sent to Smolny (Bolshevik headquarters). Don't permit consideration for my personal safety to influence government action.

A few weeks previous, in September, the anarchists had held a meeting and had put out "posters" according to their usual plan of presenting their views. In these posters they demanded the release of Berkman. At that time an inquiry was made of the Embassy by the Provisional Government to know who Berkman was and what offense he had committed.

To this I replied that Berkman was utterly discredited by organized labor in the United States; that he had been an opponent of all kinds of government and an enemy of society. I said that he had been arrested for interfering with or attempting to interfere with the enforcement of the draft law and was awaiting trial on that charge. He had served in the penitentiary for the attempted assassination of Henry C. Frick, who at the time was a partner of Andrew Carnegie.[18]

This information was given to the Petrograd newspapers and printed. Apparently it was not satisfactory to the anarchists, but beyond an anonymous communication

---

[18] Henry C. Frick (1849–1919), chairman of the Carnegie Steel Company who organized the cruel suppression of the labor strike (which killed ten workers) at the Homestead Works of the Carnegie Company in 1892. In response, Alexander Berkman tried to assassinate him and was sentenced to twenty-two years in prison, of which he served fourteen years.

sent to the Embassy nothing more was heard from them until the Bolsheviks had set up their government. The anonymous communication was signed, "The Black Point," and was addressed "Ambassador." It was to this effect:

> You appear too often in the press, and especially in the newspaper *Russkoe Slovo*[19] with your anecdotes of a true American model. You irritate the nerves. Our advice is to finish up with this childish occupation. Pack the trunk with anecdotes and leave for your native country, via Archangel, to your wise Solomons. It would be desirable to leave not later than December 15th, 1917, in order to arrive in time for Christmas Eve.

With the dispersal of the Constituent Assembly the anarchists began to threaten. Meetings were held and violent addresses were made. In a letter addressed to my son, dated four days after the dispersal of the Constituent Assembly, I wrote:

> The morning of Saturday, January 19th, an article appeared in the *Bureauvestnik*,[20] the anarchistic organ. I paid little more attention to this than I did to the resolution passed by the Helsingfors anarchists, of which I sent you a copy. The next morning, however, I learned about 11 o'clock that two well-known men, Ex-Ministers. named Shingarieff and Kokoshkin, had been murdered in a hospital about four blocks from the Embassy.[21] After confirming this report which I was enabled to do by sending the Commercial Attache[22]

---

[19] *Russkoe Slovo* (Russian Word), influential Moscow daily newspaper published from 1895 to 1918.

[20] *Burevestnik* (Stormy Petrel), anarchist paper created as a weekly publication of the Petrograd Federation of Anarchist Groups. The first issue appeared on November 11, 1917; distributed daily from December 5, 1917. It continued as an organ of the Petrograd Federation of Anarchist-Communists, and was closed by the Soviet government on May 21, 1918.

[21] Fyodor F. Kokoshkin (1871–1918), graduate of Moscow University, lawyer, professor of constitutional law, one of the founders of the Constitutional Democratic Party. After the February Revolution, a chairman of the Judicial Conference under the Provisional Government; chairman of the committee for preparation of rules of election of the All-Russian Constituent Assembly; state controller, July–August 1917; deputy of the Constituent Assembly. After the October Revolution, he was arrested and killed in Mariinsky Hospital by anarchist sailors on January 7, 1918, along with Andrei I. Shingarev. The hospital was located at Liteyny Prospekt, 56.

[22] William Chapin Huntington (1884–1958), graduate of Columbia University (1907, ME), served as a metallurgist in the US Steel Corporation. He spent three years in Germany and Belgium, studied in the Royal Technical College in Aix la Chapelle (1914, Doctor of Engineering); served as a commercial agent in the Chicago office of the Department of Commerce, 1915–16. Appointed commercial attaché to the US embassy at Petrograd on May 26, 1916.

to look at the bodies, I began to think that the threat of the anarchists should be guarded against. During the afternoon when I was presiding at a meeting of the Allied Chiefs of Missions a woman telephoned to the Embassy saying she had some important information to impart but was afraid to come to the Embassy and desired that I send someone to meet her at the intersection of two streets about eight blocks from the Embassy. Earl Johnston, and Doctor Huntington, Commercial Attache, went and met her and heard from her the following story:

She had been approached the night before by a soldier who was under obligation to her, and who professed to have some wine for sale. Upon being asked where he got the wine he replied it was from the Italian Embassy and he was one of the soldiers who had done the looting the night or several nights previous. He told her that the American Embassy would be attacked that evening, and the building burned and the Ambassador killed.

I had arranged a reception or tea that evening to which 200 guests had been invited, to say good-by to General Judson, the Military Attache who will leave tomorrow morning for America. I concluded to permit General Judson to send to a barracks not far from the Embassy for a guard. A guard of ten soldiers (Bolshevik) was secured after considerable time, and came to the Embassy about 9 p.m. They did not look or deport themselves as soldiers, but I told Phil to give them cigarettes and tea, soup and bread, which he did—he had to give them white bread which is very scarce here and a great luxury. They consumed that rapidly and asked for more, which Phil provided. The guests began to arrive about 9:30, but mostly in uniform as they were military attaches of the other Diplomatic Missions. Two of them, however, were Russian officers and came in uniform, not knowing there was a guard in the Embassy, as there never had been one before since the last Revolution. The music box was brought into use—it is a great luxury, tell your Mother—and some of those who were not playing bridge began to dance. Phil provided a most excellent supper which all the guests seemed to enjoy greatly. It was unfortunate that there was an entertainment here that evening, and more unfortunate that the two Russian officers came in uniform. I heard the following day from the dvornick at the door that he had difficulty in preventing the Bolshevik soldiers on guard from invading the salon to take the shoulder straps off of the Russian officers. The order has been issued by the Bolshevik Government that shoulder straps should be abolished and officers now get no more pay than soldiers, which is five or seven roubles per month. I gave each one of the soldiers five roubles when they left the Embassy for their barracks the following morning, but was told that they regarded the gifts contemptuously. Under these circumstances I have concluded not to request any additional guard for the Embassy; consequently, am attempting to protect it by its attaches. To-day two members of the marine corps who were serving as couriers and were about to leave to-morrow morning were ordered by me to remain and to live in the Embassy. They remonstrated, but I was very emphatic—don't know at this writing whether they will remain or not. If they should go after my order to remain I shall cable the Department and demand that they be punished.

Later in the month, January, 1918, I wrote home as follows:

At an anarchist meeting held not a great distance from the Embassy about two weeks ago a resolution was passed demanding the release of Berkman, Mooney, Emma Goldman, et al., and threatening "local American Ambassador" with a hostile demonstration in front of the Embassy if he did not procure the desired liberations. That resolution was sent to Trotzky, the Peoples' Commissaire for Foreign Affairs; Trotzky was at Brest-Litovsk negotiating a separate peace, and his assistant, a Russian Jew named Zalkend,[23] forwarded the resolution to me saying he felt it his duty to do so. His note contained no comment whatever, not even an offer of protection, but indicated "save yourself if you can," or might be construed that way. When Lenin heard of it he was incensed and directed Zalkend to write me a note of apology, which Zalkend failed to do, but thought he had smoothed the situation over by sending a messenger to the Embassy last evening at seven o'clock, who stated that the anarchists had planned an attack for last night but that Trotzky had attended to it, or prevented it. I have six guards at the Embassy—all Americans and well-armed, whom I kept on duty last night; furthermore, Earl Johnston and American Consul Treadwell[24] and two or three others and myself were here on hand in case of necessity. No attack or demonstration occurred. I have been communicating or keeping in touch with Smolny through Raymond Robins, a Chicago man who is in charge of the American

---

[23] Ivan A. Zalkind (1885–1928), graduate of the Sorbonne (Doctor of Biology). Returned to Russia after the February Revolution and took part in the October Revolution. First assistant people's commissar for foreign affairs from November 3, 1917; director of the Western Countries Division, December 1917–January 1918.

[24] Roger Culver Tredwell (1885–1961), graduate of Yale University (1907); attended university at Grenoble, France (1908). Entered the consular service in 1909, served in Japan, England, Germany, the Netherlands, Italy, and the Department of State. Appointed consul general at Petrograd on July 17, 1917. He was detailed to Tashkent and arrested there on October 26, 1918, but was released on March 27, 1919, due to the efforts of William C. Bullitt, who visited Moscow on a special mission.

Red Cross Mission here.²⁵ He says no one believes that any demonstration was planned at all. Anyhow Lenin has removed Zalkend and put in his place Tchecherin,²⁶ a Bolshevik who was interned in London and whose release was demanded by the Bolsheviks a month ago when Trotzky announced that no British would be permitted to leave Russia until Tchecherin and his colleague, Petrov, were released. The British Ambassador recommended the release of these men, and they were set free. The anarchists are now attempting to frighten me into recommending the release of Mooney and Berkman and Goldman but as you know I don't scare very easily. On the contrary I have wired the Department not to permit consideration for my safety to influence the action of the Government.

I received last night from the Department a long cable evidently composed by the President giving a summary of the report of the Commission appointed by him to investigate the Mooney case. The Department wired that the President had instructed that I be authorized to publish the cable if I saw fit. It has not been published yet and may not be.

The Bolsheviks seem to be gaining all over Russia but as our only source of information is the Bolshevik press,—the anti-Bolshevik newspapers having been suppressed,—it is difficult to tell what is going on outside of Petrograd and Moscow. I received to-day a telegram from American Consul at Odessa²⁷ which was 21 days enroute. I sent two telegrams to the American Consul at Vladivostok²⁸ the 29th of December, or two copies of the same telegram, one

---

[25] Raymond Robins (1873–1954), graduate of the Columbian (later George Washington) University, lawyer, businessman, prominent social worker, activist of the Progressive Party. Officer of the American Red Cross Mission to Russia with rank of major from August 1917. Promoted to lieutenant colonel in late November 1917 and was in charge of the ARCM till May 1918.

[26] Georgy V. Chicherin (1872–1936), graduate of St. Petersburg University, served in the archival section of the Russian Ministry of Foreign Affairs, 1897–1903. Emigrated to Germany in 1904, joined the Mensheviks. After the outbreak of the World War, he settled in Great Britain and was arrested by British authorities for revolutionary activities in August 1917; released along with another Russian Social Democrat, P. M. Petrov, in exchange for permission for British subjects to leave Russia. Returned to Petrograd on January 3, 1918, joined the Bolsheviks, was made assistant people's commissar for foreign affairs on January 29; made acting commissar for foreign affairs instead of Trotsky on March 13; appointed commissar for foreign affairs on May 30, 1918.

[27] John Author Ray (1879–1977), graduate of Yale University (1903, MA), Docteur de l'Université de Paris (1906). He entered the consular service in 1909, served in Masqat, Venezuela, and England; appointed consul at Odessa on July 25, 1914; detailed for Bushire (Persia) on February 8, 1918.

[28] John Kenneth Caldwell (1881–1982) entered the diplomatic service in 1906, served in Japan. Appointed consul at Vladivostok on August 1, 1914; appointed to Kobe (Japan) on July

of which was sent direct, and the other around the globe,—or via Washington. To the former I have as yet received no reply, but to the latter received reply to-day. This shows you how difficult it is to communicate with interior points in Russia. I don't know how long our cables will be in transmission to the United States or any foreign country. Not one of the Foreign Missions here has recognized the Bolshevik government, which is making every effort to obtain recognition and consequently is making it more disagreeable for the Foreign Missions from day to day. It is possible that our cable communications may be cut off. If so, most or all of the Foreign Missions will have to leave. The Department has not only complied with every request I have made, but when I suggested a change of policy in regard to the Bolshevik government which it had not recognized in accordance with my advice, it declined to follow the suggestion saying my course had met with approval of the Department and it saw no occasion to change it. I suggested such a change because I was disgusted with all political parties and all capitalistic interests in Russia for not organizing and deposing the Bolshevik government, whose principles were so reprehensible. My advice up to December 24th was to await the convening of the Constituent Assembly which was the supreme power to which all Russia and all civilized countries had looked; but the time for its assembling, November 28th, passed and when the Bolsheviks arrested many of the prominent men elected to that Assembly and intimidated others from coming I began to feel that the only way to keep Russia in the war was by supporting the people in authority. One reason for the bourgeoisie, as they are called, offering no resistance to the Bolsheviks was that the latter had control of the army which numbered 10,000,000 or more men, with guns, who had been held in subjection so long that they could not appreciate liberty when they gained it. All ranks in the army and navy were abolished, even shoulder straps being prohibited and officers drawing the same pay as men after being selected by their comrades but subject to removal by the same authority. I don't know what is to become of this country as 80 per cent of the people are uneducated and many are inclined to follow the false teachings of Bolshevism. The ignorant believe that they can divide the property and live in idleness if not in luxury. It is a great pity that Russia is, in view of these circumstances, richer in resources than the United States or any other country on the globe. I would write at greater length on this subject but have not the time.

A telegram just received from Helsingfors, Finland, says that the Bolsheviks have driven out the bourgeois Senate and assumed control of Finland—a country which declared itself independent about a month ago and whose independence has just been recognized by France and five or six other gov-

---

1, 1920; on special detail at Chita (Siberia), October 1921–February 1922.

ernments. Finland has been a part of Russia for about a century, but the Finns, many of whom are in the United States, have preserved their own identity by speaking their own language, having their own schools, customs, etc. They deserved independence and I was in favor of their having it, but like the Russians they don't seem to know how to use it.

I have just been called to the phone and heard that Smolny Institute, Bolshevik Headquarters, has formally announced that a revolution similar to that in Russia has begun in Germany. The Bolshevik leaders here, most of whom are Jews and 90 per cent of whom are returned exiles, care little for Russia or any other country but are internationalists and they are trying to start a worldwide social revolution. If such a revolution can get a foothold in Germany where the people are obsequious to those above them and domineering and tyrannical to those beneath them and where organization and system has obtained such a foothold as it never had in history before, I begin to fear for the institutions not only of England but of the Republic of France and the thought arises in my mind whether our own institutions are safe.

The relationship between the Bolsheviks and the anarchists grew closer as the weeks passed. On April 15th our Consul-General Summers in Moscow cabled the Secretary of State:

By decrees March 21st Moscow Commissariat Military Affairs incorporated anarchist forces into socialistic army on equal footing. Since then de facto authorities have requisitioned and given to official anarchist groups approximately thirty large private residences for publication newspapers and other propaganda. As result of protection present government anarchism has openly spread over Russia. As a result of growing power and insults offered Colonel Robins of the American Red Cross, who is on very intimate terms with Lenin and Trotzky, orders were given on the 13th to arrest all anarchists. This was done after considerable resistance and partial destruction by artillery of the houses occupied by anarchists. It is understood also that Count Mirbach, the German Ambassador,[29] who is expected in Moscow daily, warned the local authorities that anarchism must cease before he arrived.

---

[29] Count Wilhelm von Mirbach (1871–1918), a German diplomat, served as counselor in the St. Petersburg embassy, 1908–11, then in Romania and Greece. He headed the special German mission to Petrograd, December 16, 1917–February 10, 1918, and was the first German minister to Soviet Russia from April 2, 1918. On July 6, 1918, he was killed in Moscow by Left Socialist Revolutionaries in protest of the Treaty of Brest-Litovsk.

Figure 5. The American Embassy, Petrograd, 1909–17.

TERESTCHENKO
Minister of Finance and later Minister of Foreign Affairs under the First Provisional Government

PAUL MILIUKOFF
First Minister of Foreign Affairs under the Provisional Government

MICHAEL RODZIANKO
Formerly President of the Russian Duma

Figure 6. Russian statesmen with whom Francis had the closest contact: Terestchenko, Minister of Finance and later Minister of Foreign Affairs under the First Provisional Government; Paul Miliukoff, First Minister of Foreign Affairs under the Provisional Government; and Michael Rodzianko, Formerly President of the Russian Duma.

Figure 7. The American Railway Commission to Russia and Ambassador Francis at the American Embassy, Petrograd. Left to right: Commissioners Darling, John F. Stevens, Ambassador Francis, and Commissioner Henry Miller.

Figure 8. Alexander Kerensky. The writing across the picture reads in translation: "In memory of friendly conversations through bright but difficult days."

N. PREBENSEN
Norwegian Minister to Russia

SIR GEORGE W. BUCHANAN
British Ambassador to Russia

COUNT DIAMANDI
Roumanian Minister to Russia

T. NOULENS
French Ambassador to Russia

Figure 9. Members of the Diplomatic Corps at Petrograd: N. Prebensen, Norwegian Minister to Russia; Sir George W. Buchanan, British Ambassador to Russia; Count Diamandi, Roumanian Minister to Russia; and [Joseph] Noulens, French Ambassador to Russia.

Figure 10. Ambassador Francis and his staff before the American Embassy, Vologda, Russia.

Figure 11. Last conference of the Allied chiefs in the American Embassy, Vologda, July 23, 1918.

Chapter XV
THE DIAMANDI INCIDENT

I never saw Trotzky. I saw Lenin on one occasion. It was when I went as Dean of the Diplomatic Corps, accompanied by all Allied and Neutral Chiefs, to demand the release of the Roumanian Minister, Diamandi. The British Ambassador, Sir George Buchanan, had left Petrograd two weeks before. The Roumanian Minister had been arrested and put in the fortress on the Russian New Year's Evening, our 14th of January, 1918. I called the Corps to meet at the American Embassy the following day. There were twenty of us altogether, thirteen representing the Allied and seven the Neutral countries. All of us signed the demand for the release. Some of the others were disposed to have me go accompanied by two Neutrals and two Allied Chiefs. There was some delay about agreement on the four members besides myself, and I proposed that we all go in a body. I had arranged a meeting through the telephone with Lenin, who speaks English.

The Bolsheviks had been in control of the government about two months when the Roumanian Minister was arrested. They retained the same headquarters that they occupied when the Provisional Government was overthrown, which was Smolny Institute. Smolny had been used as a girls' school. When Lenin appointed the time for the Diplomatic Corps to call upon him, he informed the leaders of the Bolshevik Party thereof. Some of these leaders suggested that Smolny Institute should be furnished with rugs and new furniture for the occasion.

Others advised Lenin to receive the Diplomatic Corps in his own office, without rising and without inviting them to take seats, and to cut the interview short by asking the Diplomats in a curt tone of voice what they wished. A compromise was decided on by Lenin, who did not procure any additional furnishings, but met us at the door of his office.

I, as Dean of the Corps, accosted him first, saying to him I was the American Ambassador and Dean of the Diplomatic Corps. I introduced the other Ambassadors and the Ministers by their official titles. Lenin thereupon invited us into a room about twelve by fifteen feet, and showed the Ministers and Charges to seats upon a wooden bench. He showed the Ambassadors to chairs, and said: "Be seated, gentlemen." I read in English, and while standing, the demand which we had all signed, and then had Livingston Phelps[1] read it in French.

Lenin said: "Let us discuss the matter. "I immediately replied: "No discussion on the subject whatever." I said that the person of a diplomatic representative was inviolate and was immune; that we stood on this principle recognized in international relations and demanded the release of Diamandi. The French Ambassador began to talk. A discussion ensued lasting at least an hour. Lenin was pleasant in manner throughout the meeting. At the close of the talk I got up and said: "We'll end this discussion here."

The Serbian Minister had made a very impassioned speech in French in which he had said the Germans and Austrians had invaded his beloved land, killing many innocent citizens, women and children. He said that the Serbians did not revenge themselves on the German Minister or the Austrian Minister, when they could have done so, observing the custom, which had never been violated, of giving ministers of the belligerent countries safe conduct through the border. It was evident that the Bolsheviks saw they were in a very embarrassing position. The Diplomats would have left Petrograd if Diamandi had not been released.

Lenin said he would refer the demand to the Council of Commissars, that is to say practically the Bolshevik Executive Committee, and would let us know by twelve o'clock that night, or as soon as the matter was passed upon. I told Lenin I would be in the Embassy throughout the evening. He phoned me about midnight that the Central Soviet had concluded to release Diamandi. The release took place the next day about one o'clock, but the Roumanian Minister was ordered to leave Petrograd within ten days after that, and was given only twenty-four hours' notice. I went to the Roumanian Legation[2] to say good-by, but found that Minister Diamandi had already gone to the Finnish Station. I followed him there, and caught the train before he left. He was going to Sweden. He crossed at Torneo, which was about thirty hours' distance by regular schedule, but he was three weeks in getting there. I heard afterwards that the Bolshevik Commissar who had the Minister in charge carried a communication to the local Commissar ordering that the Roumanian Minister be shot when they reached Torneo; but a revolution had taken place there and the Whites were in control, having taken Torneo out of the hands of the Reds the day previous. The Whites arrested the Bolshevik Commissar when he came into Torneo and it was reported that they shot him instead of Minister Diamandi.

---

[1] Livingston Phelps (1885–1960), a non-career diplomat born in France to American parents. He received his primary education in Austria, France, and England, and graduated from École Libre des Sciences Politique (Paris, 1903) and Harvard University (1907, AB). He served as private secretary to Ambassador Thomas N. Page at Rome, 1914–15, and was appointed third secretary of the embassy at Petrograd on October 26, 1916.

[2] The Romanian legation was located on Zakharevskaya Street, 23, not far from the US embassy.

The arrest and imprisonment of Diamandi will pass into diplomatic history as an act of most extraordinary character. It was an incident which gained in significance through later developments.

On the day following the call of the Diplomatic Corps at Smolny, the organ of the Bolsheviks *Pravda*[3] (Truth) printed an astonishing statement that Zalkend, the Assistant Commissar (Trotzky being down in Brest-Litovsk) had received by telephone information to this effect:

> American Ambassador assures he will immediately after the release of Diamandi go to him with protest against the treatment of the Russian troops in Roumania, and will make through the American Representative at Roumania, a necessary statement to the Roumanian Ministry. He regards the act of Diamandi's arrest as a formal expression of protest of the Russian Government against the activities of the Roumanian Commander-in-Chief.

As a matter of fact, I had sent no statement and had authorized no one to make any statement for me, by telephone or otherwise, to Zalkend. Apparently the statement had been given out by Zalkend to save the face of the Bolshevik Government. It was not until some time later that I learned what was behind this action of Zalkend's. Diamandi after his release referred to this publication in Pravda and expressed to the Diplomatic Corps his surprise and regret on account of it. I immediately addressed to him a letter in which I said:

> My dear Colleague:
> I am surprised and pained to learn from you that you for a moment think that I would or could justify your arrest and confinement in Peter and Paul Fortress as I have had only one opinion on the subject, and have made no expressions concerning it other than to deplore such an unprecedented infraction on diplomatic immunities. I have concurred in the sentiment of our colleagues, allied and neutral chiefs of missions, and as the doyen of the Diplomatic Corps accompanied by all the members thereof presented to the President of the Commissars the demand for your immediate and unconditional release and stated in doing so that we could not enter into any discussion concerning the causes of your arrest.
> I have had no communication direct nor indirect, nor have I sent any message to anyone connected with the Soviet Government on the subject of your arrest or your release. The dragoman of the Embassy by my direction

---

[3] *Pravda* (Truth), a Bolshevik daily paper founded in 1912. It was shut down in July 1914 and resumed publication on March 5, 1917, as an official organ of the Bolshevik Central Committee. After March 1918, when the Russian capital was transferred from Petrograd to Moscow, *Pravda* became the main newspaper of Soviet Russia.

telephoned to Smolny Institute about midnight of the 14th to ask whether the decision concerning your release had been determined, but he was not instructed nor authorized to make any other inquiry and certainly no condition concerning your release, and he informs me that he did not do so or even think of doing so.

There was an echo to this Diamandi incident at the meeting of the Bolshevik Councils some weeks later. Rabovski, one of the Bolshevik leaders,[4] in that congress expressed regret that the Roumanian Minister had spent only twenty-four hours outside the walls of his Embassy. "This matter can be righted," he said, "and we will give the most active assistance to Roumanian workmen and peasants to help them hide away the Messrs. Diamandis where they should be."

The circumstances which led the Bolsheviks to arrest and imprison the Roumanian Minister came to my knowledge some time after the visit of the Diplomatic Corps to Lenin. Those circumstances went to show not only that the Bolsheviks were acting in the interests of the Germans in this matter, but under special requests from them.

A letter from A. Joife,[5] and marked "confidential" was sent from Brest-Litovsk, dated December 31st (Old Style), 1917, addressed "To the Council of People's Commissars of Petrograd." A. Joffe was President of the delegation representing the Bolshevik Government in the peace negotiations at Brest. This letter opened with: "Comrade L. D. Trotzky instructed me to bring to the knowledge of the Council of People's Commissars the motives of his telegraphic order about the arrest of the Roumanian diplomatic representatives at Petrograd." The letter stated that General William Hoffmann[6] of the German Peace Delegation[7] "pointed out the necessity of

---

[4] Khristian G. Rakovsky (1873–1941), Romanian and international revolutionary of Bulgarian origin. He arrived in Russia after the February Revolution, joined the Bolsheviks in November 1917, and led revolutionary activities on the Romanian border on the eve of and during the Diamandy Affair. He was appointed a member of the delegation sent to negotiate peace with Ukraine in April 1918. He was sent with a diplomatic mission to Berlin in September and was deported from Germany in early November. From January 1919, he was chairman of the Council of People's Commissars of Soviet Ukraine.

[5] Adolf A. Ioffe (1883–1927), studied medicine at Berlin University and law in Zurich University; graduated from Vienna University (DM). Originally a nonfactional Social Democrat, he joined the Bolsheviks in the summer of 1917 and headed the Bolshevik faction in the Petrograd City Duma. A member of the Petrograd Military Revolutionary Committee, which organized the overthrow of the Provisional Government. The first chairman of the Soviet delegation at the Brest-Litovsk peace negotiations, November–December 1917; the first Soviet diplomatic representative to Germany, April–November 1918.

[6] Max Hoffman.

[7] Carl Adolf Maximilian Hoffman (Max, 1869–1927), graduate of the Prussian War Academy; studied Russian at the German embassy in St. Petersburg; served in the Russian and Northern States Department of the German General Staff (1899–1901); an observer with the Japanese

sending of sure agents into the Roumanian Army and the possibility to arrest the Roumanian Legation at Petersburg (Petrograd) in whole; also to take repressive measures against the Roumanian King and the Roumanian Chief Command. After this conversation Comrade L. D. Trotzky ordered in a telegraphic way the arrest of the Roumanian representative at Petersburg (Petrograd). The above-mentioned report is sent with a special courier, Comrade I. G. Brosoff, who will give to Commander Podvoyski[8] secret information concerning the sending to the Roumanian Army of persons, the names of whom Comrade Brosoff will tell. All of those persons will be paid from the fund of the German Kerosene-Trade Bank, which bought near Borislave the stock society Fanto & Co. The chief direction of the agents will belong according to General Hoffmann's indication to the well-known Wolff Venigel, who has under his observation the military missions of the Allied countries."

Very significant was the conclusion of this Joffe letter: "What concerns the British and American representatives, General Hoffmann said that the German staff approved the measures taken by Comrade Trotzky and Comrade Laziniroff[9] concerning looking after their activities."

Still more convincing evidence, perhaps, of Lenin's employment as the agent of Germany was afforded in a newspaper interview with General William Hoffmann, Chief of Staff of the Eastern Army of Germany, which appeared in the newspapers of December 24th, 1920. General Hoffmann was quoted as saying:

> As Chief of Staff of the East Army during the war, I directed the propaganda against the Russian Army. The General Staff naturally made use of every possible means to break through the Russian front. One of these means was poisoned gas, another was Lenin. The Imperial regime dispatched Lenin to Russia from the Swiss frontier. With our consent, Lenin and his friends disorganized the Russian army. Von Kuehlmann (former German Secretary for

---

army in Manchuria during the Russo-Japanese War of 1904–05. From the beginning of the World War, he fought against Russia alongside Hindenburg and Ludendorff; chief of staff of the Eastern Front from August 1916; promoted to major general in October 1917. Deputy chairman of the German delegation at the Brest-Litovsk peace negotiations.

[8] Nikolai I. Podvoisky (1880–1948), head of the Military Organization of the Petersburg Bolshevik Committee and one of the organizers of the Red Guard in 1917. Assistant chairman of the Military-Revolutionary Committee and one of the most active figures in the October Revolution; commander of the Petrograd Military District in fall 1917; people's commissar for military and naval affairs, November 23, 1917–March 13, 1918.

[9] Probably Pavel E. Lazimir (1891–1920), Left Socialist Revolutionary who headed the Soldiers' Section of the Petrograd Soviet's Executive Committee; chairman of the Petrograd Military Revolutionary Committee during the October Revolution; afterwards an active member of Soviet military leadership.

Foreign Affairs),[10] Count Czernin (Austro-Hungarian Foreign Minister),[11] and I then closed the Brest-Litovsk Treaty so that we could throw our army against the West front. While at Brest we were convinced that the Bolsheviks could not hold power more than three weeks.

On my word of honor as a German general, in spite of the valuable service Trotzky and Lenin rendered, we neither knew nor foresaw the danger to humanity from the consequences of this journey of Bolsheviks to Russia.

Shortly after the appearance of this interview, General Hoffmann attempted to repudiate it. While I was in Washington, early in March, 1921, to present my resignation as Ambassador to Russia to the outgoing Administration, I was told that this interview with General Hoffmann was shown to him before publication, and that he signed his name to it in token of approval.

---

[10] Baron Richard von Kühlmann (1873–1948), German secretary of state for foreign affairs, August 6, 1917–July 9, 1918, who headed the German delegation at the Brest-Litovsk peace negotiations.

[11] Count Ottokar Theobald Otto Maria Czernin von und zu Chudenitz (1872–1932), Austro-Hungarian minister of foreign affairs from December 1916 to April 1918.

Chapter XVI
THE BREST-LITOVSK PEACE

The Bolsheviks acted quickly after announcing their new government under the form of the "Council of Commissars of the People."

On the 7th of November, 1917, Trotzky as "the Commissary of the People for Foreign Affairs," addressed this communication to the American Embassy:

> In drawing your attention to the text of the proposition for an armistice and a Democratic peace without annexations or contributions, founded on the rights of people to dispose of themselves, proposals approved by the Congress of the Council of Workmen and Soldiers, I have the honor to beg you, Mr. Ambassador, to be good enough to regard the above-mentioned documents as a formal proposal for an armistice without delay on all the fronts, and for the opening without delay of negotiations for peace—a proposal which the plenipotentiary government of the Russian Republic is addressing simultaneously to all the belligerent nations and to their governments.
>
> I beg you, Mr. Ambassador, to be good enough to accept the assurance of the perfect consideration and very profound respect of the government of the Councils for the people of the United States, who also, like all the other peoples exhausted by this incomparable butchery, cannot help but ardently desire peace.

The armistice between the Bolsheviks and the Germans took effect at the end of November, 1917.[1] Trotzky announced that hostilities had ceased on the Russian front and that preliminary negotiations would be started on the 2nd of December. His announcement said:

> The Allied governments and all diplomatic representatives in Russia are kindly requested to reply whether they wish to take part in a negotiation.

---

[1] The first Russian-German armistice was concluded on December 2 (15), 1917, and went into effect two days later.

The British Ambassador, who at that time was Dean of the Diplomatic Corps, made public a statement that Trotzky's letter with the proposal of a general armistice was not received until nineteen hours after the receipt by the Russian Commander-in-Chief of the Bolsheviks of the order to open immediate negotiations for an armistice. I transmitted the communication from Trotzky to the American Government, but made no answer to Trotzky, as the United States had not recognized the Bolshevik Government. Lieut.-Col. Kerth, representing the Military Mission of the United States at the front in Russia,[2] did address the Commander-in-Chief of the Russian Army this protest:

> In accordance with definite instructions of my Government, transmitted to me by the Ambassador of the United States of America in Petrograd, I have the honor to inform you that in view of the fact that the Republic of the United States is carrying on a war in alliance with Russia, which war has as its basis the struggle of democracy against autocracy, my Government categorically and energetically protests against any separate armistice which may be made by Russia.

It was not until the 12th of March, 1918, that the terms of this peace were approved by the Soviet Congress at Moscow,[3] but in the meantime Lenin and Trotzky had not delayed the work of demoralizing the Russian Army. Lenin, it must be remembered, had come into Russia from Switzerland, traveling through Germany in a private car and being abundantly supplied with means. When I went to Russia there was an army enlisted of 12,000,000 men. It was increased to 16,000,000 before the revolution against the Monarchy in March, 1917, and there was a call for 3,000,000 additional. Of those 16000,000 men, 2,000,000 had been captured and 2,000,000 had been killed or died from disease, so that the army at the time of the armistice

---

[2] Monroe Crawford Kerth (1876–1936), graduate of the US Military Academy, served in the Philippines, took part in the China Relief Expedition. Major of infantry, detailed to General Staff Corps on March 11, 1916. Appointed assistant military attaché to the Petrograd embassy on July 23, 1917; promoted to temporary lieutenant colonel on August 5, 1917, served as the US military representative at the Stavka (headquarters of the Supreme High Command of the Russian army). Promoted to temporary colonel on February 8, 1918, transferred to the American Expeditionary Forces in Europe, served on the staff of General Pershing.

[3] The Extraordinary Fourth All-Russian Congress of Soviets of Workers', Peasants', Soldiers', and Cossacks' Deputies convened in Moscow on March 14–16, 1918, for ratification of the Brest-Litovsk peace treaty. Ratification followed on March 15 and caused the breaking of a governmental coalition of the Bolsheviks with the Left Socialists-Revolutionaries, who bitterly opposed the Brest-Litovsk treaty. The Fourth Congress also approved the decision to move the Russian capital from Petrograd to Moscow.

entered into by the Bolsheviks with the Germans numbered about 12,000,000 men, not equaled in numbers by any other nation in any war.

With the signing of the armistice this army demobilized itself. It melted away like snow before a summer's sun. Disintegration continued during the period of negotiations at Brest-Litovsk, and while the treaty was awaiting approval by the Soviet Congress. The soldiers left their regiments in large bodies. They would get on trains and the trains would start before they asked where they were going. Some of these soldiers sold their arms for a trifle; others threw their arms away, and some took their arms home.

As soon as the armistice had been agreed to by the Bolsheviks, the Germans moved more than 100 divisions from their Eastern front to France,[4] and began to prepare for their drive, in March, 1918, against the Allied armies. History records how nearly successful this drive was. Had it not been for the demoralization of the Russian army by the Bolsheviks, hundreds of thousands of lives of French and British and American soldiers would have been spared. Lenin and Trotzky demoralized the Russian army and thereby caused the war to be prolonged.

In various ways the Bolsheviks promptly contributed directly or indirectly to strengthen the Germans during that period immediately following their armistice. In March I received through Consul-General Madden Summers, of Moscow, reports from our consuls,—Macgowan at Irkutsk, Nielson at Samara,[5] Jenkins at Chita,[6] and others, showing the movement of released prisoners and of material from Russia to Germany. Nielson from Samara reported many cars of cotton loaded and being shipped by German firms.

The Bolsheviks went through the form of inviting England, France, Italy and America to enter into negotiations for peace under the armistice with Germany. They waited ten days, professedly to give the other countries time to come in. Then they proceeded with the negotiation of a separate peace. Trotzky was at the head of the Bolsheviks in the first negotiations. Lenin remained in Petrograd and was practically

---

[4] There were fifty-nine German divisions on the Russian Front at the moment, and only part of them might be removed to the Western Front. Another part continued their offensive on the local fronts from Finland through Ukraine to the Caucasus. In March 1918, there were sixty-two German divisions altogether in France.

[5] Orsen Norman Nielsen (1892–?), graduate of Wisconsin University, afterwards engaged in newspaper work. He was appointed clerk in the US Consulate General in Moscow on December 28, 1916; vice consul in Moscow from March 15, 1918; on special detail at Samara; transferred to Stockholm on September 14, 1918.

[6] Douglas Jenkins (1880–1961), entered the consular service in 1908, served in Sweden. He was appointed consul at Riga on November 24, 1913, and evacuated to Petrograd when the city was captured by the Germans in August 1917. In December 1917, he was sent by Francis to Kiev on special detail and then moved to Chita. He was detailed to Harbin on August 16, 1918, and later detailed to the State Department on December 23, 1921.

the whole Bolshevik Government. While I have no doubt that Lenin was a German agent from the beginning and disbursed German money, I believe, and so wired the Department, that his real purpose was promotion of worldwide social revolution. He would have taken British money, American money, and French money and used it to promote his purpose. He told a man who asked what he was doing in Russia that he was trying an "experiment in government" on the Russian people. Germany's desire to demoralize Russia and break up the Provisional Government gave Lenin his opportunity, of which he made good use.

When Trotzky demurred to the hard terms offered by the Germans in the first peace negotiations, General Hoffmann, the head of the German delegation, notified him and his Bolshevik associates that Germany would not prolong the negotiations more than two or three days further, and said: "You will have to say definitely whether you will accept these terms or not." Then it was that Trotzky showed real ability. He made that dramatic stand and replied in effect: "We decline to sign those severe peace terms, but Russia will fight no more."

This was the situation which rather stunned the Germans. Trotzky carried out his declaration[7] by leaving Brest-Litovsk and returning to Petrograd. A few days later the Germans gave out that they were going to march on Petrograd and Moscow. Trotzky replied to them that they could not move without violating the terms of the armistice, which required twelve days' notice before resumption of hostilities. The Germans' reply was, as the armies advanced, "You have already terminated the armistice by refusing to sign the peace terms."

From Brest-Litovsk on the 5th of February, 1918, Karl Radek[8] sent a long statement of the purposes of the Bolshevik delegation in the negotiations for peace with Germany. In the course of that he said:

> We Revolutionary-Internationalists not only emphatically refused to aid our own Bourgeoisie to gain a victory over the proletariat of a neighboring country, but we pointed out that a peace which would be the result of an agreement between the great capitalistic powers would be a peace concluded at the expense of small nations and their international proletariats. The small nations will represent "small change" for such a peace, and the international proletariat will pay the expenses of the war. What is it that you want?—we are asked by the Centrist elements; by the Minimalist Internationalists in

---

[7] Trotsky's response to the German ultimatum on January 28 (February 10), 1918: "No war, no peace." Trotsky's declaration resulted in the breaking of the armistice with Germany, a new German offensive on Petrograd, and the signing of a peace treaty on conditions much more detrimental for Russia.

[8] Karl B. Radek (1885–1939), Social Democratic activist and newspaperman in Poland and Germany. He arrived in Russia after the October Revolution, entered the People's Commissariat of Foreign Affairs, and took part in the Brest-Litovsk peace negotiations.

Russia. Do you demand that the war shall be continued until capitalism is overthrown in all countries and all colonies liberated?—and they ridicule us as visionaries, who are prepared to consent to the proletariat being drained of blood for the sake of India being liberated from the English yoke. Yes, this would be insanity; and we answered them, therefore: No, we do not want to continue the war until socialism has conquered but we want to use, with all our might, the world war—the world crisis of capitalism—for directing the maturing forces of the labor class to the object of tearing out once for all, the roots of war and capitalism. We want to transform the war of nations into a civil war.

The formal notification which the Trotzky delegation handed to the Germans at Brest was a curiosity:

In the name of the People's Commissaries, which is the government of the Russian Federated Republic, we hereby bring to the knowledge of the governments and peoples at war with us, to our allies and to the neutral countries, that refusing to sign an annexationist treaty, Russia declares on her part the state of war with Germany, Austro-Hungary, Turkey and Bulgaria has ceased. That the Russian troops are simultaneously given orders to demobilize completely on all fronts.

When Trotzky returned to Petrograd after making this grandstand play, which dumbfounded the Germans, Lenin reprimanded him and told him the Russian Soviet Government would be compelled to agree to terms still more severe, whereupon Trotzky resigned as Minister of Foreign Affairs and was made Minister of War and organized the Red Army,[9] which organization is in existence up to the present time, and waged war successfully for a time against Poland and is now threatening Esthonia. The Red Army is composed of Lettish and Chinese troops[10]

---

[9] The Workers' and Peasants' Red Army was created in accordance with the Soviet decree of January 15, 1918, and was originally a volunteer force comprised of Red Guard detachments, Latvian regiments, Chinese, Hungarian, and other international units. On June 12, 1918, the Council of the People's Commissars decreed the first call-up for military service, and afterwards the Red Army was made up by way of compulsory mobilizations including former officers of the Imperial Army ("military specialists").

[10] Red Latvian Riflemen (see n. 8, p. 161). During the revolution and Civil War, they fought on the Bolshevik side and were the most efficient force of the Red Army at the initial stage of its formation. Chinese troops consisted mostly of the former Chinese laborers who joined the Red Army during the Civil War. There were a lot of small Chinese units throughout Soviet Russia, numbering about 50,000. Some Chinese units fought on the White side as well. The whole strength of the Red Army was about 800,000 by October 1918, and almost three million by the end of 1919.

and conscripted Russians. It has the reputation of being the most strictly disciplined and the most cruel army in history.

The actions of these Bolsheviks in these peace negotiations were without precedent as far as I know in the history of international relations, but it may be said that Lenin and Trotzky have disregarded many precedents. While I have no agreement whatever with Lenin's views, my judgment credited him with sincerity. (This sentence was written soon after my return. I have changed my mind in regard to Lenin's sincerity.) He proved ruthless and unscrupulous, however, in attempting to carry out his convictions. When his power was threatened and could not be maintained in any other way, he permitted the Reign of Terror. It will be recalled that Trotzky refused to be a party in person to the second negotiations with the Germans, and that Tchecherin represented the Bolsheviks.

While the peace negotiations were going on at Brest one of my "scouts," whose duty it was to look, listen and report, brought to the Embassy this memorandum:

> The anarchist movement strengthens daily. During a visit to the Foreign Office, the anarchist representative said that in case the anarchists condemned in America are not released the American Embassy at Petrograd and the Ambassador would pay the penalty.

A short time before the Brest-Litovsk peace was ratified at Moscow by the All-Russian Soviet Congress I had cabled the State Department that the Congress would meet to act upon the peace treaty, and that I thought the Russian people should have some expression of interest on the part of the American people. President Wilson cabled a message addressed to the Russian people through this Soviet Congress.[11] He said:

> May I not take advantage of the meeting of the Congress of the Soviets to express the sincere sympathy which the people of the United States feel for the Russian people at this moment when the German power has been thrust in to interrupt and turn back the whole struggle for freedom and substitute the wishes of Germany for the purpose of the people of Russia?
>
> Although the Government of the United States is, unhappily, not now in a position to render the direct and effective aid it would wish to render, I beg to assure the people of Russia through the Congress that it will avail itself of every opportunity to secure for Russia once more complete sovereignty and independence in her own affairs, and full restoration to her great role in the life of Europe and the modern world.

---

[11] Woodrow Wilson's open letter of March 11, 1918, aiming to prevent the ratification of the Brest-Litovsk treaty by the Extraordinary Fourth All-Russian Congress of Soviets.

THE BREST-LITOVSK PEACE 199

The whole heart of the people of the United States is with the people of Russia in the attempt to free themselves forever from autocratic government and become the masters of their own life.

On the same day Samuel Gompers, President of the American Federation of Labor, cabled the All-Russian Congress of Soviets as follows:

> We address you in the name of world liberty. We assure you that the people of the United States are pained by every blow at Russian freedom, as they would be by a blow at their own. The American people desire to be of service to the Russian people in their struggle to safeguard freedom and realize its opportunities. We desire to be informed as to how we may help.
>
> We speak for the great organized movement of working people who are devoted to the cause of freedom and the ideals of democracy. We assure you also that the whole American Nation ardently desires to be helpful to Russia and awaits with eagerness an indication from Russia as to how help may most effectively be extended.
>
> To all those who strive for freedom, we say: Courage! Justice must triumph if all free people stand united against autocracy! We await your suggestions.

President Wilson's message was presented to the Congress. Zinoviev, who was the head of the Bolshevik Government in Petrograd,[12] was in Moscow when the cable from President Wilson was printed. He returned to Petrograd two or three days later and said in a speech: "We slapped the President of the United States in the face."

The reply to the President's message to the Republic of Russia was intended by the Bolsheviks for effect on the workingmen of the United States. It was practically an invitation to revolution in the United States. It is a fair illustration of what Bolshevism means.

> The All-Russian Congress of Soviets expresses its appreciation to the American people, and first of all to the laboring and exploited classes in the United States for the message sent by the President of the United States to the Congress of Soviets in this time when the Russian Socialistic Soviet Republic is living through most difficult trials.
>
> The Russian Republic uses the occasion of the message from President Wilson to express to all peoples who are dying and suffering from the horrors of this imperialistic war its warm sympathy and firm conviction that the happy time is near when the laboring masses in all bourgeois countries will

---

[12] Grigory E. Zinoviev (1883–1936), Bolshevik leader who returned to Russia from emigration on April 3, 1917, in company with Vladimir I. Lenin. Chairman of the Petrograd Soviet of Workmen's and Soldiers' Deputies from December 13, 1917.

throw off the capitalistic yoke and establish a socialistic state of society, which is the only one capable of assuring a permanent and just peace as well as the culture and well-being of all who toil.

Immediately following the ratification of the peace treaty at Moscow, I gave out a statement for publication, March 16, 1918. The Bolshevik papers at Moscow were closed against communications from the American Embassy, but in other cities the statement was printed. I had it translated into Russian:

> I shall not leave Russia until forced to depart. My government and the American people are too deeply interested in the welfare of the Russian people to abandon the country and leave its people to the mercies of Germany. America is sincerely interested in Russia and in the freedom of the Russian people. We shall do all possible to promote the true interests of the Russians and to protect and preserve the integrity of this great country. The friendship between Russia and the United States which has existed for a century or more should be augmented rather than impaired by Russia becoming a Republic, and all Americans are sincerely desirous that Russians should be permitted to continue free and independent and not become subjects of Germany.
>
> I have not yet seen an authentic copy of the peace treaty but am sufficiently acquainted with its provisions to know that if the Russian people submit thereto Russia will not only be robbed of vast acres of her rich territory but will eventually become virtually a German province and her people will lose the liberties for which their ancestors have struggled and sacrificed for generations past. My Government still considers America an ally of the Russian people, who surely will not reject the proffered assistance which we shall be prompt to render to any power in Russia that will offer sincere and organized resistance to the German invasion. If the Russian people who are brave and patriotic will hold in abeyance for the time being their political differences and be resolute and firm and united they can drive the enemy from their borders and secure before the end of 1918 for themselves and the world an enduring peace.

I issued the above address to the Russian people. I appealed to them to organize and repel the Germans. I said we Americans and our Government still considered the Russian people our allies, that we were not going to observe the peace.

About four days after this appeared, Kuehlman, the German Minister of Foreign Affairs, made a demand on the Bolshevik Government that I be sent out of Russia. The German demand said:

"He is not only violating the laws of neutrality, but he has issued an address to the Russian people which is a virtual call to arms."

The Bolsheviks said nothing to me about this demand of the German Government. I was not in communication with them at the time. I learned, however, that their reply to Kuehlman was to the effect that I had not said any more than President Wilson had said in his message to the Bolshevik Congress.

Kuehlman, in conversation with Karahan, Secretary of the Russian Peace Delegation at Brest in February,[13] had said that the Foreign Embassies would have to leave Petrograd on short notice from the Germans. One of the reports which reached us at the time was that the Allied Missions might be arrested. It was even rumored that the American Ambassador might be made a prisoner by the Germans and held to be exchanged for the German ship, The Vaterland, then held in New York harbor. There were German officers in Petrograd at the time.[14] One of them shot and killed two Russian soldiers at the Grand Hotel "for being rude to him," as the report made to the Bolshevik officers stated.

At this time cable communication with my Government was severed; it had been very unreliable and irregular since the Bolsheviks came into power. I had no authority from my Government to make the foregoing address to the Russian people, but assumed the responsibility, advising the Department of State of the exact wording of this appeal to the Russian people. I did not learn until two months later that the Department of State approved of this address, and then I was informed only through a newspaper clipping sent to me by Ira Nelson Morris, American Minister to Stockholm. That newspaper clipping stated the Associated Press correspondent in Washington had called at the Department of State and inquired whether the address I had issued to the Russian people had been authorized by my government. The reply, according to the clipping, was: "No, but it was thoroughly approved."

---

[13] Lev M. Karakhan (1889–1937), originally a Menshevik. After the February Revolution, he was elected to the Petrograd Soviet and joined the Bolsheviks in May 1917. Secretary of the Soviet delegation at the Brest-Litovsk peace negotiations from November 1917; assistant people's commissar for foreign affairs from March 1918.

[14] Military members of the special German mission, which stayed at Petrograd from December 15, 1917 to February 14, 1918. The chief military representative was Vice Admiral Walter von Keyserlingk (1868–1946).

Chapter XVII
VOLOGDA—THE DIPLOMATIC CAPITAL

I had received authority from my government to leave Petrograd whenever my judgment so dictated, and all of my colleagues had received similar authority from their governments. We were meeting in the American Embassy daily, not all of the Allied Chiefs, but the British, the French, the Italian and the Japanese Ambassadors. The Germans were approaching Petrograd. The Bolshevik Government was preparing to move to Moscow. I had remained some four weeks after receiving instructions to act upon my own discretion about leaving Petrograd. At one of these conferences of the Ambassadors toward the end of February, 1918, we decided that the time had come to leave. I said to them: "I am not going out of Russia."

"Where are you going?" one of them asked.

"I am going to Vologda," I said.

"What do you know about Vologda?"

"Not a thing except that it is the junction of the Trans-Siberian Railway and the Moscow-Archangel Railway and that it is 350 miles farther away from the Germans."

"Well, if it is unsafe there, what are you going to do?"

"I am going east to Viatka, which is 600 miles east, and if it is unsafe there, I am going to Perm. If it is unsafe at Perm, I am going to Irkutsk, and if it is still unsafe, I am going to Chita, and if necessary from there I am going to Vladivostok, where I will be protected by an American man-of-war, the *Brooklyn*,[1] under Admiral Knight."[2]

We discussed the situation, and I told my colleagues:

"You ought not to leave Russia now."

They wanted to get out of Russia and return to their own countries. All of them declined to join me in my plan except the Japanese Embassy and the Chinese Legation. They were willing to go to Vologda, which would be on their way home.

The other missions attempted to get away by going west. The British, French, Italians, Belgians, Serbians, Portuguese and the Greeks left on trains, attempting to go through Finland. They found themselves in the midst of civil war between the

---

[1] The USS *Brooklyn*, armored cruiser, flagship of the Asiatic Fleet from 1915–19. It supported the American Siberian Expedition during the Allied intervention in the Russian Far East.

[2] Austin Melvin Knight (1854–1927), rear admiral, commander in chief of the Asiatic Fleet, May 22, 1917–December 7, 1918.

Bolshevik element and the Bourgeoisie. The Bolsheviks had occupied Helsingfors. After considerable negotiation it was arranged that these Allied Missions be permitted to go through the lines, but through some misunderstanding the British Embassy in its special train was the only mission that got through. The lines were again closed and the remaining six missions were left on the Red Guard side of Finland. After remaining several weeks on their special trains, some of them were instructed by their respective governments to return to Russia, which they did and joined me at Vologda, The French, Italian and Serbians arrived first, and the Belgians about a week later. They lived in cars on the tracks at the railway station for some time.

Having discretionary authority to leave Petrograd the natural thing, perhaps, for me to do was to have gone with the other missions and stopped in Norway or Sweden for orders from Washington, but I did not like to abandon the Russian people, for whom I felt deep sympathy and whom I had assured repeatedly of America's unselfish interest in their welfare.

Just before leaving Petrograd, I wrote my son Charles,[3] under date of February 23rd, 1918:

My plan is to stay in Russia as long as I can. If a separate peace is concluded, as I believe it will be, there will be no danger of my being captured by the Germans. Such a separate peace, however, will be a severe blow to the Allies, and if any section of Russia refuses to recognize the authority of the Bolshevik Government to conclude such a peace I shall endeavor to locate in that section and encourage the rebellion. If no section is opposed to same I shall go to Vladivostok and endeavor from there to prevent supplies from falling into the hands of the Germans, and if there are any people organizing in Russia for armed resistance to Germany, I shall encourage them and recommend our Government to assist them. You may not conclude, therefore, that I am planning to return to America.

I left Petrograd on the morning of February 27th, and arrived at Vologda about twenty-six hours later. The railroad connections offered the main reason for the selection of this stopping place, notwithstanding my information was to the effect that the Bolshevik spirit in Vologda was deep-rooted and widespread. I lived nearly a week on the train, which was very much crowded with the Embassy staff and the military mission. After being in Vologda two days, I cabled the Department I had concluded to remain as long as it was safe. To this conclusion I was encouraged by the local

---

[3] Charles Broaddus Francis, the ambassador's third son (1881–1957).

treatment received. The Mayor,[4] the President of the City Duma,[5] the President of the local Soviet[6] and the local representatives of the Central Soviet at Moscow called upon me. Although I had never had any official relation with the Soviet or Bolshevik government because the United States had not recognized the Bolsheviks, these local officers were very courteous and accommodating. They offered me the use of a club house,[7] a commodious and an imposing structure, for the American Embassy. I accepted and began living there and conducting the chancellery therein from March 4th. I inaugurated the custom of giving a tea every Saturday afternoon to which the officials mentioned, my colleagues and their families and the stationmaster were invited. In an after-dinner speech made by me when I was a guest of the Mayor, I designated Vologda as "the diplomatic capital of Russia." The Russians present seemed very much pleased when this was translated to them.

This action taken by me in selecting Vologda and remaining there was rather unique in diplomatic history. I recall that the French Ambassador to the United States, Jusserand,[8] when I met him in Paris, during the peace negotiations, referred to it and commented. He said, "You discovered Vologda. You put it on the map. You made it the diplomatic center of Russia for five or six months."

Vologda was founded 1147 A. D., or about 345 years before Columbus discovered America. It is the great or one of the great lace centers of Russia. Some very fine samples of lace are to be had there. I am told they are all handmade and of very fine linen.

After becoming settled at Vologda, I told in a private letter to one of my sons of the gradual development of friendly relations. The letter was dated March 19th:

> I have never recognized this Bolshevik Government, but have established a quasi business or working arrangement with it, and to that do I attribute the

---

[4] Aleksei A. Alexandrov (1876–?), Menshevik, city head of Vologda, September 1, 1917–June 27, 1918.

[5] Ivan P. Galabutsky, Socialist Revolutionary, chairman of the City Duma from August 9, 1917.

[6] Shalva Z. Eliava (1883–1937), Bolshevik, chairman of the United Executive Committee of the Vologda Soviet, January–April 1918, and regional commissar for provisions, April–December 1918. Afterwards, Eliava was chairman of the Council of People's Commissars of Georgia, 1923–27, and of the Trans-Caucasian Republic, 1927–31.

[7] The two-story wooden building of the Vologda Society of Mutual Aid to Private Service Labor (commonly known as the Shopmen Club) at 35 Ekaterinsko-Dvoryanskaya (now Hertzen) Street. From 1997 to 2012, the building housed the private Museum of the Diplomatic Corps.

[8] Jean Jules Jusserand (1855–1932), French diplomat and student of English literature. He entered the Foreign Service in 1876 and served in Great Britain, Tunis, and Denmark. Ambassador to the US, 1902–25.

courtesy shown us by the municipal authorities and by the local Commissar[9] and by the President of the local Soviet. There are local Soviets throughout Russia composed of workmen, soldiers and peasants; they assume and exercise the right to commandeer whatever residences they desire to live in, ordering the owners or occupants therefrom. There has been no violence here that I have heard of; in fact the town is remarkably quiet and I have enjoyed my stay here, being domiciled in the club house, very well adapted to the Embassy's uses. Last night I entertained the local Commissar, the Mayor, President of the Local Soviet, President of the City Duma, and five other officials, at a dinner in the club house, which has become known through the town as the American Embassy.

At one time I spoke to the Mayor about his affiliations. I asked him if he was a Bolshevik. He said he was not a Bolshevik, and that he was authorized by the municipal assembly—as we would call it in the United States—to invite us to remain there; that we would be protected. He continued to administer affairs until we left Vologda, although the local Soviet was disposed to dispute his authority some time before we left.

On May 5th, 1918, 1 was shocked to hear that Consul General Madden Summers had died the day before after an illness of twenty-four hours. I had not yet regained my strength from ten days' illness and was still on diet, but I decided to go to Moscow and did so on the first train. At the funeral I delivered an address in which I endeavored to bring out the significance of Summers' splendid work, to emphasize his record as a faithful, efficient representative of his country. In the course of this address I said:

> He who gives his life for a cause can contribute no more. Whether such tribute be rendered on sea or on land or in the clouds, whether it be at the cannon's mouth or in defense against an assault or even by some of the other horrible devices of modern warfare, whether it be in military or civil service, none the less, he has given his all and no man can make greater sacrifice than this.
>
> Madden Summers yielded his life in his country's service and did so as effectually as if he had been taken off by the enemy in ambush and as courageously as if he had fallen in attack on the enemy's works. He realized as fully as does an officer leading his troops in a battle that his very life was in jeopardy and that realization nerved him to renewed effort.

---

[9] Viktor A. Kudryavy (1860–1919), graduate of St. Petersburg University, lawyer, Constitutional Democrat; chairman of the Vologda Regional Zemstvo Board, 1900–04 and 1909; member of the State Council of the Russian Empire from 1906. He was appointed Vologda regional governing commissar by the Provisional Government on March 6, 1917. On January 26, 1918, he was dismissed by the Vologda Soviet, his powers being usurped by Shalva Z. Eliava.

On the 4th of July, 1918, 1 gave a reception which was attended by the members of the Diplomatic Corps then in Vologda, all of the attaches of the Allied Missions, and by quite a number of Russians. The Mayor was present—nominally Bolshevik, but at heart "anti." He had been elected by a direct vote of the people before the Bolshevik regime. The assistant mayor, Mr. Zuboff, a Cadet, was present.[10] Both the mayor and the assistant mayor had been suspended from office the week before by a representative of the Bolshevik Government at Moscow, named Kedroff.[11] The latter, after arresting and sending to Moscow the City Duma of Archangel, stopped at Vologda on his return and had placed a local Bolshevik "in the saddle" of municipal affairs.

I made this Fourth of July reception the occasion of an address to the Russian people, which was published in the Vologda paper, Listok.[12] I ordered 50,000 copies printed in Russian circular form, for general distribution.

At this time the Bolshevik Government at Moscow had a representative at Vologda in the person of Vosnesenski, who occupied the position of Chief of the Far Eastern Division in the Ministry of Foreign Affairs.[13] Vosnesenski was a shrewd Jew. He had, as we used to express it in Kentucky immediately after the Civil War, "the cheek of a government mule." He had been sent to Vologda by the Bolsheviks to ascertain whether the Allies had concluded in principle to intervene, but he got no satisfaction from me, and I do not think he received any definite information from any of my colleagues.

There were at this time many rumors afloat concerning the advance of the Allied detachments. We had authentic reports to the effect that the landing of the Allied

---

[10] Pavel Y. Zubov (1871–1942), former theatrical actor, landowner, marshal of nobility of the Vologda district (*uezd*), joined the Constitutional Democratic Party after the February Revolution. He was assistant city head of Vologda, September 1917–June 1918. Afterwards, a member of the Northern Government (see n. 27, p. 238).

[11] Mikhail S. Kedrov (1878–1941), Bolshevik leader noted for his extraordinary cruelty. He studied law at Moscow University and medicine at Bern and Lausanne, and served as a military surgeon on the Caucasian Front from 1916. A member of the Bolshevik military organization in Petrograd from May 1917; after the October Revolution, he served as commissar for demobilization of the old army in the People's Commissariat for Military and Naval Affairs. From May 18, 1918, he headed the so-called Soviet Inspection in the Arkhangel'sk, Vologda, and Yaroslavl' regions, which carried out Sovietization of the local authorities. From August, he was the main organizer of the Red forces on the Northern Front, which resisted the Allied intervention. From September 1918, he headed the military division of All-Russian Emergency Commission for Combat with Counterrevolution and Sabotage (CheKa).

[12] *Vologodskii Listok* (Vologda Sheet), the city non-party newspaper, published from 1909–18.

[13] Arseny N. Voznesensky (1881–1937), graduate of St. Petersburg University, orientalist and lawyer. He entered the Foreign Service and served in China. Socialist Revolutionary, later Bolshevik. Chief of the Eastern Division of the People's Commissariat for Foreign Affairs, 1917–20.

forces would be resisted by Bolsheviks at Archangel. Those forces were, as we knew, in possession at Murmansk,[14] and the local Soviet there was friendly to the Allies, because it had seen what had been evident to the Allied representatives at Vologda for some time, that the Bolshevik Government was absolutely under the domination of Germany. At the same time the Bolsheviks at Moscow were manifesting a strong desire to appear on good terms with the Allied missions, and especially the American Embassy.

The Fourth of July address to the Russian people follows:

On this July 4th, the natal day of the American Republic, I feel constrained to say a few words of encouragement to the Russian people for whom my country cherishes deep sympathy. One hundred and forty-two years ago to-day the thirteen American Colonies proclaimed their independence; they had a population of about three million souls occupying a narrow strip along the Atlantic seacoast. After a struggle of seven years their independence was acknowledged; then followed a critical period of internal dissension which ended in the adoption of a Constitution and the formation of the Government which exists to-day.

Americans throughout the world celebrate this day in commemoration of the achievements of our ancestors, to express our pride in our institutions, to renew our pledges of fealty to the principles on which our Government is based and to inspire our descendants with love of country and with appreciation of the liberty they enjoy.

France assisted us to gain our independence and we have always felt sincerely grateful therefor—and I am pleased to note that the French Chamber of Deputies has decided to observe the day in testimony of "indissoluble and fraternal friendship."

The Father of our Country warned us against entangling foreign alliances and we observed that injunction for a hundred and forty years, or as long as our self-respect, our sense of duty and our obligations to humanity permitted. We were much farther removed from Europe when our independence was achieved than we are to-day; the application of steam as a motive power had not then been discovered, there were no ocean steamers, no steam railroads; there were no telegraph lines, no telephones, no machine guns, no aeroplanes, no submarines.

Within that period our population has grown by rapid strides until it now numbers considerably over one hundred millions, and many millions of the increase have come from European lands.

---

[14] The Allied forces landed at Murmansk as early as March 6, 1918. American marines joined them in early June.

We are engaged in the greatest war of history—a world war in fact—and so earnestly have we taken part that the spirit of our people is aroused as never before. We have not the slightest doubt as to the outcome. Russia is interested in this war as no other country is interested because she will lose most in the event of the victory of the Central Empires. My country and all of the Allies consider the Russian people still in the struggle. We do not observe the Brest-Litovsk peace. Surely no Russian who loves his country and looks with pride upon her greatness is going to submit tamely to her dismemberment and humiliation.

President Wilson has said feelingly and impressively on several occasion that he has no intention of deserting Russia, in fact that he is resolved not to do so. That means that we will never consent to Germany making Russia a German province; that we will never stand idly by and see the Germans exploit the Russian people and appropriate to Germany's selfish ends the immense resources of Russia. We take this stand not because we ourselves seek territorial aggrandizement; not because we have commercial ambitions in connection with Russia; nor because we wish to dictate to the Russian people or to interfere in the internal affairs of Russia. We assume this position because we wish the Russian people to have the right to dispose of themselves and not be compelled to submit to the tyrannical rule of Germany, even though such a disposition might result in a temporary peace. It is moreover my opinion that all of the Allies agree with America on this subject.

Therefore, on this day, which is celebrated in every city, in every village and in every hamlet in America, I appeal to the Russian people to take courage, to organize to resist the encroachments of Germany. The Allies are your friends and are willing and able to assist you notwithstanding your superb army has been demobilized. The United States, which had an army of about two hundred thousand when we entered the war less than fifteen months ago, has already sent to France nine hundred thousand well-armed, disciplined men and is making rapid progress toward raising an army of five million. The strength of the American Navy and of the American shipping has been increased many fold and is continuing to grow at a wonderful rate which exceeds all calculations and expectations. There is not a craft on the broad seas that dares float the German flag or the colors of one of the Central Empires.

On May 29th, last, my Government authorized its representatives throughout the world to express its sympathy with the nationalistic aspirations of the Czechoslovaks and Jugo-Slavs, and within three days past I have received instructions to announce that the position of the United States Government is "that all branches of the Slav race should be completely freed from German and Austrian rule."

What an inspiration this should be to Russians!

When my appeal to the Russian people reached Berlin, the German Minister of Foreign Affairs again demanded my deportation, on the same ground he had previously urged, that I had not only violated the rules of neutrality but had criticized the Central Soviet Government of the Republic. I do not know what reply was made to this by the Bolsheviks.

At the same time I made my Fourth of July appeal to the Russian people to resist the Germans, conditions in Russia favored it. The time was opportune for action. Prompt and decisive intervention by the Allied Powers might have had far-reaching results. I received from a reliable source this account of what was going on at Moscow:

> The Fifth All-Russian Congress of the Soviets opened on the 4th of July at the Grand Theater in Moscow.[15] Strict measures were taken not to allow anybody without special permit to enter the theater. The Grand Duke's box on the left side of the theater was occupied by representatives of the German Embassy with the Counselor von Bassovitzat the head.[16] The President of the Central Executive Committee, Sverloff,[17] announced the Congress opened at 5 p.m., and stated that up to that moment 1,035 deputies had arrived, of whom 678 belonged to the Bolshevik party; 269 to the party of the Left Social Revolutionists; about 30 Maximalists, and about six Internationalists. The floor was given to Alexandroff, delegate of the Ukrainian Peasants' Congress. His appearance on the platform was met with loud applause. He said:
>
> "We have (in Ukrainia) against us the overwhelming power of German bayonets. We have no more professional Unions, no Cooperatives, and no Workmen's Clubs. The regulation respecting the eight-hour day has been annulled (shame, shame). When the Ukrainian Rada opened the doors to Germany (traitors) we lost even that which we gained by the February revolution. Germans are destroying with artillery fire whole villages, people are executed without trial."

---

[15] The Fifth All-Russian Congress of Soviets of Workers', Peasants', Red Army, and Cossacks' Deputies convened in Moscow on July 4–10, 1918. It was interrupted by the Left Socialist Revolutionaries' mutiny on July 6, and resumed its meeting on July 9. The defeat of the Left SRs' mutiny meant the end of their governmental coalition with the Bolsheviks and paved the way for one-party rule in Soviet Russia. The Fifth Congress adopted the first constitution of the Russian Socialist Federative Soviet Republic (RSFSR).

[16] Count Rudolf von Bassewitz (1881–1951), secretary of the German embassy at St. Petersburg, 1909–10; counselor of the German legation at Moscow, 1918–20.

[17] Yakov M. Sverdlov (1885–1919), Bolshevik since 1903, chairman of the All-Russian Central Executive Committee of Soviets, November 8, 1917–March 16, 1919.

"But," exclaims Alexandroff, "the Ukrainian proletariat are not giving up their struggle with their enemy. Peasants refuse to give Germany grain. Trains loaded with grain for Germany are blown up by us. Practically all stores of munitions have been blown up by us. The aeroplane works in Odessa were set on fire. The Ukrainia is on the verge of rising against Austro-Germany."

These words of Alexandroff were met with continuous applause. The Left Social Revolutionists, standing up from their seats and turning in the direction of the box occupied by von Bassovitz shouted, "down with the Germans." Movement in the box could be noticed.

"I implore you," continued Alexandroff, "to come to our assistance." Shouts again: "Down with the Germans!"

"I want you to reply with yes or no. We are confident that you will come," continued Alexandroff, "and the sooner you come will our Baron von Mumm[18] be driven out from the Ukrainia, as well as your Baron von Mumm, Count Mirbach, will be driven out by you from Moscow." Stormy applause: "Down with Mirbach! Down with the Germans!"

After a speech by Karelin, a Left Social Revolutionist,[19] protesting against capital punishment, and his second speech disclosing forgeries practised by the party of Bolsheviks during the election in order to insure their majority at this Congress, the floor was given to Trotzky.

Trotzky stated that some agitators have resumed their work against the Soviet Government in different parts of the front line. Under the influence of these agitators, several Red Army detachments have crossed the demarcation line. Several commissars have been murdered, and the President of the Bolshevik Peace Delegation to the Ukrainia, Rakoffsky,[20] was threatened with a bomb. "If you will ask me who are these agitators, I say that I do not know, but presume that among them are Right Social Revolutionists, agents of the German war party, as well as agents of those that landed troops on the White Sea coast."

Trotzky further stated that he had given orders that agitators belonging to parties that want Russia to be drawn into war by provoking Germany to occupy Moscow and Petrograd should be sent to prison in Moscow and

---

[18] Baron Philip Alfons Mumm von Schwarzenstein (1859–1924), German diplomat who served in Washington 1888–92 and 1899–1900. Ambassador at Kiev, 1918.

[19] Vladimir A. Karelin (1891–1938), one of the organizers and leaders of the Party of Left Socialists-Revolutionaries; people's commissar for state property in December 1917; member of the Soviet delegation at the Brest-Litovsk peace negotiations in January 1918. He resigned in March in protest of the Brest-Litovsk treaty. He was also one of the organizers of the abortive Left SRs mutiny on July 6–7, 1918.

[20] Rakovsky (see n. 4, p. 190).

Petrograd. Agents of foreign governments who resist the government with arms in their hands should be shot on the spot. Trotzky requested the congress to give sanction of this, his order.

Kumkoff, a Left Social Revolutionist Deputy,[21] replying to Trotzky, stated that the latter had misrepresented the actual facts. That the events referred to were not perpetrated by agitators, but were an actual result of a policy of national treason favored by the Bolsheviks; that the men at the front cannot be silent spectators of workmen and soldiers being shot by German imperialists; that they do not want to take any part in these deeds of Cain, and mean to fight the scoundrels which have also come here. Kumkoff pointed to the box occupied by German representatives. Shouts, "down with Mirbach!"

On the 6th of July, two days later, the German Ambassador to Russia, Count Mirbach, was assassinated in Moscow. An official statement issued by the Bolshevik Government said:

Two scoundrels, agents of Russian-Anglo-French Imperialism,[22] having forged the signature of Dzerjinsky,[23] sneaked through to the German Ambassador, Count Mirbach, under a false certificate, and, under the protection of this document, they threw a bomb, killing Count Mirbach.

The Bolsheviks attributed the assassination to the Russian Monarchists and Counter-Revolutionists. They claimed to have identified one of the assassins as a member of the Left Social Revolutionists Party.

---

[21] Boris D. Kamkov (1885–1938), graduate of Heidelberg University; returned to Russia after the February Revolution and was elected to the Petrograd Soviet. One of the leaders of the Left Socialist Revolutionaries; collaborated with the Bolsheviks during and after the October Revolution; was a member of the Council of People's Commissars without a portfolio. He resigned in March 1918 in protest of the Brest-Litovsk treaty; elected chairman of the presidium of the Central Committee of the Party of Left SRs in April; took part in the abortive Left SRs mutiny on July 6–7, 1918.

[22] Mirbach was assassinated by members of the staff of the All-Russian Emergency Commission for Combat with Counterrevolution and Sabotage (CheKa), Nikolai A. Andreev (1890–1919) and Yakov G. Blumkin (1898–1929), who were Left Socialist Revolutionaries and implemented the decision of their party to execute the ambassador in order to incite a war between Russia and Germany. Both terrorists escaped to Ukraine, where Andreev died the next year. Blumkin was pardoned and made a brilliant career as a secret agent of the Soviet intelligence service, operating in Persia, Mongolia, Turkey, Palestine, and other eastern countries. He was executed in the fall of 1929 for relations with Trotsky.

[23] Felix E. Dzerzhinsky (1877–1926), Polish socialist, later Bolshevik, chairman of the CheKa, which was created on December 7, 1917. He was nicknamed "Iron Felix."

About four or five days after this assassination of Count Mirbach, Tchecherin, Minister of Foreign Affairs of the Bolshevik Government at Moscow, sent me a telegram marked "urgent," addressing me as Dean of the Diplomatic Corps, and saying:

> Taking into consideration the present situation and possibility of danger for representatives of Entente powers Soviet Government looks upon Moscow as town where security of named representatives can be assured. Considering as its duty safeguarding ambassadors' security Government sees in their coming to Moscow a necessity. We hope that highly esteemed American Ambassador will appreciate this step in friendly spirit in which it is undertaken. In order to execute this measure and to remove any difficulties People's Commissariat for Foreign Affairs delegates to Vologda as its representative, Citizen Radek.

To this I made immediate reply, hoping to forestall the coming of Radek:

> Immediately on receiving your urgent message last midnight, I called a meeting of the Chiefs of Allied Missions, as their Dean. I am requested by them to ask you why you think our remaining in Vologda unsafe or inadvisable. We have no fear of the Russian people, whom we have always befriended and whom we consider our Allies, and we have full confidence in the population of Vologda. Our only anxiety is concerning the forces of the Central Empires with whom we are at war and, in our judgment, they are much more likely to capture Moscow than Vologda. We realize that in a country suffering as Russia is at present there are unreasonable and desperate men, but we are confident that they are not more dangerous at Vologda than elsewhere. At Moscow, on the other hand, we hear that the Germans have already received permission to introduce their troops to safeguard their representatives, and in any case the town is directly threatened by the Germans. If you mean by your message that the government of Soviets has taken without consulting the Allied Missions the decision that the latter should come to Moscow and that you are sending Mr. Radek to carry such a decision into execution, we desire to inform you that we consider that would be offensive to us and we would not comply therewith.

Radek arrived the next day and about 3 p.m. inquired at what time I could receive him, and was told at four o'clock new time. Radek did not call until after five o'clock, when the Allied Diplomats were in session at he American Embassy. Leaving my colleagues in session I went to the reception room of the Embassy, and, after hearing from Radek that the object of his mission was to arrange for the removal of the Allied Missions from Vologda to Moscow, I told him that such an invitation had already been received by wire from Tchecherin and had been declined by wire. He disclaimed any intention on the part of the Soviet Government of forcing the Allied Missions to remove from Vologda to Moscow, but after mentioning the responsibility of the Soviets for the safety of the Allied representatives, stated that if this declination would be persisted in he would demand a statement in writing from the Allied representatives absolving the Soviet Government from all responsibility for their safety. I said to Radek that as the Allied Chiefs were in session in the American Embassy at that moment, perhaps he should himself make this statement to them. I returned to the Allied conference and reported the interview with Radek. The Allied representatives decided that I, as the Dean, should state to Radek that they stood upon their reply made by wire to Tchecherin until authoritatively advised as to the demands of Germany consequent upon the killing of Mirbach, having heard by wire from Moscow that armed Germans and Austrians were guarding the embassies and consulates of the Central Empires in Moscow. The Allied Conference thereupon adjourned.

I returned to the reception room and had a talk with Radek lasting about an hour. Radek was accompanied by an interpreter, Arthur Ransome,[24] the correspondent of *The Manchester Guardian*. I called my stenographer, Mr. Johnston, who was also my private secretary, and he took down the conversation. I told Radek, after listening to his argument, that we had decided to refuse the invitation to go to Moscow. His reply was: "I will station guards around all of your embassies." They called all of our legations embassies. "And no one will be permitted to go in or out without a passport." I said: "We are virtually prisoners then?" "No," he said, you are not virtually prisoners, you can go in and out and the chiefs can all go in and out, but when you desire anybody to come in here, you will have to tell the local Soviet the name of the man and they will give him a pass to enter through your guards."

The guards came there the next morning, or perhaps the same evening, but they did not disturb us. They were hungry and we gave them food. They were very accommodating to us. Radek was in uniform, and carried a pistol. He was a newspaper man, an Austrian. He was intensely devoted to the Bolshevik purpose of a worldwide revolution. I understood that Lenin and Trotzky depended upon Radek for the composition of many proclamations which they signed. After the armistice, Radek went to Berlin, and was active in the efforts to overturn the German Government and in the attempted spread of Bolshevism throughout Germany.

The day after sending the decision of the Allied Missions not to leave Vologda, I received from Tchechein this message, marked "Urgent":

---

[24] Arthur M. Ransome (1884–1967), English writer and journalist. The first time he visited Russia in 1913 was to study Russian language and folklore. The next year, he arrived in Russia as a newspaper correspondent to cover the war on the Eastern Front, and then stayed in Russia from 1915–19. He covered the events of the Russian Revolution, coming to sympathize with the Bolshevik cause. He married Trotsky's private secretary, Evgenia P. Shelepina.

Thanks for telegram. You are obviously badly informed. It is absolutely false that Germans have received permission to introduce troops at Moscow. This is monstrous distortion of true situation. How is it that somebody from Moscow deliberately misrepresents to you our policy and real state of things? When you will be in Moscow no intriguers will be able to create such trouble between us. Moscow is not threatened by Germans. If this was the case, we would at once warn you and take steps necessary for your departure. You are insufficiently informed situation Russia. People are for us but conspiring groups like that which acted lately systematically create trouble. Such conspirators prepare stroke. Your remaining Vologda impossible. We have responsibility to bear we cannot otherwise. Radek goes consult you first.

I replied to Tchecherin as follows:

I have received your telegram in response to mine which was sent in reply to your first telegram concerning the removal of the Allied Missions from Vologda to Moscow. Mr. Radek, representative of the Soviet Government, arrived and had conference with me before the receipt of this telegram. He informed me that your first telegram was intended for invitation or advice to the Allied Missions in Vologda and not a command or a decision to be enforced by him as your representative. After conferring with Mr. Radek I submitted his proposition to the Allied Diplomatic Corps, which decided to stand on its former reply and to decline your invitation to come to Moscow until hearing what further demands or movements Germany is likely to make as the German press and many prominent Germans charge the Allies with inspiring, planning and carrying into execution assassination of the German Ambassador, Mirbach. Mr. Radek when informed by me of this decision demanded a written statement from the Allied Missions that we absolve the Soviet Government from all responsibility for our safety. When again informed that the Allied Missions stand on their reply telegraphed you until they learn what Germany demands or proposes to do, Mr. Radek stated that he would station guards around every Allied chancery or residence in Vologda who would be instructed to admit no one without his approval or ours, as he proposed to remain in Vologda until receiving further instructions from you or the Soviet Government. While we have not asked for guards and would appreciate guards stationed around our residences and chanceries solely for our protection we look upon the plan as proposed by Mr. Radek as a virtual arrangement to place us under espionage or to make us prisoners. We trust such is not your intention; if it is we protest against the plan proposed by Mr. Radek as incompatible with the dignity of our Governments. Your telegram states that our remaining in Vologda is "impossible." While Mr.

Radek disclaimed any intention on the part of the Soviet Government to compel us to come to Moscow your telegram fails to reply to that portion of my message to you based upon the theory that Mr. Radek has been sent to Vologda to carry into execution a decision of the Soviet Government. We await your reply to this telegram.

Radek remained in Vologda some days. He made a bad impression upon the people of Vologda, who showed their opposition to him and their preference for the Allies against the Germans in many ways. The Bolshevik element called a meeting of about 2,000 workmen, including the railroad employees, for the purpose of hearing a speech from Radek on the evening of July 15th. This speech was intended to incite feeling against the Allies. Radek even went so far as to say that the workmen must unite with the German troops to oppose the Anglo-French soldiers. This was too much for the audience, who immediately cried out: "We won't do it. The Germans have shown what they will do by their conduct in the Ukraine. We prefer the Allies, and we will join them and fight the Germans." Radek was very much incensed, and threatened that the Bolshevik Government would treat Vologda as it did Yarsolave,[25] and would destroy both cities.

While this pressure was being brought to bear to induce the Allied diplomats to go to Moscow, I was visited at 11 o'clock at night, July 17th, by a British captain, named McGrath,[26] who had come down that same afternoon from Archangel. Lindley, the British Charge,[27] brought McGrath to the Embassy. I had already heard from Riggs, who came down from Archangel on the same train with McGrath, that General Poole, in command of the British,[28] was in closer touch with the situation at Archangel than we had previously known. Captain McGrath, after telling me in a general way of the military plans of the Allies for the occupation of Archangel, said he had come down to make a proposition to the Allied missions in Vologda, but he knew I would be opposed to it. His proposition was that the missions leave Vologda for Archangel.

---

[25] The city of Yaroslavl' was heavily damaged by artillery and aerial bombardment in the course of suppressing the anti-Bolshevik uprising organized by the Union of Defense of Motherland and Freedom on July 6–21, 1918.

[26] Representative of the British Military Supply Mission at Arkhangel'sk.

[27] Francis Oswald Lindley (1872–1950), British diplomat. He entered the Foreign Service in 1896 and served in Austria, Persia, Egypt, Japan, Bulgaria, and Norway. He was appointed counselor of the British embassy at Petrograd in July 1915 and served as chargé d'affaires after the departure of Ambassador Buchanan till March 1918. He was sent back to Russia in June 1918 as special British commissioner and stayed there till May 1919.

[28] Frederick Cuthbert Poole (1859–1936), major general, commanding the British and Allied expeditionary forces in northern Russia, August–October 1918.

I immediately replied that I was not opposed to leaving Vologda or making any other strategic move, but that I was opposed to going to Moscow on the "invitation" of the Bolsheviks, and would not leave Vologda by order of the Bolsheviks, and would under no circumstances leave Russia unless forced to do so, or recalled by my Government.

Captain McGrath's face lighted up and he said General Poole thought the continued presence of the Allied Embassies at Vologda would hamper his military plans. General Poole feared the Soviet Government would capture the Allied chiefs and hold them as hostages, and possibly some desperate Bolsheviks might commit violence upon the Allied Ambassadors.

I asked Captain McGrath what his plan was and he said he wanted us to leave Vologda in time to meet General Poole, who was at Murmansk when the British arrived in Archangel, but he was not definitely advised as to when that would be. Lindley, the British Charge, had told me previously when he arrived in Vologda that Poole would reach Archangel the first week in August, but McGrath said the British plans had been hastened by our safety being threatened at Vologda.

I arranged for McGrath to come to the conference of the Allied chiefs the following day. He did so and stated in effect what he had told me the night before. I then outlined to my colleagues the plan that we should be prepared to leave for Archangel on short notice, but should not ask consent of the Bolshevik authorities, and should distinctly state that we were not going to leave Russia, but were only withdrawing to Archangel temporarily for safety, and to prevent being taken by the Bolsheviks as hostages. I proposed that we would leave our Embassies and Legations at Vologda functioning as usual. I reminded the chiefs that the invitation of the Bolsheviks to come to Moscow for protection had been accompanied by the statement that they could not protect us at Vologda from unreasonable and desperate Russians or from five thousand German and Austrian prisoners in the Vologda district. Radek had said that these prisoners were likely to be incensed by the assassination of Mirbach, the German people and the German leaders having charged the Allied Ambassadors with instigating and having carried into execution that dastardly act.

Captain McGrath said there could be no possible doubt about the ability of the Allies to land when they arrived at Archangel, and went into sufficient detail to convince me that he was justified in making such statement.

The diplomatic representatives at Vologda agreed for the time being that it was best for them to stay there. We had entire confidence in the good will of the Vologda people, and we believed that Moscow was an undesirable residence place for us. We refused to change our location. Tchecherin's telegram to me and my reply thereto were given to the press before the arrival of Radek and had been published in Vologda and Petrograd papers. The party headed by Radek was known as "the

Extraordinary Revolutionary Staff."[29] This staff issued an order addressed to the journals of the city, prohibiting publication of communications or interviews with us unless they were previously censored by the staff. We endeavored to reach the Russian people through a pamphlet containing a copy of the order from the staff, but another order was issued prohibiting the distribution of these pamphlets. The conclusion of the Diplomatic Corps was that the Bolsheviks desired to have us in Moscow and hold us as hostages in event of intervention. It seems as if our refusal to leave Vologda had settled the matter, but on the 23rd of July this message marked "Urgent" was received by me from Tchecherin:

> I entreat you most earnestly to leave Vologda. Come here. Danger approaching. To-morrow can be too late. When battle rages, distinction of houses cannot be made. If all smashed in your domiciles during struggle of contending forces responsibility will fall upon your making deaf ear to all entreaties. Why bring about catastrophe which you can avert?

After consulting with my colleagues, and finding them of the same mind with me, that the plan was to hold us as hostages at Moscow, or at any rate to hold us against the German and Austrian representatives at Moscow, I replied to Tchecherin:

> Thank you for your telegram. We fully appreciate the uninterrupted interest you have taken in our personal safety and have decided to follow your advice and are leaving Vologda.

Our determination was to go to Archangel, but I did not state in the telegram where we proposed to go.

When we finally decided to go to Archangel, I sent word to my colleagues to have their baggage down to the train before six o'clock, that the train would leave at eight o'clock in the evening. I had held a special train on the Vologda tracks for five months. My transportation man, Mason,[30] had told me that the stationmaster, with whom we had made friends, would furnish me a locomotive on an hour's notice to take that train on any road that we wished. I sent for my transportation man and said: "You told me that the stationmaster promised you a locomotive for this train. I want that locomotive attached to the train tonight at 7:30 and I want to leave at 8." He left me, but came back in an hour and said that the stationmaster had left on a vacation,

---

[29] The Extraordinary Revolutionary Staff was established in Vologda after the anti-Bolshevik uprising erupted in Yaroslavl´ in July 1918. It was invested with all powers in the Vologda region and was headed by Chairman of the Vologda Regional Executive Committee of Soviets Mikhail K. Vetoshkin.

[30] Frederick Mason, an American resident of Petrograd who assisted the Stevens Commission and then joined the American Red Cross Mission with the rank of lieutenant.

and that the one he had left in charge could not get a locomotive without submitting his request to Moscow. The stationmaster said that Tchecherin had given orders to the Director of Locomotive Power that he must not put a locomotive on this train without getting his permission. I told the substitute stationmaster to submit the matter to Moscow. He did so and the reply was: "Who wishes the locomotive?" I replied through my transportation man, "the American Ambassador."

"Where does he wish to go?"

"To Archangel."

When the Diplomatic Corps went to the station we were shown a telegram signed by Zaikin, Commissar of Exploitation Department of the Bolshevik Government and addressed to the Vologda stationmaster, reading:

> In accordance with an order from People's Commissar for Foreign Affairs, Tchecherin, I request information immediately as to who from the American Embassy and for what purpose is demanding a special train to Archangel. Until the receipt of this information and the receipt by you of a permit to dispatch the train, same should not be dispatched.

I replied to this:

> The American Ambassador as Dean of the Diplomatic Corps, received about noon to-day a telegram from Tchecherin entreating the Diplomatic Corps to leave Vologda "as to-morrow can be too late," and it is unsafe for them to remain there. This train is desired by the American Ambassador for the entire Diplomatic Corps to convey them to Archangel.

Then came a longer message from Tchecherin still urging that the Corps decide to come to Moscow:

> Having heard of your resolve to leave Vologda for Archangel, we feel ourselves compelled whilst appreciating your clear comprehension of the untenable situation in Vologda to be kindly informed by you about some particulars of your decision. If your intention is to leave Russia, we are powerless to hinder you in doing so, but we express our sincerest regrets at your departure from our soil together with our hope to see you soon in our midst here in the hearts of Soviets of Russia. In case you really wish to depart we beg to emphasize that in our view the relations between our two countries are not going to be affected by an event to which we will not ascribe any political symptomatic character. If, however, the idea of exchanging Vologda for Archangel was not altogether removed from your mind it is unfortunately necessary to draw your attention to the fact that in the expectation of a siege Archangel cannot

VOLOGDA—THE DIPLOMATIC CAPITAL

be a residence fit for Ambassadors and that such a question cannot possibly be answered in the affirmative. I cannot but repeat that under the present condition when our foes seeing their impotence to take place in the political inclinations of the great masses seek to conspire and to create artificial outbursts and to provoke civil war, we can, with complete earnestness, point to Moscow, where as experience shows our forces are and cannot but remain in undisturbed control of the city and to its peaceful gay suburbs with their splendid villas as to an appropriate abode which our government deliberately proposes to the Ambassador of friendly America. We must at any cost avoid the danger of your departure being misinterpreted in the eyes of our great masses and of American public opinion and of its being understood in a sense altogether dissimilar to that in which you and myself would understand it. That at the present juncture would be a fatal mistake, and the best means of averting this danger would be your coming to the official center of Russia, where a warm, friendly reception awaits you. The special train is at your disposal, but we do not lose the hope that your decision will be to come to Moscow.

I replied with a detailed statement covering the situation, showing how communication with the American Government had been practically cut off and referring to the censorship which prevented the Corps from printing anything without first submitting it to the Soviet Government. I give this communication in full:

On receipt of your urgent telegram of the 22nd, addressed to me as Dean of the Diplomatic Corps, and received about noon of the 23rd, I called the Corps in conference. After deliberating, we decided to leave Vologda, but considered that our previous telegraphic correspondence had fully settled the question of our going to Moscow and that conclusion was negative. As Dean of the Diplomatic Corps, I replied to your telegram, expressing appreciation for your continued interest in our personal safety and advising that we had concluded to leave Vologda. Consequently the entire Diplomatic Corps repaired to their train at Vologda Station, but on giving directions for the train to move we were informed by the railroad officials that no motive power could be furnished without authority from Moscow. We were under the impression and had been informed from reliable sources that these trains were at our disposal and locomotives would be furnished upon our request. When such request was forwarded to Moscow the reply was received after some delay that locomotives could not be furnished without your consent and you desired to know who had asked for the train for the American Ambassador and for what purpose he wished to go to Archangel. I promptly directed that reply be made that the locomotive was desired to take the entire Diplomatic Corps to

Archangel as they had concluded to quit Vologda upon receipt of your urgent telegram entreating them to leave because unsafe to remain in Vologda, and stating that postponing departure until to-morrow might be too late.

In reply to this statement you wired me at length.

The correspondence up to this time had been between myself as Dean of the Diplomatic Corps and yourself as Commissar of Foreign Affairs.

This telegram while sent by me as Dean of the Diplomatic Corps is meant also for my reply as the American Ambassador.

Permit me to say to you that while your message is appreciated because expressing friendly feeling for the people I represent and a desire on your part to maintain relations with them and with my government, your treatment of me as their representative does not accord with such expressions. While refraining from interfering in all internal affairs in Russia I have considered that the Russian people were still our Allies, and have more than once appealed to them to unite with us in resisting a common enemy. I have furthermore recommended to my government many times to send food to relieve the sufferings of the Russian people and to ship agricultural implements to meet the requirements of Russia. A wireless message sent from Washington July 18th, received at Moscow, was delivered to me after last midnight. It stated that no message had been received from me of later date than June 24th, except one sent through Archangel July 7th, advising of the killing of the German Ambassador; it furthermore stated that it had cabled me often and fully. I have received no cables from my government that were sent after July 3rd, except two wireless messages inquiring why they did not hear from me; I have cabled fully every day. Moreover the press of Vologda and doubtless the entire press of Russia has received orders to print nothing from any Allied Ambassador or representative without first submitting same to the Soviet Government. Some journals in Vologda and some in Petrograd did print your first telegram inviting or ordering the Diplomatic Corps to come to Moscow and our reply thereto; these were given to the press by myself for the information of the Russian people and because I thought secret diplomacy had been abolished in Russia. Upon learning that the press was forbidden to publish further correspondence concerning our removal to Moscow, the Diplomatic Corps decided to have printed in pamphlet form in Russian the entire correspondence on the subject together with some excerpts from a stenographic report of the interview between your representative Radek and myself. These pamphlets have been ready for delivery for two days past, but we are informed that the Central Soviet Committee or the Extraordinary Revolutionary Staff of Vologda has prohibited delivery of same to us.

Your last telegram addressed to myself while expressing friendly sentiments toward America and consideration for its Ambassador makes no mention of my colleagues representing America's Allies in Vologda. This is to inform you if you entertain any doubt on the subject that the Allied representatives in Vologda are acting in concert and in perfect harmony.

The Allied missions and staffs have been living for twenty-four hours in special train on track of Vologda station, awaiting a locomotive to transport them to Archangel. Your telegram to me states that if permitted to go to Archangel it would be only for the purpose of their leaving Russia which you "are powerless to hinder." Your telegram states that Archangel is not a fit residence for Ambassadors in the event of a "siege." Do you expect a German siege of Archangel? You certainly do not anticipate Allied siege of that city or you would not insist upon the Allied representatives coming to Moscow. If you mean a siege of Archangel by Russians I can only repeat what I have said to you and to the Russian people many times, and that is that the Allies have nothing to fear from the Russian people whom they have constantly befriended and with whom they consider themselves still in alliance against a common enemy. Speaking for myself I have no desire or intention of leaving Russia unless forced to do so, and in such event my absence would be temporary. I would not properly represent my government or the sentiment of the American people if I should leave Russia at this time. The Brest-Litovsk peace the Allies have never recognized, and it is becoming so burdensome to the Russian people that in my judgment the time is not far distant when they will turn upon Germany and by their repulsion of the invader from the Russian borders will demonstrate what I have continuously believed, and that is that the national spirit of great Russia is not dead but has only been sleeping.

The above are my personal views and feelings and I think that in cherishing such I am properly representing my government and my people.

The Allied Diplomatic Corps of Vologda await your immediate approval of the locomotive to draw their train to Archangel. If local authorities at Archangel consider the situation does not allow us to remain, we shall leave with deep regret and with the hope of soon returning.

After the receipt of this telegram, Tchecherin said he would go to the direct wire and wished the American Ambassador or his representative at Vologda to be there. I sent Mr. Lehrs, an attache of the Embassy,[31] with instructions to inform Tchecherin that the Diplomatic Corps reiterated with emphasis its request for a locomotive in order to go to Archangel. Mr. Lehrs reported that Mr. Tchecherin had given orders that when a definite reply from the ambassadors came a locomotive should be

---

[31] John A. Lehrs, of Baltimore, appointed vice consul in Moscow on April 5, 1918. In early July, he was reassigned to Vologda for service at the embassy.

immediately provided. Tchecherin also said to Lehrs that he would telegraph Mr. Popoff[32] of the Bolshevik Government at Archangel instructing him to prepare a steamer for the Allied Ambassadors.

Mr. Lehrs reported this conversation with Tchecherin, and at my direction sent the following:

> I am instructed by the Dean of the Diplomatic Corps to inform you that the diplomats of the Allied missions at Vologda after considering your message decided to request you to furnish at your earliest convenience a locomotive to draw their special train from Vologda to Archangel.

The correspondence, part of it by wireless, was completed at 11:20 p.m., July 24th, with the following from Tchecherin:

> We will give instructions that a locomotive be put at your disposal at Vologda and that a boat should be prepared for you in Archangel. Once more we emphasize that we do not ascribe a political meaning to this individual leaving of Allied representatives, which we profoundly regret and which was caused by a sorrowful —— of circumstances independent of our will.

Tchecherin seems to have been under the impression that after our departure from Vologda the Soviet Government had disposed of the American Ambassador. He sent this wireless message to Archangel July 29th, 1918:

> American Ambassador Francis,
> Archangel.
>
> I take the opportunity of this last moment before your departure to express once more my profound regret and sorrow at the unfortunate circumstances which have had as a result your present journey across the sea and also my best thanks for your kindness and courtesy and for your good feeling toward the Russian popular masses whose most adequate and faithful representatives are the Soviets, the councils of the poor and of the toiling. Please convey our affection and admiration in the messages you will send across the ocean to the great people of pioneers on the new continent and to the posterity of Cromwell's revolutionaries and of Washington's brothers-in-arms.
>
> Tchecherin.

---

[32] Stepan K. Popov (1893–1941), chairman of the Arkhangel'sk Regional Executive Committee of Soviets from June 30, 1918.

This telegram was evidently meant for consumption by American pacifists, and fearing it would be given to the American people by the Department of State, I failed to transmit it.

Chapter XVIII
ARCHANGEL AND THE NORTHERN GOVERNMENT

The plan had been to leave Vologda on the 23rd of July but we did not get away until after midnight of the 24th; the telegraphic correspondence with Moscow taking that interval. The Diplomatic Corps had slept on the train and waited.

I had received a telegram from Kedroff, the Bolshevik Commissar, who had removed the City Duma of Vologda and the City Duma of Archangel, saying he would meet us at a station between Vologda and Archangel, naming the station. Our train arrived there before his, but after we waited ten or fifteen minutes his train pulled into the station. I sent Riggs to ascertain what Kedroff wished in requesting us to wait, thinking he might probably detain us, and possibly by force take us back to Moscow. Riggs, who was second in rank to Col. Ruggles[1] of the Military Commission, had learned to speak Russian, and had by this time become a major. He was only a lieutenant when I arrived in Petrograd, and was my Military Attache until he was supplanted by General Judson. He returned after a short conference with Kedroff, and reported that Kedroff desired to inform us that a steamboat was awaiting our arrival at Archangel.

This intelligence was communicated to us and relieved us greatly, as we were on our way out of Bolshevik jurisdiction of Russia.

On our arrival at Archangel, we were met by a delegation of local Bolsheviks, accompanied by a representative of the Moscow government. These officers pointed to a boat on the Dvina River and said:

"There is a boat. We are instructed to direct your attention to that boat, to put you on that boat and to say you can use that boat to go where you wish."

I said: "We refuse to go on that boat."

"Why?"

"Well," I said, "we do not intend to leave Russia until we can communicate with our governments. Cable communication has been severed for three weeks."

---

[1] James A. Ruggles (1869–1948) entered the US Army during the Spanish-American War and served in the Philippines. A graduate of the Artillery School, he served in the Coast Artillery Corps. Temporary lieutenant colonel; appointed assistant military attaché at Petrograd on October 25, 1917; assigned to duty as military attaché on February 8, 1918; promoted to colonel of National Army on June 20, 1918.

The Bolsheviks replied: "Well, we have no other orders."

The Diplomatic Party numbered about 140 persons, counting attaches and domestics. I said to the Bolsheviks: "Moreover that boat is not big enough for us."

They said: "We will give you an additional boat."

In the course of further conversation these local Bolsheviks seemed to be perplexed as to their own course, and asked us: "What are we to do?"

I replied: "I do not know what you are to do except to go and report what we say to the people at Moscow, to Lenin, Trotzky and Tchecherin."

They stationed guards around the train and left. That was on the 26th of July. In about thirty hours they returned. We learned that they had been wiring Moscow and received answer. The purport of this correspondence had been made known to us through confidential sources. We knew that the Moscow people, while professing to desire us to leave Russia, were telling the local Bolsheviks to hold us as hostages. About two or three o'clock in the afternoon of the 27th of July, the Bolsheviks came back to the train where we were. By that time, acting upon the information we had received as to the communications from Moscow, and also upon information of local trouble, we had determined that our best plan was to get away to Kandalaksha. Information had reached us through confidential channels that an anti-Bolshevik revolution was about to take place at Archangel. We felt that we would not want to be there when it occurred.

When the Bolshevik officers came back to the train, we assumed a firm attitude before them, and insisted on leaving Archangel for Kandalaksha, which was under Allied control. The Bolsheviks, realizing local conditions and at the same time having their instructions from Moscow, were frightened. They did nothing to actually detain us, but they threw all the obstacles in the way they could. For example: when we had expressed our determination to go to Kandalaksha, they said our baggage did not have diplomatic seals on it. I said to my colleagues: "We will go down and identify the baggage." After this the baggage was transferred to the boat about eight o'clock in the evening. Then the Bolsheviks insisted that we must all come off the boat and show our passports when we reembarked. We complied with this. By that time it was midnight. The next excuse was that the Bolshevik officers must go across the river to have our passports vised. The railroads do not enter Archangel. They stop at the south side of the Dvina River, which is about a mile wide. The Bolsheviks went over to Archangel, and were gone until four o'clock in the morning. Then they came back, and at that hour on the 29th of July, we cleared for Kandalaksha.

If the Bolsheviks had not given permission for us to leave for Kandalaksha, we intended to go anyway.

There was a British merchantman in the harbor, and I had asked the British Commissioner Lindley, "What boat is that?"

His reply was: "It is one of ours."

I asked: "Will it obey your instructions?" He said: "I think so." I said: "If the Bolsheviks do not come by seven o'clock, we will get on that boat and go to Kandalaksha," but the Bolsheviks came at four o'clock. I had had the conversation about the British merchantman two hours previous.

At Kandalaksha we heard that General Poole, in command of the British forces, was at Murmansk, which is a port of the railroad that is open all year around as the Gulf Stream flows by that port. Kandalaksha is about 150 miles south of Murmansk. General Poole with about 2,000 men cleared for Archangel. The forces arrived at Archangel on the 2nd of August. Not knowing whether he was to be opposed in his plan to land there, he telephoned in from the pier: "What government is in control here?" The reply was: "The Provisional Government of Northern Russia."[2]

It seems that the anti-Bolshevik revolution, of the plans for which we had learned before we left Archangel, had taken place about four hours before the arrival of the troops. The General inquired: "Will you permit us to land?" The Bolshevik Government, under instructions from Moscow, had been prepared to resist the landing. The reply of the new government was: "Yes, come quick." The landing at Archangel was made on the 2nd of August.

The first landing of Allied troops on the North coast of Russia came about without opposition by the Bolsheviks through an interesting combination of circumstances. It will be remembered that Trotzky refused to participate in the second negotiations for the Brest-Litovsk treaty. He sent Tchecherin in his place. Tchecherin wired for a special train to return from Brest-Litovsk without saying whether he had signed the treaty. The terms of the treaty were far more severe than those which Trotzky had rejected during the first negotiations, and Trotzky supposed Tchecherin had refused to sign them. Just at the time of Tchecherin's request for a train on which to return, Trotzky received an inquiry from the local Soviet at Murmansk wishing to know whether the Bolsheviks there should permit Allied troops to land. Trotzky, thinking Tchecherin had not signed the treaty because of its severe terms, replied to the inquiry: "Yes, permit the Allied troops to land without resistance." Whereupon the local commissars, or Bolsheviks, at Murmansk informed the Allied troops of Trotzky's instructions, and even invited the Allied troops to land.

Captain Martin, of the American Military Mission,[3] just before his departure for Murmansk to meet the Allied forces, called upon me at the American Embassy

---

[2] Actually, it was the Supreme Administration of the Northern Region, created on August 2, 1918, and replaced by the Provisional Government of the Northern Region on October 7, 1918. Both bodies were headed by Nikolai V. Chaikovsky.

[3] Hugh S. Martin (1891–1931), an American resident of Petrograd who enlisted in the US Army during the World War and served for the Military Information Division. Lieutenant; in January 1918, he was sent to Murmansk to serve as an American passport control officer. Captain; assigned to duty as assistant military attaché at Archangelsk on November 15, 1918; headed the American counterintelligence service in northern Russia.

in Petrograd, and asked if I had any message to send to Captain Bierer,[4] who was in command of the cruiser *Olympia* in Murmansk harbor. I replied: "Tell Captain Bierer that I do not assume authority to command him to land his marines, but if I were called upon to give advice, I should want American marines to land, provided the British and French and Italian troops were landed."

I subsequently met Assistant Secretary of the Navy, Franklin D. Roosevelt,[5] who informed me that Captain Bierer in command of 200 American marines, was instructed to obey my orders. These marines were the first American troops to be landed in Russia.

The Allied missions had held the boats on which they had come from Archangel to Kandalaksha. The British Commissioner, the Italian Ambassador and the French Minister and I went from Kandalaksha to Murmansk and were able to communicate with our governments from there. I cabled Washington my plan, that I was going back to Archangel, and received approval of the plan. So I went back to Archangel, and remained then until November 6th.

The revolution against the Bolsheviks at Archangel established what was known as the Sovereign Government of the Northern Region.[6] This government not only welcomed the landing of the Allied forces, but invited the Allied missions to return to Archangel. The head of that government was Tchaikovsky.[7] In a letter written from Archangel, August 29th, 1918, to Charles R. Crane of Chicago, I wrote of Tchaikovsky:

> He spent four years, 1875–79 in America, and was Russian exile in England from 1879 to 1907. When in America he lived at Independence, Kansas, where he attempted to form a new religious sect, but failed therein. He told someone a few days ago that he still cherished the belief that God is in every man's soul, and that is the sole existence of what the religious denominations call the Supreme Being, but that he had abandoned all effort to found such a

---

[4] Bion Barnett Bierer (1869–1936), captain of US Navy commanding the cruiser *Olympia*. He was awarded with the Navy Cross "for distinguished service in the line of his profession as commanding officer of USS *Olympia* engaged in important and exacting duty in the waters of northern Russia, operating under the senior British naval officer in those waters." (Home of Heroes [website], "Navy Cross—WWI—US Navy A to C," https://homeofheroes.com/distinguished-service-cross/service-cross-world-war-i/navy-cross-world-war-i/navy-cross-wwi-navy/navy-cross-wwi-navy-a-to-c/.)

[5] Franklin Delano Roosevelt (1882–1945), assistant secretary of the navy, 1913–20.

[6] Supreme Administration of the Northern Region (see n. 2, p. 226).

[7] Chaikovsky, famous Russian revolutionary (see n. 27, p. 155). Chairman of the Supreme Administration of the Northern Region from August 2, 1918, and of the Provisional Government of the Northern Region from October 7, 1918. He left Arkhangel´sk for Paris in January 1919.

sect because the race has not arrived at that stage of development where it can appreciate such beliefs. He is an able writer, a fine character and a valuable man.

To my son, Sidney,[8] I wrote on the 30th of July from Kandalaksha:

The Russian people are divided between a Monarchy and a Socialistic Republic, and I am not interfering in the slightest degree in any way. Their national pride seems to be awakening, and they are so disgusted with the Bolshevik rule that they would make an alliance with Germany if we don't intervene. Have written you that I recommended the intervention in cable of May 2nd, but have not been advised whether this principle has been passed upon. It is true that American marines have been landed at Murmansk, and I believe that American troops are enroute to Archangel. Suffice it to say that Russia is an immense country abundant in resources, and nearly two hundred million people who are uneducated but who love the land devotedly. I have issued a number of statements or pronunciamentos trying to arouse the Russian people against Germany and have gotten limited circulation therefor. The general instructions to diplomats are to do nothing at this time without instructions from the Department. I have not been "called down" thus far.

I very soon established close relations with the American Expeditionary Forces which had been landed at Archangel. The information came to me one day that our American soldiers were manning the street cars. There had been a general strike in Archangel. When the workmen heard of the kidnapping of the Tschaikovsky Ministers, some 30,000 of them quit work, including all those in the factories. The street car forces joined the strike. As soon as I heard that American forces were manning the street cars instead of the strikers, I called up Col. Stewart, the commanding officer, or rather attempted to call him up, but could not find him. I then called for Major Nichols,[9] who was in command of the American battalion still remaining in Archangel,—the one I had reviewed. I asked Major Nichols, "Is it true that American soldiers are manning the street cars?"

"Yes."

---

[8] Sidney Rowland Francis, the ambassador's sixth son (1888–1960).

[9] Major Jesse Brooks Nichols (1883–?), commanding the Railway Detachment of the 339th Infantry in northern Russia. He was awarded with the highest Russian, French, and British decorations "in recognition of meritorious service rendered the Allied cause." ("Detroit's Own" Polar Bear Memorial Association [website], "Citations of Foreign (French, British and White Russian) Military Decoration Recipients," http://pbma.grobbel.org/decorations.htm#foreign.)

"Do you know that will raise commotion in America? By whose orders has this been done?"

"Well, G. H. Q." (General Headquarters.)

"Was it in writing?"

"No, it was not in writing. I was called up by phone and asked if I had any men here who could act as motormen and conductors in the street cars here. As my battalion was recruited in Detroit, and about one-half of them are motormen and conductors, I said 'Yes.' I sent some of the men down to the car sheds to take the cars out."

"Where is Col. Stewart?" I asked.

Major Nichols replied: "Mr. Ambassador, we are charging no fares." I said: "That is different, but I want Col. Stewart anyway."

For twenty-four hours or perhaps thirty hours, Americans were conducting the street cars, or acting as motormen, and at every stopping place, which in Archangel is every two or three blocks, there were two or three American soldiers to keep the crowds from overloading the cars. That was because no fares were being charged. In connection with this street car incident, I made an announcement of America's position in Archangel. I said, "In connection with this street car strike, there is one thing I want understood." I said it with the emphasis of an oath, I believe. "There is one thing I want understood."

"What is that?" I was asked.

I said: "Civil strife in the rear of our front. I am not going to permit the lives of our soldiers to be jeopardized by Bolsheviks on one side and a civil war in the rear. I will order them back from the railroad, and from up the river, and if there is a gun fired we will participate in the firing ourselves, if we have to kill Russians."

After that there was no fear of civil strife.

Right here, I would like to say a word about the American soldiers who landed at Archangel. They showed the same spirit that they did on the Western front. They were just as anxious to get into a fight. They understood the cause of the war.

I had a personal experience with a group of these American soldiers, most of whom were from Michigan and Minnesota, and seemed to know me by reputation.

One day while walking along the principal thoroughfare, the Broadway of Archangel, I saw three or four soldiers engrossed with a war map. I stopped and said to them, in English, of course, "You are American soldiers." They turned around and smiled at me, and I said, "I never was so glad to see American soldiers in my life as I was when you landed here a few days ago." They looked pleasant, but did not make any answer, and I continued, "I am the American Ambassador." They looked more interested and opened their eyes wider, but did not reply or ask me any questions. I said something more to them—four or five more remarks in an interrogative way—and they answered respectfully, "yes," and "no," but did not develop the conversation. I turned to go away, when the soldiers stopped the man who was with me, and asked "Who is that fellow?" The man replied, "That is Governor Francis." They said, "Why in hell didn't he say so."

Archangel is on the White Sea—a place of about 50,000 or 60,000 people. It has very substantial structures, more substantial than Vologda, although it is not so old. On the night of the 5th of September, 1918, occurred a coup d'état. Americans would call it a plain case of kidnapping. All ministers but two of the new Northern Government were taken from their homes and conveyed on a steamer to the Soliovetski Monastery on Soliovetski Island,[10] which was about thirty hours from Archangel. The kidnapping was done by a party of Russian officers, counter-revolutionists, who were against the Tchaikovsky Government, because the ministers were Socialists. The head of the kidnapping party was a man named Chaplin, a Russian naval officer,[11] attached to the staff of General Poole.

On the morning of the 5th of September, following the kidnapping, I was reviewing a battalion of American troops. Three American battalions had been landed, one of them had been sent down the railroad toward Vologda, one was up the Dvina River, toward Kotlas, and the other one was held at Archangel. I had just finished reviewing this battalion that was left in Archangel, when General Poole, who with me on the Government steps had received the salute, turned to me and said: "There was a revolution here last night." I said: "The hell you say! Who pulled it off?" He replied: "Chaplin." Chaplin, as I have said, was a Russian naval officer on General Poole's staff. I said: "There is Chaplin over there now." I motioned for him to come over and join us. General Poole remarked, "Chaplin is going to issue a proclamation at 11 o'clock." It was then 10:15. I said: "Chaplin, who pulled off this revolution here last night?" He said: "I did."

Chaplin had done very good work against the Bolsheviks, getting them deposed and out of Archangel. He went on to say: "I drove the Bolsheviks out of here, I established this Government"—meaning the Tchaikovsky Government. "The ministers were in General Poole's way, and were hampering Col. Donop," who was the French Provost Marshal. "I see no use for any government here anyway."

I replied: "I think this is the most flagrant usurpation of power I ever knew, and don't you circulate that proclamation that General Poole tells me you have written until I can see it, and show it to my colleagues."

---

[10] Solovetsky Monastery, a fortified Orthodox monastery on the Solovetsky Islands in the White Sea.

[11] Georgy E. Chaplin (1886–1950), captain of the Russian navy and leading figure of the anti-Soviet coup d'etat in Arkhangel'sk on August 2, 1918, which paved the way for the Allied intervention. He was the first commanding officer of Russian military and naval forces in the Northern Region. On September 6, 1918, he led another coup against the Chaikovsky government, which failed due to the active intervention of Allied diplomats headed by Ambassador Francis. Afterwards he commanded rivers and lakes flotillas of the White forces in northern Russia.

The Representatives of the Allied Missions met at my apartment that day. They came up there at 12 o'clock. I had Chaplin there. When the troops landed, I had sent for Col. Stewart, who was the commander of 4,700 American soldiers, and asked him: "Have you any communication for me?" He said, "No." I said, "What are your orders?" He said, "To report to General Poole, who is in command of the Allied forces in Northern Russia." I said, "I interpret our policy here. If I should tell yon not to obey one of General Poole's orders what would you do?" He said, "I would obey you."

This conversation had taken place before the kidnapping. I had arranged beforehand through the Department of State the relations between the Ambassador and the American forces. I had cabled the State Department that as I was interpreting the American policy in North Russia, I requested that the ranking officer in command of the American troops be put in close touch with me. Basil Miles, who was head of the Russian Bureau in the State Department,[12] told me when I arrived in Washington six months later that he had taken my cable over to General March,[13] who manifested great annoyance on reading the cable, and said: "I didn't want the Ambassador to have anything to do with these troops." Mr. Miles returned to the State Department, and told Assistant Secretary Long[14] of his interview with General March. Assistant Secretary Long wrote a letter to the President expressing the opinion that I had made a proper request in desiring the ranking officer in command of American troops to be in close touch with me, as I was interpreting American policy in Russia. The President evidently agreed with Assistant Secretary Long, as in a war council held the following day, he told General March that he thought I had made a reasonable request and ordered that request complied with. General March immediately cabled Col. Stewart to get in close touch with me, which accounts for Col. Stewart's reply to me when I asked him whose orders he would obey.

We brought back the Tchaikovsky ministers composing this "socialistic government" as Chaplin and his associates called it. It seems those ministers had been aroused at their apartment about 12:30 at night, and had been told to put on their clothes. They asked, "What are you going to do with us?" Chaplin's party replied, "We are going to put you in a monastery." The ministers were taken to a boat, and the boat cleared about 4:30 in the morning. It was after ten when I heard of the

---

[12] The Division of Russian Affairs in the State Department was created in fall 1917 by Basil Miles, who had built up the division from its initial one staff member and two secretaries to a staff of thirteen by fall 1919. DeWitt Clinton Poole headed the division, with intervals, from October 1, 1919 to October 1, 1923.

[13] Peyton C. March (1864–1955), general, May 20, 1918; chief of staff of US Army, March 1918–June 1921.

[14] Samuel Miller Breckinridge Long (1881–1958), lawyer born in St. Louis, MO. He supported Woodrow Wilson in the 1916 campaign; appointed third assistant secretary of state responsible for Asian affairs, January 29, 1917–June 8, 1920.

coup d'état, or kidnapping, through General Poole. The boat on which the Ministers had been taken away had no wireless apparatus, and we could not communicate with them. We wired to Kem, which is a station down the Murman Railroad, about twenty-five miles below Kandalaksha, to get a boat over there and get these ministers when they landed there and bring them back to Archangel.

There was something significant about the time chosen for his kidnapping. The American troops had landed on the 4th of September, and the kidnapping took place, as I have said, on the night of the 5th. It was timed, I think, to make the impression upon the people up there that it had the sanction, if it was not at the instigation of the American Ambassador, occurring as it did almost simultaneously with the landing of the American troops. I soon gave them to understand that I did not sanction the kidnapping at all.

As soon as the news was spread of the kidnapping, petitions and delegations and telegrams were coming to me as Dean of the Diplomatic Corps, asking that the deposed government of ministers be reinstated. The Tchaikovsky administration, I think, was well disposed, and intended to administer a very good government. As to the position of General Poole, I am satisfied he did not want to establish a government of his own, but British soldiers have been colonizers for so long that they do not know how to respect the feelings of socialists. I do not mean to say that is the policy of the British Government, but British officers have had to do so much with uncivilized people, and Great Britain has done so much colonizing that its officers do not feel as American officers do. We brought back the Tchaikovsky Government on Sunday night, and the ministers were reinstalled on Monday morning at 9 o'clock. The confused conditions which prevailed in Archangel after I learned that Tchaikovsky and his fellow ministers had been kidnapped and taken to the monastery are thus described in my report to the Secretary of State, dated September 10, 1918:

> I asked Chaplin if he had gone with those detailed to arrest the Ministers and was told he had not, but he had given a written order to the officer in command, and that officer had arrested the Ministers and taken them to the steamer in the harbor and they had cleared for the monastery between 2 a.m. and 4 a.m. General Poole had told me that Chaplin was going to issue a proclamation explaining to the people that the Sovereign Government had been deposed and that he was in command of the situation. Chaplin's manner indicated that he was proud of the deed, and expected commendation. I told General Poole not to permit any proclamation to be circulated before submitting it to the Allied Ambassadors, whom I requested to meet in my apartment at 12 noon. They assembled at that hour, when General Poole brought me a copy of the proclamation by Chaplin, and said he had held up its circulation until the Allied Ambassadors could pass upon it. The Allied Ambassadors immediately decided to bring back the kidnapped ministers and

sent for Chaplin, who came with Startseff, Commissar of Archangel under the Sovereign Government,[15] who had joined with Chaplin in deposing it. We told Chaplin to issue no proclamation; that we had ordered the ministers brought back, and I told him that I considered his act a flagrant usurpation of power, and an insult to the Allied Ambassadors. That evening about 10 p.m., September 6th, Chaplin issued a proclamation, appointing Ignatieff[16] to the position from which the Sovereign Government had removed him three days previous, and appointing Durop, Assistant Minister of War under the Sovereign Government, to be Minister of War.[17]

Durop came to the ambassadors' meeting on the following day, September 7th, and said he had been offered the post of Minister of War, but had declined it, and would not serve under Chaplin, as he considered Chaplin an adventurer. Meantime the strongest man in the Ministry, Dyedushenko, who held three portfolios,[18] had escaped arrest by not sleeping in his apartment.

---

[15] Nikolai A. Startsev (1873–1940), graduate of St. Petersburg University, lawyer, founder and leader of the Constitutional Democratic Party in the Arkhangel'sk Region. Deputy of the Fourth State Duma, 1912–13; assistant chairman of the Arkhangel'sk city administration from the summer of 1917; and governing commissar of the Northern Region after the Allied occupation of the country. On September 6, 1918, he joined Captain Chaplin in the failed coup d'etat against the Chaikovsky government, which ended his political career.

[16] Vladimir I. Ignatiev (1887–1937), graduate of Warsaw University, lawyer. Originally a Socialist Revolutionary, then SR-Maximalist. From 1917, People's Socialist, chairman of the Petrograd Party Committee. Governing commissar of the Northern Region from September 1918; manager of the Interior Division of the Provisional Government of the Northern Region, January–August 1919. Afterwards he went to Siberia and headed the All-Siberian Peasants' Union.

[17] Boris A. Durov (1879–1977), colonel of the Imperial Army. He arrived at Arkhangel'sk from the Macedonian Front in August 1918 and was appointed assistant chief of the military division of the Supreme Administration of the Northern Region; chief of the division from September 6. He was governor general and commander of the military forces of the Northern Region, September 18–November 3, 1918; also the manager of the military, interior, ways of communication, and post and telegraphs divisions of the Northern Government, October–November 1918.

[18] Yakov T. Dedusenko (1890–1936), graduate of the St. Petersburg Agronomical School, Socialist Revolutionary. After the February Revolution, he was a deputy of the Petrograd Soviet, the assistant chairman of the Petrograd City Administration, and the most active member of its Extraordinary Attendance on Provisions, September 22–December 3, 1917; deputy of the All-Russian Constituent Assembly. In June 1918, he was sent by the Union for the Revival of Russia to Arkhangel'sk via Vologda to organize anti-Bolshevik resistance. After the Allied occupation of Arkhangel'sk, he was made manager of the divisions of provisions, industry, and commerce in the Supreme Administration of the Northern Region. In the fall of 1918, he left Arkhangel'sk for Siberia to establish connections with local anti-Bolsheviks, was arrested by Kolchak's forces, and ceased his political activities after his release.

He had sent word to me that he would like to call if I would guarantee him against arrest, which I promptly did. He came while the ambassadors were in session and was invited in. He and another minister, who had escaped arrest, Evanoff,[19] by name, had prepared a proclamation, calling upon laborers, peasants and citizens to resist the Chaplin domination and charging it with being monarchistic, stating that the Grand Duke Michael, brother of the murdered Czar, was in Archangel, and implying, if not asserting, that the Chaplin movement was in concert with the Grand Duke's followers. We told Dyedushenko not to circulate the proclamation, and he went to the telephone in my apartment and gave an order to that effect. The four Allied Ambassadors issued a statement which was circulated, a copy of which is enclosed. The morning of September 7th, crowds were gathered around these three declarations, namely: The Ambassadors, and the one from Chaplin and Startseff and the third from Dyedushenko and Evanoff. To say that the populace was confused inadequately expresses the condition of their minds.

Meantime I had been visited by delegations of workmen, of peasants, of Zemstvos and of Cooperatives, all of which protested against the Chaplin government, and stated they were in favor of the deposed ministers. I also received telegrams and petitions from organizations of Zemstvos and peasants in the outlying districts, some of them stating that organizations were arming and coming to Archangel to reinstate the Sovereign Government. The strike committee ordered a general strike of the workmen, including those at the electric light plant and conductors and motormen of street cars. I thought that the situation justified and demanded that the Allies should assume control. My colleagues and General Poole agreed thereto, and a proclamation or statement was prepared setting forth such conclusion. By the time this proclamation was translated into Russian it was 8 p.m., and upon sending it to the printers we were informed that the printers were on strike, consequently the proclamation was never published.

The Ministers returned at 9 p.m. on Sunday, September 8th, and were held on the steamer in the harbor until a representative of the Allied Ambassadors, Lindley, could tell them of the action of the Ambassadors. Lindley returned to my apartment about 11 p.m., and reported that President Tchaikovsky appeared grateful that he and his colleagues were so promptly returned

---

[19] Aleksei A. Ivanov (1891–1937), Socialist Revolutionary, leader of the young people's SR organization in St. Petersburg from 1911. After the February Revolution, deputy of the Petrograd Soviet; went to Arkhangel'sk in March 1917 and headed the regional SR organization; was chairman of the Arkhangel'sk Regional Soviet of Peasant Deputies and elected to the All-Russian Constituent Assembly. Manager of the agricultural division of the Supreme Administration of the Northern Region from August 1918.

and promised to perform no act of government until meeting with the Ambassadors at 11 a.m., the following day, September 9th.

After we succeeded in bringing them back the Allied Ambassadors conferred with them in the hope of being able to reestablish the Tchaikovsky Government on a firm basis.

The report made by me on September 12th, 1918, to the Secretary of State sets forth the discouragement that attended our efforts:

Yesterday afternoon the three Ministers who attended the conference with the four Ambassadors surprised us very much by reading a declaration to the effect that they were going to abdicate and appoint a Governor General, who would report direct to the new government combination, whose headquarters are at Samara.[20] The main cause given for the abdication was that their decree of mobilization had been a failure. It appears that Chaplin had assembled in Archangel about 300 Russian officers, who were completely under his control, with, I suspect, the encouragement of some British and French military officers. Tchaikovsky, who was an old man and unaccustomed to the responsibilities of the position he had held for six weeks, appears 75 years of age. He told us in tremulous tones that only three officers, of the 300 or more he had expected, had obeyed the call for mobilization. That call specified that officers desiring to serve in the army should report first to the Sovereign Government and fixed dates therefor. Furthermore, he stated that while the Allied Diplomatic Chiefs were well disposed toward the new government, friction was constantly arising between the British Military control, represented by the British Intelligence Bureau under Colonel Thornhill,[21] and the Russian Military officials. He drew out the official newspaper of the government and exhibited the work of the censor commission, which had condemned over half of the matter in the proposed issue of the paper, and consequently it was not issued.

---

[20] The Committee of Members of the All-Russian Constituent Assembly (KOMUCh), consisting mostly of Socialist Revolutionaries, was established on June 8, 1918, at Samara after its seizure by the mutinous Czecho-Slovak troops. KOMUCh created the so-called People's Army which, in alliance with Czecho-Slovaks, opened the Eastern Front against Soviet Russia. After military defeats, KOMUCh went to Ufa, where its members took part in establishing the Provisional All-Russian Government (Ufa Directory) on September 23, 1918. The government moved further to Omsk, where it was overthrown by Admiral Kolchak in November 1918.

[21] Cudbert John Massy Thornhill (1883–1952), major of the British Indian Army, an officer of the Secret Intelligence Service in Russia during the World War; assistant military attaché at Petrograd, 1916–18. Lieutenant colonel; chief intelligence officer of the British Expeditionary Force in northern Russia, 1918–19.

I have just written to General Poole a note demanding American representation on this censor commission. General Poole appointed a French Military Governor, Colonel Donop, for the city of Archangel, and he has had friction not only with the ministry but with the ministry's military appointees; this French Colonel is sustained by the French Ambassador, who has suggested a modus vivendi which leaves the Sovereign Government a government in name only. I have not consented to this project, and shall not without modifications. The Ministry planned to announce to the Zemstvo meeting at six p.m. this intention of abdicating and appointing a Governor-General to report to the head of the new movement at Samara, but we prevailed upon them not to do so. Tchaikovsky went to the Zemstvo meeting and at my request, translated, sentence by sentence, a speech I delivered there. While Tchaikovsky, who preceded me, spoke in Russian, I had an interpreter who told me that Tchaikovsky said nothing about the intention of abdicating. This new Government at Samara is under three directors who are higher than the Ministers in Archangel, in Samara and in Siberia; these three directors are: Avksentieff, Aleksieff and Stapenoff.[22] I told Tchaikovsky as we were going to the Zemstvo meeting that he knew I was friendly to him and his Government and that he should not take such a serious step without consulting me. I have been waiting for a call from him, but up to this hour, noon, he has not phoned or called. The objection I have to the new Government abdicating is that it will give an appearance to the presence of the Allied troops here of a decided military character and may possibly arouse opposition among the peasants and Zemstvos and Cooperatives against the Allied forces.

After deciding to abdicate, the Ministers of the Sovereign Government appointed a Governor-General, but on the 25th of September reconsidered that decision and decided to remain in office. Tchaikovsky also continued as President. The selection for Governor-General was Duroff.[23] He was appointed on the 18th of September, but issued no orders until several days thereafter. President Tchaikovsky, the Governor-General, and General Poole met with the ambassadors in my apartment, and reached an understanding as thorough as seemed possible under the circumstances.

On the 24th of September, President Tchaikovsky telephoned me he would like to meet the ambassadors, and I called them in session at my apartment at five o'clock that day. When they were all assembled, Tchaikovsky said that the government in

---

[22] Actually, Nikolai D. Avksentev headed the Provisional All-Russian Government, created in Ufa on September 23, 1918 (Ufa Directory). General Mikhail V. Alekseev was appointed assistant war minister of the same government in his absence, but he died in Ekaterinodar on September 25, 1918. Colonel Alexander P. Stepanov commanded the northern group of the KOMUCh's People's Army.

[23] Durov (see n. 17, p. 233).

view of conditions in Samara could not abdicate without vesting the Governor-General with dictatorial power. This the government could not think of doing on account of its responsibility to the people.

"Of course," I said, but my colleagues were not so prompt, and while they made no objections I thought they were disappointed that the government had concluded to continue.

Three ministers after the "irrevocable decision" of the government left Archangel by boat for Omsk. These were the three ministers most objectionable to the opposition, and also the ministers least liked by my colleagues. As the vessel on which they sailed had no wireless apparatus and could only be reached at some place on the Ob River, where they might make their first landing, Lindley and Noulens advised that no effort be made to reach them. I did not object to permitting them to remain away, as I knew their return would bring discord, or promote any that already existed. President Tchaikoysky did not say what he would do, but I learned that he attempted to reach them by wire and failed, because he expressed great concern lest they might be shot by the Bolsheviks, who had captured the town to which he wired.

After the abdication of the Sovereign Government took place Tchaikovsky was thoroughly disheartened. He came to my apartment several times during the effort we were making to reestablish the Sovereign Government of Northern Russia. Impressed with his sincerity and believing that he had the confidence of a great many Russians, we endeavored to persuade him to accept some official position. One suggestion made to him was that he become Military Governor. He put this aside. The French Ambassador suggested that Tchaikovsky become the Diplomatic Representative of the Government of Samara. This proposition was taken under advisement by Tchaikovsky, and when he came to see me the next day he told me that he had concluded not to accept, and said he would like to go to England if I would assist, which I promptly agreed to do if he had fully decided to go, but expressed the hope that he would remain in Archangel.

I took advantage of this private conference with Tchaikovsky to ask him the real reason for the Government abdication. He told me that another coup d'état was being planned and when I assured him that I would take steps to prevent same and to protect the Ministers in the discharge of their duties, he replied that the Sovereign Government could not get along with General Poole, who, while apparently desirous of doing the right thing, was constantly under the influence of the British officers surrounding him and the French officers also, and that the British especially and he thought the French also were discouraging Russians from joining the Russian army, and doing propaganda work to induce them to join the British army. He said the French had recently opened a recruiting station also. He was confident that the British officers together with some of the French officers had planned a coup d'etat, or kidnapping, of himself and associates; that General Poole was approving orders issued by his subordinates which sent all Russian soldiers of democratic inclinations out of Archangel to the front, and consequently the Russian soldiers remaining were friends of Chaplin and opposed to the Sovereign Government or to any regeneration of Russia that did not look to the restoration of monarchy. At this juncture Lindley entered and Tchaikovsky told him that he had decided not to accept the diplomatic post which Noulens had suggested the previous evening.

Of the events which followed, I wrote the Department of State on the 4th of October:

> I advised President Tchaikovsky to fill the vacancies with representatives of elements not represented, such as commerce and shipping interests, etc., and to agree to make effort to do so. At the next meeting, held two days later, he informed us that he was unable to fill the vacant portfolios because he could find no members of the Constituent Assembly among those interests and was impervious to our arguments that it was not essential that ministers should be members of the Constituent Assembly, which had been dissolved by the Bolsheviks when it attempted to meet in Petrograd in January last and had never met since. Furthermore, the membership of that Constituent Assembly was depleted by assassination and flight and some of the members, such as Rodzianko, were open advocates of monarchy, and others, such as Miliukoff, had made terms with the Germans. He was immovable, but was finally prevailed upon to reduce the Ministry to five members, Matushin, Minister of Finance;[24] Ivanoff, Minister of Agriculture;[25] Goukovsky, Minister of Justice;[26] Zouboff, Minister of Post and Telegraph[27]—Zouboff was not a member of the Constituent Assembly, but was Secretary of the Government,

---

[24] Grigory A. Martushin (1884–1938), a prominent Socialist Revolutionary; one of the organizers of the First All-Russian Congress of Peasants' Deputies; assistant chairman of the Executive Committee of the All-Russian Soviet of Peasants' Deputies; deputy of the All-Russian Constituent Assembly. He went to Arkhangel'sk in the summer of 1918, where he headed the finance division of the Supreme Administration of the Northern Region. He was sent to the US in early 1919 as a representative of the Northern Government; testified before the Overman Committee.

[25] A. A. Ivanov (see n. 19, p. 234).

[26] Alexander I. Gukovsky (1865–1925), lawyer, Socialist Revolutionary, deputy of the All-Russian Constituent Assembly. Manager of the justice division of the Supreme Administration of the Northern Region, August–September 1918; city head of Arkhangel'sk, 1918–19. In the fall of 1919, he left Arkhangel'sk for Paris.

[27] Pavel I. Zubov, former assistant city head of Vologda (see n. 10, p. 206). He went to Arkhangel'sk from Vologda in the wake of foreign diplomats as a representative of the Union for Revival of Russia. Secretary of the Supreme Administration of the Northern Region and manager of its Division of Interior, Post and Telegraphs from August 3, 1918; acting chairman of the Provisional Government of the Northern Region, January 25, 1919–February 10, 1920.

and while he met with the Ministers he had not the privilege of voting on their decrees.

At the next meeting President Tchaikovsky informed us that Matushin, Ivanoff and Zouboff had resigned. Consequently he and Goukovsky were the only remaining members of the Constituent Assembly. He said that he had attempted to persuade Grudestoff, a well-known commercial man representing timber interests,[28] to become a minister without a vote, as he was not a member of the Constituent Assembly, but that Grudestoff had pleaded want of time, whereupon the Ambassadors asked me to attempt to persuade Grudestoff, whom I knew, to consent to become a member of the Government. I telephoned Grudestoff and he came to my apartment about 11 p.m.; instead of my convincing him, he convinced me that it was better that he should remain outside of the government, and organize an executive commission of fifteen, who would represent all interests and to such commission the government would refer financial, economic, and all questions other than military over which the Governor-General had supreme control, subject to the approval of the Ministry.

The next meeting held at 11 a.m., the following day, was attended by the Ambassadors, President Tchaikovsky and Grudestoff. The Ambassadors advised that a minister be appointed from the bourgeois classes; several names were suggested, but as the bourgeoisie who were active and influential had been arrested and taken to Moscow by the Bolsheviks, or fled from Archangel before the Sovereign Government was installed, the supply of available men was limited. Several were suggested during that day and the following day, but everyone declined.

At the next meeting of the Ambassadors with Tchaikovsky, it was agreed that he and Goukovsky would represent the Government and cooperate with the Executive or Advisory Commission, of which Grudestoff was to be Chairman, and with Col. Duroff, who in the meantime had talked with General Poole, as I had, and arranged for harmonious action. At this juncture the subject which I had avoided at previous meetings was brought up, and that was punishment of the Russians who had planned and executed the kidnapping. General Poole was present and in his defense of these men was very emphatic and insistent, saying he knew that if effort were made to punish them there would be greater discord than ever. I then told General Poole that I had heard confidentially from President Tchaikovsky, previously, that the Government Secret Service had informed President Tchaikovsky that another coup d'etat or kidnapping of Colonel Duroff had been planned. The

---

[28] Nikolai V. Grudistov (1867–1939), director of the Russian Forest Department from 1915; assistant minister of agriculture, 1916–17.

result of this conference was that General Poole guaranteed there would be no more coups d'etat and President Tchaikovsky agreed to issue a proclamation of amnesty and appeal to all Russians to unite in the formation of an army for the restoration of order, the expulsion of the Germans and the regeneration of Russia.

At the next meeting President Tchaikovsky informed us that Goukovsky had resigned because they had differed over the form of the proclamation which Duroff had drawn up and Tchaikovsky had approved with a few alterations. He read the proclamation to us and we commended it. He thereupon said that Goukovsky, who is a lawyer and a Jew, a man of fifty-odd years, insisted on stating in the proclamation in legal phraseology all the reasons why this amnesty was granted and they had argued four hours without coming to any agreement. I related a story of an old St. Louisan who said that he employed lawyers not to tell him what to do, but to arrange methods for his doing what he had concluded to do. Tchaikovsky said that the Ministers when they had all resigned several days previously had empowered him to form a new ministry, but he could find no members of the Constituent Assembly to whom he could assign portfolios, and as no supreme power could exist outside of the Constituent Assembly there would be no branch of the government authorized to legislate.

The next and final meeting of the Ambassadors with Tchaikovsky was held two days ago, and he then stated that he had "ordered" Matushin and Zouboff to resume their former positions in the government, and was now looking around for the fourth man, or a fifth counting Duroff, who would confer and advise without a vote. For two days past he had been endeavoring to find such a man, and when he succeeds will inform the Ambassadors. I think now he will not appoint a minister to whom we object.

In the meantime quiet prevails throughout the city, and the forces up the Dvina and down the railroad toward Vologda seem to be resting on their arms, as no engagements have been reported by General Poole for three days past—the warfare has been of a guerrilla character from the beginning. A few days ago three British sailors were surprised and captured on the railroad by the Bolsheviks, were killed after they had surrendered, and their arms severed from their bodies. A French interpreter was captured about ten days ago, was killed after capture and his head cut off and his heart taken out.

Roger Simmons[29] and Peter Bukowski,[30] have just arrived in Archangel, but I have not seen them. Simmons told my secretary that Lockhart[31] was in prison and would surely be shot; that a young Jewish lawyer whom I knew well—but Simmons could not remember the name—was in the same cell with Simmons and was taken out and shot because he had been the legal adviser of the British Embassy. Simmons said he would have been shot the next day, if Poole, Acting Consul-General, had not intervened. Simmons also says that the doctor who attended me during my illness of ten days in April in Vologda, Dr. Gortaloff,[32] a man of sixty years, was arrested because he gave him a certificate of illness, and has probably been shot ere this. The Bolsheviks are inhuman brutes. Simmons says they have heard that General Poole said he would kill every commissar he could capture, and that numbers of innocent people had been killed in anticipation of the execution of General Poole's threat. I do not blame General Poole for feeling that way, but if he made the threat, which I do not believe, it was indiscreet. I have been satisfied from subsequent developments as well as from what I heard at the time of cabling you, that it was the intention of the Soviet Government at Moscow to hold us Allied diplomats as hostages at Archangel when we arrived the first time and remained there two days before leaving for Kandalaksha. The reason why we were not detained was because the local Soviet knew that a revolution was brewing here and feared it would be successful with the aid of Allied forces, who were reported as coming from Murmansk for days before they left that place, July 31st.

---

[29] Roger Edwin Simmons (1868–1958), special agent of the Department of Commerce who traveled throughout Russia from July 1917 to November 1918, studying the lumber industry and the exploitable forests of the country.

[30] Peter I. Bukowski (1894–1956), assistant commercial attaché, 1916–17; then assistant military attaché, 1917–19, with rank of first lieutenant of the National Army.

[31] R. H. Bruce Lockhart (1887–1970), British diplomat and Secret Intelligence Service agent. After some private adventures in Malaya, he joined the Foreign Service and was appointed vice consul at Moscow, 1912–15, then consul general, 1915–17. He left Russia shortly before the October Revolution, but in January 1918, he was sent back as British special representative in Soviet Russia. He was arrested in September 1918 and deported the next month in exchange for Maxim M. Litvinov.

[32] Sergei F. Gortalov (1862–1937), graduate of the St. Petersburg Military-Medical Academy, senior physician of the Vologda regional hospital from 1899–1926. He was again arrested and executed in the course of the Stalin Great Purge.

I think I did not write you or cable that the Moscow Central Soviet ordered the Siberian Government[33] to arrest the Japanese Ambassador Uchida (now Minister of Foreign Affairs in Japan), when he left me at Vologda, March 4th and started for Vladivostok. The Siberian Government replied that they would not arrest the Japanese Ambassador, because they feared it would bring the Japanese army in Siberia. These Bolsheviks have persistently endeavored by special favors and hypocritical expressions of friendship to American representatives to create discord between the Allies. They are in my opinion German agents and have been from the beginning.

As cabled you yesterday, if the American troops had not arrived when they did this Government of the North would have been overthrown and a civil war in the rear of our front, which would have been the result, would have left the few British and French soldiers on the Dvina and on the railroad toward Vologda completely at the mercy of the Bolsheviks, and we diplomatic representatives would have been forced to leave Russia. As General Poole stated to me, before the arrival of the 4,500 American soldiers, he was playing a great game of bluff; he had less than 2,000 soldiers all told. If the Allied forces had numbered 50,000 when they first landed, they could have advanced to Vologda, could have taken Kotlas and possibly Viatka, but now the Bolsheviks have had time to get reenforcements and are commanded by German officers, who are directing them how to offer spirited resistance. Only four American soldiers have been killed in battle, but about sixty have been wounded and brought back to Archangel.

Personal letters written by me from Archangel give possibly more detailed and intimate descriptions of the confusing situation than do the official reports.

To Thomas H. West, St. Louis,[34] in a letter dated Archangel, August 27th, I wrote:

This letter is written from Archangel and is dictated from my bed. My colleagues come to my apartment, as do members of the new government and the British General and the Military Governor also. I am determined, as Mr. Britling said, "to see it through" even although it may cause a shortening of my life, which I hope it will not do. But if it did, I would be willing to remain

---

[33] The first Provisional Siberian Government was established in January 1918 in Tomsk; it soon went to Harbin and then to Vladivostok. Another Provisional Siberian Government was created in Omsk in June 1918. That same month, the Vladivostok government was renamed the Provisional Government of Autonomous Siberia. Both governments were dominated by Socialist Revolutionaries and subordinated to the Provisional All-Russian Government, which was created in Ufa and removed to Omsk in October 1918.

[34] Thomas Henry West (1846–1926), president of the St. Louis Union Trust Company.

here if I thought I could best serve my country by doing so. My whole heart and soul is in this war, and I am hoping and praying that I may be spared to see Germany defeated.

At Murmansk I received newspapers from America for six months back, and although I have not been able to read them carefully, have gathered therein information that is very gratifying to me, and that is that our people are aroused and determined to succeed in this struggle which is one between force and humanity, between autocracy and democracy, between feudalism and civilization, between the old and the new, in fact a struggle between the old theory of classes and the new and broadening, principles of Christianity; a struggle between slavery and freedom, between a favored few who think they can exploit their fellows, by their own superiority if not by divine right on the one side, and individual responsibility to God and society on the other. I feel that if Germany is successful in this war, not only will our liberties in America be jeopardized and all of our principles subverted, but that this world will not be a desirable place for an intelligent freeman to live in.

On the 29th of August, 1918, I wrote from Archangel to Festus J. Wade of St. Louis[35] a letter describing the conditions then existing in Northern Russia.

The situation here is critical. Cable communication is very irregular and unreliable, and connection with Moscow, Petrograd, Vologda and Siberia is absolutely severed. The new government in the saddle here is sincere but not strong. I am having difficulty in lessening the friction between the Military Governor, a Britisher, General Poole, and the new civil government. None of the Allied governments have yet recognized this "Sovereign Government of the Northern Regions" as it calls itself, but its principles are correct, and that is more than could at any time have been said of the Bolshevik Government. The new government is attempting to organize an army with which to fight Germany, and it has the sincere motive of attempting to resurrect Russia. At the same time it has its enemies in Russia, the Bolsheviks and the Monarchists are persistently endeavoring to undermine and overthrow it. As I said to the President of the new government, Tchaikovsky, in a conversation a few days ago, "The situation at Archangel is anomalous, unprecedented, difficult and delicate." American representatives here are less disliked than the representatives of any other foreign country. There is some prejudice against the Allied governments, as their objects are suspected. It is believed by some Russians, and they are a suspicious race, that England, France

---

[35] Festus John Wade (1859–1927), St. Louis banker, president of the Mercantile Trust Company.

and Japan are planning to subordinate the resources and the man power of Russia to their own interests, and the Bolsheviks are doing all in their power to foster this suspicion. Thanks to the expressions of our President and the American Ambassador in Russia to a limited and less extent, our objects are not considered selfish. Lenin and Trotzky called the American Government imperialistic and capitalistic and all Bolshevik orators do likewise, and find thousands of hearers who believe them, as it is difficult for Europeans to understand why a people thousands of miles away are interfering in affairs which do not affect their material welfare. It has been very difficult to make clear to them that America is unselfishly fighting for a principle, for humanity, for civilization, for society itself as it should be constituted. I flatter myself that I have made some impression on the Russian people by the addresses I have issued and the interviews I have given. All that I have said and done, however, cannot be compared with the utterances of President Wilson, whose speeches and messages I have assiduously circulated and with good effect. I must close now as the Financial Adviser of the British Embassy[36] is waiting for me in an outer room. I hear him coughing as if he were impatient.

In a letter to Breckinridge Jones of St. Louis, dated Archangel, September 4, 1918, I wrote of the confusion and difficulties attending the establishment of government in Russia:

The British Empire was not diplomatically represented in Russia from February to July, when on the 7th or 10th of that month F. O. Lindley, who had been Charge after the departure of Sir George Buchanan in January, came to Vologda. The Allied forces here, numbering only about 3,000 are under the command of a British General, named Poole. About 4,000 American soldiers are expected to-morrow, but the State Department has not advised me specifically of their coming. Reconciling their presence with our Governments declaration of Russian policy is a delicate task. The British and French are impatient with the Russians and have lost patience with the latter's ability to govern themselves. The new government here, calling itself "Sovereign Government of the Northern Region" has an exaggerated judgment of its importance and power and is constantly complaining to me of the encroachments of the military on the civil prerogatives. I am Dean of the Diplomatic Corps, by reason of being longest in service as Ambassador, and have my hands full in endeavoring to reconcile these discordant elements. The new government, it is true, has declared that it does not recognize the Brest-Litovsk peace and is attempting to mobilize an army with which to fight

---

[36] Francis probably meant commercial attaché Henry Arthur Cooke (1862–1946).

Germany. I had to tell the President a few days ago in answer to some grievance he presented that if the Allied forces should withdraw from Archangel, the officials of the new government would be driven into the Arctic Ocean, if they escaped being killed by the Red Guard of the Bolsheviks. This is not the only menace of the new government; officials of that government are Socialists and are considered by the Monarchists as little better than the Bolsheviks, consequently the Monarchists are constantly attempting to undermine the Sovereign Government of the Northern Region and to supplant it with a dictatorship.

On the first of October, 1918, I wrote to my son Charles:

My request for additional American troops to come to Archangel has not met with favor. In fact, I am in receipt of a cable, dated September 26th, stating, "You are advised that no more American troops will be sent to the northern ports of Russia." The same cable contains the following: "The course that you have followed is most earnestly commended. It has the entire admiration of the President, who has characterized it as being thoroughly American. I highly approve of your actions. They have been very consistent and have been guided by a very sound judgment, exercised under the most trying and complicated circumstances." Of course, this is confidential. I replied, "Thanks for personal commendation but am not resting on past efforts,"— and then went on to say that I did not despair of inducing the Russians to form a republic.

In a letter of September 23rd from Archangel to Miss Isabel F. Hapgood,[37] Atlantic City, who visited Russia while the Root Commission was in Petrograd, and who took great interest in Russian affairs, I wrote of the fate of the Czar, giving the official information which had come to me direct from the American Consulate at Ekaterinburg.[38]

The Emperor was shot by the Bolsheviks on the 16th of July, last, after having been removed from Tobolsk to Ekaterinburg. He was killed by order of the

---

[37] Isabel Florence Hapgood (1851–1928), American writer, journalist, and translator, especially of Russian literature. She was traveling through Russia in 1887–89 and 1916–17 to collect material for her books about the country and its culture.

[38] The consulate in Ekaterinburg (Central Urals) existed in the person of Henry Palmer, the US citizen who was appointed vice consul there on April 3, 1918. From April to July 1918, the city was a place of imprisonment for the imperial family. At the time of their execution, an American military intelligence officer, Major Homer H. Slaughter (1885–?), also was at Ekaterinburg and reported on the event.

local Soviet, whose action was subsequently approved by the Central Soviet at Moscow. A courier from the American Consul at Ekaterinburg to myself, who left Ekaterinburg August 2nd, and after many vicissitudes arrived in Archangel, August 24th, told me that the Emperor was shot July 16th, but nobody knew it until July 18th, when it was officially announced. He said that the disposition of the body was not known but the rumor was that it had been thrown into a coal mine and burned. He said that the members of the Red Guard or Red Army who were ordered to shoot the Emperor refused to do so, and a detachment of Lettish soldiers was ordered to shoot him, but when they found it was the Emperor, they declined to shoot, and thereupon the local Commissar himself shot him. The killing of the Emperor, whom the people of Russia once looked upon with affection and reverence as the "Little Father" aroused no resentment on the part of the people whatever. In fact, it was forgotten within a short time—so accustomed have these people become to killing.

Of events at Vologda, following our departure on July 25th, a letter sent from Stockholm, September 12th, to me at Archangel by Norman Armour,[39] the Second Secretary of the American Embassy whom I left in charge at Vologda, gave the following account:

> After receiving your telegram instructing me to remain in Vologda, until it should be possible to join you, I went to the Soviet and explained to Vitoshkin,[40] as President of the Extraordinary Revolutionary Committee, that I had received orders from you to stay. Things went all right for three days, when suddenly we were ordered by an officer sent by Kedroff to leave town immediately for Moscow. I flatly refused, saying that having twenty nationals I should have to remain in order to protect them. If it was dangerous

---

[39] Norman Armour (1887–1982) was born in England of American parents, graduated from Princeton University (1909, BA; 1915, MA) and Harvard Law School (1913, LLB). He served in US embassies at Vienna (1912) and Paris (1915–16). He was appointed to Petrograd on May 22, 1916, as third secretary of the embassy; promoted later to second secretary. He stayed in charge of the American embassy building at Vologda after Francis's departure to Arkhangel'sk, but was forced by the Bolsheviks to remove to Moscow. He left Russia for Sweden in September 1918.

[40] Mikhail K. Vetoshkin (1884–1958), graduate of St. Petersburg University, lawyer, Bolshevik, deputy of the All-Russian Constituent Assembly. Chairman of the Vologda Regional Executive Committee of Soviets and of the Vologda Bolshevik Regional Committee from April 1918 to January 1920; chairman of the Extraordinary Revolutionary Staff, created in July 1918. Afterwards, he led revolutionary activities in Crimea and Ukraine, and held responsible positions in the Soviet government. Professor of history at Moscow University from 1953.

for me to remain it was equally dangerous for them. However, Kedroff refused to see this point of view and a train was prepared and we were told to go on board. Upon our again refusing, troops entered the Embassy during the night (the French, as you know, had already moved into our building) and forced us to enter an automobile, which took us to the station, and put us on board the train. On the train was a guard of ten soldiers. Before our departure, we were informed by the Commissar of War that our train would stop 40 versts away where we could await our nationals. Contrary to this promise, the train continued to Daniloff, from which station I sent a telegram to the Commissar of War, telling him he had broken his word and demanding the train to remain there. He complied with this request, and I was able three days later to see the Y.M.C.A. and National City Bank pass through safely.

Secretary Armour requested to remain with me upon my leaving Petrograd. He is at the present Secretary of the American Legation at The Hague. I saw him in London when I was confined in the hospital there, immediately before he returned to Stockholm, where he married the Russian Princess Koudachev.[41] I was confined to my apartment in Archangel during almost my entire stay in that city, and in my bed the most of the time. Five surgeons, who were called in, two Americans, two British, and a French-Russian, agreed upon the diagnosis of my ailment and said it required a major surgical operation for my relief. I said to them, "Perform it here and now." But they refused. After suffering ten or twelve days longer, I advised the State Department of my condition and of my exasperation at the surgeons for refusing to perform the surgical operation. The Department replied in a very complimentary cable, which is set forth in the Introduction, and a subsequent cable informed me that it had obtained the consent of Admiral Sims[42] and Secretary Daniels[43] to send the *Olympia* for me. The cruiser arrived on the 28th of October, under command of Rear Admiral McCully[44] and Captain Bierer, but was held in the Archangel harbor

---

[41] Princess Maria S. Kudasheva (1895–1990), who became Myra Armour. Norman Armour had managed her escape from the Soviet Russia with great adventures and married her on February 2, 1919, in Belgium.

[42] William S. Simms (1858–1936), former naval attaché at Paris and St. Petersburg, 1897–1900. Temporary vice admiral, commander of US naval forces operating in European waters during the World War.

[43] Josephus Daniels (1862–1948), secretary of the navy, 1913–21.

[44] Newton A. McCully, former naval attaché at Petrograd (see n. 47, p. 17). He was promoted to temporary rear admiral on September 21, 1918, and appointed commander of US naval forces in northern Russia; served there from October 24, 1918 to July 13, 1919. He was designated a special agent of the Department of State in south Russia on December 23, 1919; arrived in Novorossiisk in January 1920; left Crimea in November 1920. He brought back to

until the 6th of November, just five days before the Armistice was signed, when I was carried on board on a stretcher, borne by eight sailors.

Terestchenko, former Minister of Finance and Minister of Foreign Affairs in the Provisional Government, came to Archangel and dined with me twice. He was going under the name of Titoff. He came from Stockholm, having gone there from Norway, where he had been living quietly with a peasant since his release from prison in Petrograd, about March 4th. He was attempting to join Kolchak, traveling as a courier of Goulkevitch, the Russian Minister to Sweden.[45] He was decidedly anti-German and pro-Ally in his feelings, but like most Russians was suspicious of the intentions of the British. He thoroughly approved of the American policy, and told me at our second meeting that while living in Archangel incognito he had seen many of his bourgeoisie friends and was pleased to inform me that not only the local government, but the people generally considered the American Ambassador the best friend they had in the Diplomatic Corps. He told me that he and Kerensky were not friends, or did not agree in their policies after the Korniloff affair. He furthermore assured me that about August 1st, 1917, he received advantageous peace proposals from Germany; that he showed them to no one in the Ministry except Kerensky and gave Kerensky the credit of siding with him against a separate peace. He was very proud of his position on that issue and claimed credit therefor, correctly saying that if Russia had concluded a peace at that time, four months after America entered the war, the Central Empires would have been able to concentrate their strength against the Allied armies before America could transport troops to France. If this was true, and I have no reason to doubt it, the course of Terestchenko, supported by Kerensky, not only brought the war to an earlier end than it would otherwise have had, but it cost the Allies less blood and far less treasure. I always had faith in the sincerity and loyalty of Terestchenko. He is a more practical man than Kerensky, and is much more highly esteemed in Russia.

The reasons which inspired Terestchenko to reject the proposal of the Central Empires for a separate peace were the same reasons that inspired me to sustain the Provisional Government to the extent of my influence, because I knew that when the Bolsheviks came into power they would withdraw Russia from the conflict and thereby permit Germany and Austria to send their forces on the Eastern front to the Western front. It is possible that our Government's recognition of the Provisional Government on my recommendation perpetuated the Provisional Government during its administration of affairs. If the Provisional Government had been shorter-

---

the US seven Russian orphans, five girls and two boys, and their nurse Olga A. Krundisheva. He adopted the children in 1921 and married Krundisheva in 1927.

[45] Konstantin N. Gulkevich (1865–1935), Russian minister to Sweden from March 1917; member of the Russian Political Conference created in 1919 to represent Russian interests at the Paris Peace Conference.

lived, Germany would have sent 105 divisions to the Western front sooner than they were sent, and that would have been before Pershing[46] and his men could have gotten to France from America.

In my Archangel cables of October to the Department of State, I reported in detail the friction existing among the different forces there and especially the attitude of the British, who were inclined to be overbearing, and who attempted to conduct all affairs in the Archangel region according to their own ideas. The State Department informed me that General Poole had been cautioned regarding his policy in Russia, and to keep in touch with me. Immediately following receipt of this cable from the Department, I noticed a change in the General's attitude. However, it was reported to me that he was going to England and would not return unless I was removed or recalled from Archangel, and that that was one of the objects of his visit to England.

Under date of October 19, 1918, I cabled from Archangel to the Department:

> The general conduct and bearing of all British representatives, military and civil, at Archangel and Murmansk indicate a belief or feeling on their part that if they do not have exclusive privileges at these ports, they should have, and they will not be contented with not having a decided advantage. Every move on their part indicates a desire to gain a strong foothold. There were 20,000 tons of flax in Archangel and the British, after stating to the French and our representatives that we should not compete therefor and thus advance the price to unreasonable figures, and after we consented thereto, contracted for the entire holdings of the cooperatives. Three thousand tons were apportioned to us, and as the same is shipped Captain Proctor, the British representative,[47] demands payment for purchase shall be in pound sterling in London,—notwithstanding shipments are made to America, and the cooperatives or the sellers wish and request payments to be made in dollars in America. At this writing I have instructed Consul Poole and Berg's representative (Berg is making purchases for a linen thread company of America) to inform the cooperatives and Captain Proctor that the sellers of this flax when shipped to America can receive purchase money in dollars in America.

> I cabled you that Lieut. Hugh S. Martin, our representative at Murmansk, had sent me confidential information by Crawford Wheeler, ranking Secretary

---

[46] John J. Pershing (1860–1948), general, October 6, 1917; commander of the American Expeditionary Force in Europe during the World War, 1917–18.

[47] Captain Alex Proctor, representative of the British Military Supply Mission at Arkhangel'sk.

of the Y. M. C. A. in Russia,[48] that he had proof the British were attempting to negotiate commercial treaties of an exclusive, preferential character with the Russians at Murmansk. I cannot believe this is true, but am waiting the arrival of Lieut. Martin before making up my mind on the subject. The British have been experienced in international commerce for centuries and consequently they have the advantage over others who have less experience.

Under date of October 18th, 1918, I cabled the Department of State, as follows:

General Ironsides,[49] the successor of General Poole, dined with me last evening; he told me he had made two or three quick tours of inspection to the fronts, and while he realized that the soldiers on both fronts should have more relief than he is able to give them, on account of the small number of soldiers at his disposal, he had arranged that each company at the front should spend eight days in the month in Archangel. Acting Naval Attaché Riis[50] returned from the railroad front and reported that American soldiers there were very dissatisfied and the French were more so. The French, having heard that there was an armistice, had openly declared that they would not fight any more in Russia if the hostilities had ceased in France, because they did not see why they should fight for British interests in Russia. The American soldiers and officers were partially inoculated with the same sentiment, but Riis told them that no armistice had been agreed upon and hostilities had not ceased.

General Ironsides is six feet four inches tall without shoes, weighs 270 pounds, and is only thirty-seven years old. He is descended direct from the last Saxon king of England, was dismissed from St. Andrew's School when he was ten and one-half years old because he whipped the teacher. He was the first British officer to land in France; in fact he landed on the night of

---

[48] Crawford Wheeler, war prisoners' aid secretary for the American YMCA in Germany during the World War. He went to Russia in 1917, and worked in Moscow and Arkhangel'sk until 1919.

[49] Brigadier General William Edmund Ironside (1880–1959), commander in chief of the British and Allied Expeditionary Forces in northern Russia from October 1918.

[50] Sergius Martin Riis (1883–1963), son of a Danish immigrant who was engaged in trade at St. Petersburg. He was appointed lieutenant of the Naval Auxiliary Reserve on November 20, 1917; was ordered to Russia in the summer of 1918; arrived at Petrograd when the Red Terror started; escaped the city with great adventures and finally reached Arkhangel'sk. He was awarded with the Navy Cross "for distinguished service in the line of his profession attached to various vessels of the U. S. Naval Forces in Northern Russia, acting Naval Attaché to the American Embassy at Archangel." (Home of Heroes [website], "Navy Cross—WWI—US Navy M to R," https://homeofheroes.com/distinguished-service-cross/service-cross-world-war-i/navy-cross-world-war-i/navy-cross-wwi-navy/navy-cross-wwi-navy-m-to-r/.)

August 2nd, before England had entered the war, on August 6th. He was in command of a division on the French front, when he was ordered to Russia. He relinquished his command and cleared in an aeroplane for England. After a flight of three and one-half hours he landed somewhere in England, spent three days acquainting himself with Russian conditions and arrived in Archangel September 20th; he does everything that way. He speaks six languages with equal fluency—English, French, Russian, German, Italian, Swedish, and can converse although not fluently in eleven other languages. In other words, he has studied seventeen languages, and has mastered six of them sufficiently to be able to converse therein fluently and grammatically. He told me that the War Office had turned down his request or appeal for permission to transfer 5,000 or 6,000 troops from Murmansk to Archangel, but he said that while greatly disappointed thereat he was making the best of the troops under his command, few as they are.

Under date of October 23rd, 1918, I cabled the Department:

General Ironsides seems to have impressed everybody favorably. President Tchaikovsky told me he was pleased with General Ironsides, and believed him to be a sincere man and more disposed than his predecessor was to respect the rights of the civil government. General Ironsides told me that he was encouraging in every way the mobilization of an army by the Archangel Government, and President Tchaikovsky confirmed this by saying that he was experiencing less difficulty in procuring clothing and supplies for the mobilized army since General Ironsides came. General Poole or his staff were delaying honoring such requests with the view to forcing into the British-Slav legion[51] all men desiring to enlist.

Almost my last act before I was taken on board the *Olympia* was to issue an address to the American soldiers in North Russia in which I gave a short account of the work they had done, the hardships they had suffered, the illness and deaths among the men, calling attention to their splendid response in spite of all these difficulties and expressing my appreciation of their spirit of service and sacrifice with which they had performed every duty. I said:

I trust you do not underestimate the importance of the service you are performing as American soldiers in Russia. Our Government has no desire for territorial conquest anywhere, especially in Russia, in whose welfare and

---

[51] Slavo-British Allied Legion, a British raised and sponsored military unit which was created in northern Russia in the summer of 1918.

integrity President Wilson has repeatedly assured the world of his deep and abiding interest.... President Wilson reflects the views and feelings of the American people when he says he proposes to stand by Russia. Regardless of sympathy with the people who have been oppressed for centuries, if the Allies had consented for Germany to appropriate Russia, German methods would have begun immediately to organize the immense man power of this country and to develop itself immeasurable resources in preparation for another effort to establish Deutschland Uber Alles...[52]

The Bolsheviks, who control the Soviet Government, are completely under the domination of Germany and consequently in resisting them you are not only performing a humanitarian service but you are preventing Germany from securing a much stronger foothold in Russia than she has up to this time been able to establish. Your service is as important as that which any American soldiers or Allied troops are performing anywhere. I have no doubt that you would prefer to be in France or in Italy, but like soldiers you are performing the duty to which you are assigned and are entitled to all the more credit therefor.

---

[52] The slogan derived from the refrain "Deutschland, Deutschland über alles" of the first stanza of "The Song of the Germans," written in 1841 to the Joseph Haydn's melody of 1797. Originally, the song meant that the imagined united Germany should be above any particular interests of separate German states. The song became widely known by this refrain, which replaced its original title in popular imagination. "The Song of the Germans" was made the national anthem of Germany in 1922.

Chapter XIX
ALLIED POLICIES IN RUSSIA

In December, 1917, the Bolsheviks in a series of decrees began to develop their strange financial policies.[1] These decrees declared the banking business to be a "monopoly of the government," instructed all proprietors of safes in safe deposit institutions to present themselves immediately with their keys "in order to be present at the revision of the safes," otherwise all property contained therein would be confiscated and become the property of the nation. Later decrees announced the cancellation of all loans contracted by former Russian governments, all guarantees for these loans, and all loans made from abroad. There were nine other decrees: nationalization of land, of factories and works, of banks (including the opening of all safe deposit boxes); the suspension of payment of all bond coupons; taxation amounting to confiscation of buildings, whether or not belonging to foreigners; annulment of all loans; confiscation of shares of stock in former private banks; and nationalization or confiscation of every ship belonging to private individuals or corporations.

The diplomatic corps was unanimous with the exception of myself, in approving a protest to the Bolshevik government against all these decrees. I believed that with the decrees pertaining to domestic affairs we had nothing to do and consequently we should not protest in the form proposed. As for the decree abolishing debts to foreigners, or to foreign countries or interfering with the property rights of our nationals, I was willing to join in the protest.

Finally a protest was agreed upon by all of us and served on the Soviet Government. This protest stated that we regarded the repudiation of state debts, confiscation of property, etc., in so far as they concerned the interests of foreign subjects, as non-existent and that our governments reserved the right to demand satisfaction for all damage or loss which may be caused foreign states in general and their subjects who live in Russia in particular, by the operation of these decrees.

On the 2nd of May, 1918, I cabled the State Department that the time had come for the Allies to intervene in Russia, and gave my reasons in detail:

---

[1] Decree on Establishment of the Supreme Council of National Economy, December 2, 1917; Decree on Nationalization of Banks, December 14, 1917; decrees of nationalization of some plants, factories, and joint-stock companies.

In my opinion the time has arrived for Allied intervention. I had hoped Soviet Government would so request and have discreetly worked to that end.

First, by remaining here with the approval of the Department when other Allied Missions had departed.

Second, by fostering friendly business relations with the Bolsheviks and allowing Robins to remain in Moscow for that purpose—this although Summers objected, saying he was humiliated thereby.

Third, by taking position against Japanese intervening alone.

Fourth, by suggesting and arranging for Allied military advice in forming new army; as stated to you I was confident I would be able at proper time to influence such army; I also persuaded my French and Italian Colleagues to permit their military chiefs to cooperate. This movement, however, had not been carried into effect when your cable was received prohibiting its execution until advised of the object for which the new army was to be organized; that object was never varied from Trotzky's first statement that it was to defend and promote the world-wide social revolution not only against existing monarchies but against our government also.

Fifth. I requested that six railroad units be sent to Vologda for consultation with me and an experienced Soviet Railroad official. Stevens at first wired he was sending six units and I so advised the Soviet Government, but later Stevens having opposed the sending of any men whatever these units were not directed to come and I was embarrassed by having to explain to Trotzky through Robins and Riggs their failure to come as promised. I later asked that Emerson be instructed to bring three able engineers to Vologda and you replied April 24th that Emerson had been ordered to come or send Goldsmith and advise me of their leaving Harbin. Receiving no advice from Harbin of the departure of Emerson, I did not advise Trotzky or the Soviet thereof, fearing I might be again embarrassed. I am not complaining or criticizing Department action concerning military and railroad matters but merely stating facts.

Sixth. I have in every way encouraged international commercial relations between America and Russian merchants while throwing around the same proper safeguards.

I was ill nine days, from April 19th to April 28th, possibly from ptomaine poisoning, by which I was greatly weakened, being confined to my room if not to my bed, but I never ceased to work or lost spirit; am fully recovered now.

Seventh. I informed the Soviet Government of the Department's action concerning Chinese Embargo and ignored the offensive prohibition issued to

American Consul at Irkutsk[2] concerning cipher messages and overlooked the demand for recall of the American Consul at Vladivostok[3] notwithstanding there were no evidences that he was guilty of charges made which if proven were not incriminating. I furthermore paid no attention to the demand of the Soviet Government to define the American view of the landing of Japanese and British marines at Vladivostok but gave two carefully worded interviews on the subject. I have herein made a hasty resume of my policy since arriving in Vologda.

Am not aware of the Department's view concerning Allied intervention, while knowing American and Russian opposition to exclusively Japanese invasion which I heartily endorse. Last information on this subject received by me was from the Ambassador at Tokio[4] and was to the effect that Japan would not intervene against our wishes. Since then Motono has resigned but if our Japanese policy has been altered I am not advised. It is possible that Japan may not intervene without being compensated but any reasonable compensation other than territorial if demanded by Japan I think should be granted.

I fully realize the import of this recommendation which is given now for the following reasons:

First. Germany through Mirbach is dominating and controlling Bolshevik Government and Mirbach is practical dictator as all differences even between Russians are referred to him.

Second. I call attention to Consulate-General's No. 439 of April 29th, which contains an account of Soviet protest and appeal to Berlin against violation of Brest Treaty and contains also Mirbach's reply of April 30th that German encroachments would cease when Allies evacuated Murmansk and Archangel; this last information was obtained through the French Embassy who say it was received from Lockhart, British Representative in Moscow. In my opinion such evacuation would be very unwise.

Riggs, just arrived from Moscow, says the Soviet Government won't oppose Germany in absence of Allied encouragement and is confident that the Soviet Government will approve Allied intervention when it knows the same is inevitable; he furthermore says that if the Military Missions are informed of the proposed intervention previous to occurrence thereof the

---

[2] David B. Macgowan, acting consul at Irkutsk while on special detail in Siberia (see n. 34, p. 160). In May 1918, Ernest L. Harris was appointed consul general in Siberia and detailed to Irkutsk.

[3] John K. Caldwell (see n. 28, p. 177).

[4] Roland S. Morris (1874–1945), the US ambassador to Japan, October 30, 1917–May 15, 1920.

Missions can probably influence Bolsheviks to become reconciled thereto. Possibly the Soviet Government when informed of Allied intervention would advise Germans; we must take that risk. Riggs advises the Embassy moving from Vologda to Moscow or that a diplomatic representative be established there. I do not concur because I think it would result in recognizing Soviet Government or widening existing breach.

Russia is passing through a dream or orgy from which it may awaken any day, but the longer awakening is delayed the stronger foothold will Germany acquire. Robins and probably Lockhart also have advocated recognition but the Department and all Allies have persistently declined to recommend it and I now feel that no error has been committed.

I have postponed this recommendation of Allied intervention not only because I hoped the Soviet Government would request intervention but expected that the Department would approve my requests for purchasing supplies to prevent such falling into the hands of Germany and also in the hope that Russian people would awaken from their lethargy and request Allies to intervene. Many organizations in Russia have informed the Allied Missions and myself that Russians would welcome Allied intervention but whether such sentiment would result in material physical assistance I much doubt as the Bolshevik policy has been severe and has inflicted death penalty upon all charged with being counterrevolutionary.

Lenin is the ablest intellect in the Bolshevik party and tyrannizes the situation. In every speech he calls the Brest-Litovsk peace only a breathing spell and predicts success of world-wide social revolution, exulting over the exhaustion of what he calls capitalistic-imperialistic governments by their bloody struggle. In an address of April 28th he glorified the struggle for territorial aggrandizement and said that by such conflict the dictatorship of the proletariat was brought nearer. Lenin's last utterances are devoted to what he calls the danger to the proletariat from small bourgeois, as he claims the rich bourgeoisie are already exterminated. He has said that he was trying an experiment in government in Russia; is relentless and far-seeing and appreciates the danger from the middle classes and the desire on the part of the peasants to own their own homes and till their own soil.

Finally I doubt the policy of the Allies longer temporizing with a Government advocating the principles of Bolshevism and guilty of the outrages the Soviet Government has practised.

I await instructions or information.

On the 15th of May I saw Colonel Raymond Robins who was on his way to the United States. We had a private conversation of about twenty minutes. After our conversation Robins told Rennick, the Associated Press representative at Vologda,[5] and a man named Groves who was one of the employees of the Embassy, in charge of the telegraph department,[6] that if he could get one hour with President Wilson he would persuade the President to recognize the Bolshevik government. He made the remark, "I have the goods on my person." I heard afterwards that Colonel Robins was the courier for the Soviet Government of proposals to our government to grant us the same concessions, privileges, and advantages that it had been forced to grant Germany in the Brest-Litovsk treaty.

I received no reply to my May 2nd cable, recommending Allied intervention, for a month thereafter. I concluded to go to Petrograd. I wished to demonstrate to the Germans and Austrians that the American Government still had a representative in Russia who was not afraid; and besides I wished to see what progress was being made in removing munitions and supplies out of the possible reach of the Germans. These were the ostensible objects of my journeying to Petrograd. The real object was to see what organized opposition, if any, existed to the Bolshevik Government. I found Petrograd a very different city from the Petrograd I had left a little over three months previous. The streets presented a deserted appearance, a great many of the shops were closed. The Central Soviet Government had removed from Petrograd to Moscow, and the office buildings were deserted or only partially occupied. After remaining four days in Petrograd, I returned to Vologda. The two women and the dvornick that I left in charge of the American Embassy in Petrograd[7] were very much pleased at my return there. My first act was to have the Stars and Stripes raised over the Embassy and the Norwegian flag taken down. This was my last visit to Petrograd. I understand that at this writing, April, 1921, it is a deplorable sight, and a travesty upon its former greatness as the capital of all the Russias and the gayest city in Europe.

To my son, Tom,[8] I wrote from Vologda, June 4th, 1918:

> I am now planning to prevent if possible the disarming of 40,000 or more Czecho-Slovak soldiers, whom the Soviet Government has ordered to give up their arms under penalty of death, and has prohibited their transportation by every railroad line and threatened to penalize every railroad official who violates such instructions. The Czecho-Slovaks were Austrian prisoners of war, confined in Russian military prison camps; they were conscripted men,

---

[5] Henry L. Rennick, the *Associated Press* correspondent at Petrograd, Vologda, and Arkhangel'sk.

[6] Philip Groves, of Indiana, cipher officer of the US embassy; arrived in Russia in October 1917.

[7] A Finnish girl, Karin Sante, was in charge of the Petrograd embassy after Francis's departure.

[8] Thomas Francis, the ambassador's fifth son (1884–1964).

and have long felt themselves to be oppressed by Austria,—consequently were serving against their wishes in the Austrian Army. They will be treated as deserters now if they return to Austria. They are well disciplined soldiers, good fighters, and hate bitterly the Austrian rule and more bitterly, if possible, Prussian militarism. I have no instructions or authority from Washington to encourage these men to disobey the orders of the Soviet Government, except an expression of sympathy with the Czecho-Slovaks sent out by the Department of State. I have taken chances before, however.

I was visited last week by Vosnesinski,[9] an attaché of the Soviet Foreign Office, who has charge of the Division of the Far East. He is a shrewd, talkative little Russian. He came to me on a "fishing expedition" to ascertain whether Allied intervention is likely to occur soon if at all, and whether if it should occur it would interfere with the present Soviet Government. I told him as you will see from the enclosed cable that I did not know, but when he told me that he would return this week I informed him that I would not be as candid with him again and on his return would not tell him whether I knew or not. When he asked my individual opinion, I told him that sometimes I thought Allied intervention would take place, and other times thought otherwise, sometimes changing opinion several times a day during these long Russian days.

From Vologda under date of June 20th, 1918, I wrote to my son Talton:[10]

Affairs are approaching a crisis here. The last report is that the Bolsheviks have made an agreement with the Germans which contemplates the latter taking possession of Moscow with two army corps immediately and joining in an effort to suppress the Czecho-Slovaks. These Czechs are in control of various cities throughout Siberia and are encouraging the organization of a new Siberian Government. Tchecherin, the Commissar for Foreign Affairs, has addressed a note to the American, French and British representatives here demanding that their war vessels leave Russian ports. I have forwarded the American note to the Department at Washington, but have recommended that the demand be not complied with, and I think it will not be. It has been a question for some weeks past whether the Bolsheviks would come to terms with the German Government, or whether the Intelligencia, or educated and thinking people, would form a German alliance. I have been in fear that the latter would be effected. Consequently, am not displeased with the reported agreement between the Bolsheviks and the Germans. I have cabled the

---

[9] Voznesensky (see n. 13, p. 206).

[10] Talton Turner Francis, the ambassador's fourth son (1882–1955).

Department that the sensible, patriotic Russians who are inclined to favor the Allies are getting weary in waiting for Allied intervention and are likely to make terms with Germany,—in fact, as cabled, they would make terms with the devil himself in order to get rid of the Bolsheviks.

I have recommended Allied intervention and the Government at Washington has it under consideration. We have no forces, however, to send to Russia as we are sending all of our available men to France. The only country that can send a formidable army into Russia at this time is Japan, against which there is a strong prejudice among the Russians, who fear that Japan will have a covetous eye toward Siberia. If the Germans move into Moscow, they will probably come to Vologda, which is only about 300 miles from Moscow. If the Germans should approach Vologda, of course I shall have to leave. It is possible I may have to go to Archangel, but I prefer to go East, or to Siberia, as I am determined not to leave Russia until compelled to do so.

Chapter XX
BOLSHEVISM AND THE PEACE CONFERENCE

I sent a dispatch to the Department of State after the Armistice, in which I recommended that I be sent back to Petrograd as soon as my operation was performed and I was strong enough. My plan, as I recommended, was to occupy the Embassy at Petrograd. I said I would require not more than 50,000 American soldiers. I was satisfied that as soon as the English, the French and the Italians learned I was returning to Petrograd they would send their Ambassadors to join me. Our soldiers would be strengthened by a detail of at least 50,000 French, 50,000 English, and 20,000 Italian soldiers.

The plan as I outlined it was that I, as Dean of the Diplomatic Corps, would announce in Petrograd to the Russian people that we had not come for the purpose of interfering in their domestic affairs, but for the protection of our Embassies and to enable the Russian people to hold a free election with a fair count for members of a constituent assembly, that assembly to choose a form of government preferred by the majority of the Russian people.

During the visit of President Wilson to London I endeavored to secure an audience with him, and to take up this recommendation, but was unable to do so. I sent a note to the President by my private secretary, Earl M. Johnston, and had it delivered at Buckingham Palace. The President's reply to this note was that his mind had been running in the same lines as mine, and while he could not fix any date or time to give me an audience, he would undoubtedly see me before his return. I supposed that meant before his return to Paris from England.

I attended a dinner that King George V. gave to the President at Buckingham Palace, one or two days after Christmas, 1918. At the dinner the President remarked to me that he had hoped to have some opportunity there to talk with me about Russia. But we were not thrown together. While he was talking to the King and the Premier, Lloyd George,[1] and the former Premier, Asquith, I was talking to the ladies. As the President took his departure from the dinner, he offered his arm to the Queen.[2] King George, who was escorting Mrs. Wilson out of the reception room, when he met me, said:

---

[1] David Lloyd George (1863–1945), British prime minister, 1916–22.

[2] Queen Mary (1867–1953), the wife of King George V. Born as Princess of Teck (Württemberg); married Prince George, Duke of York, in 1893; queen consort from 1910.

"Mr. Ambassador, what do you think we ought to do about Russia!"

I replied I thought the Allies should overturn the Bolshevik Government.

The King rejoined by telling me he thought so, too, but President Wilson differed from us.

The next day being Saturday a luncheon was given at the Mansion House, which is the residence of the Lord Mayor. President Wilson spoke. I attended the luncheon and heard the President speak. That afternoon, following the luncheon, Mr. Wilson went to Carlisle, England, where his grandfather, Rev. Woodrow, had a Presbyterian congregation. The next day, Monday, he visited Manchester, returning to London late that evening. As he had not fixed a time for giving me an audience, I instructed my private secretary to get Admiral Grayson[3] on the phone at Buckingham Palace and to say to him that although I had been confined to my bed, I would journey to Dover with the President, if agreeable, as the itinerary provided for a special train to convey him there. As Dover was about two hours' ride from London, I thought I could in one hour discuss with him my recommendations concerning Russia,—my plan to return to Petrograd with a military support as outlined in the recommendation made to the Department of State.

Admiral Grayson replied over the phone to my private secretary that he would confer with the President and call me later, asking where I could be found. Admiral Grayson did call up about half an hour thereafter, and said that as the Hyde Park Hotel was not far from Buckingham Palace, he would come over to see me if I would receive him. He came about half past eleven o'clock that night, bringing with him Captain Jones, of Houston, Texas. Admiral Grayson told me that the President had made other arrangements about his trip to Dover, and asked what my plans were. I told him they would depend on whether Dr. Hugh H. Young[4] would consent to perform the operation for me that my ailment required. I explained that a celebrated British surgeon had refused to perform it; that Dr. Young had been in London since the 22nd of December, having been ordered to report to me as soon as possible by Secretary Lansing.

The operation was performed in a London hospital by Dr. Young on the 4th day of January, 1919. I left the hospital four weeks to a day after the operation, and arrived in Paris at 11 p.m., February first. On arriving there I got in touch with Admiral Grayson and told him that I desired an audience with the President. The Admiral promised me to secure an audience with the President if possible. In the meantime I stated my recommendation and plan to return to Petrograd in conversations with

---

[3] Cary Travers Grayson (1878–1938), naval surgeon close to President Wilson. He was promoted to rear admiral on August 29, 1916, and then appointed White House physician. He accompanied Wilson during his travel to the Paris Peace Conference in 1919.

[4] Hugh Hampton Young (1870–1945), American surgeon, medical researcher, and inventor. Major of the US Army during the World War; served in France.

Secretary Lansing, General Bliss,[5] Colonel House,[6] General Pershing, and Henry White.[7] With each of them separately I went over the recommendation, and each one of those men said to me, "You tell that to the President." Not one of them, however, told me, if he knew it, about the President's contemplated return to America. I asked my chief, Secretary Lansing, if he had any orders for me. He requested me to remain in Paris, because, he said, the Peace Conference would probably wish me to come before it.

Not hearing from Grayson during the next week and seeing him at a dinner at the Ritz, I accosted him and remarked to him that I was only awaiting the President's pleasure in Paris, but if I did not hear from the President during the following week, I would proceed to America. Thereupon the Admiral said: "We are going to America, leaving Paris on the 14th, and clearing from Brest on the 15th of February. Come and go on the steamer *George Washington* with us."

I replied to the invitation that I had orders from the Secretary to remain in Paris until further instructed, but that I would call on the Secretary and tell him that I had been unable to secure an audience with the President, and inform him of the invitation that the Admiral had extended to me to go to America on the steamer. I saw Secretary Lansing the next day, and he advised me by all means to accept the invitation to accompany the President to America, because he thought that was the only way I could secure an audience, as the President had engagements that would consume his entire time up to his departure. Admiral Grayson had asked how many there were in my party, and I had told him my son Perry and his wife, my private secretary, and a colored valet.

I left Paris on the special train with the President the evening of February 14th. We went on the steamer the next day and cleared immediately. In a note to the President, I said to him I awaited his pleasure for an audience. The President did not reply in writing, but two or three days later came to the cabin I was occupying. I outlined my recommendation about Russia to him. He replied that sending American soldiers to Russia after the armistice had been signed would be very unpopular in America. I ventured to differ with him; I expressed the opinion that many of the 2,000,000 soldiers he had in Europe were disappointed that the armistice was signed before they could engage in a battle. I said: "You could get 50,000 volunteers out of the 2,000,000

---

[5] Major General Tasker Howard Bliss (1853–1930), chief of staff of the US Army, September 22–December 31, 1917; general, October 6–December 30, 1917; the US military representative at the Supreme War Council of the Allies from November 17, 1917; brevet general, May 20, 1918; the US plenipotentiary at the Paris Peace Conference of 1919.

[6] Edward M. House (1858–1938), influential Texas politician. Having no official position, he was Woodrow Wilson's chief adviser on European politics and diplomacy and representative of the president on special missions to Europe during the World War.

[7] Henry White (1850–1927), American diplomat, ambassador to Rome and Paris before the World War; one of five US peace commissioners who signed the Treaty of Versailles in 1919.

of American soldiers who would be glad to go to Russia to protect a representative of their government in that country." The President replied that he had mentioned my recommendation to Lloyd George and that Lloyd George's expression was, if he should order any British soldiers to go to Russia they not only would object but refuse to go. The President furthermore stated that he had mentioned the same subject to Clemenceau,[8] and he had met with the reply that if Clemenceau should order French troops to go to Russia they would mutiny, but the President said he would give further consideration to my recommendation. I never broached the subject again to the President, and did not see him after landing in Boston until his term expired, except for a moment when he arrived in New York from Paris July 8, 1919.

I think that if the recommendation had been carried out it would have saved Europe from Bolshevism, which came near overturning the German Government, and did succeed in deposing the Austrian and Hungarian Governments, and menaced France, and threatened England and was the cause of unrest in America and throughout the world.

From the *George Washington* I sent by radio to Secretary Lansing, General Bliss, Colonel House and Henry White this report of my conversation with the President:

> I had a thorough talk with the President concerning Russia. I presented the plan that the Allied Missions return to Petrograd to occupy their domiciles accompanied by 100,000 Allied troops and abundant food supplies. I also suggested that the proposed Prinkipo investigation be transferred to Petrograd and that all professed Russian governments be summoned there and their statements be confined to replying to questions asked. I further proposed that the Allied Missions issue an address to the Russian people disclaiming any intention of interfering in the internal affairs of Russia and stating that the Russians were still considered Allies and that the object in reoccupying domiciles was to assist Russia in her misfortunes and difficulties and to afford them unawed the opportunity for a free election and a fair count for the election of a constitutional assembly to select a form of government by the majority. In order to accomplish this, order would necessarily be restored. The President said he would give the plan consideration; he admitted that the withdrawing of Allied forces from Russia would mean the deplorable slaughter of the Russian friends of the Allies, but repeated the statements of Lloyd George and Clemenceau concerning the difficulty of ordering British and French troops to Russia.
>
> I expressed the opinion that an army of 200,000 composed of American, British, French and probably Italian soldiers would volunteer when the

---

[8] Georges Clemenceau (1841–1929), French prime minister and minister of war, November 16, 1917–January 20, 1920.

appeal was made to them to go to Russia to protect the representatives of their governments, but stated that I thought 100,000 would be ample.

Radios indicate that Secretary of War Baker[9] has said the Allied troops will be withdrawn from Northern Russia early in the spring; my judgment is that such a policy would be a mistake and would delay peace negotiations because no peace treaty would be effective with Russia left out. If treaty is signed with Bolsheviks dominating Russia or disorder prevailing there, Germany will so utilize Russia's immeasurable resources and so organize Russian manpower as to convert defeat into victory in ten years or shorter time. Furthermore, Bolshevism prevailing in Russia would extend its baneful influence to other countries and become a more potential menace than it is now not only to organized governments but to society itself. Bolshevik doctrines destroy family relations and if they predominate they will mean return to barbarism.

I shall not return with the President but shall keep in touch with the State Department and can be in Paris on two weeks' notice.

While I was in the hospital at London, I received through the American Embassy this cable addressed to me and signed "Polk, Acting":

Kindly telegraph the American Ministry which has already received the text of the following telegram full comments on the points which are raised therein. Embassy and Consulate cables relating to these questions have been received by the Department but it now wishes to have such a collective statement as you could furnish. It is urgent to have an answer as soon as possible.

The telegram he enclosed was from Tchecherin, People's Commissar of Foreign Affairs at Moscow. The comments on the points in the telegram were desired for the use of the American Peace Commission then in session in Paris. Tchecherin began by referring to the reasons for sending American troops to Russia as they had been presented in the United States Senate by Senator Hitchcock, Chairman of the Foreign Relations Committee.[10] Tchecherin took up these reasons, giving the Bolshevik answer to them, and then made his argument for the recognition of the Soviet Government by the United States. This long dispatch by Tchecherin was manifestly intended for effect in connection with the peace negotiations going on at Paris.

Tchecherin's cable stated:

---

[9] Newton Diehl Baker, Jr. (1871–1937), secretary of war, 1916–21.

[10] Gilbert M. Hitchcock (1859–1934), Democratic politician, US senator from Nebraska, 1911–23. As chairman of the Senate Foreign Relations Committee, he was the leading advocate of the Treaty of Versailles.

First reason given is desire prevent establishment of German submarine base Archangel. Whether previously justified or not, at any rate this reason exists no longer.

As to second reason, namely, safeguarding Allied stores, I beg to remind that already in Spring of last year we entered into negotiations with view guaranteeing interests of Entente in this respect, and we are ready now to give every reasonable satisfaction on this question. As to danger of the stores falling into hands of Germans, whether previously justified or not, danger exists no longer.

Third reason given is maintaining gateway for arrival and departure of diplomats and others. I beg submit that best way attain that end is to enter into an agreement with my Government. Mr. Francis, American Ambassador, at time of leaving our country was able to depart and arrive unhindered, our sole reason for asking him not remain Vologda was the great danger which threatened his personal safety, and we offered him most appropriate residence in or near Moscow.

Fourth reason given is guaranteeing safety of Czecho-Slovaks, but there is nothing to prevent this being attained by agreement with my Government. We have officially proposed Czecho-Slovaks free passage home through Russia on conditions guaranteeing their safety and we have come to complete understanding with Professor Maxa, President Czecho-Slovak National Council in Russia,[11] who has now gone to Bohemia to communicate our proposal to Czecho-Slovak Government.

Last reason given by Senator Hitchcock is prevention of formation of army composed of German-Austrian prisoners. At present only obstacle barring way home to all prisoners of war is presence of Entente troops or White Guard under their protection. We are therefore at loss to understand what justification there can be for further maintenance of American troops in Russia. As can be seen from above-mentioned radiogram, some prominent leaders of principal political parties of America equally fail understand the reason. They expressed desire that American troops be withdrawn from Russia as soon as possible. We share their desire for resuming normal relations between two countries and are ready to remove everything that can be hindrance to such relations. It is not first time we make such offer. In October we sent communication to that effect through Norwegian Minister in Russia. A week later we made similar verbal offer through Mr. Christensen, Attaché Norwegian Legation,[12] when he was leaving Moscow. On November 3rd we invited all

---

[11] Prokop Maxa (1883–1961), representative of the Czechoslovak National Council in Russia, 1917–18.

[12] Thomas Christensen, attaché to Norwegian legation and chargé d'affaires in 1918.

neutral representatives in Moscow requesting them transmit written proposal to Entente Powers to enter negotiations for putting end to fighting Russia. On November 26th all-Russian Congress of Soviets[13] declared to the whole world and to Entente Powers that Russia wished to open peace negotiations. On December 23rd, our representative, Mr. Litvinoff,[14] informed Entente Ministers in Stockholm once more of desire of Russian Government of peaceful settlement all outstanding questions. He also appealed to President Wilson in London. Responsibility, therefore, lies not with us if settlement not yet been reached. We had opportunity of hearing some American officers and soldiers expressing perplexity at their presence in Russia, especially when we pointed out to them this to be attempt to put upon Russian people yoke of oppression, which it cast away. Result of this explanation was not unfavorable to our personal relations with these American citizens. We hope that peaceful aspirations of above-mentioned Senators shared by whole American people and we request American Government kindly make known place and date for opening peace negotiations with our representatives.

I made my comments on the above dispatch from Tchecherin, dictating what I had to say from my bed in the hospital. In accordance with Acting Secretary Polk's request, on January 22nd, I sent to the American Peace Commission at Paris this statement:

Neither we nor any of the Allied governments nor any Neutral have recognized (with possible exception of Persia) the Tchecherin message from Soviet Government, which message is absolutely false in its claim that it represented Russian people. In spite of the importunities of Robins and some other Americans I refused to recommend recognition. I always maintained, as shown by the records, that world-wide social revolution was the object of the Soviet Government and also as subsequent developments proved, their efforts were entirely directed to that end. It was clearly established that Lenin accepted German money and used it to corrupt Russia, but to gain the same

---

[13] The Extraordinary Sixth All-Russian Congress of Soviets of Workers', Peasants', Cossacks', and Red Army Deputies was held in Moscow on November 6–9, 1918, in order to sum up the general result of the first year of the Soviet rule and to discuss the international and military situation created by the nearing defeat of Germany in the World War.

[14] Maxim M. Litvinov (1876–1951), Bolshevik who lived in England from 1910. He was secretary of the London Bolshevik group and the party representative in the International Socialist Bureau. After the October Revolution, he was appointed Soviet diplomatic representative in the United Kingdom but was not recognized officially. On September 6, 1918, he was arrested by British authorities and exchanged later for a British special representative in Soviet Russia, Bruce Lockhart. Soviet ambassador to the US, 1941–43.

end he would have accepted American, British or French money. Lenin is a fanatic. He openly stated that he was trying an experiment on Russia in government. Trotzky is an adventurer, absolutely without conviction and saturated with personal ambition. Until the Brest-Litovsk Peace I encouraged Soviet opposition to Central Empires, after which peace I made an address trying to arouse Russian spirit and saying that the United States still considered herself the ally of the Russian people and would not recognize such a peace. The German Government demanded that I be sent out of Russia. This they demanded of the Central Soviet Government because of the above address referred to and the one to the Russians of July 4th. In the meantime I had left Petrograd on February 27th on account of threatened German approach and stopped at Vologda, in which place I remained five months, being joined there subsequently by Belgian, French, Serbian and Italian missions. As shown by the records my requests that railroad engineers be sent from Vladivostok to me at Vologda and that American officers be sent to aid Trotzky in organizing army had ulterior objects.

Answering Tchecherin message, while first reason is dissipated it unquestionably existed when Allied troops were sent into North Russia.

Second reason: While Soviet Government was negotiating for retention of supplies at Archangel it was removing such supplies at the rate of a hundred cars daily and the British and French assured me was breaking faith by doing so in addition to having repudiated obligations given for purchase of such supplies. I refrained from participation in such negotiations as America had little if any supplies there. Undoubtedly the Soviet Government would now negotiate for retention of such supplies at Archangel or make other promises for recognition.

Third reason: A few days after Mirbach's assassination the Soviet Government wired Allied Diplomats at Vologda, inviting or ordering them to Moscow and saying Radek was sent to Vologda to "execute" removal. The Allied chiefs unanimously declined the invitation or order, saying if order was meant they considered it offensive. Furthermore, German press was charging Mirbach's death to Allied instigation and demanding of Soviet Government that German and Austrian troops be permitted to come to Moscow for protection of their Embassies and Consulates. Ten days later, after midnight July 23rd, I received as Dean of the Diplomatic Corps telegram from Tchecherin urging that Allied Diplomats quit Vologda and saying another day might be too late. To this we replied we had concluded to accept the advice and would leave Vologda, requesting a locomotive to convey the special train on track at Vologda to Archangel. When Tchecherin heard we contemplated going to Archangel he wired going there meant leaving Russia. I replied, repeating the request, stating we would not leave Russia unless compelled by force and then absence would be temporary. A locomotive was furnished after twenty-four hours' delay and the Diplomatic Corps arrived in Archangel July 26th. When told by the Local Soviet and the representative of the Central Soviet that a boat was waiting to convey us where we elected we replied refusing to embark before communicating with our governments, with which communication had been severed for three weeks or more. After some colloquy our decision was wired the Soviet Government at Moscow, who replied that communication was impossible. We decided to go Kandalaksha which was occupied by Allied troops if furnished an additional steamer because one was inadequate. The additional steamer was provided July 28th, but many useless obstacles prevented clearing until four a.m. July 29th. Meanwhile we heard from credible sources that while the Central and Local Soviet professed willingness for our departure the Central Soviet was secretly urging Local Soviet to detain us as possible hostages to prevent landing of Allied troops, which I have heard since was their object in insisting on our removing to Moscow rather than regard for our safety. The Local Soviet, however, was afraid to detain us as a local Anti-Bolshevik revolution was impending. This was not the first evidence we had of Tchecherin's hypocrisy. The Anti-Bolshevik revolution occurred August 2nd, Allied troops landed four hours later and the Allied Missions returned to Archangel August 9th.

Fourth reason: Czecho-Slovak detention no longer obtains. It was a burning issue when Allied troops landed at Archangel. Permitting Czecho-Slovaks to depart now is no reason why Soviet Government should be recognized, and it should be remembered that when the Czecho-Slovaks started leaving Russia they were promised safe conduct with their arms and all Czecho trouble was caused by the treachery of Trotzky, who issued a secret order that they should not be permitted to leave without giving up their arms and, when given up, they should be detained notwithstanding.

Answering the last reason: Allied missions had positive evidence that German-Austrian war prisoners were being armed and German officers were instructing Bolshevik forces. While German-Austrian prisoners may now be free to return home, the fact remains that Bolsheviks are propagandizing among prisoners and offering every inducement to join the Red Army. Probably the Soviet Government did send communications, written and verbal, to us through Norwegian representatives that if American troops were withdrawn they would establish diplomatic relations, but that involved recognition of Bolshevik Government, which neither we nor any other well-ordered government could afford as Bolshevik orators not only charged our Government with being capitalistic but openly advocated opposition to all organized government everywhere. I was compelled to leave Archangel for a surgical operation November 6th, but the Soviet Government had already instituted a reign of terror to maintain themselves in power; they were pillaging and murdering inoffensive citizens without trial and when they could not find men they were arresting wives, mothers and sisters as hostages for the appearance of the men to serve in Red Army. I recommended weeks before leaving Archangel armed intervention for restoration of order knowing that the same would involve extinction of Bolshevism, which I considered not only irreparably injurious to Russia but a disgrace to civilization and a reflecting on Allies. I consider Bolshevism as practised in Russia means a return of the race to barbarism if it should prevail throughout society. That is why I studiously avoided encouraging the Soviet Government, refused going to Moscow and failed to establish even a modus vivendi with it. I have never doubted its willingness to make any arrangement that would secure our recognition as Tchecherin's message demonstrates. I heard through Radek after Robins' departure that the latter was the messenger from the Soviet Government to extend to our Government all of the privileges and concessions granted Germany in the Brest-Litovsk treaty, but Radek said that the offer did not include England and France. I never heard that Robins was permitted to present this proposition to our Government.

I think furthermore that if peace is consummated with the disorder prevailing in Russia or if the Bolsheviks are permitted to dominate there, that Russia will be exploited by Germany so completely as to effectually recoup her losses by war and become again a menace to civilization.

Three days after my statement had been sent to the American Peace Commission, Mr. Poole, whom I had left in charge of the Embassy at Archangel, forwarded his comments upon the Tchecherin communication. He wrote:

The entire absence of good faith on the part of the Bolsheviks would render futile Tchecherin's proposal of an agreement for the establishment of diplomatic relations even if it were not acceptable for other reasons. No reliance can be placed on the solemn assurances of the Bolshevik party. For example, the Consulates-General of Great Britain and France were forcibly violated, as reported from Moscow on August 5th and 6th, two hours after Tchecherin had most earnestly assured the Japanese and Swedish Consuls-General and myself that under all circumstances the immunities of foreign representatives would be respected. You will no doubt hear from Mr. Francis about his "unhindered private movements" during the latter part of July. Even now Tchecherin is constantly lying about the circumstances relating to the departure of the Ambassador. First proof of this is an intercepted wire communication between him and Radek while the latter was working on this matter at Vologda, a copy of which has been given the Department; second proof lies in a subsequent admission made by Tchecherin in his report to the All-Russian Soviet Congress held in September, translation of which was sent me from Moscow, to the effect that 400 German soldiers were admitted during July to Moscow as a German Embassy guard. On at least two occasions Karahan and Tchecherin solemnly assured me, in reply to a categorical inquiry on my part, that there were no German soldiers in Moscow and none would be admitted. When these men spoke the soldiers were in Moscow. The third proof is contained in a letter addressed to Karahan by Larin, the Bolshevik negotiator in Berlin,[15] translation of which was forwarded from Stockholm. There is an admission in the next to last paragraph of this letter that one of the true motives in forcing the Ambassadors to go to Moscow was to play them off against the German Government in connection with negotiation of the treaties by which the treaty of Brest-Litovsk was supplemented.

The problem is gravely complicated by the utter bad faith of the Bolsheviks. Even were it possible to disregard the virtual alliance which existed between the Imperial German Government and the Government at Moscow after conclusion of the treaties supplementary to that of Brest-Litovsk[16] (which differed from the latter in that they were actively sought after rather than accepted under constraint) or the nauseous and destructive butchery of the terrorism and other evils,—even if it were possible to overlook all these,— it would still be impracticable to renew de facto relations with the Moscow Government because of the impediment of complete and proven bad faith on their part. The President found this an insuperable obstacle to peace negotiations with the German Government. The futility of Bolshevik engagements is due, not only to the dishonesty of their leaders, but to the natural disorderliness of a loose knit Government, many of whose most active members are anarchists by temperament. At the caprice of Trotzky and the Commissariat of War or the Extraordinary Commission against counter-revolution or of any other strong personality of the moment, the most democratic decision or engagement of the Commissariat of Foreign Affairs may be altered.

The Czecho-Slovak matter has given Department evidence of Bolshevik bad faith. Unfortunately my files on this were burned.

---

[15] Yu Larin (Mikhail Z. Lure, 1882–1932), leader of the Mensheviks-Internationalists during the World War; joined the Bolsheviks in August 1917. After the October Revolution, he held responsible posts in the Supreme Council of National Economy.

[16] Russian-German supplementary treaty to the peace treaty, August 27, 1918, which stipulated that "Russia will at once employ all the means at her disposal to expel the Entente forces from North-Russian territory." That same day, the supplementary Russian-German financial agreement was concluded, the main article of which read as follows: "Russia shall pay Germany six billion marks as compensation for losses sustained by Germans."

It is of interest to note following representative statements regarding Tchecherin's proposal. These are taken at random from "The Fall is Near of Lloyd George and Wilson," a piece of Bolshevik propaganda prepared for distribution among our troops here:

"Pitiless conditions which are more cruel than those of Brest-Litovsk and which are more threatening to the world's peace have been imposed by the Allies on the enemy which they have vanquished."

"The League of Nations which Wilson proposes is a fake."

DeWitt C. Poole, Jr., was sent to Russia by the Department of State. I recommended him for Acting Consul-General after the death of Madden Summers at Moscow in May, 1918. The Department followed my recommendation and gave him that appointment. He was a fearless, loyal and able representative of his government. I had known his mother and grandfather, who formerly lived in St. Louis. I was not acquainted with his father, who was an army officer. Old residents of St. Louis will remember well the firm of Pettus & Leathe. Poole was a grandson of that Mr. Pettus.

Poole remained in Moscow until he was forced to leave by the Bolsheviks. He succeeded me as Chief Representative of the American Government at Archangel, after my health necessitated my leaving Russia. He was Chief of the Russian Bureau in the Department of State at Washington[17] for a number of months, and was given a long leave of absence. He is connected with the Department of State at this writing, assisting Mr. Carr, the head of the Consular Bureau.[18] His special duty is teaching new consuls as well as those not new to the service their duties and responsibilities.

On the 22nd of January, President Wilson presented to the Peace Conference what is known as the "Prinkipo Proposal."[19] This was an invitation to "every organized group that is now exercising or attempting to exercise political authority or military control anywhere in Siberia or within the jurisdiction of European Russia" to send representatives to a conference on the Princes Islands. The invitation included the Bolshevik Government.

The official report of a conference held by members of the Peace Conference the preceding day, January 21st, 1919, represented President Wilson as saying: "That if on the other hand the Allies could swallow their pride and the natural repulsion

---

[17] See n. 7, p. 5, and n. 12, p. 231.

[18] Wilbur John Carr (1870–1942), graduate of Georgetown University (LLB) and Columbian (George Washington) University (LLM). Joined the Department of State in 1892; served in the Consular Bureau from 1902; charged with the direction of the Consular Service on August 15, 1907; director of the Consular Service, November 30, 1909–July 1, 1924.

[19] A failed attempt made in early 1919 in connection with the Paris Peace Conference to arrange a meeting of representatives of the Allies and rival Russian factions on Princes' Islands (Turkey).

which they felt for the Bolsheviks and see the representatives of all organized groups in one place, he thought it would bring about a marked reaction against Bolshevism."

This action of the President drew from Acting Chief Poole the following protest, which included the offer of his resignation, and which was received by the American Peace Conference at Paris on the morning of February 5th:

> It is my duty to explain frankly to the Department the moral perplexity into which I have been thrown by the statement of Russian policy adopted by the Peace Conference January 28th, on the motion of the President. The announcement very happily recognizes the revolution and confirms again that entire absence of sympathy for any form of counter-revolution which has always been a keynote of American policy in Russia; but it contains not one word of condemnation for the other enemy of the revolution—the Bolshevik Government. However, this Government is accepted apparently on the same footing for the purpose of the invitation to Princes Island. Those other groups which, however weak they may be, are inspired with reasonable decency and patriotism and have been loyal in the fight against growing Imperialism. Having reread within the past few days practically every pronouncement of the President on foreign policy and having remarked especially his statement at Mobile, October 27th, 1913,[20] that we dare not turn from the principle that morality and not expediency is the thing that must guide us and that we will never condone iniquity because it is most convenient to do so, I feel that some further utterance of the Conference must follow which will reveal the United States and its associates as the outspoken champions of right aligning our Russian policy in the future with that of the past as exemplified in the note of September 20th to the Neutral Powers. The Department knows that I am not a stubborn or obstinate advocate of any specific course of action against the Bolshevik Government. I had thought only that unceasing condemnation of its evil methods had been accepted beyond all changing as a part of our policy. I have given all there is in me to reveal, and possibly thereby slightly to counteract, the utter wickedness of much the Bolsheviks have done and are still doing. I had thought that I might be contributing in some slight way to better the world's affairs. Knowing as I do, possibly better than any other American, the complete unmorality of the Bolshevik leaders—though the aspirations of a few be sincere—and the demoralization which their cynicism and cruelties work upon those whom they lead, I cannot in honesty or self-respect do other than protest against any course of action which does not take unmistakable account of these facts. If I have misconstrued the Paris

---

[20] Woodrow Wilson's address before the Southern Commercial Congress in Mobile, AL, in which his program of Latin American policy of the United States was outlined.

announcement, or any subsequent action is to give it a different color, I know that the Department will set me right with the same understanding and indulgence which it has invariably shown me. Affairs at Archangel are critical. I should be loath to evade responsibility and my departure would add uncertainty and conjecture to a situation already overwrought. In tendering my resignation, therefore, I desire not only to express the sorrow which the necessity for this action causes me and my deep appreciation of the kindness which I have always met at the hands of my superiors, but also my readiness to abide by the Department's determination of the moment when it will be opportune to let me go. My only purpose is to avow readily to the Department my state of mind, in order that it may determine the possible future value of my services, and secondly to assure my early disassociation from any Russian policy which does not include, regardless of its other components, unremitting public denunciation of, or in any other way seems to condone, the methods by which the Bolsheviks have come into power, which they have continued to employ and are still to-day employing in order to maintain themselves.

I cabled to Poole on February 8th, as follows:

I am inclined to think you misconstrue therein the President's policy as he offered the resolution as a compromise for the proposition of Lloyd George which was to invite representatives of all Russian Governments to appear before the Peace Conference in Paris. I consider the Prinkipo suggestion merely an investigation or inquiry court to enable the Conference to officially acquire knowledge of Russian conditions as the Commission would have no power to act but would refer back findings to the Conference accompanied or unaccompanied by recommendations. The Commission can make rules of procedure designating hours for each delegation and thereby preventing delegates from even seeing each other. I have stated in interview here that patriotic Russians put themselves no more on a level with the outlaw Bolsheviks than you would put yourself on the level with a burglar when subpoenaed as witness to identify stolen property.

Your cable is very able, clear and creditable, but I regret its presentation at this juncture. Confidentially I am reliably informed that the British, French, and Italian members of the Conference told the President that if their armies were ordered to Russia they would not obey.

I am here under Department instructions, but no specific duty has been assigned as yet. I have recommended that the Allied Missions be sent to Petrograd, which from their viewpoint is still the Russian capital, accompanied by sufficient troops to protect and sufficient food to subsist, with the announcement that they are sent to reoccupy domiciles there, to befriend the Russian people, whom we still consider Allies, and to enable Russia after order is restored to make untrammeled choice of the form of Government preferred by the majority. This would mean extinction of Bolshevism, would save our faces and would probably induce troops to obey orders. What think you? Would 100,000 troops be sufficient?

I think, and stated at the time, that the Russian representatives of the anti-Bolshevik factions who were in Paris and the Soviet Government itself made a mistake in not accepting this Prinkipo invitation. In the light of subsequent events, I have not changed my mind in that respect up to the present time. As I told the Russians in Paris at a luncheon given to me the Monday before my departure for America, they did not have to cross their legs under a table with murderers and robbers, as the Commission appointed by the Peace Conference would summon as witnesses the representatives of every government in Russia, including Lenin and Trotzky, and the commission would make rules for its procedure and report to the Peace Conference.

I furthermore stated in a speech at the luncheon given to me in Paris on the 10th of February, 1919, as I did in the above-quoted cable to Acting Consul Poole that they would no more degrade themselves by appearing before this commission and would no more associate with murderers and robbers than I would if summoned by a court to identify stolen property when the burglar was being tried.

All of the Russian factions declined to appear before the commission, so the Prinkipo Conference was abandoned. Notwithstanding, however, the President appointed William Allen White,[21] Italy appointed Terretti,[22] who had been with me in Russia, and some other Italian of prominence to represent Italy on the commission. I cannot recall whom England appointed to represent the British Government, nor whom France appointed to represent the French Government, if, indeed, they appointed representatives at all.

The Russians in Paris notified the Peace Conference that they would not associate with murderers and robbers representing the Soviet Government of Russia, evidently thinking they would have a general conference instead of a commission making its own rules for procedure and summoning witnesses to appear before it. The Soviet Government also declined to participate in the Prinkipo Conference, but not until after refusal of the Anti-Bolshevik factions in Paris had resulted.

Tchecherin was one of the two Bolsheviks who had been interned in England. A letter from Trotzky to the British Ambassador conveyed the thinly veiled threat that unless these men were released, public opinion in Soviet Russia would turn against

---

[21] William Allen White (1868–1944), famous journalist, newspaper editor, author, and nationally recognized spokesman for the Progressive cause. Editor of the *Emporia Gazette* (Emporia, KS); correspondent at the Paris Peace Conference of 1919.

[22] Marquis della Torretta (see n. 7, p. 169).

the many Englishmen living in Russia who openly expressed counter-revolutionary attitudes.

That this letter was not entirely a bluff may be seen in the fact that on August 31st Captain Cromie, a British officer, was killed by the Bolsheviks in an attack on the British Embassy.[23] On the sixth of September Balfour[24] addressed a note to Tchecherin strongly protesting against this attack and demanding immediate satisfaction and severe punishment of all those responsible: "If the Russian Soviet Government will not give complete satisfaction or if violence be used against British subjects," he said, "the British Government will consider every member of the Russian Government individually responsible, and will take measures to insure that all the governments of civilized nations shall consider them outside the law and that there shall be no asylum for them to go to."

While in Archangel, Lindley told me that every civilized government in the world had been notified they could not become a harbor for Lenin and Trotzky without incurring the serious displeasure of the British Government; that the British Government would pursue Lenin and Trotzky to the ends of the earth. Yet, notwithstanding this statement of the British High Commissioner and the announcement of Minister of Foreign Affairs Balfour, less than three years after that the British Government entered into a commercial treaty[25] with Lenin, Trotzky, Tchecherin and Krassin,[26] representing the Bolshevik Government of Russia. Selah!

Two weeks after this note was sent the American Government issued under date of September 21st, 1918, a note addressed "To all the Associated and Neutral Governmerits" to be communicated through American representatives. This note referred to the state of terrorism then existing in Russia in which thousands of persons were executed without trial and numberless barbaric crimes committed, and asking

---

[23] Francis Newton Allen Cromie (1882–1918), acting captain of the British Navy in command of the submarine flotilla in the Baltic Sea from 1915. He was appointed naval attaché to the British embassy at Petrograd in May 1917; killed by Soviet agents in the course of the attack on the embassy on August 31, 1918.

[24] Arthur James Balfour (1848–1930), British secretary for foreign affairs, December 10, 1916–October 23, 1919.

[25] Anglo-Soviet Trade Agreement signed in London on March 16, 1921.

[26] Leonid B. Krasin (1870–1926), activist of the Bolshevik Party from its foundation; headed its Fighting Technical Group, which delivered weapons to Russia from abroad and organized expropriations of money from banks to finance the party's activities, 1905–08. He emigrated to Europe, ceased his political activities for many years, and made a successful career as a civic engineer in Germany, becoming a wealthy man. He returned to Russia in 1912 as representative of the German engineering firm Siemens-Schuckert. He rejoined the Bolsheviks after the October Revolution, and was a member of the Soviet delegation at the Brest-Litovsk peace negotiations and of the delegation sent in the summer of 1918 to Berlin. From November 1918, he was people's commissar for trade and industry.

what action, if any, each of these governments expected to take to show the attitude with which civilization regarded such acts.

On the 24th of October, 1918, Tchecherin addressed a long open letter to President Wilson sneering at the President's professed sympathy for the Russian people and the League of Nations, charged the Allies with inspiring counter-revolution, and protested against the arrival of Allied troops. The note concluded a denunciation of capitalists and stated that the source of war could be destroyed by transferring the control of banks and industries into the hands of the masses.

Chapter XXI
BOLSHEVISM IN PRINCIPLE AND IN PRACTICE

How has it been possible for the Bolsheviks to maintain themselves in power when they represent a small part of the Russian population, certainly not one-fourth, probably not more than one-tenth? This question has been put to me many times. My reply is that the "bourgeoisie," who include the middle classes, and all the land-owning peasants, have been so unjustifiably and cruelly treated by the Bolsheviks that they have lost all courage. Many of the Bolshevik followers, or those who were followers when the Bolshevik Government first came in power, have deserted them. Bolshevism would not have gained such headway in Russia had not the army been demoralized by General Order No. 1, which permitted the soldiers to select their own officers, and this was followed by Kerensky, when he became Minister of War, issuing a decree abolishing the death penalty. It is true that Kerensky afterwards restored the death penalty; it was made a condition by Korniloff upon his accepting the position of Commander-in-Chief.

The Russian army, when Trotzky made the dramatic statement at Brest-Litovsk in February, 1918, that the peace treaty would not be signed but that Russia would fight no more, numbered about 12 million men, according to the records, but it had probably been reduced 25 to 33% or more by desertions, as the soldiers had been going home ever since the Bolshevik Government had come into power in the previous November, 1917. After Trotzky's statement that there would be no more fighting every freight and passenger train was filled with soldiers who paid no fare and did not ask where the train was going until after embarking on it; they were on the roofs, and on the trucks and on the platforms.

The Bolshevik army, which has been estimated variously from two hundred thousand to seven hundred thousand, is scattered through Central and Western and Northern Russia and is composed of Letts and Chinese, together with conscripted Russians. The Bolshevik leaders arrest women and hold them as hostages until their husbands, and sons and brothers reappear and accept service in the Bolshevik army. The discipline in this army is very strict. The Russians act from impulse and that accounts for the following that Bolshevism had in the beginning. The leaders, Lenin and Trotzky and Radek, Peters[1] and Zinovieff and others promised peace to the army wearied by three years of fighting—peace, food, and land.

Russia is inhabited largely by the Slav race; a race possessed of more than ordinary common sense, with good impulses, but with paradoxical characteristics. When I first arrived in Petrograd, I was impressed by the religious sentiment of the people. That sentiment, however, has grown smaller by degrees and beautifully less under Bolshevik rule. I could see a decided change even in the cab drivers. Under the Czar, who was the head of the Greek Church, a driver would not pass a church or cathedral without crossing himself, although he might pass the same cathedral thirty times during the day; under the Bolshevik rule it was a rare thing for a cabby to cross himself, although he might come into the very shadow of St. Isaac's or the Kazan Cathedral. The Provisional Government attempted to foster the church, but the Bolshevik Government recognizes no religious sentiment and no Supreme Being. With the abdication of the Czar, the church lost its titular head, but the ministry of the Provisional Government still recognized the existence of the church by appointing a Procurator of the Holy Synod. Russians are naturally sympathetic and tenderhearted, but they are fatalists; they are superstitious to a degree. I have never visited a country where human life was held as cheaply as it is in Russia. During the first Revolution and during the attempted Bolshevik Revolution of July 17th-18th, 1917, and during the Bolshevik Revolution of November, 1917, and during the whole period from that time to the present when a murdered person was found on the streets no questions were asked, no effort was made to apprehend the murderer, but the corpse was taken to the morgue (provided the deceased had no friends cognizant of the murder) and interred in the public burying ground. I remember one incident when a woman came out of a house chasing a man and yelling that he had stolen her pocketbook. The woman was soon joined by an angry mob who pursued the fleeing man and captured and cruelly murdered him. Meantime the woman had returned to her apartment and had found her purse which she accused the man of stealing, and attempted to restrain the mob saying she had found her pocketbook. Thereupon the crowd turned upon the woman and put her to death. Occurrences of that character were frequent from Nov., 1917, to Nov., 1918, when I left Archangel and I learn from well authenticated sources that they have continued with increasing frequency since, as the Bolshevik rule has been characterized by augmented cruelty and mercilessness.

---

[1] Yakov K. Peters (1886–1938), Latvian revolutionary who emigrated to London in 1910 and married the daughter of a British banker. He returned to Russia in May 1917 and was a member of the Military Revolutionary Committee; after the October Revolution, he was assistant chairman of the All-Russian Emergency Commission to Combat Counter-Revolution and Sabotage (CheKa), 1917–19.

In the midst of the strenuous effort to form a stable government out of the uncertain elements at Archangel, I received a letter quoting from Lovat Fraser,[2] a traveler and writer and considered one of the best authorities on the Russian people:

> The only possible course for the Allies until stability has been restored is to insist on the Russians obeying their orders. There must be no speechifying, no more quarreling with rival parties, no more meetings of the illiterate rank and file to consider whether they will or will not do this or that. I do not in the least believe that there will be a recrudescence of Bolshevism as a result of Allied action. The Russian people will obey strength, and the nearest strength, and nothing else. That Russian general who said the other day that many of his countrymen would fight for any man with a big stick knew what he was talking about.

Germany understood the Russian character better than any other country. Until the beginning of the war Germany was making rapid progress toward monopolizing the foreign trade of Russia, and if the war had been postponed or deferred for ten years, Germany would have had such a firm foothold in Russia that it would have been impossible to dislodge her; Germany was better acquainted with Russian resources than was the Russian government itself. Germany took advantage of Russia's misfortunes to end the Russo-Japanese War and of the threatened revolution to negotiate a very advantageous commercial treaty of ten years' duration. Under the treaty Germany had succeeded in capturing more than fifty per cent of the entire foreign commerce of Great Russia. The Russian merchants and manufacturers, and the Russian people who were not under the domination of Germany, became very restive under the commercial treaty of 1905, which had been in operation for nine years when the war began. Germany well knew that this treaty on its expiration would neither be renewed nor extended, and that was one of the potential reasons why Germany thought she could subjugate Russia and France, and consequently did not hesitate to bring on the war, little thinking that England would come to the rescue of Belgium, and not dreaming that America would be involved in the contest. The world war was waged with the loss of eight millions of lives and untold and incalculable treasure. After four years of struggle, hostilities nominally ceased. Almost two and a half years have elapsed since the armistice was signed, and the work of reconstruction in the victorious countries has made slow progress. Germany, familiar as she was with the deplorable result of an invaded domain, took care when she saw the tide of war turning against her that her industries should not be destroyed

---

[2] Lovat George Fraser (1871–1926), British journalist, war correspondent of the weekly *War Illustrated*.

as she had dismantled and stolen those of France and Belgium; took care that her fields should not be laid waste and her cities, villages and hamlets leveled to the ground, as were those of the countries she had invaded. It was the boast of the German Emperor that "the soil of the Fatherland was not desecrated by the tramp of hostile armies."

The Military Party in Germany had used Lenin and Trotzky to demoralize Russia's immense army, and had succeeded in withdrawing Russia from the contest. This was done in the face of the protests of the conservative element of the German population, but was aided by the Socialists in Germany. Little did the General Staff of the Imperial Government think when the fatal dose was handed to Russia that the poisoned chalice would be commended to her own lips within twelve months. Germany was defeated on the battlefield, and her armies have been subjugated and shorn of their power, but it is not so with industrial Germany. Germany is using the same means and pursuing the same policy in her economic war, which has not only begun but has made considerable headway with Russia. Germany's commercial agents are the only ones admitted into Soviet Russia. Germany is making her plans to wage an economic war by the same unscrupulous methods which she used in waging the world war. She has quit the manufacture of poisonous gases which had physical effect, but she has not abandoned her devious ways by which she hopes through neutral and deceitful agencies to capture the commerce of the world. She has been prohibited from constructing submarines with which to prey upon the commerce of the neutral countries and destroy innocent lives, but she has not forsaken her manufacturing power; on the contrary she is rapidly utilizing it in her efforts to extend German trade.

The German people have changed their form of government, but it is as difficult for a leopard to change his spots as it is for the Germans to change their character. The present government of Germany is following in the footsteps of the Imperial government in all matters pertaining to German domination in the commercial world.

I was astounded upon returning to this country to find a much larger number of advocates of Bolshevism than I thought possible. The basic principle of the Bolshevik government is what they call the "dictatorship of the proletariat,"—which means the severe oppression of a class or of certain classes. It is a worse form of tyranny than absolute monarchy—bad as that is. This basic principle put in practice is that no man or woman is allowed to vote who does not perform manual labor. The Bolshevik constitution prohibits from the exercise of suffrage all merchants, or dealers in securities, or professional men who are not in the employ of the government, and even domestics or servants who work for the proscribed classes. The Bolshevik theory strikes at the home as Americans understand it. The decrees of Bolshevism made marriage and divorce so easy that they were to be had for the asking. Simply a verbal announcement to an irresponsible citizen legalized both marriage and divorce under the Lenin and Trotzky regime.

After I returned to the United States, still being Ambassador to Russia but on the inactive list, I was asked repeatedly as to the reports of the Bolshevik theories on personal or domestic relations. I replied it was true that in some part or parts of Russia local authorities had issued decrees nationalizing women. I saw nothing of the application from my own observation. I only know of such decree or decrees from having seen them in official publications of the Bolshevik government.

The Central Organization, that dominated by Lenin and Trotzky, had never nationalized women by a decree when I left, but it had issued a decree which I saw in *Izvestia*, the official publication of Lenin and Trotzky, making divorce and marriage as easy as to require only a notice to some man by a married couple that they had agreed to separate, and likewise a notice that two unmarried people had decided to marry. There was no limit of time as to how long the marriage should hold.

There are some well-meaning people in the United States who advocate leaving Russia "to stew in her own juice." Passing over for a moment the selfishness of this policy, I would call attention to the effect of Bolshevism already seen on the uneducated of every European country. All of the unrest throughout Europe and in this country and in every country on the Western hemisphere can be traced back to this Bolshevik experiment in Russia. The Allies could have exterminated Bolshevism in Russia and saved their face if they had taken steps to this end before the armistice was signed. This Bolshevism or Soviet Government as operated in Russia has been a disgrace to civilization and a reflection upon the Allies. Bolshevism even dared to show its head in this country.

It has made strenuous effort to depose the conservative administration of the labor organizations of the United States. It has presumed to induce the members of those organizations to assume control of the Government by "direct action." Lenin and Trotzky and their followers have not hesitated from the time they came into control to call the Government of the United States, under which this country has been the haven of the oppressed at all times and for all races, a "capitalistic government."

A temporizing policy with Bolshevism in the United States is not only unwise but may result in the undermining of our institutions, which have withstood the test of time, and which every American citizen should be willing to sacrifice his life to maintain. I advocated the eradication of Bolshevism in Russia because it is a blot on the civilization of the Twentieth Century, and for the additional reason that it is to our interest to exterminate it in the land of its birth. I say "our interest" from two points of view. First: If Bolshevism is permitted to thrive in Russia it will promote unrest in all countries. Second: It is our duty to the Russian people, who have always been favorable to America, and whose greatest offense is that they favored the Allies as against Germany in the world war, to relieve their country of the injury and disgrace inflicted upon it by Soviet Rule.

When I first returned to America from Russia it appears that I was misunderstood in expressions of my opinion of Lenin. I said he was not only honest commercially but honest intellectually, and a fanatic who would sacrifice his sons and his wife and his own life for the promotion of a world-wide social revolution. This was said to contrast him with Trotzky, whom I considered an adventurer pure and simple, without convictions, fond of display and luxury, liking to be in the limelight, but possessed of executive ability of a high degree.

Trotzky foresaw the outcome of the war more clearly than Lenin, which accounts for his grandstand play at the first Brest-Litovsk Peace Conference, and his refusal to attend the second conference, and his resignation as Minister of Foreign Affairs. Trotzky after accepting appointment as Minister of War flirted with the Allied Military Missions when he asked their assistance in organizing an army, professedly for the promotion of world-wide social revolution and incidentally for opposing the German advance—Germany had an imperialistic government at that time—but Lenin would never consent to fighting Germany. This move was encouraged by me, as I felt confident that the army when organized, and after checking the Germans and interesting them so that they could not send assistance to Hindenburg and Ludendorff at the Western front, could be influenced against a world-wide social revolution.

Lenin was the great intellect that dominated the Bolshevik Revolution in Russia. Every time that Lenin and Trotzky disagreed, Lenin came out victor. Lenin led a simple life, while Trotzky lived a luxurious life. They both, however, were ruthless. They agreed in the policy of instituting a reign of terror to perpetuate Bolshevik supremacy, and now, after they have inflicted untold damage on Russia, which it will require two or more generations to repair, they are professing to abandon communism. In my judgment this is camouflage, a mere pretense, a move to strengthen their tottering reign and to afford an opportunity to propagandize their pernicious doctrines in other countries.

I have sometimes wondered what would have been the result if I had not been compelled to leave Russia when I did, or had remained in Russia after the Armistice was signed. Admiral McCully, whom I saw in Washington within the last three months, said when he put me on the cruiser *Olympia* at Archangel on the 6th of November he never expected to see me alive again. Major Williams, of the Red Cross Mission to Northern Russia,[3] whom I also met in Washington, expressed the same opinion.

As narrated in the foregoing, King George of England agreed with my policy of exterminating Bolshevism, and that had been the desire of the French Government from the beginning. When on the eve of my departure from Archangel I received a

---

[3] Charles Turner Williams (1874–1932), banker of Fidelity Trust Company in Baltimore, MD. Captain of the American Red Cross Mission to Romania, having special assignment to carry the hospital supplies from Arkhangel'sk to Jassy, August–December 1917. Major in charge of the American Red Cross Mission to north Russia, September 1918–January 1919.

cable from the Department of State saying "It is the plan of our Government for you to return to Archangel when your health and strength permit," it would have been my effort as the result of my deep-seated convictions that Bolshevik supremacy should be overthrown in Russia.

It is likely that President Wilson would not have objected to sending more American troops to Archangel; and if he had consented thereto, England and France certainly would have cooperated, and Italy and the other Allies possibly would have also. I certainly would have requested additional troops, because I knew well that the Bolshevik Soviet Government did not represent more than ten per cent at the outside of the Russian people, and only maintained itself in power by the assistance of Chinese and Lettish soldiers whom they were able to pay with the Russian and Roumanian gold that they had commandeered or stolen.

The Secretary of State at that time would, I think, have been favorable, and the sending of troops there would have enabled the Allied forces in Northern Russia to depose the government of Lenin and Trotzky, and thereby have spared Russia at least two years of suffering and Europe an equal period of difficulties which came near producing chaos on the Continent and threatened England itself.

I do not mean that this Bolshevik Soviet Government should have been overthrown by any other power than the Russian people themselves, but the presence of Allied troops in Russia would have encouraged the people to hold their differences in abeyance for the time being, and I certainly would have contributed all in my power to that end.

From the first I contended that Bolshevism did not have followers in Russia exceeding twenty per cent of the Russian people, and that following has been diminishing until it is now less than five per cent. I furthermore expressed the opinion in cables and dispatches from Archangel to the State Department and from London that order could not be restored in Europe as long as there was chaos in Russia. Lloyd George recognized this by advocating that Russia should be authorized to send delegates to the Peace Conference and President Wilson recognized this by suggesting the Prinkipo Conference.

My conclusions as to the character and purposes of Bolshevism, as set forth in the private letters and official reports sent by me during my residence in Petrograd, Vologda and Archangel have not undergone changes, save that they have become intensified, if possible, since my return to the United States. I received a telegram from a prominent newspaper recently asking my opinion about Lenin's reported change of heart on world-wide social revolution. I was asked, "Do you believe Lenin sincere or that he can hold fanatical followers?" My reply, which shows my present attitude, was:

I would not trust Lenin's promises and doubt his sincerity. He has stated on more than one occasion that he would not hesitate to violate a written contract if he could promote his main object of a world-wide social revolution by so doing. I have always charged that Lenin would sacrifice his wife and children and even his own life if he thought he could promote a world-wide social revolution by doing so. He has been ruthless in his administration of Russian affairs for almost three and one-half years and when England first offered to make a commercial treaty with the Bolshevik Soviet Government on condition that the latter would cease propagandizing in British territory, he manifested willingness to enter into an agreement to this effect. But when the British Government demanded that the agreement should include the Third Internationale[4] also, Lenin said he could not control the Third Internationale, and thereby was guilty of falsifying. I agree with English sentiment that calls the commercial treaty with the Soviet Government "the unclean thing." Lenin was first sent into Russia as a German agent to demoralize the Russian army and withdraw Russia from the world war. His administration has been marked by theft and murder. I do not believe in trusting thieves and murderers.

Three days later I received from a different city this inquiry:

Russia has asked the United States to enter into a trade agreement following Great Britain. Will you kindly wire your opinion whether such an agreement should be made together with your reasons why it should or why it should not?

To this I made the following reply:

If we wish to strengthen the Bolshevik Soviet Government of Russia the most effective way to do is to enter into trade relations with it. The invariable rule of that government is that all foreign commerce is directly and absolutely under its control. I think I have answered your inquiry completely by this statement unless we desire to promote a world-wide social revolution and to assist in maintaining an experiment in government which is "the greatest failure in all history" and an experiment which is not new but has met with signal failure every time it has been tried. I think it would be a grievous mistake for any government and a stultifying crime for our government to enter into trade relations with the Bolshevik government of Russia.

---

[4] Third (Communist) International (Comintern), an international communist organization founded on March 2, 1919, at a congress that convened in Moscow, where delegates from thirty-four parties were present, including the Socialist Propaganda League and Socialist Labor Party of America.

Chapter XXII
RUSSIA—THE CHIEF VICTIM OF THE WORLD WAR

Who will gainsay that Russia was and is the chief victim of the World War? Belgium and France are rapidly recovering, as are the Balkan States; Germany and Austria were never laid waste by a hostile army, nor was England. Turkey is no worse off than before the war, and all the other belligerents were too far removed from the scene of battle to have suffered any devastation whatever. Russia not only lost more of her sons in the war than did any other nation, notwithstanding she withdrew from the contest almost a year before it ended; but no progress has been made toward her recuperation. On the other hand Russia was in the throes of civil war for two years after the Armistice; her industries have been wrecked; her transportation lines are idle for want of motive power and equipment; her intelligencia are in exile; her proud capital is deserted and infested with epidemics and racked by famine. And what is the cause? Bolshevism!

She deserves a better fate. Twice she saved the conflict before America entered the war. Twice she has defended our Government, once when England was about to recognize the Southern Confederacy, and once when our country was in the panic of 1893, by tendering three hundred million dollars in gold—true the offer was not accepted, but the good will was manifested; nor should we forget that Russia sold us Alaska for the paltry sum of $7,000,000. In my judgment too much credit cannot be given the labor unions led by Samuel Gompers and his conservative colleagues in France for not siding with the Bolsheviks in Russia. I have no sympathy with any movement which has for its object the disruption of labor unions.

On my return to St. Louis after three and one-half years' absence a banquet was given me at which I made an address which was published in full in the dailies of the city, but I do not think that speech can be summarized more tersely than it was in "America at Work," of October 16th, 1919, under the caption of, "The Message of Ambassador Francis to America":

> First, that Russia's continuation in the World War under the Provisional Government, until March, 1918, shortened the conflict by at least a year, and perhaps saved European civilization.

Second, that the issued joined by Lenin is one which the whole world will have to meet, that true democracy and sound economic development must either conquer Bolshevism or be conquered by it,

And, third, that in the hour of Russia's bitter need that help which she so richly deserves at the hands of the world by reason of her self-forgetful sacrifice of precious lives and treasure in the cause of liberty and democracy can only be rendered through the instrumentality of the League of Nations.

For three years this citizen of the United States has occupied a unique position in our diplomatic service. He has worked unafraid in the very teeth of the flames which were threatening the whole fabric of civilization. He has said, as a great missionary of liberty, of life and faith nineteen centuries ago, "This one thing I do." It was an impressive moment when at the banquet tendered him by his friends and fellow townsmen, he said, "I hold myself ready to go back to Russia at the call of my Government; I may even return without that call."

Ambassador Francis returns to America not simply as the Ambassador of the United States; he has received a commission from a higher power. He stands before his countrymen to proclaim the inexorable working of laws written not in human statute books but in the eternal constitution of men and nations by Him who "hath made of one blood all men who dwell upon the earth." He has come back to tell us that it is impossible that we should leave 180,000,000 human beings helpless and hopeless in command of a ruthless, conscienceless and bloodthirsty oligarchy, directed by a man with the brain of a sage, and the heart of a monster, without ourselves being involved in the threatened ruin of the great people which compose one-seventh of all the land of the earth.

Never was Ambassador Francis on a more truly diplomatic mission than now. Against him in his message are ranged the traditional provinciality of the people of the United States, the sense of the remoteness of the Orient, the deadening effect upon our sensibilities and sympathies of the breadth of the Atlantic and half the continent of Europe on the one side and the whole width of the vast Pacific on the other, and the narrow contractile councils of a group of blind and selfish political leaders, distributed somewhat impartially among both parties in the United States.

When I was cabling to our Government from Archangel recommending armed intervention and when I was arguing with President Wilson and appealing to him on the steamer *George Washington* to let me go back to Petrograd, accompanied by American soldiers, I used the above reasons. President Wilson suggested permitting the Russians to settle their own differences, and when I told him that would entail great human slaughter he replied that no one abhorred bloodshed more than he did, but if I was right that he thought "it must needs come." This was on his first return to America, when he made a stay of only eight days in Washington. President Wilson may have been influenced by my emaciated physical condition and apparent weakness, or he may have thought the League of Nations would be formed and America would join the League and that would serve the same purpose. He returned to New York July 8th, 1919. I met him there, but only for a moment, and did not have opportunity to broach the Russian problem. He soon started on the tour of the country, and if he had not broken down I have always thought the result would have been different—America would have joined the modified League and Russia would have been saved.

In my opinion Woodrow Wilson will live in history as one of the greatest of Presidents, as a lover of his fellows, and as a patriotic American!

Chapter XXIII
RETROSPECT

The foregoing pages, with the exception of a few interlineations, were written over two years ago, but were not published because I was still nominal American Ambassador to Russia. I presented my resignation to President Wilson on March 3rd, 1921, in the following communication:

> My dear Mr. President: "I beg herewith to tender my resignation as American Ambassador to Russia. I have made effort to resign three or more times since my return from Russia, but have been asked by the Secretary of State not to do so—have drawn no salary since April 26th, 1919, since which time have been on the inactive list of ambassadors.

Shortly after Secretary of State Hughes[1] announced his Russian policy, I wrote congratulating him thereon, and called attention to my resignation with the request that it be accepted. Secretary Hughes replied that the letter of resignation could not be found in the State Department nor at the White House, and that if I would forward my resignation he would submit it to the President and have it promptly accepted. I did so in two communications, a copy of the one presented to President Wilson, and one dated May 18th, 1921, which was an exact copy thereof, addressed to President Harding, who chose to accept the latter, and a letter dated 31st of May, 1921, of which the following is a copy:

> My dear Mr. Francis:
> There has come to my attention yours of May 18th, tendering your resignation as Ambassador for the United States to Russia. I beg to advise you of the acceptance of your resignation, and at the same time thank you for the signal service which you rendered to your country in that capacity.
> Very truly yours,
> (Signed) Warren G. Harding.

---

[1] Charles Evans Hughes (1862–1948), secretary of state, 1921–25.

This much in explanation of the delay in publication of "Russia from the American Embassy." In correcting the proof of this book there is one thought that impresses me, and that is the horror of Bolshevism and how Russia is to be saved from its curse and all other countries from its menace.

I still believe that Germany employed Lenin to demoralize the Russian Army, that fact having been proven by General Hoffmann, and that the entente would have been justified in deposing the Bolshevik-Soviet Government of Russia before the armistice was signed, as recommended in my cable of 2nd of May, 1918, from Vologda, framed after I had given the Soviets every encouragement to resist the encroachments of Germany.

When I arrived in London from Archangel, during all the two weeks I spent in Paris, in my home-coming on Steamer *George Washington*, in my testimony before the Overman Committee of the Senate on Bolshevism,[2] in all my public addresses, interviews, magazine articles, I endeavored to impress my hearers and readers with the menace of Bolshevism. I argued that it was impossible to restore peace to Europe with chaos prevailing in Russia. These predictions have all been fulfilled. You cannot pick up a newspaper or periodical without seeing a dispatch or an article about the deplorable plight of Russia under Bolshevik rule, or the growing danger of the spread of Bolshevism into some other country. The I. W. W. chief, "Big Bill" Haywood,[3] has gone to Russia and forfeited his bond by doing so; I was told by a well-informed man that the I. W. W. organization had four million members in the U. S. and the cables inform us that Haywood received an ovation in Moscow. Furthermore, at the national meeting of the Socialist Party held in Detroit in July, 1918, a resolution was introduced to the effect that the convention should yield obedience to the Soviet Government of Russia, and that resolution had such enthusiastic support that it was laid over for consideration.

At the American Federation of Labor now in session in Denver, Gompers had the fight of his life for reelection to the Presidency. He was opposed by the radicals in the organization because he had courageously stood against Bolshevism—the opposition polled over 12,500 votes. The Bolsheviks are propagandizing continuously and zealously. I have changed my mind about Lenin; upon returning to America I expressed belief in his sincerity, while a fanatic and ruthless and unscrupulous. I have

---

[2] Special subcommittee of the US Senate Committee on the Judiciary, chaired by North Carolina Democrat Lee S. Overman (1854–1930). From September 1918 to June 1919, it investigated German and Bolshevik activities in the US. Francis testified before the Overman Committee on March 8, 1919.

[3] William Dudley Haywood ("Big Bill," 1869–1928), a founding member and leader of the Industrial Workers of the World (IWW) and member of the Executive Committee of the Socialist Party of America. He was arrested in 1917 on the charge of seditious conspiracy and sentenced to twenty years' imprisonment. He made an escape and fled to Soviet Russia in 1921.

lost confidence in his honesty and think him as great a hypocrite as Tchecherin, who, while professing to pursue the policy of establishing friendly commercial relations with all countries, secretly instructs his representatives therein to do all in their power to stir up revolution and opposition to the governments to which they are accredited. Lenin is quiet at the Third Internationale, which is meeting in Moscow at this writing, while the radicals seem to have captured the Assembly—Trotzky, Zenovieff and Radek and that ilk. Lenin has always been able to have his own way in Russia.

If the Russians opposed to the Bolsheviks had consented to go into the Prinkipo Conference as President Wilson proposed, this state of affairs might, and most likely would, have been avoided; they may say that the Soviet Government refused to go to Prinkipo also; if they had stayed away, their very absence would have been the death knell to Bolshevism. The Kolchak, Deniken,[4] and the Tchaikovsky Governments should have been present, and their attendance would have encouraged the peasants and the intelligencia to organize and overthrow the Soviet Government and would have justified the Peace Conference in establishing some kind of a protectorate over Russia, as the Peace Conference called the Prinkipo meeting and at that time Russia was considered an ally by the victors in the world war, notwithstanding the peace of Brest-Litovsk. I cabled the State Department to inquire whether the President included Russia when he demanded that all the territory of the allied countries should be evacuated, and received a prompt reply that Russia was included and Roumania also.

The situation might have been saved, had President Wilson permitted me to return to Petrograd, accompanied by 50,000 troops, but he doubtless felt that some antidote to Bolshevism would be found by the Peace Conference.

It would have inspired the Russians with some courage to organize and depose the Bolshevik Soviet Government, which represented at that time not over three per cent of the people.

Do you ask why the Kolchak and Deniken and Wrangle[5] movements failed? I will tell you why, notwithstanding they were aided by the British and by the French also. The Bolsheviks were propagandizing all the while by telling the peasants if Kolchak or Deniken or Wrangle were successful they would restore the big estates to the barons, and that England and France would take Russian territory for the

---

[4] Anton I. Denikin (1872–1947), lieutenant general, chief of staff of the commander in chief of the Russian army, March 28–May 31, 1917. After the October Revolution, he took part in the formation of the Volunteer Army, succeeding Lavr G. Kornilov as commander on April 13, 1918; commander in chief of the Armed Forces of south Russia, January 8, 1919–April 4, 1920. He emigrated to the US in 1945 and died near Ann Arbor, MI.

[5] Baron Peter N. Wrangel (1878–1928), major general, commander of the Combined Cavalry Corps in 1917. He joined the Volunteer Army in August 1918, was promoted to lieutenant general but dismissed in February 1920 by General Denikin. Commander in chief of the Armed Forces of south Russia, April 4–November 14, 1920.

RETROSPECT

assistance which those governments were rendering. The Russian peasant loves the land which he tills, and all Russians cherish a pardonable pride in the magnitude of their country.

Only America could have assisted Kolchak or Deniken or Wrangle without her motives and her objects being impugned.

But what is to be done now? The wounds of millions of Russians cry trumpet tongued to save their beloved land from the curse of Communism. Are we allies of this afflicted country going to persist in ignoring these appeals? As I have said in these pages, Russia was the chief victim of the world war. We owe her a duty which gratitude should prompt us to discharge. But beyond that, if we could but realize it, we owe it to ourselves, if we would preserve our institutions, to eradicate this foul monster—Bolshevism—branch, trunk and root. We owe it to society. We owe it to humanity. If we would save society from barbarism and humanity from slaughter.

America saved civilization and thus became the moral leader of the world. Let us retain this leadership by saving Russia, because we are the only government on the face of the earth that can do it. The League of Nations is in active operation and forty-eight or forty-nine governments have joined it. Let us join also. By that course we can save Russia and put an end to Bolshevism.

INDEX

Alaska, 285
Alexander III, 8n7, 90, 122
Alexandrinsky Theater, 142–143
Aleksandrov, Aleksei A., 204n4
Alexandrov, delegate of the Ukrainian Peasants' Congress, 209, 210
Alexandrovsky Palace, xiii, 15n37, 71
Alekseev, Mikhail V., 119, 136, 137, 236
Aleksei Nikolaevich, Tsarevich, 13n30, 20, 60, 62, 63, 65, 70, 71
All-Cossacks Congress, 129
All-Russian Congress of Soviets of Peasants' Deputies, 122
All-Russian Congress of Soviets of Workers' and Soldiers' Deputies, First, 73n2, 129
All-Russian Congress of Soviets of Workers' and Soldiers' Deputies, Second, 153n17, 158, 168, 193
All-Russian Congress of Soviets of Workers', Soldiers', and Peasants' Deputies, Third, 170n11
All-Russian Congress of Soviets of Workers', Peasants', Soldiers', and Cossacks' Deputies, Extraordinary Fourth, 111n15, 194n3, 195, 198, 199
All-Russian Congress of Soviets of Workers', Peasants', Red Army, and Cossacks' Deputies, Fifth, 209, 210
All-Russian Congress of Soviets of Workers', Peasants', Cossacks', and Red Army Deputies, Extraordinary Sixth, 266n13
Allies, xviii, xx, xxvi, xxvii, xxviii, xxxi, 12, 18, 22, 23, 29, 31, 35, 37, 38, 49, 51, 69, 76, 77, 82, 91, 92, 93, 94, 100, 101, 102, 103, 104, 109, 116, 132, 133, 134, 135, 145, 149, 156, 158, 163, 169, 175, 187, 193, 195, 197, 201, 203, 206, 206, 207, 208, 209, 212, 213, 214, 215, 216, 220, 221, 222, 225, 226, 231, 232, 233, 234, 235, 236, 241, 242, 243, 244, 245, 248, 252, 253–59, 261, 263, 264, 265, 266, 267, 268, 269, 271, 273, 274, 276, 279, 281, 282, 283
American ambassador at Tokyo (Roland S. Morris), 255
American Bolsheviks, 143
American colony in Petrograd, xvi, xvii, xxv, xxvi, xxx, 14, 109, 136, 156
American Commission. *See* Root Mission
American consul at Chita. *See* Jenkins, Douglas
American consul at Harbin. *See* Moser, Charles K.
American consul at Irkutsk. *See* Macgowan, David B.
American consul at Odessa (John A. Ray), 177
American consul at Samara. *See* Nielsen, Orsen N.
American consul at Vladivostok (John K. Caldwell), 177, 255
American consulate at Ekaterinburg, 245
American consulate general at Moscow. *See* Lehrs, John A.; Macgowan, David B.; Poole, DeWitt C., Jr.; Summers, Maddin; Thomas, Edward B.
American consulate general at Petrograd. *See* Tredwell, Roger C.; Vezey, Harry C.; Winship, North
American embassy at Arkhangel'sk, 231, 232, 234, 236, 237, 239, 247, 269
American embassy at Petrograd, xii, xiii, xiv, xv, xvi, xvii, xix, xxii, xxiii, xxiv, xxv, xxvi, xxvii, 7, 12, 13, 14, 19, 20, 44, 45, 48, 50, 51, 52, 53, 54, 55, 56, 57, 58, 60, 63, 64, 66, 72, 74, 77, 87, 88, 90, 91, 100, 107, 109, 115, 125, 126, 136, 137, 138, 140, 143, 151, 152, 154, 155, 156, 157, 158, 159, 168, 169, 172, 173, 174, 175, 176,

187, 188, 189, 193, 198, 200, 202, 226, 257, 260
American embassy at Vologda, xxviii, 203, 204, 205, 207, 212, 213, 215, 218, 246, 247, 254, 256, 257
American Expeditionary Forces in northern Russia, 5n6, 228, 231, 242, 251
American Federation of Labor, 84, 108, 199, 289
American hospital in Petrograd, xvii, 14n34, 56n9
American Methodist Episcopal Chapel, xvii
American minister at Stockholm. *See* Morris, Ira N.
American Peace Commission at Paris, 15n36, 262n7, 264, 266, 269, 272
American Press Bureau in Russia, xxiii, 160n35
American Red Cross Mission to north Russia, 282
American Red Cross Mission to Romania, 147, 282n3
American Red Cross Mission to Russia, xxiii, xxiv, xxvii, 147, 161, 162, 176–77, 179. *See also* Robins, Raymond; Thompson, William B.
American Refuge for Refugee Women and Children from the War Zone, xvii, 14
American-Russian Chamber of Commerce, 22n1
anarchists, 87, 96, 172, 173, 174, 175, 176, 177, 179, 198, 270. *See also* "drunken sailor"; Shatov, Vladimir S.
Andreev, Nikolai A., 211n22
Anglo-Soviet commercial agreement, 275, 284
Arctic Ocean, 245
Arkhangel'sk, x, xviii, xxvi, xxviii, 5, 6, 101, 111, 174, 206, 207, 215, 216, 217, 218, 219, 220, 221, 222, 224–52, 255, 259, 265, 267, 268, 269, 271, 273, 275, 278, 279, 282, 283, 286, 289
Armenians, 93
Armistice, European, xxviii, 3, 248, 250, 260, 262, 279, 281, 282, 285, 289
Armistice, German-Russian, 111, 193, 195
Armour, Norman, xiii, 46n34, 81n19, 246, 247
Artzimovich, Vladimir A., xvii

Asquith, Herbert H., 92, 260
Associated Press, The, 140, 201, 257. *See also* Macgowan, David B.; Rennick, Henry L.
attachés on special mission. *See* Miles, Basil; Sands, William F.
Aurora, Russian cruiser, 152
Austria (Austria-Hungary), 18, 86, 93, 105, 197, 248, 258, 285
Austrian prisoners, xix, 7, 8n5, 257
Austrian-Hungarian embassy, 8, 53, 54, 55, 57
Avksentev, Nikolai D., 121n10, 155, 171, 236
Azef, Evno F., 10
Azov-Don Commercial Bank, 39

Bailey, James G., xiii, 54, 81n19
Baker, Henry, xiii, 14n34, 17, 75n7
Baker, Newton D., Jr., 264
Bakhmetiev, Boris A., 89
Balfour, Arthur J., 275
Baltic railway station, 60
Bark, Peter L., 29
Belgian minister, 49
Belgium, 23, 104, 105, 106, 279, 280, 285
Belosselsky-Belozersky, Prince, 59
Belosselsky-Belozersky, Princess (née Susan Tucker Whittier), xvii, 59
Berg, American trader, 249
Berkman, Alexander, 139, 140, 141, 172, 173, 176, 177
Bernatsky, Mikhail V., 75n7, 121
Bertron, Samuel R., Jr., 108, 109
Bierer, Bion B., 227, 247
Birzhevye Vedomosti (Stock Exchange News), business newspaper, 116, 118
Björkö, Treaty of, 9
Black Sea Fleet, 93, 109
Bliss, Tasker H., 262, 263
"Bloody Sunday," 10–11
Blumkin, Yakov G., 211n22
Bobrinsky, Aleksei A., 43
Bolshevik Revolution. *See* October Revolution
Bolsheviks, xxiv, xxv, xxvi, 20n54, 27, 73, 74, 107, 111, 116, 119, 121, 122, 125, 131, 132, 135, 141, 142, 143, 144–63, 167, 168, 169, 170, 174, 177, 178, 179, 187, 188, 190, 192, 193, 195, 198, 199, 201, 203, 204, 206, 207, 209, 210, 211, 216, 217, 224, 225, 226, 229, 230, 237, 238,

239, 240, 241, 242, 243, 244, 245, 248, 252, 253, 254, 256, 258, 259, 264, 268, 269, 270, 271, 272, 275, 277, 285, 289, 290
Bolshevism, xxviii, xxx, 3, 6, 30, 132, 172, 178, 199, 201, 213, 256, 260–76, 277–84, 285, 286, 289, 290, 291
"Bourse Gazette." See *Birzhevye Vedomosti*
Breckenridge, James C., xiii, 17, 46n34, 81n19
Brest-Litovsk peace negotiations, xxiv, xxvi, 176, 189, 190, 195, 196, 197, 198, 201, 226, 277, 282
Brest-Litovsk, Treaty of, xxvii, 111, 192, 193–201, 208, 221, 226, 244, 255, 256, 257, 267, 269, 270, 271, 290
Briand, Aristide, 92
British ambassador. *See* Buchanan, Sir George W.
British commissioner to Russia. *See* Lindley, Francis O.
British embassy, 45, 49, 81, 109, 134, 136, 202, 203, 241, 244, 275
British military attaché (Sir Alfred Knox), 154
British socialists in Russia, 86
British-Slav legion (Slavo-British Allied Legion), 237, 251
Brooklyn, USS, 202
Brosoff, I. G., 191
Brusilov, Aleksei A., 25, 119
Bryant, Louise (Mrs. Jack Reed), 140n20, 141
Bryce, James, 27
Bublikov, Alexander A., 68
Buchanan, Lady Georgina, 125
Buchanan, Sir George W., xviii, xxi, xxv, 38, 44–45, 49, 78, 81, 94, 125, 133, 134, 135, 143, 156, 169n6, 177, 187, 194, 244, 274
Buisseret Steenbecque de Blarenghien, 49
Bukowski, Peter I., 241
Bulgaria, 197
Bullard, Arthur, xxxiii, xxivn75, xxv, 160
Burevestnik (Stormy Petrel), anarchist newspaper, 174

Cantacuzène-Speransky, Princess (née Julia Dent Grant), xvii
Carlton, Newcomb W., 29
Carlotti di Riparbella, Marquis Andrea, 38n8, 45, 49, 78, 81, 125, 133, 134

Carnegie, Andrew, 173
Carr, Wilbur J., 271
Chaikovsky, Nikolai V., xxviii, 75n7, 155, 156, 226n2, 227, 228, 230, 231, 232, 234, 235, 236, 237, 238, 239, 240, 243, 251, 290
chairman of the Council of Ministers of the Russian Empire. *See* Golitsyn, Prince Nikolai; Stürmer, Boris V.; Trepov, Alexander F.
Chaplin, Georgy E., 230, 231, 232, 233, 234, 235, 238
Chernov, Viktor M., 109n8, 118, 121n10, 126, 171
Chicherin, Georgy V., 177, 198, 212, 213, 214, 216, 217, 218, 221, 222, 225, 226, 258, 264, 266, 267, 268, 269, 270, 271, 274, 275, 276, 290
China, 32, 48, 50, 108, 120, 136
Chinese legation, 50, 202
Chinese minister (Liu Tszin Jen), 48, 50, 87
Chinese soldiers, 197, 277, 283
Chita, 195, 202
Chkheidze, Nikolai S., 61n24, 73, 84
Christensen, Thomas, 265
Circus Modern, 114, 139
Clemenceau, Georges, 263
Cleveland, Grover, x
Club House (Vologda Society of Mutual Aid to Private Service Labor), 204, 205
commercial attaché. *See* Baker, Henry; Huntington, William C.
commercial treaty, negotiations of, xviii, xix, 11, 12, 13, 18, 31
Committee of Members of the All-Russian Constituent Assembly (KOMUCh), 235n20
Committee for the Salvation of the Motherland and the Revolution, 155n28
Committee on Public Information, xxiii
communism, 291
Constantinople, 32n3, 77, 93, 94. *See also* Straits
Constituent Assembly (All-Russian Constituent Assembly), 75, 77, 78, 117, 132, 137, 144, 145, 146, 148, 154, 159, 164–79, 238, 239, 240, 260, 263. *See also* Committee of Members of the All-Russian Constituent Assembly

Constitutional Democratic Party. *See* Kadets
Consular Bureau, 271
Cooke, Hamilton, 27
Cooke, Henry Arthur, 244n36
Corse, Frederick M., xi, xvii
Council of People's Commissars, 4n2, 153, 168, 169, 170, 171, 188, 190, 193, 197
counselor of the embassy. *See* Dearing, Fred M.; Wright, J. Butler
Cramm, Matilda de, 125n20, 127
Crane, Charles R., xi, 108, 227
Cromie, Francis N. A., 275
Crosley, Pauline S., xxvin94, 124n13
Crosley, Walter S., 116n10, 124, 135
Czecho-Slovaks, xxvii, 8n10, 93, 94n22, 112, 208, 257, 258, 265, 268, 270

Dan, Fyodor I., 153
Daniels, Josephus, 247
Danish minister (Harald Scavenius), 48
Dardanelles, 38, 94. *See also* Straits
Darling, William L., 110
Dean (Doyen) of the Diplomatic Corps, xxv, 133, 169, 187, 189, 194, 212, 213, 218, 219, 220, 222, 232, 244, 260, 267
Dearing, Fred M., xiii, 12, 15, 16, 19
Declaration of War Aims of the Provisional Government, 91n17, 93, 101, 103
Dedusenko, Yakov T., 233n18, 234
"Defeatists," 113, 197
Delo Naroda (People's Cause), Socialists Revolutionaries' newspaper, 170
Democratic Conference (All-Russian Democratic Conference), 137, 145
"Democratic débauche," xii
Denikin, Anton I., 290n4, 291
"Deutschland, Deutschland über alles," 252
Devine, Edward T., xiv, 8n5
Diamandy, Count, xxvi, 125, 187, 188, 189
Diamandy Incident, 187–92
Dillon, Emile Joseph, 20
"Diplomatic Capital of Russia," xxvii, xxviii, 202, 204
Diplomatic Corps, xxv, xxviii, xxx, 44, 46, 47, 48, 78, 133, 169, 187, 189, 190, 194, 206, 212, 214, 217, 218, 219, 220, 221, 222, 224, 225, 232, 235, 244, 248, 253, 260, 267, 268

Dmitry Pavlovich, Grand Duke, 13n30, 41, 42
Donetzk railroads, 111
Donop, French colonel, 230, 236
"drunken sailor" (Anatoly G. Zheleznyakov), 171
Duncan, James, 108, 109
Durov, Boris A., 233n17, 236, 239, 240
Dutch minister (Arthur-Marin-Désiré Sweerts de Landas Wyborgh), 48
Dvina River, 224, 225, 230, 240, 242
"dvornick," 56, 57, 175
Dvortsovaya Embankment, 26n5, 134n8
Dzerzhinsky, Felix E., 211n23

Economic Conference of the Allies, 12, 26, 33
Edward VII, King of Great Britain, xi
Ekaterinburg, 8n10, 245, 246
Ekaterininsky Palace, 44n29
Eliava, Shalva Z., 204n6
Emerson, George H., 111, 112, 148, 254
Emperor's Station, 16, 44, 46
Empress (Alexandra Fyodorovna), 9, 10, 13, 15, 19, 20, 21, 23, 33, 40, 41, 42, 43, 56, 60, 65, 67, 69, 70, 71
Empress Dowager (Maria Fyodorovna), 8, 10, 21, 42, 70
England, xxviii, 15, 23, 26, 27, 29, 49, 127, 163, 179, 195, 227, 237, 243, 249, 250, 251, 261, 263, 269, 274, 279, 282, 283, 284, 285, 290
Entente. *See* Allies
Estonia, 197
Extraordinary Commission against counter-revolution (All-Russian Emergency Commission for Combating Counter-Revolution and Sabotage (CheKa), 270. *See also* Blumkin, Yakov G.; Dzerzhinsky, Felix E.; Kedrov, Mikhail S.; Peters, Yakov K.; Uritsky, Moisei S.
Extraordinary Revolutionary Staff, xxviii, 217, 220, 246

February Revolution. *See* March Revolution
Finland, 22, 105, 178, 179, 202, 203. *See also* Helsingfors; Torneo
Finland railway station, 7, 188
"Ford," 57, 159

INDEX

Fourth of July reception, xvii, xxviii, 109, 206, 207, 209
France, 9, 23, 26, 27, 102, 104, 105, 106, 113, 178, 179, 195, 207, 208, 243, 248, 249, 250, 252, 259, 263, 269, 274, 279, 280, 283, 285, 290
Francis's reception by the emperor and empress, xiii, 13, 15–19, 45
Francis, Charles, 203, 245
Francis, David R., Jr., 96, 122
Francis, Jane (née Jane Perry), x, xivn17, xviin35, 44, 159
Francis, Perry, 11, 91, 98, 106, 135, 143, 149, 159, 262
Francis, Sidney, 228
Francis, Talton, 258
Francis, Thomas, 257
Frantsuskaya Embankment, 51n15, 57n13
Fraser, Lovat G., 279
Frederiks, Count Vladimir B., 67, 70
French ambassador. *See* Noulens, Joseph; Paléologue, Maurice
French embassy, 57, 81, 109, 202, 203, 255, 267
French military attaché (Jean Guillaume Lavergne), 154
French socialists in Russia, 86
Frick, Henry C., 173
Furshtatskaya Street, xv, 12n27, 14, 51, 53, 54, 72n1, 138

Galabutsky, Ivan P., 204n5
Gapon, Georgy A., 10
Gardner, Frederick D., 4, 5
Gaylord, Franklin A., xvii, 14n34, 162n36
George V, King of Great Britain, 20, 260, 261, 282
George Washington, steamer, 262, 263, 286, 289
German embassy at Petrograd, 8, 24
German legation at Moscow, 209, 212, 213, 217, 267, 270
German officers in Petrograd, 201
German prisoners, xix, 7, 8n5
German propaganda, 156
German-Russian commercial treaty (additional convention to the Treaty of Commerce and Navigation between Russia and Germany), 9, 15, 279
German-Russian supplementary treaties, 270

Germany, xx, xxii, xxv, xxviii, 9, 15, 18, 23, 24, 25, 27, 28, 30, 31, 32, 33, 36, 37, 49, 50, 76, 82, 86, 92, 93, 96, 102, 105, 106, 113, 114, 120, 123, 127, 146, 147, 156, 179, 191, 194, 195, 196, 197, 198, 200, 203, 207, 208, 209, 210, 213, 214, 221, 228, 243, 245, 248, 249, 252, 255, 256, 257, 259, 264, 269, 279, 280, 281, 282, 285, 289
  declaration of war, 8, 14, 31
Gibbs, George, 110
Glasberg, Valentin N., 121
Glennon, James H., 101n6, 108, 109
Goldman, Emma, 139, 176, 177
Golitsyn, Prince, 43
Gompers, Samuel, 84, 199, 285, 289
Gorky, Maxim, 149
Gortalov, Sergei F., 241n32
Grabbe, Michael N., xv, 12n27
Grant, Ulysses S., US president, xvii
Grayson, Cary T., 261, 262
"great rally," 95
Greek (Orthodox) Church, 278
Greiner, John E., 110
Grekov, Konstantin F., 67, 68
Grey, Sir Edward, 92
Grigorovich, Ivan K., 59
Groves, Philip, 257
Grudistov, Nikolai V., 239n28
Guaranty Trust Company of New York, xvii
Guchkov, Alexander I., 70, 78, 79, 81, 88, 91n17, 94, 95, 98, 99, 100, 165
Guchkov, Nikolai I., 79n13
Gukovsky, Alexander I., 238n26, 239, 240
Gulkevich, Konstantin N., 248n45

Hague, The, 247
Halifax, 114
Hapgood, Isabel F., 245
Harbin, 112, 120, 136, 143n27, 254
Harding, Warren G., 288
Harper, Samuel N., xi, xii, xiii, xx, xxiv, xxv, xxvi
Harte, Archibald C., xiv, 162n36
Haywood, William D., 289
Helsingfors, 172, 173, 174, 178, 203. *See also* Finland
Hillquit, Morris, 141, 142
Hitchcock, Gilbert M., 264, 265

Hoffman, Max, 190n7, 191, 192, 196, 289
Holbrook, Frederick, 115
Holy Synod (Most Holy Governing Synod), 131, 278. *See also* Lvov, Vladimir N.
Hôtel Astoria, 125
Hôtel de France, 55
House, Edward M., xxv, 262, 263
Hughes, Charles E., 288
Hungary, 93
Huntington, William C., xiii, xiv, xxv, 46n34, 81n19, 174n22, 175
Hurd, Eugene, 27
Huysmans, Camille, 141, 141

Ignatiev, Pavel N., 43n22
Ignatiev, Vladimir I., 233n16
Industrial Workers of the World (IWWs), 289
International Bank of Commerce (St. Petersburg International Commercial Bank), 39
International Socialist Bureau, 142
Ioffe, Adolf A., 190n5, 191
Irkutsk, 195, 202, 255
Ironside, W. Edmund, 250n49, 251
Italian ambassador. *See* Carlotti di Riparbella, Marquis Andrea; Torretta, Marquis Pietro della
Italian embassy, 57, 81, 109, 175, 202, 203, 267
Italy, 32n3, 93, 195, 252, 274, 283
Ivanov, Aleksei A., 234n19, 238, 239
Ivanov, Nikolai I., 68n38
Izvestiia (News), Soviet newspaper, 166, 281

Japan, 9, 23, 31, 32, 86, 111, 242, 244, 255, 259
Japanese ambassador. *See* Motono Ichiro; Uchida Kosai
Japanese chargé d'affaires (Marumo Naotosi), 45
Japanese embassy, 45, 46, 51n15, 202
Japanese intervention, 254, 255
Jenkins, Douglas, 195
Johnston, Earl M., 56, 60, 61, 74, 77, 173, 175, 176, 213, 260, 261, 262
Jones, American captain, 261
Jones, Breckinridge, 26, 244
Jordan, Philip, xii, xv, 7, 61, 87, 159, 175, 262

Judson, William V., xxiii, xxiv, xxv, 105n10, 135n9, 154, 155, 175, 224
Jugo-Slavs, 208
July Crisis (July Revolution), 90, 109, 113–19, 121, 162, 163, 167, 278
junkers (cadets), 152, 154, 155, 157, 158, 160
Jusserand, Jean Jules, 204

kadets (Constitutional Democrats), 3n1, 34n6, 75n10, 76, 117, 121, 142, 143, 168
Kaledin, Aleksei M., 74
Kamkov, Boris D., 211n21
Kandalaksha, 225, 226, 227, 228, 232, 241, 268
Karakhan, Lev M., 201, 270
Karelin, Vladimir A., 210
Kazan Cathedral, 34, 87, 278
Kedrov, Mikhail S., 206n11, 224, 246, 247
Kem, 232
Kerensky, Alexander F., 3n1, 71, 76, 77, 85, 87, 88, 89, 90, 94, 99, 100, 101, 104, 106, 107, 109, 120, 121, 122, 124, 125, 126, 127, 129–43, 144, 146, 150, 151, 152, 157, 162, 163, 167, 168, 171, 248, 277
Kerth, Monroe C., 194
Khvostov, Alexander A., 29n11
Kiev, 10, 42, 62, 70n42
Kirochnaya Street, 60n21, 116
Knight, Austin M., 202
Kokoshkin, Fyodor F., 121n10, 174
Kolchak, Alexander V., 101, 248, 290, 291
Kollontai, Alexandra M., 157
Korf, Pavel P., 15, 17, 19
Kornilov Affair, 88n7, 129–43, 144, 151, 162, 248
Kornilov, Lavr G., 66n28, 88, 119, 120, 122, 123, 129–37, 162, 277
Kotlas, 230, 242
Kovanko, Lev E., 151
Krasin, Leonid B., 275
Krasnov, Peter N., 151
Kronstadt, 107, 115, 140, 152, 153
"Kronstadt Republic," 107, 152
Krylov, S., 173
Kseshinskaya, Matilda F., 20, 114
Kseshinskaya's mansion, 20, 114
Kudasheva, Princess (Myra Armour), 247n41
Kudryavy, Viktor A., 205n9
Kutzy, K., 173

Lansing, Robert, xvi, xixn14, xxn51, xxn54, xxi, xxiin68, xxiin69, xxv, xxvii, 5, 6, 22, 28, 37, 49, 153, 261, 262, 263
Larin, Yu, 270
Lazimir, Pavel E., 191n9
League of Nations, 271, 276, 286, 287, 291
Lebedev, Vladimir I., 120
Lee, William H., 99
Left Socialists Revolutionaries, xxviii, 85n3, 169, 171, 209, 210, 211. *See also* Socialists Revolutionaries
Lehrs, John A., 221, 222
Lenin, Vladimir I., x, xxvi, 4, 89, 90, 91, 96, 97, 113, 114, 116, 119, 120, 121, 126, 132, 153, 154, 156, 157, 158, 159, 162, 163, 167, 168, 169, 170, 171, 176, 177, 179, 187, 188, 190, 191, 192, 194, 195, 196, 197, 198, 213, 225, 244, 256, 266, 267, 274, 275, 277, 280, 281, 282, 283, 284, 286, 289, 290
Lenin's brother (Alexander I. Ulyanov), 90
Leopold II, King of Belgium, xi
Lettish soldiers (Latvian riflemen), 169, 170, 197, 246, 277, 283
Lindley, Francis O., 202, 215, 216, 225, 227, 234, 237, 238, 244, 258, 275
Liteiny Bridge, 115, 116
Liteiny Prospekt, 14n35, 53, 54, 58, 60, 115, 174n21
Litvinov, Maxim M., 266n14
Livadia, 68, 69
Lloyd George, David, 260, 263, 271, 273, 283
Lockhart, Bruce, 241, 255, 256
London, 3, 5, 6, 101, 177, 247, 249, 260, 261, 264, 266, 283, 289
Long, Breckinridge, 231
Looga Workers' and Soldiers' Council, 170
Lorraine, 23, 102
Loubet, Emile, xi
Lukomsky, Alexander S., 136
Lvov, Georgy E., 3n1, 63, 77, 80, 81, 90n15, 104, 116, 118, 119, 131, 164, 166
Lvov, Vladimir N., 131, 132

Macgowan, David B., 75n7, 160, 195, 255n2
Manchester Guardian, The, 213
March, Peyton C., 231

March Revolution (February Revolution), x, xx, xxi, xxii, xxiii, xxx, 20, 51, 53–71, 126, 146, 194, 209, 278
Mariinsky Palace, 80, 95
Mariinsky Theatre, 88
Marines, xiii, 176, 207n14, 227, 228
Martin, Hugh S., 226, 249, 250
Martushin, Grigory A., 238n24, 239, 240
Marye, George T., xi, xix, xxx, 14n34
Mason, Frederick, 217, 218
Maxa, Prokop, 265
Maximalists (members of the Union of Socialists-Revolutionaries Maximalists), 171, 209
Mayak (Lighthouse) Society, xvii, 162n36. *See also* Young Men's Christian Association
McCormick, Cyrus H., Jr., 108n7
McCully, Newton A., xiii, xxviii, 17, 46n34, 55, 81n19, 247, 282
McGrath, British captain, 215, 216
McRoberts, Samuel, xvi, 22
Mensheviks, 121n6, 153, 171
Mensheviks-Internationalists, 153, 196, 209
Meserve, H. Fessenden, xvi, 14n34
Mikhail Alexandrovich, Grand Duke, 61, 63, 65, 69, 70, 166, 234
Miles, Basil, xiv, xxv, 8n5, 46n34, 54, 55, 64, 81n19, 105n10, 231
military attaché. *See* Judson, William V.; Riggs, E. Francis; Ruggles, James A.
Military Revolutionary Committee, 146, 149, 154, 155
Miller, Henry, 110, 111
Milyukov, Pavel N., xxi, 34, 37, 73, 75, 76, 77, 78, 80, 81, 83, 85, 86, 91, 93, 94, 95, 96, 99, 100, 104, 109, 124, 126, 127, 130, 168, 238
Milyukov note, 91n17, 93, 94
minister of agriculture. *See* Bobrinsky, Aleksei A.; Chernov, Viktor M.
minister of commerce and industry (Alexander I. Konovalov), 95n25
minister of finance. *See* Bark, Peter L.; Bernatsky, Mikhail V.; Nekrasov, Nikolai V.; Tereshchenko, Mikhail I.; Witte, Sergei Y.
minister of foreign affairs. *See* Milyukov, Pavel N.; Pokrovsky, Nikolai N.; Sazonov, Sergei

D.; Stürmer, Boris V.; Tereshchenko, Mikhail I.
minister of the Imperial Court and Household. *See* Frederiks, Count Vladimir B.
minister of internal affairs. *See* Khvostov, Alexander A.; Protopopov, Alexander D.; Stürmer, Boris V.; Tsereteli, Irakli G.
minister of justice. *See* Kerensky, Alexander F.
minister of navy. *See* Grigorovich, Ivan K.
minister of people's education. *See* Ignatiev, Pavel N.
minister of posts and telegraphs. *See* Tsereteli, Irakli G.
minister of war. *See* Shuvaev, Dmitry S.; Sukhomlinov, Vladimir A.; Verkhovsky, Alexander I.
minister of war and navy. *See* Guchkov, Alexander I.; Kerensky, Alexander F.
minister of ways of communication. *See* Nekrasov, Nikolai V.; Trepov, Alexander F.
minister president of the Provisional Government. *See* Kerensky, Alexander F.; Lvov, Georgy E.
Mississippi Valley Trust Company, 26
Mogilev, 69, 70
Molotov, Vyacheslav M., 146n2
Mooney, Thomas J., 87, 90, 176, 177
Morris, Ira N., 156n30, 201
Morskaya Street, 39n14, 39n15, 55n7, 57n12, 125n15, 157
Moscow, xxvi, xxviii, 5n7, 44, 56, 62, 63, 79, 96, 97, 109, 111, 129, 130, 137, 156, 157, 159, 160, 163, 177, 179, 194, 195, 198, 200, 202, 205, 206, 207, 209, 210, 211, 212, 213, 214, 215, 216, 217, 218, 219, 220, 221, 224, 225, 226, 239, 241, 242, 243, 246, 254, 255, 256, 257, 258, 259, 264, 265, 266, 267, 268, 269, 270, 271, 289, 290
Moscow Political Conference, 129n2, 130
Moser, Charles K., 120, 136
Motono Ichiro, 31, 255
Mott, John R., xi, 108, 109
Muraviev, Mikhail A., 154
Murmansk, xxvii, 111, 163, 207, 216, 226, 227, 228, 241, 243, 249, 250, 251, 255
Musin-Pushkin, Vladimir A., 16n40

Narodny Dom (People's House), 123
Naryshkina, Elizaveta A., 15
National City Bank of New York, Petrograd Branch, xvi, xvii, xxvii, 14n34, 22, 26, 247
National Socialists (members of the Labor People-Socialist Party), 121
naval attaché. *See* Crosley, Walter S.; McCully, Newton A.; Riis, Sergius M.
Nekrasov, Nikolai V., 89, 95, 118, 120, 121, 126
Neva, 13, 20, 41, 51, 55, 59, 114, 115, 152
Nevsky Prospekt, 39n13, 58, 75n7, 80, 87, 95n24, 96, 143, 162n36
New York Call, 142
New York City, 6n8, 68n36, 75n8, 108, 109n8, 114, 118n14, 120n3, 140, 153n19, 155, 156n29, 201, 263, 287
New York Life Insurance Company, xvii, 27n8
Nicholas II, x, 8, 14n32, 17, 20, 21, 23, 41, 42, 43, 44, 45, 46, 51, 56, 60, 62, 63, 65, 67, 68, 69, 70, 71, 79, 245, 246
Nichols, J. Brooks, 228, 229
Nielsen, Orsen N., 195
Nikolayevsky railway station, 67
Nikolaevskoe Cavalry School, 155
Nikolai Nikolaevich, Grand Duke, 10, 55, 56
Nilov, Konstantin D., 67, 68
"no war, no peace" declaration, 196n7, 197, 277
Nolde, Baroness, 74
Nolde, Boris E., 74
Northern Government. *See* Provisional Government of the Northern Region; Supreme Administration of the Northern Region
Norway, 48, 101, 163, 203, 248
Norwegian attaché. *See* Christensen, Thomas
Norwegian legation, 8n5, 50, 265
Norwegian minister. *See* Prebensen, Nikolai
Nostitz, Countess (née Lilie Bouton), xvii, xix, xx, 56, 59
Nostitz, Grigory I., 56n9, 59
Noulens, Joseph, 133, 134, 188, 202, 227, 236, 237, 238, 254, 258
Novocherkassk, 74n4
Novoe Vremia (New Times), Petrograd newspaper, 118, 170

Ob River, 237
October Revolution, x, xxiv, xxviii, 89n12, 90, 101, 111, 112, 119, 159, 171, 278, 282
Octobrist Party (Union of October 17), 33n4, 43n26, 63n25, 70n41, 79
Odessa, 106, 177, 210
Officers' Assembly of the Army and Navy, 59–60
Olympia, USS, xxviii, 101, 227, 247, 251, 282
Omsk, 237
Order No. 1, 80, 89, 277
Overman Committee, xxix, 238n24, 289

Paléologue, Maurice, xviii, 38n10, 45, 49, 78, 81
Pankhurst, Emmeline, 124, 125, 127
Paris Peace Conference, 3, 15n36, 87, 248n45, 260–76, 290
Pavel Alexandrovich, Grand Duke, 41
"Peace Without Victory," 47–49, 92, 93
Peirce, Herbert H. D., xiii, 16, 75n7
people's commissar for foreign affairs. *See* Chicherin, Georgy V.; Trotsky, Lev D.
people's commissar for war and navy. *See* Trotsky, Lev D.
Perm, 202
Pershing, John J., 249, 262
Persia, 41n18, 42, 266
Peter and Paul Fortress, 10, 34, 38, 59, 90, 101, 114, 151, 152, 163, 189
Peters, Yakov K., 278
Petrograd, x, xii, xiii, xv, xvi, xvii, xviii, xx, xxii, xxiii, xxv, xxvi, xxvii, xxxi, 3, 4, 5, 7, 8, 10, 11, 14, 19, 22, 24, 25, 29, 33, 34, 39, 42, 44, 46, 51, 58, 61, 65, 67, 68, 73, 75, 79, 86, 90, 96, 98, 99, 101, 108, 109, 110, 111, 113, 114, 118, 121, 122, 123, 124, 130, 131, 135, 136, 137, 138, 139, 149, 151, 154, 155, 156, 157, 159, 162, 169, 177, 188, 196, 199, 201, 202, 203, 210, 211, 216, 220, 224, 238, 243, 245, 247, 248, 257, 260, 261, 263, 267, 273, 274, 278, 283, 286, 290
Petrograd City Duma, 95, 154
Petrograd side, 114
Petrograd Soviet of Workers' and Soldiers' Deputies, 61n24, 62–63, 64, 65, 66, 71n43, 73, 76, 79, 80, 81, 83–97, 98, 99, 100, 107, 114, 115, 116, 122, 131, 137, 139, 153, 154, 157, 158, 162, 165, 167
Petrograd telephone station, 157, 158
Pettus & Leathe of St. Louis, 271
Petrov, P. M. (Bolshevik emigrant), 177
Phelps, Livingston, xiii, 46n34, 81n19, 173, 188
Plekhanov, Georgy V., 113
Podvoisky, Nikolai I., 191n8
Pokrovsky, Nikolai N., xivn14, 28, 47, 59
Poland, 22, 197, 117n12
Polar Star, imperial yacht, 172
Polish soldiers, 155
Polk, Frank L., 15, 40, 264, 266
Polovtsev, Alexander A., 64
Poole, DeWitt C., Jr., xxii, 5, 160, 231n12, 241, 249, 269, 271, 272, 273, 274
Poole, Frederick C., 215, 216, 226, 230, 231, 232, 234, 236, 237, 239, 240, 241, 242, 243, 244, 249, 250, 251
Pope (Benedict XV), 147n6
Popov, Stepan K., 222n32
posts and telegraphs, general administration, 29
Potemkinskaya Street, 50n12
Pravda (Truth), Bolshevik newspaper, 189
Prebensen, Nikolai, 48n4, 50
Priest, Henry S., 132, 137
"Prinkipo Proposal," 263, 271, 272, 273, 274, 283, 290
Proctor, Alex, 249
Protopopov, Alexander D., 33, 34, 39, 42, 43, 56, 59, 62, 69, 76, 77
Provisional Committee of the State Duma, 34n6, 43n26, 58, 60, 62, 63, 64, 65, 68n36, 70n42, 71n43, 73, 78, 89n10, 95n25, 131n3
Provisional Government, xviii, xxi, xxii, 3, 28, 34n6, 57, 62, 63, 64, 65, 68, 70, 71, 72–82, 83, 85, 86, 88, 90, 94, 95, 96, 98, 99, 100, 101, 102, 104, 107, 108, 109, 113, 114, 117, 118, 119, 120–28, 132, 133, 134, 135, 136, 137, 138, 144, 145, 146, 147, 149, 150, 152, 157, 164, 165, 166, 167, 168, 173, 187, 196, 248, 278, 285
Provisional Government, second coalition, 3n1, 118, 120, 121n10

Provisional Government of the Northern Region, 226n2. *See also* Supreme Administration of the Northern Region
Pskov, 70, 79
Purishkevich, Vladimir M., 13n30, 39, 40, 41, 42

Queen Dowager of Greece (Olga Konstantinovna), 42
Queen Mary of the United Kingdom, 260

Radek, Karl B., 196, 212, 213, 214, 215, 216, 220, 267, 269, 278, 290
Radical Democrats (members of the Russian Radical-Democratic Party), 121
Railroad Commission (Advisory Commission of Railway Experts to Russia), xxii, xxvii, 98, 109–12, 147, 148
Railway Union (All-Russian Executive Committee of the Railway Trade Union), 153
Rakovsky, Khristian G., 190n4, 210
Ramsay, Baroness (née Frances Sheldon Whitehouse), xvii, 59
Ramsay, Konstantin A., 59, 150, 151
Ransome, Arthur M., 213
Rasputin, Grigory E., 13, 33, 39n11, 40, 42, 56, 69
Rech' (Speech), kadet newspaper, 75
Red Army, 112, 197–98, 210, 246, 254, 268, 269, 277
Red Guard, 152, 154, 155, 158, 170, 203, 245, 246
Reed, John, 140, 141, 142
Relief Corps. *See* Second Division
Rennick, Henry L., 257
Repin, Ilya E., 100
Riggs, E. Francis, xiii, 17, 46n34, 63, 81n19, 99, 110, 215, 224, 254, 255, 256
Riis, Sergius M., 250
Robins, Raymond, xi, xxiiin70, xxiv, xxvi, 147n4, 176, 179, 254, 256, 257, 266, 269
Rodzianko, Mikhail V., 43, 55, 58n14, 60, 64, 68, 69, 72, 73, 74, 75, 77, 78, 85, 109, 238
Romania, xxvi, 32n3, 37, 39, 93, 189, 283, 290
Romanian legation, xxvi, 188, 190, 191
Romanian minister. *See* Diamandy, Count

Romanovs' dynasty, 46, 63, 69, 76
Roosevelt, Franklin D., 227
Root, Elihu, xxii, xxiii, 105, 108, 109
Root Mission (Special Diplomatic Mission of the United States to Russia), xxii, xxiii, 54n4, 54n5, 105, 108–09, 135n9, 147, 245
Rosen, Roman R., xvii, 75, 88
Roshal, Semen G., 152, 153n16
"round robin," 42
Ruggles, James A., 224
Ruhl, Arthur, xi, xii
Russell, Charles Edward, 108, 109
Russia, x, xi, xii, xiii, xiv, xv, xvi, xvii, xviii, xix, xx, xxi, xxii, xxiii, xxv, xxvi, xxvii, xxviii, xxix, xxx, xxxi, 3, 4, 6, 7, 8, 11, 13, 14, 15, 22, 23, 24, 25, 26, 27, 28, 30, 31, 32, 34, 35, 36, 37, 38, 39, 44, 50, 51, 53, 56, 64, 65, 68, 77, 78, 81, 83, 84, 93, 94, 96, 98, 99, 101, 102, 103, 104, 106, 109, 110, 111, 113, 114, 116, 119, 122, 123, 127, 130, 131, 132, 134, 135, 136, 137, 144, 145, 147, 148, 149, 156, 158, 159, 163, 167, 177, 178, 179, 192, 194, 195, 196, 197, 198, 199, 200, 202, 208, 209, 212, 214, 216, 218, 220, 221, 224, 225, 227, 228, 238, 240, 242, 243, 244, 245, 248, 249, 250, 251, 252, 253–59, 260, 261, 262, 263, 264, 266, 267, 269, 271, 272, 273, 275, 278, 279, 280, 282, 283, 284, 285–87, 288, 289, 290, 291
Russian ambassador at Washington. *See* Bakhmetiev, Boris A.; Rosen, Roman R.
Russian-American Chamber of Commerce, xvii, 79n13
Russian-American Treaty of Commerce and Navigation, 11n25
Russian army, 10n16, 23, 24, 25n4, 27, 28, 32, 39, 56, 77, 78, 80, 88n7, 97, 98, 99, 102, 104, 105, 106, 107, 113, 119, 120, 137, 156, 162, 178, 191, 194, 195, 237, 277, 280, 284, 289
Russian Bank for Foreign Trade, 39
Russian Bureau in the Department of State (Division of Russian Affairs), 5n7, 54n4, 231, 271
Russian Daily News, The, Petrograd English-language newspaper, 143
Russian New Year's Day, 43, 44, 187

INDEX 303

Russian Purchasing Committee in America, 10, 89n11
Russian Revolution of 1905, 11n21, 14n32, 33n5, 36, 76n11, 89n12
Russkoe Slovo (Russian Word), Moscow newspaper, 174
Russo-American Society (Society for Promoting Mutual Friendly Relations between Russia and America), xvii, 75, 95n23
Russo-Japanese Agreement, 31
Russo-Japanese War, 9, 15, 16n41, 17n47, 58, 75n8, 135n9, 279
Ryan, John L., xiii, 17

Samara, 195, 235, 236, 237
Sands, William F., xiv, xxv, 8n5, 46n34, 81n19
Sante, Karin, 257n7
Savinkov, Boris V., 120, 131
Sayler, Oliver M., xxvii
Sazonov, Sergei D., xix, 11, 12, 13, 22, 23, 24, 25, 27, 31
Scott, Hugh L., 108, 109
Second Division, xiv, xv, 8n4, 8n5, 13, 53, 54, 55
secret treaties, 32, 77, 103, 149, 158
secretary of state. *See* Hughes, Charles E.; Lansing, Robert
secretary of the embassy. *See* Armour, Norman; Bailey, James G.; Dearing, Fred M.; Phelps, Livingston; Ryan, John L.; Sterling, Frederick A.; White, John C.; Whitehouse, Sheldon
Serbia, 48, 93, 104
Serbian minister (Miroslav Spalajković), 48, 188
Sergievskaya Street, 8n4, 14n34, 50n13, 53, 56n9, 58, 60
Sevastopol, 106
Shatov, Vladimir S., 140n18, 141
Shidlovsky, Sergei I., 63
Shingarev, Andrei I., 75n7, 163, 174
Shpalernaya Street, 58n16
Shulgin, Vasily V., 75n7, 163, 174
Shuvaev, Dmitry S., 39n12
Siamese minister (Visan Botchanakan), 48, 49, 50
Siberia, xix, 236, 242, 243, 258, 259, 271

Siberian Government, 61n24, 242, 258
Simmons, Roger E., 241
Simms, William S., 247n42
Simons, George A., xvii
Sisson, Edgar, xxiii, xxv
Skobelev, Matvey I., 121n10, 155, 156
Smith, M. McAllister, xvii, 75n7
Smith, Mercedes Lee (Mrs. McAllister Smith), 125
Smolny Institute (Imperial Educational Society of Noble Maidens), xvi, 61n24, 115, 154, 157, 173, 176, 179, 187, 189, 190
Social Democrats (members of the Russian Social Democratic Workers' Party), 121. *See also* Bolsheviks; Mensheviks
Socialist Party of America, 142, 289
Socialists Revolutionaries (Party of Socialists-Revolutionaries; SRs), 10n19, 10n20, 71n43, 85, 88, 121, 153, 168, 169, 170, 171, 210. *See also* Left Socialists Revolutionaries; Maximalists.
Solovetsky Monastery, 230
South African War (Anglo-Boer War of 1899–1902), 80
Spanish ambassador (Marquis Luis Valera y Delavat de Villâsinda), 45, 87
special assistant to the ambassador. *See* Miles, Basil; Peirce, Herbert H. D.; Poole, DeWitt C., Jr.; Sands, William F.
Stackelberg, Gustav E., 58
Startsev, Nikolai A., 233n15, 234
State Department, xii, xiii, xxiii, xxv, 4, 5, 6, 12, 47, 49, 72, 80, 110, 111, 159, 177, 178, 198, 201, 223, 228, 231, 238, 244, 247, 249, 250, 251, 253, 254, 256, 258, 259, 260, 261, 264, 269, 270, 271, 272, 273, 283, 288, 290
State Duma, xx, xxi, 25, 27, 33, 34, 37, 38, 39, 42, 43, 46, 51, 55, 56, 57, 58, 62, 69, 72, 73. *See also* Provisional Committee of the State Duma; Rodzianko, Mikhail V.
Steklov, Yuri M., 165
St. George Cavaliers, 67, 129
St. Isaac's Cathedral, 34, 278
St. Louis World's Fair, x, xi, 26n6
Stepanov, Alexander P., 236n22
Sterling, Frederick A., xiii, 16, 43

Stevens, John F., xxii, xxiii, 98, 110, 111, 157, 254
Stevens, Walter B., 6
Stewart, George E., 5, 228, 229, 231
Stockholm, 7, 23, 24, 33, 101, 201, 246, 247, 248, 266, 270
Stockholm Conference, 141, 142
Stone, William J., 4, 50
Stowe, Lyman Beecher, 6
Straits, 32n3, 93. *See also* Constantinople; Dardanelles
Stürmer, Baroness, 13, 38
Stürmer, Boris V., 11, 12, 13, 22, 23, 24, 25, 34, 36, 37, 38, 59, 76
Sukhomlinov, Vladimir A., 10, 59
Sukhomlinova, Ekaterina V., 10
Summers, Maddin, 56, 63, 96, 129, 157, 159, 179, 195, 205, 254, 271
Supreme Administration of the Northern Region, 226n2, 227, 230, 232, 233, 234, 235, 236, 237, 238, 239, 242, 243, 244, 245
Sverdlov, Yakov M., 209n17
Sweden, 48, 101, 110, 188, 203, 248
Swedish minister (Edvard Brändström), 48
Switzerland, 8, 96, 113, 194

Taurida Palace, xvi, 58, 59, 61, 85, 170
Tereshchenko, Elizaveta M., 100, 152, 153
Tereshchenko, Mikhail I., 89, 99, 100, 101, 104, 109, 119, 121, 122, 126, 129, 133, 134, 135, 137, 149, 150, 152, 153, 155, 248
Third International (Komintern), 284, 290
Thomas, Albert, 103
Thomas, Edward B., 74n3
Thompson, William B., xxiii, xxiv, 147n4
Thornhill, Cudbert J. M., 235
Tobolsk, 245
Torneo, 188
Torretta, Marquis della, 169, 202, 227, 254, 274
Trans-Siberian Railroad, 94n22, 110, 112, 202
Tredwell, Roger C., 176n24
Trepov, Alexander F., 38, 43
Tretyakov, Pavel M., 79
Tretyakov Gallery, 79

Trotsky, Lev D., 61n24, 89, 90, 96, 97, 113, 114, 116, 119, 120, 122, 126, 132, 153, 154, 156, 157, 158, 159, 162, 163, 167, 168, 176, 177, 179, 187, 189, 190, 191, 192, 193, 194, 195, 196, 197, 198, 210, 211, 213, 225, 226, 244, 254, 267, 268, 270, 274, 275, 277, 278, 280, 281, 282, 283, 290. *See also* "no war, no peace" declaration
Tsabel, Sergei A., 67, 68
Tsarskoe Selo, xiii, 13–14, 16, 41, 44, 60, 69, 71
Tsereteli, Irakli G., 118, 122, 126
Turkey, 32n3, 93, 100, 197, 271n19, 285

Uchida, Baroness, 51, 52, 202
Uchida Kosai, 51, 52, 87, 124, 242
Ukraine, 93, 111n15, 209, 210, 215
Ukrainian question, 90n15, 117
Union of Zemstvos (All-Russian Union of Zemstvos), 63n26, 77. *See also* Zemstvo
United States, xviii, xx, xxii, xxix, 3, 13, 15, 18, 26, 27, 28, 29, 32, 46, 49, 50, 51, 75, 77, 81, 84, 91, 96, 104, 105, 136, 139, 142, 146, 147, 163, 172, 173, 179, 193, 194, 198, 199, 200, 204, 208, 256, 264, 267, 272, 281, 283, 284, 286, 288, 289
Uritsky, Moisei S., 170
US Military Mission, xxiii, xxiv, xxvii, 59n20, 194, 203, 224, 226

Vasilchikova, Mariya A., 69
Venigel, Wolff, 191
Verkhovsky, Alexander I., 137, 157
Versailles, Treaty of, xxxi
Vetoshkin, Mikhail K., 217n29, 242n40
Vezey, Harry C., 143n27
Vladimirskoe Military School, 158
Vladivostok, xxvi, 94, 98, 108, 110, 111, 112, 148, 177, 202, 203, 242, 255, 267
"vodka edict" ("Dry Law"), 18
Voeikov, Vladimir N., 67, 68, 69, 70
Volodarsky, V., 146
Vologda, x, xviii, xxvi, xxvii, xxviii, 4, 5, 111, 112, 162, 202–23, 224, 230, 240, 241, 242, 243, 244, 246, 254, 255, 256, 257, 258, 259, 265, 267, 269, 283, 289
Vologda City Duma, 204, 205, 224

Vologda mayor, 204, 205, 206
Vologodskii Listok (Vologda Sheet), local paper, 206n12
von Bassewitz, Count, 209n16, 210
von Bernstorff, Count, 49, 86
von Hindenburg, Paul, 106, 282
von Kühlmann, Baron, 205n9
von Ludendorff, Erich, 106, 282
von Mirbach, Count Wilhelm, xxviii, 179, 210, 211, 212, 213, 214, 216, 255, 267
von Pistohlkors, Erich Gerhard, 41
von Schwarzenstein, Baron Mumm, 210
von Stoedten, Helmuth Lucius, 23, 24
von und zu Chudenitz, Count Czernin, 192n11
Voskresensky Prospekt, 53
Voznesensky, Arseny N., 206n13, 258n9
Vrasky, Stepan B., 164n1
Viatka, 242

Wade, Festus J., 243
Warsaw railway station, 118
Washburn, Stanley, xi, 105n10
West, Thomas H., 242
Western Union Telegraph Company, 29
Wheeler, Crawford, 249
White, Henry, 16n42, 262, 263
White, John C., xiii, 16
White, William Allen, 274
White Sea, 210, 230
Whitehouse, Sheldon, xiii, xvii, 46n34, 59n20, 63, 81n19, 150, 151
Wilhelm II, German Kaiser, xi, 8, 69
Williams, Albert Rhys, xxiv
Williams, Charles T., 282
Williams, Walter, 138
Wilson, Charles S., xv
Wilson, Woodrow, xi, xii, xix, xx, xxii, xxiii, xxx, xxxi, 47, 49, 50, 91, 92, 93, 108, 147, 156, 177, 208, 244, 252, 257, 260, 261, 266, 271, 276, 283, 286, 287, 288, 290
  address in Alabama, 272
  communication to the belligerents, 47
  message to the Soviet Congress, 198, 199, 201
  war address, 81, 83, 86, 146, 147
Wilson, Mrs., 260
Winship, North, xv, 14n34

Winter Palace, 13, 67n33, 108, 122, 126, 149, 150, 152, 158
Witte, Sergei Y., 9
Women's Battalion, 152
World War, x, xi, xiii, xiv, xxviii, 27, 32n3, 48, 77, 99, 103, 106, 127, 136, 156, 197, 208, 279, 280, 281, 282, 284, 285–87, 290, 291
Wrangel, Peter N., 290n5, 291
Wright, Harriet Rodman (Mrs. Butler Wright), 125
Wright, J. Butler, xiii, xiv, xxiv, 44, 46n34, 81n19

Yaroslavl', xxviii, 215
"Yellow Peril," 32
Young Men's Christian Association (YMCA), xiv, xvii, xxvii, 8n5, 108, 162, 247, 250. See also *Mayak* (Lighthouse) Society; Mott, John R.; Wheeler, Crawford
Young, Hugh H., 261
Yusupov, Felix F., 13n30, 40, 41, 42
Yusupov Palace, 40, 41, 42

Zaikin, Bolshevik commissar, 218
Zalkind, Ivan A., xxvin89, 176n23, 177, 189
Zemstvo, 77n12, 234, 236. See also Union of Zemstvos
Zinoviev, Grigory E., 199, 278, 290
Zubov, Pavel Y., 206n10, 238, 239, 240